LIBRARY OF NEW TESTAMENT STUDIES

691

formerly the Journal for the Study of the New Testament Supplement series

Editor
Chris Keith

Editorial Board
Dale C. Allison, Lynn H. Cohick, Kylie Crabbe, R. Alan Culpepper,
Craig A. Evans, Jennifer Eyl, Robert Fowler, Juan Hernández Jr.,
John S. Kloppenborg, Michael Labahn, Matthew V. Novenson,
Love L. Sechrest, Robert Wall, Catrin H. Williams, Brittany E. Wilson

Intergroup Conflict, Recategorization, and Identity Construction in Acts

Breaking the Cycle of Slander, Labeling, and Violence

Hyun Ho Park

t&tclark

LONDON • NEW YORK • OXFORD • NEW DELHI • SYDNEY

T&T CLARK
Bloomsbury Publishing Plc, 50 Bedford Square, London, WC1B 3DP, UK
Bloomsbury Publishing Inc, 1385 Broadway, New York, NY 10018, USA
Bloomsbury Publishing Ireland, 29 Earlsfort Terrace, Dublin 2, D02 AY28, Ireland

BLOOMSBURY, T&T CLARK and the T&T Clark logo are trademarks of
Bloomsbury Publishing Plc

First published in Great Britain 2024
Paperback edition published in 2025

Copyright © Hyun Ho Park, 2024

Hyun Ho Park has asserted his right under the Copyright, Designs and Patents Act, 1988,
to be identified as Author of this work.

For legal purposes the Acknowledgments on p. xii constitute an extension of this
copyright page.

All rights reserved. No part of this publication may be: i) reproduced or transmitted
in any form, electronic or mechanical, including photocopying, recording or by means
of any information storage or retrieval system without prior permission in writing from
the publishers; or ii) used or reproduced in any way for the training, development or
operation of artificial intelligence (AI) technologies, including generative AI technologies.
The rights holders expressly reserve this publication from the text and data mining
exception as per Article 4(3) of the Digital Single Market Directive (EU) 2019/790.

Bloomsbury Publishing Plc does not have any control over, or responsibility for,
any third-party websites referred to or in this book. All internet addresses given in
this book were correct at the time of going to press. The author and publisher regret
any inconvenience caused if addresses have changed or sites have ceased to exist,
but can accept no responsibility for any such changes.

A catalogue record for this book is available from the British Library.

Library of Congress Cataloging-in-Publication Data

Names: Park, Hyun Ho, author.
Title: Intergroup conflict, recategorization, and identity construction in Acts :
breaking the cycle of slander, labeling and violence / Hyun Ho Park.
Description: London ; New York : T&T Clark, 2024. | Series: The library of
New Testament studies, 2513-8790 ; 691 | Includes bibliographical
references and index. | Summary: "Hyun Ho Park analyzes Acts 21:17-23:35
in which the vicious cycle of slander, labeling, and violence is finally broken and the
Lukan construction of Christian identity is challenged"– Provided by publisher. Identifiers:
LCCN 2023019964 (print) | LCCN (ebook) | ISBN 9780567713278 (hb) |
ISBN 9780567713315 (pb) | ISBN 9780567713285 (epdf) |
ISBN 9780567713308 (epub)
Subjects: LCSH: Bible. Acts. | Intergroup relations.
Classification: LCC BS2625.53 .P365 2024 (print) | LCC BS2625.53 (ebook)
| DDC 226.6/07–dc23/eng/20230831
LC record available at https://lccn.loc.gov/2023019964
LC ebook record available at https://lccn.loc.gov/2023019965

ISBN: HB: 978-0-5677-1327-8
PB: 978-0-5677-1331-5
ePDF: 978-0-5677-1328-5
ePUB: 978-0-5677-1330-8

Series: Library of New Testament Studies, volume 691
ISSN 2513-8790

Typeset by RefineCatch Limited, Bungay, Suffolk

For product safety related questions contact productsafety@bloomsbury.com.

To find out more about our authors and books visit www.bloomsbury.com
and sign up for our newsletters.

To my parents

Deog Sik Park
Yeong Heui Jeon

I would not be who I am without your service and sacrifice

Contents

List of Figures and Tables	xi
Acknowledgments	xiii
Abbreviations	xv

Introduction ... 1
    Overview of the Chapters ... 4

1   Preliminary Considerations ... 7
    1.1. The Text: Acts 21:17–23:35 ... 9
        1.1.1. Boundary of Acts 21:17–23:35 ... 9
        1.1.2. Narrative Structure of Acts 21:17–23:35 ... 12
    1.2. Survey of the Scholarship on Paul in Jerusalem ... 14
    1.3. Mimesis in the Lukan Passion Narratives of Jesus and Paul ... 20
    1.4. Context and Function of Acts 21:17–23:35: An Eagle's-Eye View ... 22
    1.5. Concluding Comments ... 25

2   The Social Identity Approach and Dual Identity ... 27
    2.1. Social Identity Approach: Historical Overview ... 29
        2.1.1. Social Identity Theory (SIT) ... 30
        2.1.2. Self-Categorization Theory (SCT) ... 34
        2.1.3. Social Identity Approach: Achievements and Problems ... 37
    2.2. Dual Identity and the Proximate "Other" ... 41
        2.2.1. Models of Dual Identity ... 43
        2.2.2. The Proximate "Other" ... 44
        2.2.3. Ambivalence ... 44
        2.2.4. Social Creativity ... 45
        2.2.5. Recategorization ... 46
    2.3. Construction of Christian Identity in Luke-Acts ... 47
        2.3.1. The Jerusalem Council: Another Way to Join the People of God (Acts 15:1-35) ... 48
        2.3.2. A Eunuch Joins the People of God (Acts 8:26-40) ... 50
        2.3.3. A Gentile Man Joins the People of God (Acts 10:1–11:18) ... 52

viii   *Contents*

	2.3.4.	A Son of a Gentile-Jewish Intermarriage Joins the People of God (Acts 16:1-5)	53
	2.3.5.	A Gentile Woman Joins the People of God (Acts 16:11-15)	54
2.4.		Concluding Comments	55

3   Slander against Paul and the Labeling of Paul as an Outsider (Acts 21:17-40)   57
    3.1. Accusations against Paul and Scholarly Approaches   58
    3.2. Jewish Slander against Paul: Out-Group Stereotyping and Anti-Way Prejudice   62
       3.2.1. Refuting the Allegations   62
       3.2.2. Reading Acts 21:17-36 with SIA   63
    3.3. Interrogating Jewish Accusations against the Way   66
       3.3.1. Accusations Justified: The Temple in Luke-Acts   67
    3.4. Interaction with the Tribune: Paul, an Outsider to the Pax Romana   69
       3.4.1. The Tribune's Labeling of Paul   69
       3.4.2. Political Accusations against Jesus (Luke 23:1-5)   70
       3.4.3. Political Accusations against the Way (Acts 16:16-41; 17:1-9)   72
       3.4.4. Paul's First Defense against the Tribune   74
    3.5. Concluding Comments   75
    Excursus: Paul's Letters and Jewish Accusations in Acts   76

4   Recategorizing Paul as an Insider (Acts 22:1-21)   79
    4.1. Paul's Speech in Jerusalem: A Literary Analysis   80
       4.1.1. Structure   80
       4.1.2. Rhetorical Features   81
       4.1.3. Functions of Paul's Speech in Jerusalem   82
    4.2. Paul's Internal-External Dialectic of Individual Identification: A Social Anthropological Analysis   85
       4.2.1. Presentation of Paul's Self-Image: A Devout Jew   85
       4.2.2. (Re)presentation of Paul's Damascus Experience: Adding Nuances to Paul's Public Image   87
       4.2.3. Presentation of Jesus in the Temple: Extending the In-Group Boundary   90
    4.3. Recategorizing Paul and the Way: A Social Psychological Analysis   93
       4.3.1. Recategorization, Not Decategorization, of the People of God   93

		4.3.2. Dual Identity of the People of God	96
	4.4.	Concluding Comments	97
5	Ambivalence and the Social Creativity of Paul as an Outsider/insider (Acts 22:22–23:11)		99
	5.1.	Ambivalence toward Rome	100
		5.1.1. The Historicity of Paul's Roman Citizenship	101
		5.1.2. Functions of Paul's Roman Citizenship in Acts	103
		5.1.3. Rome in Luke-Acts: Ambivalent Portrayals	105
	5.2.	Ambivalence toward the Pharisees	107
		5.2.1. The Historicity of Paul's Pharisaic Identity	108
		5.2.2. Functions of Paul's Pharisaic Identity in Acts	110
		5.2.3. Pharisees in Luke-Acts: Ambivalent Portrayals	114
	5.3.	Social Creativity of Paul	116
		5.3.1. An SIA (Re)reading of Acts 22:22-29	116
		5.3.2. An SIA (Re)reading of Acts 22:30–23:11	118
		5.3.3. Implications of Paul's Social Creativity	121
	5.4.	Concluding Comments	122
6	Challenging the Vicious Cycle of Slander, Labeling, and Violence (Acts 23:12-35)		125
	6.1.	A Pattern of Jewish Opposition in Luke-Acts	126
		6.1.1. The Pattern of Slander, Labeling, and Violence against the Way	127
		6.1.2. The Final Cycle of Violence (Acts 23:12-15)	134
	6.2.	Breaking the Vicious Cycle	136
		6.2.1. The Pattern of Deliverance: Discovery, Development, and Destruction	137
		6.2.2. The Final Cycle of Deliverance (Acts 23:16-35)	138
		6.2.3. Breaking Free from the Second Vicious Cycle	141
	6.3.	Challenging the Portrayal of Intergroup Conflict and Identity Construction in Acts: An SIA (Re)reading of Acts 21:17–23:35	144
		6.3.1. Literary Construction of the Jews: Discursive Portrayal of the Proximate "Other"	144
		6.3.2. Identity Construction of Paul and the Way: Dual Identity and Victimization	147
		6.3.3. Inbreaking and Outbreaking of the Vicious Cycle: Beyond Lukan Anti-Jewish Slander, Labeling, and Violence	149
	6.4.	Concluding Comments	151

Conclusion 153
    Summary 154
    Avenues for Further Research 156
    Implications of this Study 156

Bibliography 159
Index of References 179
Index of Authors 197

Figures and Tables

Figures

1.1	Paul's Roller-Coaster Ride in Acts 21:17–23:35	13
2.1	Models of Dual Identity	43
6.1	The Interplay of Paul's Dual Identity	148

Tables

1.1	The Chiastic Structure of Acts 21:17–23:35	14
4.1	The Chiastic Structure of Acts 22:6-17a	83
5.1	Paul's Social Creativity	116

Acknowledgments

"In all toil there is profit" (Prov 14:23). Having this project, a revised version of my dissertation at the Graduate Theological Union, published by Bloomsbury T&T Clark—which had long been my intent and dream—is living proof of this verse to me. Yet, my labor would have never borne fruit without the help of many.

I am deeply indebted to my doctoral advisor, Dr. Jean-François Racine, who taught me not only academic excellence and intellectual rigor but also integrity, patience, and care. His presence, knowledge, and encouragement, from my presentations at Society of Biblical Literature (SBL) meetings to the class we co-taught to the writing of my dissertation, have enriched every aspect of this project. Dr. Rebecca K. Esterson's interest in Jewish-Christian relations and her timely advice helped me hearken back to the discursive voices the Lukan narrative contains and think about the ways in which the two religious traditions enrich one another. Last but not least, Dr. Darren Zook's classes at UC Berkeley were critical to the design of this work, and his questions reminded me to think outside the box.

I am also grateful to others who have been companions on this journey. Great thanks to Luke T. Johnson and Carl R. Holladay at Emory University, whose classes during my master's-level studies and commentaries continue to inspire me. I appreciate the Graduate Theological Union for allowing me, through its travel grant program, to attend various SBL meetings during my doctoral studies. I offer my sincere thanks to my friend Dominic S. Irudayaraj, who not only provided me with helpful insights in the dissertation stage but also advised me with practical tips in the publication stage. My gratitude is also due to Chris Keith, Sarah Blake, Ben Harris, and Merv Honeywood for Bloomsbury, whose generosity and kindness made the publication process smooth, not painstaking. I also wish to thank the families and friends at Atlanta Bethany United Methodist Church, Berkeley Korean United Methodist Church, San Ramon Grace United Methodist Church, and Santa Rosa First United Methodist Church for their presence and support that nurtured me not only physically and emotionally but also spiritually. And, I extend my gratitude to my proofreader, Kathy McKay, who carefully edited all my drafts.

Finally, thank you to my family. My wife, Da Hye Jung, and our children, Luke Jungan Park and Phoebe Hangul Park, have given the meaning to my existence and remind me of my calling and my identity every day. My heartfelt thanks are also due to my parents-in-law, Dong Rak Jung and Min Ja Jang, who supported and encouraged me throughout my doctoral studies. Lastly but most importantly, this book is dedicated to my parents, Deog Sik Park and Yeong Heui Jeon, whose endless love, care, and support made me who I am now and whose example showed me who I want to become. I love you more than these words can express and will remember you all the days of my life.

Abbreviations

A. Ancient Sources

Appian, *Civ. W.*	Civil Wars
Aristotle, *Rhet.*	Rhetoric
bT San	Babylonian Talmud Sanhedrin
bT RoshHaShan	Babylonian Talmud Rosh Hashanah
Cicero, *Def. Rabir.*	In Defense of Rabirius
Cicero, *Orat.*	On the Making of an Orator
Cicero, *Pro Archia*	Pro Archia Poeta
Cicero, *Verr.*	Against Verres
Dio Cassius, *Rom. Hist.*	Roman History
Dio Chrysostom, *Or.*	Orations
Epictetus, *Disc.*	Discourses
Herodotus, *Hist.*	Histories
Josephus, *Apion*	Against Apion
Josephus, *Ant.*	Antiquities
Josephus, *War*	Jewish War
Justinianus, *Dig. Just.*	Digesta Justiniani
Livy, *Hist.*	History of Rome
Ovid, *Metam.*	Metamorphoses
Philo, *Flacc.*	Against Flaccus
Philo, *Spec. Leg.*	De specialibus legibus
Plato, *Apol.*	Apology of Socrates
Plato, *Phaedr.*	Phaedrus
Plato, *Rep.*	Republic
Pliny the Younger, *Ep.*	Epistles
Plutarch, *Caes.*	Julius Caesar
Quintilian, *Orat. Educ.*	The Orator's Education (Institutio Oratoria)
Strabo, *Geog.*	Geography
Tacitus, *Ann.*	Annals
Tacitus, *Hist.*	Histories
Thucydides, *Hist.*	History of the Peloponnesian War

B. Journals, Reference Works, Series, Versions

AB	Anchor Bible
ABD	*The Anchor Bible Dictionary*. Edited by David Noel Freedman, Gary A. Herion, David F. Graf, John David Pleins, and Astrid Beck. 6 vols. New York: Doubleday, 1992.
ABRL	The Anchor Bible Reference Library

ACNT	Augsburg Commentary on the New Testament
AJEC	Ancient Judaism and Early Christianity
ANTC	Abingdon New Testament Commentaries
BBR	*Bulletin for Biblical Research*
BDAG	*A Greek-English Lexicon of the New Testament and Other Early Christian Literature*. Edited by Walter Buer, Frederick W. Danker, William F. Arndt, and F. Wilbur Gingrich. 3rd ed. Chicago: University of Chicago Press, 2000.
BDB	*The Brown, Driver, Briggs Hebrew and English Lexicon: With An Appendix Containing the Biblical Aramaic: Coded with the Numbering System from Strong's Exhaustive Concordance of the Bible*. Edited by Francis Brown with the Cooperation of S. R. Driver and Charles A. Briggs. Peabody, MA: Hendrickson, 1996.
BECNT	Baker Exegetical Commentary on the New Testament
BegC	*The Beginnings of Christianity. Part 1, The Acts of the Apostles*. Edited by Frederick J. Foakes Jackson, Kirsopp Lake, Henry J. Cadbury, and James H. Ropes. 5 vols. London: Macmillan, 1920–33.
BETL	Bibliotheca Ephemeridum Theologicarum Lovaniensium
Bib	*Biblica*
BibInt	*Biblical Interpretation: A Journal of Contemporary Approaches*
BIS	Biblical Interpretation Series
BNP	*Brill's New Pauly: Encyclopedia of the Ancient World*. Edited by Hubert Cancik and Helmuth Schneider. 22 vols. Leiden: Brill, 2002–11.
BR	*Biblical Research*
BRLJ	Brill Reference Library of Judaism
BSac	*Bibliotheca Sacra*
BTNT	Biblical Theology of the New Testament
BZ	*Biblische Zeitschrift*
BZNW	Beihefte zur Zeitschrift für die neutestamentliche Wissenschaft
CBQ	*Catholic Biblical Quarterly*
CCSS	Catholic Commentary on Sacred Scripture
CNT	Commentaire du Nouveau Testament
COQG	Christian Origins and the Question of God
CTR	*Criswell Theological Review*
ECC	The Eerdmans Critical Commentary
ESEC	Emory Studies in Early Christianity
ExpTim	*Expository Times*
FRLANT	Forschungen zur Religion und Literatur des Alten und Neuen Testaments
GH	Gorgias handbooks
HCS	Hellenistic Culture and Society
Hermeneia	Hermeneia: A Critical and Historical Commentary on the Bible
HTR	*Harvard Theological Review*
HvTSt	*Hervormde teologiese studies*
ICC	International Critical Commentary
ICNT	India Commentary on the New Testament
IJJS	*An Interdisciplinary Journal of Jewish Studies*
Int	*Interpretation*
IRS	Issues in Religious Studies
JAAR	*Journal of the American Academy of Religion*
JBL	*Journal of Biblical Literature*

JBPR	*Journal of Biblical and Pneumatological Research*
JCTS	Jewish and Christian Texts Series
JETS	*Journal of the Evangelical Theological Society*
JQR	*The Jewish Quarterly Review*
JSJSup	Supplements to the Journal for the Study of Judaism
JSNT	*Journal of Study of the New Testament*
JSNTSup	Journal for the Study of the New Testament Supplement Series
JRSSS	Journal of Religion & Society Supplement Series
KEK	Kritisch-exegetischer Kommentar über das Neue Testament (Meyer-Kommentar)
KPJT	*Korea Presbyterian Journal of Theology*
LCL	Loeb Classical Library
LD	Lectio divina
LHBOTS	Library of Hebrew Bible/Old Testament Studies
LSJ	*Greek–English Lexicon, with a Revised Supplement.* Edited by Henry George Liddell, Robert Scott, Henry Stuart Jones, and Roderick McKenzie. 9th ed. Oxford: Clarendon Press, 1996.
LTQ	*Lexington Theological Quarterly*
LXX	Septuagint
MNTC	The Moffatt New Testament Commentary
MSHACA	Mnemosyne Supplements, History and Archaeology of Classical Antiquity
NAC	The New American Commentary
NC	Narrative Commentaries
NCBC	New Cambridge Bible Commentary
NewDocs	*New Documents Illustrating Early Christianity.* Edited by G. H. R. Horsley, S. R. Llewelyn, and J. R. Harrison. 10 vols. Grand Rapids: Eerdmans, 1981–2012.
NIB	New Interpreter's Bible
NICNT	New International Commentary on the New Testament
NICOT	New International Commentary on the Old Testament
NIDB	*The New Interpreter's Dictionary of the Bible.* Edited by Katharine Doob Sakenfeld. 5 vols. Nashville: Abingdon, 2006–9.
NIGTC	New International Greek Testament Commentary
NovT	*Novum Testamentum*
NovTSup	Supplements to Novum Testamentum
NRSV	New Revised Standard Version (1993)
NTGL	New Testament and Greek Literature
NTL	New Testament Library
NTM	New Testament Monographs
NTR	New Testament Readings
NTS	*New Testament Studies*
Numen	*Numen: International Review for the History of Religions*
PCNT	Paideia: Commentaries on the New Testament
PFES	Publications of the Finnish Exegetical Society
PS	Pauline Studies
PTMS	Princeton Theological Monograph Series
ResQ	*Restoration Quarterly*
RevExp	*Review and Expositor*
RNTS	Reading the New Testament Series
RRJ	*The Review of Rabbinic Judaism*

SAC	Studies in Antiquity & Christianity
SBL	Society of Biblical Literature
SBLAB	Society of Biblical Literature Academia Biblica
SBLMS	Society of Biblical Literature Monograph Series
SBLSymS	Society of Biblical Literature Symposium Series
SCT	Self-categorization Theory
SEÅ	*Svensk exegetisk Årsbok*
Semeia	*Semeia*
SFSHJ	South Florida Studies in the History of Judaism
SHBC	The Smyth & Helwys Bible Commentary
SIA	Social Identity Approach
SIT	Social Identity Theory
SJT	*Scottish Journal of Theology*
SNTSMS	Society for New Testament Studies Monograph Series
SP	Sacra Pagina
SSRCM	Social Sciences Research Centre Monograph
STDJ	Studies on the Texts of the Desert of Judah
Strong's	*The Strongest Strong's Exhaustive Concordance of the Bible*. Edited by James Strong, John R. Kohlenberger III, and James A. Swanson. 21st century ed. Grand Rapids: Zondervan, 2001.
TPINTC	Trinity Press International New Testament Commentaries
TynBul	*Tyndale Bulletin*
WBC	Word Biblical Commentary
WUNT	Wissenschaftliche Untersuchungen zum Neuen Testament
WW	*Word & World*
ZBNT	Zürcher Bibelkommentare. Neue Testament
ZSNT	Zacchaeus Studies New Testament
ZNW	*Zeitschrift für die neutestamentliche Wissenschaft und die Kunde der älteren Kirche*

Introduction

It happened in a rush. Eight men who had been falsely accused of building a "People's Revolutionary Party" to overthrow the South Korean government were sentenced to death on April 8, 1975, in Seoul. There were no witnesses, no defense, and no justice. The prosecutor stated the charges against the eight men and the judge announced the sentences, nothing else. The condemned men's family members were allowed to be present at the court, but only one person from each family. The execution was carried out quickly, within sixteen hours. No prison visits or correspondence were allowed during their short stay in prison. Before the tears of their families had dried up, at dawn on April 9, 1975, the eight men were hanged in a Seoul prison. The family members could not look at their bodies because the military cremated them immediately, with one exception. Before the cremation, Soo Byung Lee's wife was (un)fortunate enough to see her husband's body, which was covered with scars from the torture he had endured.[1]

President Jung Hee Park's military regime, which had issued the 1972 October Revitalization emergency decree,[2] dismissed the National Assembly, and given Park presidential tenure, was facing strong resistance. College students formed student organizations, including the Democratic Youth and Student Federation, to fight against the dictatorship and to restore democracy in South Korea. Yet, by issuing Emergency Measure 4, which pressed hard against the students' dissenting voices, "The government labeled this organization a Communist front that was being used by North Korean agents to plot the overthrow of the South Korean government."[3] The killing of the eight men was a warning to all dissenters: *You will face the same fate if you challenge the dominant power.*[4]

This People's Revolutionary Party Incident was neither an isolated nor a rare incident. Slandering the out-group members, labeling them as a threat to society, and killing them have taken place repeatedly in human history, including the witch hunts

---

[1] This reconstruction of the "People's Revolutionary Party Incident" in 1975 is based on Sang Hun Choe, "In Seoul, marking a somber anniversary of executions," *New York Times*, April 11, 2005, http://www.nytimes.com/2005/04/11/world/asia/in-seoul-marking-a-somber-anniversary-of-executions.html.
[2] Wi Jo Kang, *Christ and Caesar in Modern Korea: A History of Christianity and Politics* (Albany, NY: State University of New York Press, 1997), 93.
[3] Kang, *Christ and Caesar in Modern Korea*, 94.
[4] On September 12, 2002, the Presidential Truth Commission on Suspicious Deaths in South Korea declared that the People's Revolutionary Party Incident had been fabricated by the National Intelligence Service.

that spread widely in Europe and colonial North America between 1400 and 1800[5] and the Holocaust of the early 1940s that operated within and by the same framework. Slander comes with labeling that justifies violence. Adolf Hitler, in a 1941 speech, addressed the German Parliament as follows:

> Today I will once more be a prophet. If the international Jewish financiers in and outside Europe should succeed in plunging nations once more into a world war, then the result will not be the bolshevization of the earth and thus the victory of Jewry, but the annihilation of the Jewish race in Europe![6]

The enemy is identified as agents of the Devil in witch hunts or as the cause of war in Hitler's speech. Therefore, the enemy should be eliminated. The accusers blame the outgroup for the trouble that they face. Violent reactions ensue.

Such vicious measures—*slander*, *labeling*, and *violence*—inflicted upon the Other not only are a way of fighting an internal or external threat but also reinforce group solidarity. A group and, at the same time, a group identity are formed in opposition to the Other, whether it is a pro-government group against dissenters during the military dictatorship in South Korea or supporters of Aryanism against the Jews during Nazi Germany.[7] A group's discursive rhetoric against the Other characterizes its own members as embodying the defining values of the community to which it claims to belong—what constitutes true Koreans or true Germans—in contrast to the Other, which not only lacks such values but also threatens the very existence of the community. No matter how inaccurate the portrayal, these discursive statements, whether written or spoken, have a lasting effect on the group's perception of and response to the Other. Particularly in the agonistic context in which fierce intergroup conflicts take place, group identity is based on how *we* differ from *them*.

Stories in Luke-Acts are not exempt from such a vicious cycle of slander, labeling, and violence. As a new sect within larger Jewish religious traditions, the so-called Judaism(s),[8] this sect that Luke names the Way (Acts 9:2, 19:23, 22:4, 24:14, 22), is

---

[5] It is estimated that around forty or fifty thousand people died during that period in Europe and North America due to the witch hunts. Diarmaid MacCulloch, *Christianity: The First Three Thousand Years* (New York: Penguin Books, 2009), 686.

[6] "Adolf Hitler, 'Speech to the Reichstag,' January 30, 1941," *The History Place*, http://www.historyplace.com/worldwar2/holocaust/h-threat.htm/.

[7] Adolf Hitler generated an exclusive German nationalist ethos by insisting on the genetic and ethnic superiority of the Aryan race. He labeled the Jews as supporters of ethnic mixing and explained that the greatness of the Aryan race was found in the self-sacrificing will to give one's personal labor and even life for the community. Adolf Hitler, *Mein Kampf* (The Noontide Press: Books On-Line), http://www.angelfire.com/folk/bigbaldbob88/MeinKampf.pdf.

[8] At the dawn of the first millennium, Jewish religious traditions developed in various forms. Josephus, in his *Antiquities of the Jews* (18:1:1–2) and *the Jewish War* (2:8:2–13), introduces four religious movements in Palestine: the Sadducees, the Pharisees, the Essenes, and the Zealots. It is proper to refer, therefore, to Judaisms rather than Judaism when discussing the Jewish religious world of first-century Palestine. Luke posits the Way—the Jesus/messianic movement—in the context of a hostile or troubled relationship with the Sadducees (Lk 20:27; Acts 4:1; 5:17; 23:6-8) and the Pharisees (Lk 5:17, 21, 30, 33; 6:2, 7; 7:30, 36-37, 39; 11:37, 38, 39, 42-43, 53; 12:1; 13:31; 14:1, 3; 15:2; 16:14; 17:20; 18:9-11; 19:39). The relationship between the Way and the Pharisees, however, changes after Pharisaic leader Gamaliel's speech in Acts 5:34-39. The Pharisees maintained a somewhat ambivalent attitude

persecuted. Its members are beaten, brought before the council, and killed, just as its leader, Jesus, had predicted, and Jesus himself had endured such afflictions. Jewish opponents of the Way throw slander at the sect's members, identifying them as a threat to society—for example, as "people who have been turning the world upside down" (Acts 17:6)[9]—and commit violence against them (Acts 17:5).[10] The members of the Way, however, are not just victims. They retaliate with slander against their opponents. Luke labels the Jewish people as "betrayers and murderers" of the Righteous One (Acts 7:52), even though the Jews at that time surely would not agree with such violent rhetoric. Since the Acts of the Apostles witnesses to the genesis of nascent Christianity, it is not immune to the violent rhetoric pervasive in intergroup conflicts, particularly against the Jews (e.g., Acts 13:44–14:7; 28:24-28).

This book explores the mechanics of inter/intragroup conflict and identity construction as it is manifested in Acts 21:17–23:35 and shows what those discoveries entail in terms of the narrative structure of Luke-Acts. At first, the Jewish believers accuse Paul of teaching the Jews to abandon the law during his Gentile mission. Then, the Jews from Asia accuse Paul of being a threat to the Jewish nation, the Torah, and the Temple. Paul becomes a victim of violence. Paul claims his Jewish identity, which falls between his public image as a deviant and his self-image as a devout Jew. Thus, he invites his fellow Jews to take into account God's new undertakings. Taken into captivity and brought before the Roman tribune, Paul utilizes his identity as a Roman citizen to escape the impending violence backed by Roman law. Later, Paul reveals his Pharisaic identity, turns the Jewish council into a contest of intergroup conflict between Sadducees and Pharisees, and survives. In the end, the Jews—οἱ Ἰουδαῖοι—attempt an act of intergroup violence, but they fail because an intermediary, the son of Paul's sister, intervenes. Paul is safe in the hands of the Romans. This chronology of events illuminates important aspects of the construction of Paul's identity—and thus the identity of the Way—as Paul sides with and opposes his interlocutors.

Consequently, the Lukan narrative presents Paul's identity in various ways. This is not done simply to demonstrate Paul's cleverness in slipping away from the dangers he faced or to downplay his interrogators. Rather, it serves the narrative achievement of Luke-Acts: *negating slander, labeling, and violence*. Jesus was a victim of slander and the politics of identity. His opponents accused him of claiming the following identities

---

toward the Way in the remaining narrative of Acts. The Zealot (ὁ ζηλωτὴς) as an identity marker is mentioned twice in the entire New Testament (Lk 6:15; Acts 1:13; see also Acts 21:20; 22:3; 1 Cor 14:12; Gal 1:14; Tit 2:14; 1 Pet 3:13).

[9] Yet, Luke portrays Christians as "innocent of the charges of sedition and treason." C. Kavin Rowe, *World Upside Down: Reading Acts in the Graeco-Roman Age* (New York: Oxford University Press, 2009), 136.

[10] Similarly, Malina and Neyrey analyze the conflict in Luke-Acts using labeling and deviance theory and describe a deviance process similar to the theory of slander, labeling, and violence that this study proposes: "(a) a group ... *interprets* some behavior as deviant, (b) *defines* the alleged person who so behaves as deviant, (c) *accords* the treatment considered appropriate to such deviants." Bruce J. Malina and Jerome H. Neyrey, "Conflict in Luke-Acts: Labelling and Deviance Theory," in *The Social World of Luke-Acts: Models for Interpretation*, ed. Jerome H. Neyrey (Peabody: Hendrickson Publishers, 1991), 102. Their theory speaks of elements of a vicious cycle of intergroup violence in a different way: *interpreting* (e.g., slander), *defining* (e.g., labeling), and *according treatment* (e.g., violence).

for himself: Messiah (Lk 22:67, 39), Son of God (Lk 22:67-71), and King of the Jews (Lk 23:3, 37, 38). Stephen also suffered death after being labeled as a Torah breaker and temple destroyer (Acts 6:11, 13-14). Previously, Paul's opponents had labeled Paul as a trespasser of Roman imperial symbols and Jewish socioreligious symbols and engaged in violence against him (e.g., Acts 17:1-9). Yet he no longer is a victim of the politics of group identity in Acts 22–23. He does not die, as did Jesus and Stephen, but is passionately proclaiming the Gospel "with all boldness and without hindrance" by the end of Acts (Acts 28:31). In short, the trial of Paul in Acts is a challenge to the vicious cycle of slander, labeling, and violence.

A reverse side of the Lukan rhetoric, however, should not be missed. In describing the victimization of the marginalized in-group, Luke-Acts places an equally violent label upon the dominant out-group. Members of the Way repeatedly underscore that it was the Jews who rejected God's visitation and good news (e.g., Lk 4:16-30; 19:44; Acts 7:51-53). The Lukan narrative falls into the very cycle that it attempts to break: slander, labeling, and violence. Therefore, analysis of the text requires exploration at two levels. One is the narrative dimension: the story world the narrative creates. The other is the discourse dimension: the kind of portrayal of the Other the narrative presents to its readers. This book, therefore, answers the following questions. What happens to the characters in Acts 21:17–23:35 in the context of fierce intergroup conflict? How does the text characterize the Jewish people? How does Paul react to the slandering, labeling, and violence of the Jews against him? What are the implications of Paul's survival in the broader narrative context of Luke-Acts? What are the impacts of the discursive rhetoric of Luke-Acts against the Jews?

This study argues that Acts 21:17–23:35 constructs the Jewish people caught in a vicious cycle of slandering, labeling, and inflicting violence and attempts to break this cycle by presenting Paul's multiple subgroup and/or superordinate identities (e.g., a Jew, a Roman, a Pharisee). The passage falls into the same cycle at another level in the construction of Christian identity. To demonstrate this, the inquiry employs the social identity approach to illuminate the three methodological lenses through which the text is analyzed and evaluated: *ambivalence*, *social creativity*, and *recategorization*. The proposed three methodological elements aim to illuminate the Lukan strategy for coping with intergroup conflict. The analysis of the narrative and the discourse that springs from it underscores the Lukan literary artistry that challenges the vicious cycle of slander, labeling, and afflicting violence and, at the same time, problematizes the portrayal of Luke's opponents. The project examines Luke's discursive rhetoric that slanders the Jews in his effort to defend the Way and discusses the violent nature of identity construction.

Overview of the Chapters

Chapter 1 provides readers with general background information for this study. The historiographic nature of Luke-Acts gives its implied author the freedom to revise his sources in a sociocultural milieu in which a minority group, the Way, is undergoing conflict with the dominant Jewish groups. Acts 21:17–23:35 situates the Jewish-

Christian conflicts in Jerusalem, which is the geographic center of the Jewish faith, and presents Paul's multiple attempts to reduce the animosity between the two groups. Paul's subsequent failure to reconcile their differences and his escape from Jerusalem enable the Lukan narrative to challenge the way in which the Jews killed Jesus. Following the ancient practice of mimesis, Luke adopts and adapts the Passion Narrative of Jesus in his Passion Narrative of Paul. This preliminary information prepares readers to delve into the topic of this study, which is how Luke breaks the vicious cycle of slander, labeling, and afflicting violence, constructs the identity of the Way, and yet falls into the same cycle himself.

Chapter 2 begins by outlining the social identity approach (SIA), the main methodology of this study. In order to articulate the usefulness of SIA for the proposed project, this chapter not only introduces the pivotal figures in the development of SIA and the strategies of identity construction for marginalized groups but also addresses recent debates on the common in-group identity model. Particular attention is paid to SIA's implications when applied to intergroup conflict with the *proximate "other"* and how the proposed three methodological lenses—*ambivalence, social creativity*, and *recategorization*—are apt to capture complex dynamics salient in the text as well as in the broader narrative of Luke-Acts. Then, five chosen texts are discussed to highlight the ways in which Christian identity is constructed in Luke-Acts.

Chapter 3 delves into the mechanics of the slander and labeling in Acts 21:17-40, in which Paul encounters *insiders* (believing Jews), *insiders/outsiders* (the Jewish crowd), and *outsiders* (the Roman tribune). This chapter analyzes the Jewish accusations and the anti-Roman labels leveled against Paul. The chapter brings to the fore the process of stereotyping that produces prejudices against the Way, and it also traces the rationale behind the allegations raised by the Jews and Rome.

Chapter 4 engages Paul's defense speech using the key methodological concept of *recategorization* (Acts 22:1-21). A brief discussion of the structure, rhetorical elements, and functions of Paul's speech in Jerusalem is provided. Then, the chapter delineates the Lukan dialectic of self-image and public image through which Paul (re)categorizes the people of God. The subsequent discussion analyzes Paul's new vision of the people of God and the ways in which Paul tries to reduce the Jewish intergroup bias against the Way and the Gentiles.

Chapter 5 brings two other key methodological concepts—*social creativity* and *ambivalence*—to the fore to shed fresh light on Paul's encounter with the Roman tribune and the Sanhedrin (Acts 22:22–23:11). This chapter probes the historical (im) probability of Paul's Roman citizenship and the literary functions of his Pharisaic identity in Acts. It focuses on how Paul's diverse self-presentations make him a fellow in-group member with some of his interlocutors and thus avert the impending danger. The chapter concludes by discussing how Paul's social creativity mirrors the Lukan ambivalence toward the Romans and the Pharisees and the implications those findings have in relation to the identity formation of the Way.

Chapter 6 delineates the Lukan way of breaking the vicious cycle of slander, labeling, and violence (Acts 23:12-35) and questions the Lukan identity construction of the Way. The discussion begins by exploring, at the narrative level, the pattern of Jewish opposition in Luke-Acts and the counter pattern of deliverance that arises in response.

The interplay between these two interlocking cycles helps uncover how and why the Passion of Paul in Acts differs from that of Jesus in Luke. Later, the chapter undertakes a (re)reading of the chosen text (Acts 21:17–23:35) through the eyes of SIA and unravels, at the discourse level, the pitfalls of the Lukan identity construction. In the end, a new hermeneutical cycle is proposed to help readers avoid the vicious cycle of slander, labeling, and violence and broaden their understanding of Acts and Jewish-Christian relations.

Finally, the conclusion briefly revisits the spectacles and moments that have made the text and the road trip interesting thus far. The study then opens rather than closes avenues of discussion by proposing implications of the present study and topics for future study. These final reflections invite readers to think critically about their own identity and find ways to live in peace in our increasingly diverse and multilayered society.

1

Preliminary Considerations

In *The Making of Luke-Acts*, Henry J. Cadbury quotes Alexander the Great at the tomb of Achilles: "O fortunate you, that thou hast found in Homer the herald of thy valor."[1] Homer was the author who gave life to the characters in the *Iliad* and the *Odyssey*. Luke did the same in his two-volume work, Luke-Acts. Stories in these books, featuring characters such as Agamemnon, Achilles, Hector, Jesus, Peter, and Paul, are based on events—the Trojan War and the life of (the risen) Jesus, respectively—that are thought to have occurred and to be verifiable to some extent.[2] Yet, it is difficult to (dis)prove the historicity of the details of each event that Homer and Luke narrate. Cadbury rightly asserts, "Their consequences have been dependent upon their being told more than upon their being true."[3] The characters in Luke-Acts are spokespersons for Luke, who conveys his own theological arguments through the redaction of his sources (e.g., Mark, Q, and L). In the case of the Acts of the Apostles, validating its data is like searching for missing coins in the vast ocean since no literary parallel seems to exist that can verify the details of the Lukan version of the early Christian movement or the Way (Acts 9:2; 19:23; 22:4; 24:14, 22). Even the scholarly efforts to find the unity between Acts and Paul's epistles have proven to be a fruitless endeavor because the chasm is simply too wide and deep.[4] It is not the historical Peter, Stephen, Philip, and Paul but Luke, the author, who speaks through these characters and the narrator. This literary freedom that Luke exercises characterizes Luke-Acts as a narrative and Luke as

---

[1] Cicero, *Pro Archia* X, 24. Henry J. Cadbury, *The Making of Luke-Acts* (London: Macmillan, 1927), 3.
[2] For a discussion of the historicity of the Trojan War, see Lin Foxhall, *The Trojan War: Its Historicity and Context* (Bristol: Bristol Classical Press, 1984); Barry Strauss, *The Trojan War: A New History* (New York: Simon & Schuster, 2007).
[3] Cadbury, *The Making of Luke-Acts*, 4.
[4] Although some scholars see the Acts account as supporting Paul's letters and vice versa, Luke's portrayal of Paul as a letter writer, miracle worker, and co-worker of James and Peter is differing from the portrayal of Paul found in his letters. Robert P. Seesengood, *Paul: A Brief History*, Blackwell Brief Histories of Religion Series (Chichester: Wiley-Blackwell, 2010), 33–4. On the theological difference, Philipp Vielhauer states, "The author of Acts is in his Christology pre-Pauline, in his natural theology, concept of law, and eschatology, post-Pauline. He presents no specifically Pauline idea." Philipp Vielhauer, "On the 'Paulinism' of Acts," in *Paul and the Heritage of Israel: Paul's Claim Upon Israel's Legacy in Luke and Acts in the Light of the Pauline Letters*, ed. David P. Moessner, Daniel Marguerat, Mikeal C. Parsons, and Michael Wolter, LNTS 452 (London: T&T Clark, 2012), 16. For a cautious yet favorable treatment of Acts regarding the coherence of the Pauline letters, see Martin Hengel, *Acts and the History of Earliest Christianity* (London: SCM, 1979). For a skeptical point of view, see Gerd Lüdemann, *Paul, Apostle to the Gentiles: Studies in Chronology* (Philadelphia: Fortress, 1984).

a storyteller.[5] The historical reality on which the narrative reflects and the narrative world that the narrative creates are not exactly the same.

The immense chasm between the historical world and the narrative world begs the question not only of the historicity but also of the reliability of the narrative. Luke's two-volume work has its own internal consistency and coherency, especially Acts as "a sequel to Luke."[6] Each story is an intrinsic part of the larger narrative that helps move the plot forward. But, is Luke-Acts dependable as a historical source? Luke T. Johnson comments, "In Luke's writing, the past is really past. The story of Jesus and his first followers is significant for Luke's readers, but not as a direct mirror of their situation."[7] Just as any representation is a misrepresentation and often takes a discursive turn—not embellishing but demolishing—in describing one's opponents, the Lukan narrative is both subjective and biased. When it comes to describing Jews within and without, it can even be dangerous to take what is written in the narrative at face value.

---

[5] There has been a heated debate among scholars on which genre Luke-Acts belongs to (e.g., a biography, novel, epic, bios, historical monograph, or Greco-Roman historiography). Since the purpose of this study is not to decide its genre but to analyze its narrative structure and the identity construction taking place within Acts 21:17–23:35, suffice it to say that Luke-Acts is a narrative as its prolegomenon explicitly states ("an orderly account of the events that have been fulfilled among us," Luke 1:1). For a discussion of the genre of Luke-Acts, see Charles H. Talbert, *Literary Patterns, Theological Themes, and the Genre of Luke-Acts*, SBLMS 20 (Missoula, MT: Society of Biblical Literature and Scholars Press, 1975); Thomas L. Brodie, *Luke the Literary Interpreter: Luke-Acts as a Systematic Rewriting and Updating of the Elijah-Elisha Narrative in 1 and 2 Kings* (STD diss., Pontificia Universita S. Tommaso d'Aquino, Vatican City, 1981); Richard I. Pervo, *Profit with Delight: The Literary Genre of the Acts of the Apostles* (Philadelphia: Fortress, 1987); Thomas E. Phillips, *Acts Within Diverse Frames of Reference* (Macon: Mercer University Press, 2009); Marianne P. Bonz, *The Past as Legacy: Luke-Acts and Ancient Epic* (Minneapolis: Fortress, 2000); Richard Burridge, *What Are the Gospels? A Comparison with Greco-Roman Biography* (Grand Rapids: Eerdmans, 2004); Darrell L. Bock, *A Theology of Luke and Acts: God's Promised Program, Realized for All Nations*, BTNT (Grand Rapids: Zondervan, 2012), 44–8; Luke T. Johnson, *The Gospel of Luke*, SP 3 (Collegeville: Liturgical Press, 1991), 8. For a discussion on what kind of historiography Luke-Acts would be, see David E. Aune, *The New Testament in its Literary Environment* (Philadelphia: Westminster, 1989), 77; David L. Balch, "Comments on the Genre and a Political Theme of Luke-Acts: A Preliminary Comparison of Two Hellenistic Historians," in *SBL 1989 Seminar Papers*, ed. David J. Lull (Atlanta: Scholars, 1989), 343–61; "ΜΕΤΑΒΟΛΗ ΠΟΛΙΤΕΙΩΝ—Jesus as Founder of the Church in Luke-Acts: Form and Function," in *Contextualizing Acts: Lukan Narrative and Greco-Roman Discourse*, ed. Todd C. Penner and Caroline V. Stichele (Atlanta: Scholars, 2003), 139–88; Gregory E. Sterling, *Historiography and Self-Definition: Josephos, Luke-Acts, and Apologetic Historiography*, NovTSup 64 (Leiden: Brill, 1992); Todd C. Penner, *In Praise of Christian Origins: Stephen and the Hellenists in Lukan Apologetic Historiography*, ESEC 10 (New York: T&T Clark, 2004). See also F. F. Bruce, *The Acts of the Apostles: The Greek Text with an Introduction and Commentary* (Grand Rapids: Eerdmans, 1973); Ernst Haenchen, *The Acts of the Apostles: A Commentary* (Oxford: Blackwell, 1982), 78–81; Clare K. Rothschild, *Luke-Acts and the Rhetoric of History: An Investigation of Early Christian Historiography*, WUNT 2/175 (Tübingen: Mohr Siebeck, 2004); Doohee Lee, *Luke-Acts and "Tragic history": Communicating Gospel with the World*, WUNT 2/346 (Tübingen: Mohr Siebeck, 2013); Scott Shauf, *Theology as History, History as Theology: Paul in Ephesus in Acts 19*, BZNW 133 (Berlin: de Gruyter, 2005), 50–80.

[6] Richard I. Pervo, *Acts: A Commentary*, Hermeneia (Minneapolis: Fortress, 2009), 20. For a discussion on the unity of Luke-Acts, see Joseph Verheyden, "The Unity of Luke-Acts: One Work, One Author, One Purpose?" in *Issues in Luke-Acts: Selected Essays*, ed. Sean A. Adams and Michael Pahl, GH 26 (Piscataway, NJ: Gorgias, 2012), 43–66.

[7] Luke T. Johnson, "On Finding the Lukan Community: A Cautious Cautionary Essay," in *Contested Issues in Christian Origins and the New Testament Collected Essays*, NovTSup 146, ed. Luke T. Johnson (Leiden: Brill, 2013), 141.

The present study therefore approaches Acts 21:17–23:35 as a Lukan literary construction rather than as a historical report, one that has specific functions in the wider narrative. Sometimes, the study describes the historical background of first-century Palestine and provides historical data relevant to certain issues. Yet, its primary aim is not to validate the narrative but rather to situate the events the narrative portrays in the broader history and ultimately investigate the roles of the events in the broader story.

With this preliminary comment on Lukan literary freedom as the backdrop, this chapter first presents the boundary and narrative structure of the main text, Acts 21:17–23:35. Second, it surveys the scholarship on the text, the so-called "Paul in Jerusalem," and addresses strengths as well as weaknesses of each position. Third, the chapter discusses mimesis in the Lukan Passion Narrative of Jesus and Paul. In conclusion, it offers an eagle's-eye view of the context and function of Acts 21:17–23:35 in its historical setting and in the narrative of Luke-Acts that will prepare readers to encounter the story of Paul's visit to Jerusalem in a new light.

1.1. The Text: Acts 21:17–23:35

The focus of the present study is Acts 21:17–23:35, in which Paul experiences a series of conflicts with the Jewish people. Located in Paul's Travel Narrative (Acts 13–28), the text portrays Paul's continued efforts to preach the gospel. Particular attention is paid to this story because it has a distinctive and critical place in the broad narrative of Luke-Acts.

1.1.1. Boundary of Acts 21:17–23:35

Three significant factors separate the given text from the passages that come before and after. (1) *The locus of the story*: *Jerusalem*. Jerusalem is the geographic center of Luke-Acts. It is the place of the Messiah's suffering and of the outpouring of the Holy Spirit, which are the very content and the very force, respectively, of the entire gospel mission. Paul has previously visited Jerusalem several times after his encounter with the risen Lord on the road to Damascus (Acts 9:26-30; 12:25; 15:2, 4; 18:22). Yet, just as Jesus undertakes his final journey to Jerusalem in the Gospel, Luke places Paul, the protagonist of the second half of Acts, on the way to Jerusalem one last time as a starting point for going ultimately to Rome (Luke 9:51–19:44; Acts 19:21).[8] In Acts

---

[8] Similar, if not identical, elements are found in Jesus's journey to Jerusalem (Lk 9:51–19:44) and Paul's journey to Jerusalem (Acts 19:21–21:16). (1) The narrator explicitly states that they are determined to go to Jerusalem ("He set his face to go to Jerusalem," Lk 9:51; "Paul resolved in the Spirit to go . . . to Jerusalem," Acts 19:21). (2) The protagonists predict that Jerusalem is a place of suffering (Lk 18:31-33; see also Lk 9:21-22, 44; Acts 20:22-24; 21:13). (3) Weeping precedes the entry to Jerusalem (Lk 19:41-44; 21:13). Yet, there are also dissimilarities. Shauf compares Acts 19:21-22 with Lk 9:51-53 and finds three significant differences. (1) Lk 9:51 uses συμπληρόω to denote "fulfillment," whereas Acts 19:21 uses πληρόω to convey the rather usual "accomplishment" of a past event. (2) Whereas Jesus's final destination is Jerusalem, for Paul Jerusalem is a station in which he receives a ticket—

21:17, Paul arrives in Jerusalem. In Acts 23:33, Paul is in Caesarea.⁹ Caesarea functions as a geographical intersection that connects Jerusalem with the Gentile territory in Acts.¹⁰ The narrator states that Paul stops at Caesarea on his way to and out of Jerusalem (see Acts 18:22, 21:8, 16). Though Acts 23:33 locates Paul outside Jerusalem, the present study considers Acts 21:17–23:35 as a literary unit based on the following reasons. First, with the governor Felix's remark, Paul is not going back to Jerusalem. He is confirmed to stay in Caesarea and he is safe in Herod's headquarters (πραιτώριον. Acts 23:35). Second, the temporary clause, μετὰ δὲ πέντε ἡμέρας ("after five days"), marks not only the substantial passage of time but also the beginning of the new section (Acts 24:1). A thrilling overnight escape has ended and time slows down. Third, with Acts 24:1 the narrator changes the scene. Paul is in a courtroom. Now, he has to defend himself and his gospel before a *Gentile* ruler.¹¹

(2) *The content of the story*: the *conflict* with the Jews in Jerusalem. In the Gospel, Jerusalem and the temple, in particular, are contested spaces over which different persons or groups claim to have authority: Jesus (e.g., Lk 19:45-46), the chief priests, the scribes, and the elders/leaders (e.g., Lk 19:47-48; 20:1-8; 22:66-71), the Sadducees (e.g., Lk 20:27-40), Pilate (e.g., Lk 23:1-5, 13-25), and Herod (e.g., Lk 23:6-12).¹² In this arena, Jesus at first knocks down his opponents, but finally his arrest gives leverage to his accusers or "the power of darkness" (Lk 22:53). He is beaten, mocked, and killed (e.g., Lk 22:63-65; 23:35-39, 46). The same is true for Paul in Jerusalem, except for one

---

imprisonment—to go to Rome (Acts 19:21). (3) Jesus follows the messengers whom he sent before him, whereas Paul stays in Asia after sending two delegates to Macedonia. Shauf, *Theology as History, History as Theology*, 235-7.

⁹ Later the Jews ask Festus, the new governor, to bring Paul to Jerusalem to ambush and kill him on the way, but their plan fails because Paul appeals to the emperor (Acts 25:1-12). Paul is not going back to Jerusalem. Earlier, the narrator alluded to a decisive rupture between Paul (or the Way?) and the temple. During Paul's first encounter with the Jews in Jerusalem, the narrator explicitly says, "They seized Paul and dragged him out of the temple, and immediately *the doors were shut*" (Acts 21:30). Since the temple is closed to him, there is no reason for the implied author to bring Paul back to Jerusalem.

¹⁰ Acts 8:40; 9:30; 10:1, 24; 11:11; 18:22; 21:8, 16; 23:16, 23, 33; 25:1. In particular, the narrator locates Paul's meeting with Cornelius—arguably the first Gentile convert, if not the second, to the Way in Acts—in Caesarea (see Acts 10:1-48; see also Philip's encounter with the Ethiopian eunuch in Acts 8:26-40). For the outpouring of the Holy Spirit on the household of Cornelius at the border crossing, see Hyun Ho Park, "From Jewish Mission to Gentile Mission: Triple Stories of Peter and the Border Crossing in Acts 9:32–10:48" (paper presented at the annual meeting of the SBL, San Antonio, Texas, November 19–22, 2016). Luke uses Paul's defense at Caesarea as a springboard to bring his protagonist to Rome, the heart of the Gentile world (Acts 25:6, 11-12).

¹¹ Many commentators also see Acts 21:17–23:35 as a literary unit. For example, Mikeal C. Parsons, *Acts*, PCNT (Grand Rapids: Baker Academic, 2008), 301–22; Craig S. Keener, *Acts: An Exegetical Commentary* (Grand Rapids: Baker Academic, 2014), 3113–348; Daniel Marguerat, *Les Actes des apôtres (13–28)*, CNT 5b (Geneva: Labor et fides; Paris: Diffusion Presses Universitaires de France, 2015), 247–301 (slightly differently, Acts 21:15–23:35). Parsons rightly states that Acts 24–26 is "filled with legal scenes and defense speeches." Parsons, *Acts*, 323.

¹² Luke depicts the "people" (λαὸς) wishing to follow Jesus but being swayed by the decisions of the leaders of the people (see Luke 23:13, 14, 27, 35). Yong-Sung Anh states, "Placed in-between [the power of darkness and the coming reign of God], the people function as an indicator of the power-shift. Although they are seemingly so powerful that the leaders fear them, Luke does not describe the people as anything more than the booty of the conflict." Yong-Sung Anh, *The Reign of God and Rome in Luke's Passion Narrative: An East Asian Global Perspective*, BIS 80 (Leiden: Brill, 2006), 197.

thing. The mission of Jesus in Jerusalem is to suffer, but the mission of Paul is survival. A series of conflicts ensues as Paul steps on Jerusalem soil: conflicts with Jewish believers in the Way (Acts 21:17-26), the Jews from Asia (Acts 21:27-28), the Jewish crowd (Acts 21:30-31, 35-36; 22:22-23), the Roman tribune, Claudius Lysias (Acts 21:37-40; 22:24-29), Sadducees and Pharisees (Acts 22:30-23:11), and *the Jews* (οἱ Ἰουδαῖοι. Acts 23:12-35). Paul is in a dire situation in which he is accused, arrested, beaten, mocked, and threatened to death (Acts 21:28, 31-36, 22:22-23; 23:10, 12-22). Paul's stay in Jerusalem is brief, covering a span of about six days (see Acts 21:17, 18, 26; 22:30, 12, 31, 32),[13] yet it is full of suspense—tension with Jewish believers, the threat of the Jewish mob, interventions of the Roman military, a Pharisee–Sadducee fight, a conspiracy against Paul, and a mission to rescue Paul by the Roman soldiers. The heartfelt farewell at Philip's house in Caesarea and his final speech to the Ephesian elders foreshadow what is to come for Paul; he will experience persecution by a group of Jews in Jerusalem, the antagonists in this section.[14] After fierce conflicts with Jews in Jerusalem, Paul arrives in Caesarea and stands before the governor, Felix (Acts 23:33-35). Although the Jewish opponents—the high priest Ananias, some elders, Tertullus, and *the Jews*—still accuse Paul, as he steps out of Jerusalem his main interlocutors are rulers—Felix, Festus, Agrippa, and, by allusion, the emperor (Acts 24:10-26; 25:8-12, 21; 26:1-32; 27:24; 28:19; see also Luke 12:11)—until he arrives in Rome and meets the Jews in Rome (Acts 28:17-31).[15]

---

[13] When Paul stands before Felix at Caesarea, he says, "As you can find out, it is not more than twelve days since I went up to worship in Jerusalem" (Acts 24:11). Since the hearing takes place "five days" after Paul arrived at Caesarea, Paul's stay at Jerusalem is proximately shorter than seven days (Acts 24:1).

[14] Conflict with the Jews occurs so often in Acts that it functions as a literary device to move protagonists to the next destination in the narrative (see Acts 9:23, 13:50-51; 14:5-7, 19; 17:13-15; 18:5-7). Yet, beginning in Acts 20:4, Paul neither encounters Jews nor suffers from their opposition until he arrives in Jerusalem. Paul is still constantly on the move, because he is determined to go to Jerusalem and ultimately Rome (Acts 19:21; 20:16, 22; 21:13; see also Acts 21:4, 11, 12; 25:9-12; 27:24; 28:19).

[15] There is a heated debate in Lukan scholarship regarding whether Luke is pro-imperial or anti-imperial. For many years, the scholarship has argued that Luke wrote his Gospel and Acts to convey to Roman officials that Christianity was not a threat to the empire. For example, Cadbury, *The Making of Luke-Acts*, 308–15; Paul Walaskay, *"And So We Came to Rome": The Political Perspective of St Luke*, SNTSMS 49 (Cambridge: Cambridge University Press, 1983), 25–37. This view, however, is challenged by recent scholarship. For the anti-Rome position, see, for example, Richard Cassidy, *Jesus, Politics, and Society: A Study of Luke's Gospel* (Maryknoll, NY: Orbis, 1978); Rubén Muñoz-Larrondo, *A Postcolonial Reading of the Acts of the Apostles*, Studies in Biblical Literature 147 (New York: Peter Lang, 2012). I argue with the third group of scholars (e.g., Walton, Pickett) that Luke's attitude toward the empire is ambivalent (Ch. 5.1.3). On the one hand, Luke portrays Roman officers as protectors of Paul when he is preaching the gospel in the Passion Narrative of Paul. On the other hand, Luke describes Roman officers as corrupt and full of flaws, as in Acts 24:26, in which Felix presumably is seeking money from Paul. Regarding the killing of Jesus, Luke says through the mouth of Peter, "And now, friends, I know that you acted in ignorance, as did also your rulers" (Acts 3:17). See Steve Walton, "The State They Were In: Luke's View of the Roman Empire," in *Rome in the Bible and the Early Church*, ed. Peter Oakes (Grand Rapids: Baker Academic, 2002), 1–41; Raymond Pickett, "Luke and Empire," in *Luke-Acts and Empire: Essays in Honor of Robert L. Brawley*, ed. David Rhoads, David Esterline, and Jae Won Lee, PTMS 151 (Eugene, OR: Pickwick, 2011), 1–22.

(3) *The cause of the conflict: Jewish identity*. During his missional journey, Paul experiences hostility as well as hospitality from his addressees.[16] *The Jews* (οἱ Ἰουδαῖοι), a Lukan literary character, play a critical role in this conflict as instigators, whereas Gentiles are often receptive to Paul's witness to Jesus.[17] In the Gentile territory, what causes conflict is "the proclamation of the gospel"[18] and the jealousy of *the Jews* (Acts 13:45; 17:5). For example, in Paul's preaching in Antioch of Pisidia, *the Jews* not only oppose Paul's message—"these words" (τὰ ῥήματα ταῦτα; Acts 13:42)—but also hate to see Paul's preaching gaining a broad audience, including converts to Judaism and Gentiles (Acts 13:43, 45, 48). Yet, in Jerusalem Paul never enjoys such popularity but encounters only challenges throughout his stay. At the heart of the fierce conflict is Paul's claim to have a Jewish identity or his actions that seem to contradict such claims. He is accused of not observing the law (Acts 21:21, 24) and of teaching against the Jewish nation, law, and temple (Acts 21:28). Yet he constantly insists on his Jewish identity and the Jewishness of the gospel to his audience (Acts 22:3; 23:1-6). Jewish identity is a recurring theme in Acts, as Paul restates his commitment to Jewish tradition at his defense in the following chapters (Acts 24:10-21; 25:8; 26:4-7, 22-23). In Jerusalem and with Jewish opponents, however, his battle to defend his identity is a must-win to bring himself to Rome, the heart of empire (Acts 23:11). The focus of the present study is *both* the intra-Jewish conflict *and* intergroup conflict between the Way and Jewish out-group members.

In sum, Acts 21:17–23:35 is a distinctive set of stories in which Paul, the protagonist, undergoes conflicts with various Jewish groups in Jerusalem on account of his Jewish identity.

1.1.2. Narrative Structure of Acts 21:17–23:35

The text of Acts 21:17–23:35 consists of seven scenes in which Paul encounters different interlocutors. Like a roller-coaster ride, tension exists at every turn. When it seems resolved, readers are invited to prepare for another fall until the protagonist is off the train. The constant ups and downs illustrate a point of the story. Jerusalem is a contested space for Paul.

---

[16] Acts describes Paul as beginning and ending each journey in either Antioch, his mission hub, or Caesarea, a station through which he moves to the next destination: first journey (Acts 13:4–14:28), second journey (Acts 15:36–18:23), third journey (Acts 19:1–21:14), fourth journey (Acts 21:15–23:35), and fifth journey (Acts 24:1–28:31). The first three journeys are often called "Paul's missionary journeys." Yet, since the nature of Paul's fourth and fifth journeys and his speeches in Acts 21–28 are apologetic rather than missionary, commentators are reluctant to include Acts 21:1–28:31 in Paul's missional journeys. See, for example, Darrell L. Bock, *Acts*, BECNT (Grand Rapids: Baker Academic, 2007). Holladay also states that the main concern of Acts 21–26 is "to defend Paul." Carl R. Holladay, *Acts: A Commentary*, NTL (Louisville: Westminster John Knox, 2016), 402.

[17] *The Jews*—οἱ Ἰουδαῖοι—is a Lukan literary character that constantly appears to oppose the preaching of the gospel and create confusion among the Jewish people and the Gentiles attracted to the gospel (e.g., Acts 17:5; 21:27). When referring to this specific group hostile to the gospel, this study italicizes the term, *the Jews*. This negative portrayal of *the Jews* by the Lukan narrator is contrary to the neutral and/or positive attitude that the Lukan narrator takes to the Jewish nation as in Acts 2.

[18] Holladay, *Acts*, 402.

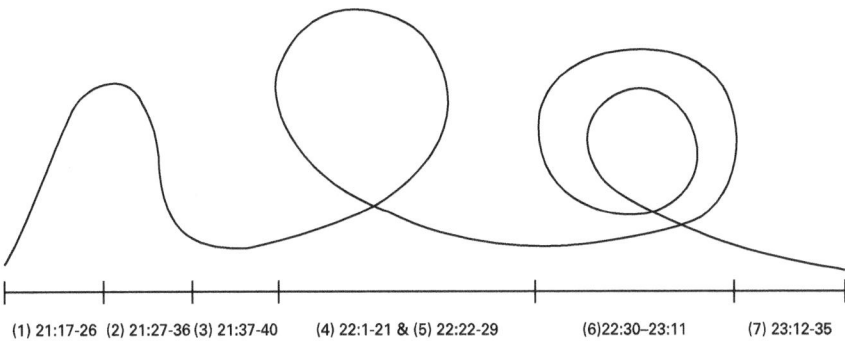

Figure 1.1 Paul's Roller-Coaster Ride in Acts 21:17–23:35.

The following is an outline of the roller-coaster ride of these seven scenes. 1) *Lift hill*: Paul's encounter with believers in Jerusalem (Acts 21:17-26). While visiting James, Paul hears that Jewish believers question his commitment to the law. He visits the temple to complete the day of purification and give a sacrifice. This existing tension between Paul and the believers is a prelude to what is to come in the following scene. 2) *Drop*: Paul's encounter with the Jews from Asia and the Jewish mob (Acts 21:27-36). Paul is accused, dragged out, and beaten by the Jews. The tribune and the soldiers intervene, but the crowd keeps shouting for his annihilation. 3) *Brake run*: Paul's first encounter with the Roman tribune (Acts 21:37-40). Paul is not only saved by the Roman tribune but is also given an opportunity to speak before the Jewish crowd. 4) *Lift hill*: Paul's speech before the Jewish crowd (Acts 22:1-21). Speaking in Hebrew, Paul explains his zeal for the law and reaches the climax of his speech. Paul seems to seize the initiative. 5) *Pre-loop*: Paul's second encounter with the Roman tribune (Acts 22:22-29). When Paul speaks of his call to the Gentile mission, he immediately experiences harsh opposition from the crowd. The tribune rescues Paul once again but attempts to examine him by flogging. Paul saves himself by revealing his identity as a Roman citizen. 6) *Corkscrew*: Paul's encounter with the Sanhedrin (Acts 22:30-23:11). Paul's initial remarks on his fidelity to Jewish tradition take an abrupt turn and cause a wild conversation with the high priest. The ups and downs do not stop here. Paul's claim to have a Pharisaic identity results in an uproar that threatens his very life. The tribune intervenes a third time, as well as the voice of the Lord, which brings Paul back to safety. 7) *High-speed section*: the plot to kill Paul and his escape (Acts 23:12-35). The scene moves swiftly *from* introducing the Jewish conspiracy to murder Paul *to* Paul's arrival in Caesarea. Everything happens in less than a day. The narrator creates suspense by introducing a series of private scenes in the barrack—Paul's nephew delivering the news to Paul and later to the tribune; the tribune ordering a secret escape mission at night and writing a letter to governor Felix.

To summarize, Acts 21:17-23:35 is Paul's wild roller-coaster ride full of *head chopper sections*. Danger lurks around every corner. Combining scenes two and three and scenes five and six, the narrative structure drawn from the preceding analysis is as follows:

Table 1.1 The Chiastic Structure of Acts 21:17–23:35

A. Intro: Paul's entry to Jerusalem and encounter with the Jewish believers (21:17-26)
  B. Paul's encounter with the Jewish crowd and the Roman tribune (21:27-40)
    C. Paul's speech before the Jewish crowd (22:1-21)
  B'. Paul's encounter with the Roman tribune and the Sanhedrin (22:22-23:11)
A'. Closing: Paul's escape from Jerusalem and encounter with the plot to kill him (23:12-35)

With this chiastic structure in view, the discussion now turns to scholarly discussions on the chosen text.

1.2. Survey of the Scholarship on Paul in Jerusalem

A formidable difficulty in tracing scholarly positions on Acts 21:17–23:35 is that scholars often differ in how they divide this section. Some treat the given narrative as an individual unit,[19] some divide it into multiple subsections,[20] and some place certain parts of the narrative under different headings.[21] A number of commentators and monographs locate Acts 21:17–23:35 within a longer section, Acts 21–28, based on Paul's status as a prisoner[22] or on trial scenes.[23] Besides the length and flexibility of the boundary, constant changes in the scene add complexities that make it difficult to identify a coherent theme undergirding the narrative. Nevertheless, scholars have ventured into the text and come out with a few findings.

The scholarship is largely divided into two groups—those who read the text non-apologetically and those who read it apologetically. A non-apologetic reading finds *a mimetic purpose* and *an evangelical purpose*, as Alexandru Neagoe summarizes in his

---

[19] For example, Parsons, *Acts*, 301–22; Michal Beth Dinkler, "The Acts of the Apostles," in *The Gospels and Acts: Fortress Commentary on the Bible Study Edition*, ed. Margaret Aymer, Cynthia Briggs Kittredge, and David A. Sánchez (Minneapolis: Fortress, 2016), 356–7.

[20] For example, Johnson, *The Acts of the Apostles*, 373–408; Holladay, *Acts*, 407–43; John B. Polhill, *Acts*, NAC 26 (Nashville: Broadman, 1992), 445–77.

[21] For example, see John W. McGarvey, *New Commentary on Acts of Apostles: Vol. 1* (Delight, AR: Gospel Light Publishing, 1892), 203–33; F. F. Bruce, *Commentary on the Book of Acts* (Grand Rapids: Eerdmans, 1976), 428–60; William S. Kurz, *Acts of the Apostles*, CCSS (Grand Rapids: Baker Academic, 2013), 317–41; Charles K. Barrett, *The Acts of the Apostles: A Shorter Commentary* (Edinburgh: T&T Clark, 2002), 321–61.

[22] For example, see F. Scott Spencer, *Journeying Through Acts: A Literary-Cultural Reading* (Peabody: Hendrickson, 2004), 212–46; Johnson, *The Acts of the Apostles*, 395–477; Gerhard A. Krodel, *Acts*, ACNT (Minneapolis: Augsburg, 1986), 396–509; Beverly R. Gaventa, *The Acts of the Apostles*, ANTC (Nashville: Abingdon, 2003), 297–348. See also Harold S. Songer, "Paul's Mission to Jerusalem: Acts 20–28," *RevExp* 71, no. 4 (1974): 499–510.

[23] Alexandru Neagoe, *The Trial of the Gospel: An Apologetic Reading of Luke's Trial Narratives*, SNTSMS 116 (Cambridge: Cambridge University Press, 2002), 175–218; Matthew L. Skinner, *The Trial Narratives: Conflict, Power, and Identity in the New Testament* (Louisville: Westminster John Knox, 2010), 133–56.

survey of the scholarship on Paul's trials.[24] Paul is setting an example of Christian witness or he is preaching, not necessarily defending, the gospel. Yet, the majority of scholars notice undeniable traces of Lukan apology and focus on identifying the object, addressees, and circumstances of Luke's defense.[25] Under the big umbrella of apologetic reading, there are eight scholarly positions worth noting.

1) *Defending Paul's long custody*. Craig S. Keener posits internal challenges coming from insiders, the Christian audience. The question stems from Paul's long custody: "If he was innocent, why did not God deliver him . . .?"[26] He argues that Paul's testimony in his defense speeches of Acts 22–26, especially Acts 22:2-21, when Paul was a prisoner, and his reenactment of Jesus' passion show not God's abandonment but God's presence with Paul.[27] Similarly, Matthew L. Skinner argues that Paul's safety and ability to witness to the gospel show that he is under God's care.[28]

This position has several benefits. First of all, Luke's apologetic efforts are probably internal since his audience is composed of members of his in-group rather than his out-group.[29] Second, the text marks the beginning of Paul's imprisonment, which lasts until the end of Acts. Third, events during his custody resemble the trial of Jesus in the Gospel.[30] There are also difficulties, however. First, it is hard to prove whether the challenges originated from within or without. Though the story opens with Paul's conflict with Jewish believers in Jerusalem, it soon spins around dealings with outsiders. Second, Paul surely defends his imprisonment (Acts 28:20), but it is the gospel and his Jewish identity that he ultimately fights for during his custody (e.g., Acts 22:3; 23:1, 6).

2) *Defending Christianity in favor of Judaism*. Hans Conzelmann finds the reason for Paul's defense not inside but outside the Christian circle—the Jewish opposition to Christianity. He argues that the belief in the resurrection is "the link between (genuine) Judaism and Christianity" and holds that "the Jews should realize their faith comes to fulfillment in Christianity."[31] Subsequent scholars also articulate the connection

---

[24] Neagoe, *The Trial of the Gospel*, 176–7. For example, reading the passage non-apologetically, Marie-Eloise Rosenblatt finds a *mimetic purpose* in this passage. She argues that Paul is "not a vehicle for Luke's opinion about the Roman government" but a "missionary faithful to his preaching vocation." Marie-Eloise Rosenblatt, *Paul the Accused: His Portrait in the Acts of the Apostles*, ZSNT (Collegeville: Liturgical Press, 1995), 94. Paul is a model whom Luke's audience should imitate when they face a similar struggle. John C. Lentz, on the other hand, discovers an *evangelistic purpose* in Luke's portrayal of Paul: "the mood of Luke's work is expansive and evangelistic, not introspective and defensive." John C. Lentz, Jr., *Luke's Portrait of Paul*, SNTSMS 77 (Cambridge: Cambridge University Press, 1993), 171.
[25] For example, see John T. Squires, *The Plan of God in Luke-Acts*, SNTSMS 76 (Cambridge: Cambridge University Press, 1993).
[26] Keener, *Acts*, 3195.
[27] Keener, *Acts*, 3196.
[28] Matthew L. Skinner, *Locating Paul: Places of Custody as Narrative Settings in Acts 21–28*, SBLAB 13 (Atlanta: SBL, 2003), 180–5.
[29] Pervo, *Acts*, 556: "Jews would not have read them and discovered that Paul was not as bad as reputed, nor would polytheists have worked through this book to learn that the Christian movement was utterly devoid of subversive tendencies." Previously, Paul is accused of not being faithful to the law, but he does not have a chance to defend himself against such a charge (Acts 18:12-17).
[30] Parallels between the passion of Jesus and the so-called passion of Paul will be discussed later in this chapter.
[31] Hans Conzelmann, *Acts of the Apostles: A Commentary on the Acts of the Apostles*, Hermeneia, trans. James Limburg, A. Thomas Kraabel, and Donald H. Juel (Philadelphia: Fortress, 1987), 192.

between the two. For example, Howard Marshall states, "Pharisaic Judaism found its fulfillment in Christianity."[32] In the same vein, Joseph A. Fitzmyer insists that Paul's speech before the Jewish crowd (Acts 22:1-21) is "a Pauline explanation of Christianity as a legitimate development of Judaism."[33]

This position emphasizes the coherence rather than the disparity between Christianity and Judaism. Paul's commitment to the Jewish tradition, particularly to Pharisaism, could give a point of contact to Luke's audience as they had witnessed the development of rabbinic Judaism after the fall of the Jerusalem temple in 70 CE.[34] The belief in resurrection could be a point of dialogue. A significant drawback, however, is that the conversation might begin, but it would never end fruitfully. The problem is twofold. First, this position is based on Jewish-Christian supersessionism, which posits Christianity's superiority to Judaism. In contrast, Paul and the Lukan narrator work toward the extension, not the contraction, of Jewishness. Second, it does not examine the discourse the narrative creates. The text clearly portrays the Way as an outcome of God's new actions (Acts 22:3-21). Yet the other side, the Jewish side, of the story is missing.[35] One cannot benignly buy into Luke's logic.

3) *Defending Christianity over against Judaism.* Gerhard A. Krodel opines that Paul's encounter with the Jewish council demonstrates the gulf rather than the union between two parties.[36] It is not Paul's disobedience of the Law of Moses but the Jewish rejection of the resurrection that separates Christianity from Judaism.[37] Richard B. Rackham identifies the Sadducees as Paul's opponents, not the entire Jewish Council nor Jews as a whole, and states that the cry of the Pharisees in Acts 23:9 is "the first sentence of acquittal of ... Paul, pronounced by his own nation."[38]

Anti-Jewish rhetoric is unquestionably present in the text. Furthermore, Paul's wild exchange with the high priest and the narrator's note on the Sadducees distance the Way from the Sadducees. A setback is also undeniable. This position does not pay attention to nuances the narrative contains toward the Pharisees. Whereas the Pharisees share a belief in the resurrection and cry out that Paul is innocent, they fail to see God's new undertaking in Jesus.[39] The Lukan ambivalence toward the Jewish people and Judaism is critical to understanding Paul's interactions in the text.

---

[32] I. Howard Marshall, *The Acts of the Apostles: An Introduction and Commentary* (Grand Rapids: Eerdmans, 1980), 364.

[33] Joseph A. Fitzmyer, *The Acts of the Apostles: A New Translation with Introduction and Commentary*, AB 31 (New York: Doubleday, 1998), 703. See also Bruce, *Commentary on the Book of the Acts*, 453; Johnson, *The Acts of the Apostles*, 400-2.

[34] See Michael Brenner, *A Short History of the Jews*, trans. Jeremiah Riemer (Princeton: Princeton University Press, 2010), 46-9.

[35] For an extensive study of anti-Jewish texts in the New Testament, see Norman A. Beck, *Mature Christianity: The Recognition and Repudiation of the Anti-Jewish Polemic of the New Testament* (Cranbury, NJ: Associated University Press, 1985), esp. 225-42.

[36] Krodel, *Acts*, 397.

[37] Krodel, *Acts*, 399.

[38] Richard B. Rackham, *The Acts of the Apostles: An Exposition* (London: Methuen, 1957), 435.

[39] Johnson, *The Acts of the Apostles*, 401-2. Tannehill also argues that Simon the Pharisee in Luke 7:36-50 is not a negative character but "an 'open' character, one who is not totally evil and is capable of change." Robert C. Tannehill, *The Shape of Luke's Story: Essays on Luke-Acts* (Eugene, OR: Cascade Books, 2005), 257.

4) *Defending the Gentile mission*. Beverly R. Gaventa stresses that what Acts is defending through Paul's defense is not Paul himself but the divine plan that extends Israel's hope "to include the Gentiles."[40] Stephen J. Strauss concurs with Gaventa that Paul's defense serves the larger purpose of Acts, which is to inform both insiders and outsiders—questioning believers and informed seekers—that "the Gentile mission is the true extension of Israel's messianic hope."[41] Attending to Paul's status as a prisoner and his movement from Jerusalem to Caesarea and ultimately to Rome, F. Scott Spencer also asserts that in spite of his imprisonment "Paul still makes notable *progress* in advancing the Christian mission."[42]

From the narrative scheme of Acts 21:17–23:35, this position first underscores the climax of Paul's defense. Paul's long defense speech before the Jewish crowd explicates the divine necessity of the Jewish mission and leads to the vehement resistance of the Jews. Second, the risen Jesus confirms not only Jesus's presence but also Paul's final destination, Rome (Acts 23:11). Unanswered questions still remain. What do the Gentile mission and its progress entail for Jewish identity? What do the wild interactions between Paul and the Jews tell us about the Jewish identity of the Way in Acts? The present study attempts to answer these inquiries.

5) *Defending Paul's proclamation*. Mikeal C. Parsons argues that Luke, by narrating the events that happened in Jerusalem slowly, vindicates not only Paul but also his message, "the hope in the resurrection from the dead (23:6)."[43] Bruce J. Malina and John J. Pilch also find evangelistic purpose in this narrative. Paul's geographic movement fulfills both Jesus's foretelling of persecution of his disciples and his call of Paul through which Paul would bring Jesus's name to the kings as well as to the people of Israel (Lk 21:12-13; Acts 9:15).[44] In a similar vein, Alexandru Neagoe maintains that what is on trial is not just the character Paul but the gospel. He points out that the trial scenes in Luke-Acts put "important tenets of the Christian faith before the reader" and are intended to confirm the gospel.[45]

A major advantage of this proposal is that it switches the focus of the discussion from the agents, Paul and/or Christianity, to the message. The narrative and its spokespeople, whether it is the narrator or Paul, are the vehicles of the gospel to its audience, as the narrator makes clear in the prologue of Luke-Acts (Lk 1:1-4). A weakness of this approach, however, is that it misses the dynamics created between Paul and his interlocutors. The message presented in the story is one, but how it is conditioned and even transformed is another. The message changes over the course of the narrative. Furthermore, the text not only fulfills the previous prophecies but also moves the narrative forward, which demands critical inquiry on the part of the reader.

6) *Defending Christianity's political harmlessness*. Frederick J. Foakes-Jackson and Kirsopp Lake argue that Luke tries to "establish the legitimacy of Christianity as the

---

[40] Gaventa, *The Acts of the Apostles*, 297. See also Talbert, *Reading Acts*, 193–202.
[41] Stephen J. Strauss, "The Purpose of Acts and the Mission of God," *BSac* 169 (2012): 459.
[42] Spencer, *Journeying through Acts*, 212, emphasis in the original.
[43] Parsons, *Acts*, 302.
[44] Bruce J. Malina and John J. Pilch, *Social-Science Commentary on the Book of Acts* (Minneapolis: Fortress, 2008), 152.
[45] Neagoe, *The Trial of the Gospel*, 22. See also Charles K. Barrett, *A Critical and Exegetical Commentary on the Acts of the Apostles: Vol. 2*, ICC (Edinburgh: T. & T. Clark, 1994), 1068.

religion of the Chosen People."[46] Luke repeatedly shows the link between Israel and the followers of Jesus and demonstrates that Christianity "contained nothing detrimental to good order."[47] In discussing Paul's speech (Acts 22:1-21), Ernst Haenchen quotes *"religio quasi licita"*—seemingly lawful religion—from Tertullian's *Apology* and states that, if continuity exists between Christianity and Judaism, "Christianity can claim to be tolerated like Judaism."[48] Along the same line, Daniel Marguerat argues that Paul's speeches in Acts 21-28 "configure the identity of Christianity by insisting on continuity with Judaism and compatibility with the Roman imperial institution."[49] Christianity is interested neither in political Messianism nor in having a political character.[50]

Accusations of insurrection are certainly made against members of the Way (e.g., Lk 23:1-5; Acts 17:5-9; 21:37-39). Luke-Acts portrays *the Jews*, not the apostles and the disciples, as instigating turbulence among people. Jesus and Paul never show overt enmity against Rome (e.g., Lk 23:3-4, Acts 21:38-39). This proposal, however, is not immune to criticism. First, the suggestion that the category *religio licita* existed when Luke composed Acts is doubted.[51] Second, it is not likely that Roman officials read Luke-Acts in the first place nor that they understood its political apology.[52] It is an apology that is, first and foremost, "addressed to the church."[53]

7) *Defending Rome*. Unlike those who understand Luke as appealing to Rome, Paul W. Walaskay proposes the opposite. He argues that Luke is persuading his readers to cooperate with Rome because, as narrated in the story, it is the "divinely guided Roman law that insures the continuation and growth of the gospel."[54] Paul's appeal to Caesar is not just a legal action that he takes to protect himself from *the Jews*. It is more than that. It is a sign of God at work in history to bring the gospel to Rome. He states, therefore, that "the Christian church and the Roman empire need not fear nor suspect each other."[55]

It is indisputable that the Romans are the guardians of Paul in this narrative. They rescue him time and again from Jews and securely deliver him to Caesarea. Besides, Paul's Roman citizenship seems to allude to a possible alliance between Rome and

---

[46] *BegC* 5.182.
[47] *BegC* 5.180. Burton S. Easton also states that "Luke desired this Roman official [Theophilus] ... should win a favorable opinion of the new religion." Burton S. Easton, *Early Christianity: The Purpose of Acts, and Other Papers*, ed. Frederick C. Grant (Greenwich, CT: Seabury, 1954), 33.
[48] Haenchen, *The Acts of the Apostles*, 631. Hans Conzelmann also understands that Luke has two apologetic concerns. Toward the Jews, Luke makes clear that "one must obey God rather than men," whereas toward the empire "one should render to Caesar what is Caesar's and to God what is God's." Hans Conzelmann, *Theology of St. Luke*, trans. Geoffrey Buswell, 2nd ed. (New York: Harper & Row, 1961), 148. Drawn from proclamations of innocence by Roman officials to Jesus and Paul, Conzelmann famously states, "to confess oneself to be a Christian implies no crime against Roman law." Conzelmann, *Theology of St. Luke*, 140.
[49] Marguerat, *Les Actes des Apôtres (13–28)*, 245.
[50] Haenchen, *The Acts of the Apostles*, 622.
[51] Robert Maddox points out that Tertullian's phrase *religio quasi licita* is used only once in ancient literature and not in a legal sense but in an ironical sense against pagan slander, "You are not allowed to exist." Robert Maddox, *The Purpose of Luke-Acts*, FRLANT 126 (Göttingen: Vandenhoeck & Ruprecht, 1982), 92.
[52] Charles K. Barrett, *Luke the Historian in Recent Study* (London: Epworth, 1961), 63.
[53] Barrett, *Luke the Historian in Recent Study*, 63.
[54] Walaskay, *"And so we came to Rome,"* 58.
[55] Walaskay, *"And so we came to Rome,"* ix–x.

Christianity. Yet, one dilemma is that the negative portrayals of Roman officials cannot go unnoticed. Lysias is quick to rescue but slow to understand. He has a hard time grasping Paul's identity and how to deal with him (Acts 21:37-39, 22-29). Felix, the governor, gives Paul some liberty during his time in custody but secretly seeks a bribe from him (Acts 24:23-26).[56] Beyond the convenient binary view of good and evil, this study explores a split view that the narrative has of Rome.

8) *Defending Paul's Jewish fidelity.* Jacob Jervell claims that Paul's speeches during his trials (Acts 22:1-21; 23:1; 24:10-21; 26:1-23) are the means by which Luke defends Paul's Jewish orthodoxy.[57] According to Robert W. Wall, Paul is "a personal exemplar of Jewish piety" as well as "a redemptive agent of Israel's God."[58] Similarly, from an ecclesiastic point of view, Luke T. Johnson argues that the story "shifts the blame for Paul's subsequent troubles entirely onto the outsiders" and explains why Paul was not helped by Christian brothers in Jerusalem.[59] Since the Jerusalem community was divided "from within concerning Paul's loyalty to Judaism," it was necessary for Luke to prove "Paul's fidelity on the terms of his critics."[60] In similar fashion, Robert C. Tannehill suggests that Paul's arrest and speech are the narrator's response to the charge against Paul: "Is Paul leading Jewish Christians to abandon their Jewish way of life?"[61] The point of Paul's imprisonment is not his ability to escape from the dangers that surround him but his "loyalty to Israel" (Acts 28:20).[62]

Undoubtedly, an enduring theme that holds different sections of the text together is Paul's devotion to the Jewish tradition. Paul is surrounded by constant challenges yet never ceases to defend his Jewish identity as well as his faith in the risen Lord (Acts 22:3, 14-21; 23:1, 6). The Lukan apology is definitely internal. Still, it is problematic to limit the springboard of the troubles to the inward dimension. There might have been challenges from outside, too, as Jews were constantly going after Paul's life. Acts may not be an accurate picture of historical events, but it is still a window through which one can see the Jewish-Christian conflict that the narrative reflects.

Although this survey does not represent all the scholarly voices on Paul in Jerusalem, it does provide a helpful guidepost for further exploration. The following elements are

---

[56] For Luke's negative portrayal of Rome, see Muñoz-Larrondo, *A Postcolonial Reading of the Acts of the Apostles.*

[57] Jacob Jervell, *The Theology of the Acts of the Apostles* (Cambridge: Cambridge University Press, 1996), 82–94; *Luke and the People of God: A New Look at Luke-Acts* (Minneapolis: Augsburg, 1972), 153–83. Robert L. Brawley states, "Paul's defense speeches vindicate him and him alone." Robert L. Brawley, *Luke-Acts and the Jews: Conflict, Apology, and Conciliation*, SBLMS 33 (Atlanta: Scholars Press, 1987), 69.

[58] Robert W. Wall, "The Acts of the Apostles: Introduction, Commentary, and Reflections" in *Acts, Introduction to Epistolary Literature, Romans, 1 Corinthians*, NIB 10, ed. Leander E. Keck (Nashville: Abingdon, 2002), 304.

[59] Luke T. Johnson, *The Acts of the Apostles*, SP 5 (Collegeville: Liturgical Press, 1992), 379–80. Stanley E. Porter also notes that Paul is abandoned by his fellow believers in Jerusalem. Stanley E. Porter, *The Paul of Acts: Essays in Literary Criticism, Rhetoric, and Theology*, WUNT 115 (Tübingen: Mohr Siebeck, 1999), 172–86.

[60] Johnson, *The Acts of the Apostles*, 379–80.

[61] Robert C. Tannehill, *The Narrative Unity of Luke-Acts: A Literary Interpretation*, 2 vols. (Minneapolis: Fortress, 1994), 2.296.

[62] Tannehill, *The Narrative Unity of Luke-Acts*, 2.271.

presumed to be key objects of the defense in the text: Paul's Jewish identity, the Gentile mission, and the gospel. The addressees are undoubtedly the Lukan audience. Yet, the circumstances can be both intergroup and intragroup conflict. Paul's encounter with Jewish believers in Jerusalem and the ensuing drama with Jews evince the dire situation that Paul and/or the members of the Way were in.

Proposal. This study accepts these gleanings from scholarship, particularly drawing from those who articulate Paul's Jewish fidelity. To add another layer to this discussion, however, this book attends to two aspects that previous scholarship has missed or has not paid much attention to: identity formation and *mimesis*. In his commentary, William S. Kurz highlights two common elements found in the text: Paul's "continuing Jewish identity" and "the striking parallels between the passion of Jesus and the 'passion of Paul.'"[63] Yet, he does not attempt to describe what this literary parallel entails in the narrative structure of Luke-Acts.

The proposal of this study is that Acts 21:17–23:35 not only defends the Jewish identity of Paul but also constructs the identity of the Way by portraying Christian conflicts with Jews. It further explores how the Lukan literary parallel between the passion of Jesus and that of Paul contributes to this process both on a narrative level and on a discourse level. Paul's arrest provides him with opportunities to present his case against his accusers and the security to exit the stage of Jerusalem through the back door. Readers find in these rapidly unfolding scenes that it is not only Jews but also Acts that slander and reveal ardent hostility to the opponents of the Way. The source of the conflict is, as previous scholarship has noted, the similarities as well as the differences between Paul and Jews. What makes cooperation possible at times, even in a quarrel, is the common elements Paul and his interlocutors share. This complex interplay between Paul and others in the narrative is the crux of this study.

1.3. Mimesis in the Lukan Passion Narratives of Jesus and Paul

To put this new proposal in perspective, a brief discussion of *mimesis*, a Greco-Roman literary technique, is necessary to highlight the literary connections between Jesus's Passion Narrative (Lk 22–23; see also Mk 14–15, Mt 26–27, Jn 18–19) and Paul's Passion Narrative (Acts 21:27–28:31).[64] As Tim Whitmarsh rightly states, in the Greco-Roman world "the dominant notion in the literary aesthetic was mimesis."[65] Models were critical and even necessary. For example, in all three stages of education, students

---

[63] Kurz, *Acts of the Apostles*, 324.
[64] The Passion Narrative in the Synoptic Gospels starts with the pericope on the plot to kill Jesus (Mk 14:1-2; Mt. 26:1-5; Lk 22:1-5). John introduces the pericope earlier in the middle of his gospel (Jn 11:45-57), but after the arrest of Jesus (Jn 18:1-11), he closely follows Mark's Passion Narrative. It is difficult to determine where the Passion of Paul starts and ends in Acts. Yet, a convenient criterion is Paul being in bondage, since this new status of Paul serves as a condition for his suffering as well as his defense. Paul loses his freedom to move around after his arrest in the temple and remains in bondage at the end of Acts. Paul's encounter with the Jews in Jerusalem in Acts 21:27-36, therefore, marks the beginning of Paul's Passion Narrative.
[65] Tim Whitmarsh, *Greek Literature and the Roman Empire: The Politics of Imitation* (Oxford: Oxford University Press, 2001), 26.

not only read, memorized, and interpreted the Homeric epics but also were encouraged to imitate them "to adorn their speeches and to express their self-presentation."[66] In other words, the goal of mimesis was for writers to imitate, adapt, and improvise what came before them for their own purpose. Quintilian states that a person who wishes to be an orator "must accumulate a certain store of resources, to be employed whenever they may be required" (Quintilian, *Institutio*, 10.1.5).[67] Luke was probably no different. He seems to have imitated his predecessors, particularly Homer and Vergil, in order to present the ministry of Jesus and his apostles in an epic fashion.[68]

The closest parallel to Acts 21:17–23:35, however, is found in the Gospel of Luke and accordingly the Gospel of Mark, Luke's primary source.[69] "The passion of Paul" rehearses the passion of Jesus, although they are surely neither doublets nor identical.[70] Yet, a few examples are noteworthy: (1) their entry into Jerusalem and immediate visit to the temple (Lk 19:28-40, 45-48; Acts 21:21-26);[71] (2) their subsequent arrest and experience of violence (Lk 22:47-53, 63-65; Acts 21:27-36); (3) their encounter with the Sanhedrin (Lk 22:66-71; Acts 23:1-11); (4) the plot to kill them (Lk 22:1-5; Acts 23:12-22); (5) their meeting with the governor (Lk 23:1-5, 13-25; Acts 24:1–25:12); and (6) their meeting with Herod (Lk 23:6-12; Acts 25:13–26:32).

Dennis R. MacDonald's six criteria on mimesis strengthen the case.[72] Mark's Passion Narrative was fairly well distributed and was accessible to Luke (*accessibility*); it was used by other authors such as Matthew, John, and Luke himself (*analogy*); the Passion of Paul shares a substantial number of parallels with the Passion Narrative in Mark

---

[66] Ronald F. Hock, "Homer in Greco-Roman Education," in *Mimesis and Intertextuality in Antiquity and Christianity*, SAC, ed. Dennis R. MacDonald (Harrisburg, PA: Trinity Press International, 2001), 77.

[67] Quintilian, *The Institutio Oratoria of Quintilian*, LCL, trans. Harold E. Butler (Cambridge, MA: Harvard University Press, 1953), 5.

[68] Since the study of the Homeric epics was a part of Greco-Roman education, it is possible that the writers of the Gospels were influenced by the epics. For a more extensive discussion on mimesis in the Gospels and Acts, see Dennis R. MacDonald, *Does the New Testament Imitate Homer?: Four Cases from the Acts of the Apostles* (New Haven: Yale University Press, 2003); *The Gospels and Homer: Imitations of Greek Epic in Mark and Luke-Acts*, NTGL 1 (Lanham, MD: Rowman & Littlefield, 2015); *Luke and Vergil: Imitations of Classical Greek Literature*, NTGL 2 (Lanham, MD: Rowman & Littlefield, 2015). Marianne P. Bonz argues that Luke created his version of the early Christian community by modeling it after Vergil's *Aeneid* to "make the Christian claim a powerful and appealing rival to the ubiquitous and potentially seductive salvation claims of imperial Rome." Bonz, *The Past as Legacy*, 86.

[69] Parallels are also found between Luke 9:51–19:28 and Acts 19:21–21:17. Talbert notes: "*Luke 9:51–19:28.* Jesus makes a journey to Jerusalem which is a passion journey (9:31; 9:51; 12:50; 13:33; 18:31-33) under divine necessity (13:33) and characterized by the disciples' lack of understanding (9:45; 18:34). *Acts 19:21–21:17.* Paul make a last journey to Jerusalem which is a passion journey (20:3; 20:22-24; 20:37-38; 21:4; 21:10-11; 21:13) under divine necessity (20:22; 21:14) and characterized by his friends' lack of understanding (21:4; 21:12-13)." Talbert, *Literary Patterns*, 16, emphasis added.

[70] James D. G. Dunn, *The Acts of the Apostles*, NC (Valley Forge, PA: Trinity Press International, 1996), 277. See also Marguerat, *Les Actes des Apôtres (13–28)*, 246.

[71] Charles H. Talbert notes: "*[Luke] 19:37* Jesus receives a good reception and the people praise God for the works they have seen. *[Acts] 21:17-20a* Paul receives a good reception and God is glorified for the things done among the Gentiles"; "*[Luke] 19:45-48* Jesus goes into the Temple. He has a friendly attitude toward it. *[Acts] 21:26* Paul goes into the Temple. He has a friendly attitude toward it." Talbert, *Literary Patterns*, 17, emphasis added.

[72] Dennis R. MacDonald, *Mimesis and Intertextuality*, 2-3. MacDonald later expands on his own criteria by adding "*ancient and Byzantine recognitions*" in MacDonald, *The Gospels and Homer*, 6-7.

(*density*); Luke closely follows Mark's sequence in this section of Acts (*order*); the Acts narrative contains similar details or "intertextual flags" (*distinctive traits*); and yet, Luke introduces differences even while imitating Mark (*interpretability*).[73]

Luke indeed mimicks the Passion Narrative in recounting Paul's Passion. Yet, the differences are undeniable. The most noticeable elements are Paul's self-defense and escape from violence. MacDonald states, in comparing *The Acts of Andrew* to Homer's *Odyssey*, that "the author's primary means of transvaluing the epic was countercharacterization: nonviolence replaces heroic violence; poverty replaces fabulous wealth; celibacy replaces adventurous sex."[74] If one is looking for the virtue—patience, non-violence, and dignity—found in the passion of Jesus, Acts is a total failure. Paul not only insults his opponents but also manipulates people into fighting each other to save his own life. If Jesus is a philosopher who faces a noble death, as many scholars argue,[75] Paul is a shrewd under trial who avoids death at any cost. The most obvious twist Luke makes in Acts is the destiny of Paul. Having gone through seemingly endless threats, Paul still remains alive, unlike Jesus, who accepted his destiny and died on the cross (Lk 22:42). This is, I argue, the Greatest Reversal of the Lukan narrative.[76] It is a twist that cannot be ignored if "Luke-Acts must ... be read as a single story."[77] What are the narrative achievements of such a change? How does this narrative (dis)symmetry that exists in Luke and Acts affect the way in which readers read and interpret Luke-Acts? How does the discursive rhetoric commending Paul and condemning Jews contribute to the construction of the Lukan version of Christian identity and Jewish identity, particularly in Acts 21:17–23:35? This book attempts to answer these questions.

1.4. Context and Function of Acts 21:17–23:35: An Eagle's-Eye View

The backdrop of the Lukan recounting of Jewish conflict is the marginalization of the Way. The *Sitz im Leben*—setting in life—that the Acts of the Apostles allegedly reflects

---

[73] To explain *distinctive traits* and *interpretability*, for example, the Markan Jesus remains silent during the trial, except for one occasion when he reveals his identity, which was hidden to the public up to this point in Mark's Gospel (Mk 14:62; see also Lk 22:67-70). In contrast, in Acts, Paul never stops speaking. He is more apologetic than Jesus and is actively defending his own case (see Acts 23:1-10).

[74] MacDonald, *Christianizing Homer*, 8. The Acts of Andrew is a New Testament Apocrypha which narrates the acts and miracles of apostle Andrew.

[75] Gregory E. Sterling, "Mors Philosophi: The Death of Jesus in Luke," *HTR* 94 (2001): 383–402. For a discussion of the crucifixion of Jesus as a praiseworthy death, see Peter J. Scaer, *The Lukan Passion and the Praiseworthy Death*, NTM 10 (Sheffield: Sheffield Phoenix, 2005).

[76] The Great Reversal is a prominent theme found in Luke. Luke opens his two-volume work with Mary's Magnificat, in which Mary praises God who "has brought down the powerful ... and lifted up the lowly" (Lk 1:52). Jesus also proclaims in the Sermon on the Plain the reversed fortune of the rich and the poor: "Blessed are you who are poor ... But woe to you who are rich" (Lk 6:20, 24). The most vivid graphic demonstration of reversal appears in the Parable of the Rich Man and Lazarus (Lk 16:19-31), in which the rich man suffers in the hell of fire whereas Lazarus stays in Abraham's bosom in the afterlife. The change is so dramatic that Justo L. González says, "We should call it 'the world upside down.'" Justo L. Gonzalez, *The Story Luke Tells: Luke's Unique Witness to the Gospel* (Grand Rapids: Eerdmans, 2015), 29.

[77] Johnson, *The Gospel of Luke*, 4.

is quite different from Jewish-Christian relations in today's world. In Acts, the Jewish people are greater in number and more powerful than they are in the contemporary context. They have a system in place not only to draw pilgrims to and offer sacrifices in the temple but also to examine and control dissenters. The dominant Jewish religious groups, which Luke provides glimpses of through Paul's opponents—the Sadducees, the Pharisees, and members of the Jewish diaspora in the synagogues—are orthodox over against a heretic group called the Way.[78] Two historical realities are worth visiting to situate and better understand the text this study addresses in its historical context.

1) *The Destruction of the Jerusalem Temple*. The First Jewish-Roman War (66–73 CE) demolished the temple and resulted in the loss of the religious autonomy Jews had enjoyed under Roman rule.[79] Yet, the Jewish nationalistic and religious fervor remained strong, as demonstrated in the subsequent Jewish-Roman conflicts, the Kitos War (115–17 CE) of the diaspora Jews, and the Bar Kokhba Revolt (132–6 CE) of the Judean Jews.[80] Acts, which was written in 80–100 CE,[81] reflects an agonistic context in which the heretical Christians were experiencing persecution or exclusion of some sort at the hands of non-Messianic Jews. Acts 21:17–23:35 is a victim's recounting of incidents in which the Jewish people oppressed members of the Way.

---

[78] A power shift took place in the Jewish religious groups after the fall of the Jerusalem temple in 70 CE. The Sadducees lost their dominance to the Pharisees, for whom the crux of the Jewish faith was a moveable object, the Torah, not an immovable temple to which the Jewish diaspora used to make pilgrimages. In Acts 21:17–23:35, the Lukan narrator places on the stage all three literary characters—Sadducees, Pharisees, and the Way—in conflict with each other.

[79] Sara Mandell, "Who Paid the Temple Tax When the Jews Were under Roman Rule?" *HTR* 77, no. 2 (1984): 223–32.

[80] Abraham Malamat, *A History of the Jewish People* (Cambridge, MA: Harvard University Press, 1976), 330–5. For details on the Bar Kokhba Revolt, see Menahem Mor, *The Second Jewish Revolt: The Bar Kokhba War, 132–136 CE*, BRLJ 50 (Leiden: Brill, 2016).

[81] I assume that Luke-Acts was written between 80 CE and 100 CE. In the early nineteenth century, Ferdinand C. Baur located Acts in the mid-second century based on the Hegelian dialectic. He argued that Acts is an outcome of "the conflict between 'Pauline' ('law-free') and 'Peterine' ('Jewish') movements." Richard I. Pervo, *Dating Acts: Between the Evangelists and the Apologists* (Santa Rosa, CA: Polebridge, 2006), 3. Yet subsequent scholars challenged his view and proposed their own: Adolf Harnack argued for 62 CE, F. F. Bruce for around 70–80 CE, Raymond E. Brown and Gregory E. Sterling for 80–90 CE, and Hans Conzelmann for 100 CE. Pervo, *Dating Acts*, 4–5. Recent scholars support a second-century dating of Acts. For example, Richard I. Pervo finds that Luke is not only familiar with the writings of Josephus that date from around 100 CE but also has common theological perspectives with the Pastoral Epistles and Polycarp that date from around 125–30 CE. Although the early second-century date seems attractive, Luke's use of the Pastoral Epistles is speculative and puts Acts distant in time from Luke, which was likely composed after its predecessor Mark, which was written around the fall of the temple in 70 CE. Mark was likely written around 70–80 CE. Hendrika N. Roskam, *The Purpose of the Gospel of Mark in its Historical and Social Context*, NovTSup 114 (Leiden: Brill, 2004), 82. I locate the composition of Luke-Acts between 80 CE and 100 CE based on the following reasons. (1) If Acts is dependent on Josephus, as many scholars argue, its dating should include the "late 90s or early 100s." Holladay, *Acts*, 6. (2) If Acts is a narrative sequel written not long after the Gospel of Luke was written, the date is likely close to 80 CE, which is Mark's date (see Lk 1:1-4). (3) The author seems to have a close connection with Paul or his colleagues, even if he himself was not Paul's travel companion. Carl R. Holladay conjectures that Luke is the one "who might have known Paul personally, and thus to have been a member of the 'Pauline school,' or at least to have direct access to Pauline traditions that stemmed from those circles." Holladay, *Acts*, 7. Luke devotes half of his second volume to Paul's ministry and depicts him, in the end, as reenacting the last days of Jesus' life. The dating of Luke-Acts around 80–100 CE encompasses all the proposed ranges of dates.

2) *The Construction of Jewish Identity*. Another historical context relevant to this study is the shift in Jewish in-group membership. Shaye J. D. Cohen argues that there was a fundamental shift in the understanding of Jewish identity in the late second century BCE during the Hasmonean era. The geographical and ethnic concept of "Judean/Judaean/Jew" (Ἰουδαῖος) gained political, religious, and cultural connotations that made possible the incorporation of other ethnic groups and individuals under the Jewish umbrella.[82] Josephus' report buttresses the historical background by describing the Hasmonean rulers forcing the Idumaeans and Ituraeans to be circumcised and calling those who observed the Judean way of life Ἰουδαῖοι, Judeans/Judaeans/Jews.[83]

> Hyrcanus also captured the Idumaean cities of Adora and Marisa, and after subduing all the Idumaeans, permitted them to remain in their country so long as they had themselves circumcised and were willing to observe the laws of the Judaeans. And so, out of attachment to their ancestral land, they submitted to circumcision and to having their manner of life in all other respects made the same as that of the Judeans. And from that time on they have continued to be Judaeans [Ἰουδαῖοι].
>
> *Ant.* 13.257–8

> He [Aristobulus] made war on the Ituraeans and acquired a good part of their territory for Judea and compelled the inhabitants, if they wished to remain in their country, to be circumcised and to live in accordance with the laws of the Judaeans [Ἰουδαῖοι].
>
> *Ant.* 13.318[84]

The Jewish identity is, now, a matter of choice as well as birth. What bestows Jewish identity is one's "way of life" and "citizenship" in the Judaean state.[85] In the first-century Palestine and diaspora setting in which Rome is the de facto political ruler, Ἰουδαῖος becomes more and more a socially, culturally, and religiously loaded term. Jews may have different geographical and linguistic backgrounds, but their adherence to the Jewish way of life ensures their Jewish identity (e.g., Acts 2:5-12). The way in which Luke-Acts claims and expands the Way's Jewishness should be understood in this historical context.

---

[82] Shaye J. D. Cohen, *The Beginnings of Jewishness: Boundaries, Varieties, Uncertainties*, HCS 31 (Berkeley: University of California Press, 1999). Erich S. Gruen summarizes this change as follows: "'Judaean' metamorphosed into a 'Jew.'" Erich S. Gruen, Review of *The Beginnings of Jewishness* by Shaye J. D. Cohen, *JQR* 92, nos. 3–4 (2002): 595.

[83] Based on this, Naomi Janowitz argues, "The Hasmoneans established the importance of circumcision in Jewish identity, clarifying the position of 'outsiders' by taking a distinct stance on 'insiders.'" Naomi Janowitz, "Rethinking Jewish Identity in Late Antiquity," *UC Davis Previously Published Works* (Davis: University of California, 2001), 10. The full text may be found at https://escholarship.org/content/qt9vx1q0xd/qt9vx1q0xd.pdf and in Stephen Mitchell and Geoffrey Greatrex, eds., *Ethnicity and Culture in Late Antiquity* (London: Duckworth 2000), 205–19. The newly circumcised received Jewish names, yet the town of Pella was destroyed by the Hasmoneans because its villagers refused to adopt Jewish customs (Josephus, *Ant.* 13.397).

[84] These translations of passages in *Antiquities* are taken from Cohen, *The Beginnings of Jewishness*, 110–11.

[85] Cohen, *The Beginnings of Jewishness*, 127.

This brief historical overview accords with the different reactions to the Way by its audiences. Some Jews as well as Gentiles welcome the gospel, whereas others reject it (e.g., Acts 2:37-42; 19:8-10; 23-41). Dissension over who is Jewish and thus is an in-group member takes place both within and outside of the Way (e.g., Acts 15:1-5; 23:6-10). The Lukan narrative, however, describes the Way's proposal as if it is ultimately rejected (Acts 28:17-28).[86] Daniel Boyarin's compelling argument complicates the Lukan portrayal. Tracing the writings of border-makers—heresiologists—such as Justin Martyr (100–65 CE), he argues that "the borders between Christianity and Judaism are as constructed and imposed, as artificial and political as any of the borders on earth."[87] It is important, therefore, to be careful not to buy into the Lukan rhetoric too quickly because Luke is not immune to the disease that will infect many historians after him: "All too often historians of ancient heresies have simply repeated negative stereotypes culled from the polemical rhetoric of the heretics' 'orthodox opponents.'"[88]

Drawing from the discussions presented so far, some introductory remarks on the functions of Acts 21:17–23:35 are useful for laying the foundation for the in-depth exploration ahead. (1) Acts 21:17–23:35 reenacts Jesus's visit to Jerusalem through its protagonist, Paul. The similarities and differences between Jesus's stay in Jerusalem and that of Paul illuminate the narrative structure of Luke-Acts, which this book will pay particular attention to. (2) Conflicts present in this text not only defend the Way but also slander the Jews. The Lukan narrator portrays a Lukan literary character, *the Jews*, along with other Jewish characters as violently attacking Paul, but the Jewish version of the story is absent in the narrative. (3) Paul's arrest serves as a critical condition for his subsequent defenses (Acts 24:10-21; 26:2-29) and ministry in Rome (Acts 28:16-31). (4) Conflict around Paul's Jewish identity illustrates the differences and similarities between the Way and other leading Jewish religious groups, including the Sadducees and the Pharisees. These stories not only construct the Jewish people in a distorted manner but also impose anti-Jewish prejudice on the Lukan audience.

1.5. Concluding Comments

"The Torah has seventy faces," Bamidbar Rabbah 13:15 states. The same is true for Acts. Given the various scenes in the present text, exploring all aspects of the text is not feasible. Discussing all the possible functions of the text is also impossible and beyond the scope of this study. Yet, by paying particular attention to conflicts within the text and to literary parallels with Luke's Gospel, this chapter has presented Acts 21:17–23:35 as a distinct literary unit with specific functions within the larger narrative structure of Luke-Acts.

---

[86] David Nirenberg, *Anti-Judaism: The Western Tradition* (New York: W. W. Norton & Co., 2013), 84: "Jewish hatred becomes proof of Paul's message, as it had been of Jesus's and of the prophets' before him. It is by Jewish persecution, according to Acts, that the gentile Christian community is defined as one of the spirit."

[87] Daniel Boyarin, *Border Lines: The Partition of Judaeo-Christianity* (Philadelphia: University of Pennsylvania Press, 2004), 1.

[88] Virginia Burrus, "The Making of a Heresy: Authority, Gender, and the Priscillianist Controversy" (PhD diss., Graduate Theological Union, 1991), 1.

To do so, perimeters that encompass diverse sections of the text were presented—its locations, issues, and events. The analogy of the roller coaster described the dynamic within the narrative and brought to the fore the central issue of Paul's visit to Jerusalem. Then, the chapter examined the pros and cons of the scholarship to date and proposed a new way of interpreting the text. To lay a foundation for this new proposal, the parallel between the passion of Jesus and Paul was discussed in light of the Greco-Roman literary technique of *mimesis*. The chapter concluded with a brief comment on the context and function of Acts 21:17–23:35 to usher readers to the wild roller-coaster ride waiting for them as well as for Paul. Before readers fasten their seat belts and step onto the ride, however, the following chapter describes the main methodology of this study, the social identity approach, a lens that readers should use in order to enjoy the spectacle that will take place before their very eyes.

2

The Social Identity Approach and Dual Identity[1]

"I pledge allegiance to the flag of the United States of America . . ." On August 17, 2017, I stood with over a thousand new citizens and a cloud of witnesses at Fox Oakland Theater in California. When the presider said, "Congratulations, fellow citizens," the crowd exuberantly applauded the new identity given to them. This transitional moment left me needing more time for reflection than celebration. I was not sure whether a simple pledge can really change one's identity. When I got home, I rather bluntly told my wife, who was feeding our two-month-old son, "Honey, I'm a U.S. citizen now. I'm not a Korean anymore." She looked at me and said, "What are you talking about? You look Korean and you *are* Korean deep in your bones!" This reminded me of the presider over the naturalization ceremony saying, "You are not abandoning your past but bringing it with you so that our nation may become more diverse and inclusive." True. My experiences, cultural heritage, and emotional attachment are too strong for me to deny my Korean-ness. I repeated to myself that day, time and time again, "I am not simply an *American*, but a *Korean American*. I am proud to be so."

At the heart of the human psyche, there lies a fundamental question: *Who am I?* This is a deeply personal question, yet the answers are overtly *social*. For example, I am a Christian, family member, pastor, Korean American, and New Testament scholar. We define ourselves by referring to the groups to which we belong, whether they are religious, cultural, familial, national—including racial and ethnic categories—or professional. Therefore, Jenkins states, "All human identities are, by definition, *social* identities."[2] At the same time, one's identity is *situation specific*. The answers to the question vary depending on one's interlocutors.[3] To my parents, I am a son. To my wife, I am a husband. To my son, I am a father. These identity claims come with certain degrees of emotional attachment that are more often positive than negative. How I choose and arrange them in words is highly selective and, at times, political because my choice reveals my allegiance to the group with which I identify: Christian > Family

---

[1] Keep in mind the following statement from Jonathan Z. Smith as this chapter unfolds: "Difference is rarely something to be noted; it is, most often, something in which one has a stake." Jonathan Z. Smith, "What a Difference a Difference Makes," in *"To See Ourselves as Others See Us": Christians, Jews, 'others' in Late Antiquity*, ed. Jacob Neusner, Ernest S. Frerichs, and Caroline McCracken-Flesher (Chico, CA: Scholars Press, 1985), 4.
[2] Richard Jenkins, *Social Identity*, 3rd ed. (New York: Routledge, 2008), 17, emphasis in the original.
[3] Charles Taylor, *Sources of the Self: The Making of the Modern Identity* (Cambridge, MA: Harvard University Press, 1989), 36.

member > Pastor > Korean American > New Testament scholar. In other words, one's identity is indicative of one's *commitment*. One may obtain a new identity by becoming a member of a previous out-group. Yet, certain differences and thus identities cannot disappear altogether but still remain salient because they constitute the very core of who one *is*. Forcing a person to erase those identities is to force them to deny their commitment and, therefore, their very existence.

Since identity is inextricably related to group membership, the core of one's identity is often questioned and challenged in the agonistic context in which one group attempts to invalidate the claims of another group. In particular, when a minority group seeks to be a part of a dominant group while maintaining its subgroup identity markers but fails to acquire the approval of the dominant group, their intergroup relationship tends to take a discursive turn. In-group members begin criticizing out-group members, just as a rejected boy often vilifies the team he once desperately wanted to join. Animosity and denigration are not the outcomes of hate but of love-hate.

I argue that this ambivalent attitude is the ethos of Acts 21:17–23:35 in which the character Paul, in spite of Jewish threats, constantly (re)categorizes himself as a Jew while maintaining his commitment to the risen Lord. After his encounter with Jesus, his Jewish identity does not go away—it only intensifies. He claims to be a law-abiding Jew *and* an apostle to the Gentiles (Acts 22:3, 21). Such a dual membership—as a devout Jew and a member of the Way—is not permissible, however, for many Jews in Luke-Acts.[4] Luke depicts the Jews as understanding themselves in terms of their ethnicity, however problematic Luke's portrayal of the Jews may be in the sociocultural milieu of his time. Any attempt to break or blur this impenetrable line is considered a threat to the Jewish nation (e.g., Acts 21:28).

A brief discussion on ethnicity is necessary here in order to clarify the use of the term "ethnicity" in this book. I define an ethnic group as one that shares at least some of the following characteristics: (1) *biological lineage*, (2) *cultural heritage and/or experience*, (3) *geographical location*, (4) *linguistic proficiency*, (5) *historical memory*, and (6) *ritual admission*. Those categories are not fixed but flexible and are not simply given but can often be adopted. I do not have American blood in my lineage (1), but my past nineteen years of living in the United States (2, 3, 4, 5) have allowed me to identify with Americans. The naturalization ceremony (6) is a legal and ritual process in which I have become *ethnically* American.

Luke-Acts seems to share a similar understanding of ethnicity. When someone is called a Jew, that person should fit one or more categories. They should have Jewish parents and/or live according to the Jewish law (1, 2). They should live in Judea or have an attachment to Jerusalem (3). They may or may not speak in Hebrew, but they should be aware of Jewish history (4, 5). If male, they should undergo circumcision which will confirm their Jewish lineage and complete the conversion process (6).[5]

---

[4] Earlier in the Gospel, the Lukan narrator describes the Jews turning to an angry mob when they hear Jesus saying that God's favor is extended to Gentiles due to the Jewish rejection of prophets (Luke 4:16-30).

[5] See, for example, Acts 2:5-42; 6:8–8:3; 15:1-29; 22:1-21.

No matter how flexible and open-ended this sounds, however, there is a fine line between Jews and non-Jews. Even after undergoing circumcision and fully adopting the Jewish way of life, a former Gentile is never called a Jew by hereditary Jews. He is simply a convert—προσήλυτος—not a Jew (e.g., Acts 2:11). The Lukan narrative has this socioculturally loaded but biologically and ritually limited understanding of ethnicity. This coincides with the Jewish practice of its time. Shaye J. D. Cohen states, "In the eyes of outsiders a proselyte not only could be called a Jew but actually became one . . . but in the eyes of the Jews did the proselytes 'become' Jews? Apparently not."[6]

Yet, Luke-Acts does not stay within the bounds of an ethnic category but employs a broader convictional and behavioral category in creating its definition of in-group membership. Whoever believes in Jesus and follows some requirements of the law is considered *Jewish*, if not an ethnic Jew (Acts 15:20, 29; 21:25). Such arbitrary amendments are not only unacceptable but also dangerous for many Jews because they seem to deprive Jews of their privilege as a chosen people and thus deny their identity altogether. Jewish resistance to the Way and counterattack are inevitable. At the heart of the text are the intergroup conflicts between the Way and the Jewish out-group(s).

In order to underscore the group dynamics and the process of identity construction found in Acts 21:17–23:35, this chapter (1) provides a brief survey of the social identity approach (hereafter SIA) from its inception to recent developments, focusing on particular aspects of SIA; (2) delineates the process of developing a dual identity with the proximate "other" and three concepts that need to be considered in an agonistic context—*ambivalence*, *social creativity*, and *recategorization*; and (3) discusses the construction of Christian identity in Luke-Acts.

2.1. Social Identity Approach: Historical Overview

The study of social identity is a distinct discipline within the field of social psychology, which focuses on "human social behavior."[7] Social psychology first appears in Gustave Le Bon's classic work *The Crowd: A Study of the Popular Mind* (1896).[8] He argues that in crowds, social conventions and norms lose their power and more primitive and instinctive behaviors come to the fore.[9] Unlike Le Bon, who sees group mentality as an extension of individual instinct, William McDougall separates the individual mind from the *group mind* (1921). He argues that in a group there emerges a new reality, the group mind, that differentiates group behavior from individual behavior.[10] Sigmund Freud (1921) argues that a group is formed by "sexual-emotional ties between members" and that people in a group setting "behave qualitatively differently" because of "'id' and

---

[6] Cohen, *The Beginnings of Jewishness*, 159–60.
[7] Michael A. Hogg and Dominic Abrams, *Social Identifications: A Social Psychology of Intergroup Relations and Group Process* (London: Routledge, 1998), 8.
[8] Hogg and Abrams, *Social Identifications*, 11.
[9] Gustave Le Bon, *The Crowd: A Study of the Popular Mind*, anonymous translation (London: T. Fisher Unwin, 1921).
[10] William McDougall, *Ethics and Some Modern World Problems* (New York: G. P. Putnam's Sons, 1924).

'repressed impulses.'"[11] This heated discussion on group psychology came to a close with Floyd Allport, who famously stated that "there is no psychology of groups which is not essentially and entirely a psychology of individuals" (1924).[12] In other words, there is no such thing as group mind; a group is just a collection of individuals. Though Muzafer Sherif (1936), Solomon Asch (1952), and Kurt Lewin (1935-52) carried out studies on the interactions between individual group members, they employed the group concept to "explain the nature of individuals," not of groups.[13] This reductionist tendency in which groups are dissolved into individuals remained the dominant perspective in social psychology until the 1960s.[14] However, with the work of Henri Tajfel and his colleagues in Europe, "a strong counter-voice" began to emerge.[15]

2.1.1. Social Identity Theory (SIT)

Henri Tajfel's study of social identity is inextricably bound up with his experience as a POW during the Second World War. Though he was a Jew, he was able to survive in German prison camps because he concealed his identity as a Polish citizen, which might have led the German guards to kill him. All those years he pretended to be French.[16] After the war, he found that all his family members had been killed and the Polish Jewish community that had been his sociocultural nest was decimated. Having experienced the formidable force of groups, Tajfel concluded, unlike Allport, that "a group is more than the sum total of its members"[17] and dedicated his life to the study of intergroup relations.

Tajfel's theories delve into the issue of group membership and its impact on the formation of the self. In a nutshell, they focus on how group membership leads to the formation of social identities that enhance self-esteem. Undertaking a series of laboratory

---

[11] John C. Turner, *Rediscovering the Social Group: A Self-Categorization Theory* (New York: Basil Blackwell, 1987), 9. For Freud's work on group psychology, see Sigmund Freud, *Group Psychology and the Analysis of the Ego* (London: Hogarth, 1921).

[12] Floyd Allport, *Social Psychology* (Boston: Houghton Mifflin, 1924), 4, as quoted in Hogg and Abrams, *Social Identifications*, 12.

[13] Turner, *Rediscovering the Social Group*, 12.

[14] Hogg and Abrams, *Social Identifications*, 13.

[15] Dominic S. Irudayaraj, *Violence, Otherness and Identity in Isaiah 63:1-6*, LHBOTS 633 (London; New York: Bloomsbury T&T Clark, 2017), 40.

[16] John C. Turner, "Henri Tajfel: An Introduction," in *Social Groups & Identities: Developing the Legacy of Henri Tajfel*, International Series in Social Psychology, ed. W. Peter Robinson (Oxford: Butterworth-Heinemann, 1996), 2. His experience at the prison camp became a source of his theory on the *interpersonal-intergroup continuum*. Regardless of his *interpersonal* relationships with German guards and his personal characteristics, his *intergroup* relationship with Poland could have ended his life. This made him live under a false identity. Tajfel explains interpersonal-intergroup continuum as follows: "We have ... a continuum which goes from the probably fictitious extreme of 'purely' interpersonal behavior to the rarely-encountered extreme of 'purely' intergroup behavior. All of the 'natural'... social situations fall between these two extremes." Henri Tajfel, *Human Groups and Social Categories: Studies in Social Psychology* (Cambridge: Cambridge University Press, 1981), 241.

[17] Irudayaraj, *Violence, Otherness and Identity*, 40. See also Philip F. Esler, "An Outline of Social Identity Theory," in *T&T Clark Handbook to Social Identity in the New Testament*, ed. J. Brian Tucker and Coleman A. Baker (London; New York: Bloomsbury T&T Clark, 2016), 16-17.

experiments, Tajfel developed "minimal group experiments."[18] He discovered that (1) a mere category, even if it is an ad hoc intergroup category, created a group; (2) membership in a particular group influences intergroup behaviors that favor the in-group and discriminate against the out-group; and (3) conflict over interest is not necessary to instigate out-group hostility.[19] The group is something that exists not out there but in one's self. When group members see a threat to their group, they consider it a threat to their social identity and subsequently to the self and their self-esteem. Conflict likely will ensue.[20] Using categorization as the point of departure and intergroup behavior as the focus of his interest, Tajfel developed the following concepts as basic tenets of SIT.

(1) *Categorization and Accentuation.* Categorization refers to a cognitive process that generalizes and accentuates certain aspects of human groups:[21] "Asians are smart," or

---

[18] Esler, "An Outline of Social Identity Theory," 14. Though Tajfel is the father of social identity theory (SIT), he has his predecessor, Muzafer Sherif. Sherif's *classic summer camp experiment* paved the way for the development of the *minimal group experiments*. In this experiment, Sherif and his colleagues divided into two groups boys who shared no interests and had had no previous contact with each other. After a week of becoming acquainted, in the second week a competition was announced with a reward being given only to the winning team. The two groups of boys demonstrated intergroup favor and outright intragroup discrimination. Muzafer Sherif, O. J. Harvey, B. Jack White, William R. Hood, and Carolyn W. Sherif, *Intergroup Conflict and Cooperation: The Robbers Cave Experiment* (Norman, OK: University of Oklahoma Press, 1961). By bringing subjects to a laboratory setting, Tajfel first eliminated the fairly extensive time for getting acquainted that Sherif and his collaborators gave to the boys in their field studies. Second, he provided no material reward. Yet, his findings were no different from Sherif's. For more on Tajfel's experiments, see Henri Tajfel, M. G. Billig, R. P. Bundy, and Claude Flament, "Social Categorization and Intergroup Behaviour," *European Journal of Social Psychology* 1, no. 2 (1971): 149–78.

[19] Tajfel et al., "Social Categorization and Intergroup Behaviour," 176.

[20] Peter Herriot, *Religious Fundamentalism and Social Identity* (London: Routledge, 2007), 28.

[21] Henri Tajfel and A. L. Wilkes's classic experiment with lines and labels (e.g., A and B) demonstrates the human tendency to exaggerate similarities and differences between different groups. Given four shorter lines and four longer lines, subjects of the experiment often exaggerated differences in the length (the focal dimension) between two groups of lines when different labels (a peripheral dimension or classification) were attached to groups of lines of the same length (e.g., A for four shorter lines and B for four longer lines). Tajfel and Wilkes found that such accentuation effects did not occur when no labels were attached to the lines or when the labeling was random, showing no correlation with the line length. Henri Tajfel and A. L. Wilkes, "Classification and Quantitative Judgment," *British Journal of Psychology* 54, no. 2 (1963): 112–13.

Michael A. Hogg and Dominic Abrams present various examples to illustrate this categorizing effect in *Social Identifications* (1998). (1) When we look at a rainbow, we tend to perceive seven colors. Unlike our seven given color categories, however, there exists almost an infinite number, of colors embedded in the rainbow. Yet our instinct to simplify complex entities and accentuate certain colors prevents us from recognizing varying degrees of the spectrum. (2) When people confront images of people with different skin colors ranging from pure "white" to pure "black" and are asked to measure a person's *blackness*, they tend to dissolve varying degrees of skin color and separate them into the two categories of *black* and *white*. (3) When an English student of Scandinavian languages sees four Japanese people who are shorter than Swedes at the airport, the perceived heights turn out to be different from the actual heights. He perceives that the height of the four Japanese is the same and is short and the height of the four Swedes is the same and is much taller than the four Japanese. The ethnicity of people (a peripheral dimension or classification) thus affects his perception of people's height (the focal dimension). (4) When people see that coins with higher value tend to be larger than coins with smaller value and when they compare their size, a coin's value (a peripheral dimension or classification) affects their perception of the coin's size (the focal dimension): "The larger coins (of higher value) are perceived to be larger than they really are, and the smaller ones (lower value) are perceived to be smaller than they really are." Hogg and Abrams, *Social Identifications*, 19–20, 69–70 (the quote is from p. 70).

"Blacks are athletic." Differences between members of the same group are dissolved, and one similarity comes to the fore to create a unified group in one's perception. Also, differences between groups are accentuated to distinguish and/or discriminate one group from the other: "Cretans are always liars, vicious brutes, lazy gluttons" (Titus 1:12).

(2) *Stereotyping*. This simplifying process leads to Tajfel's theory of stereotyping. He proposes that, first, when particular features are found continuously in selected social groups and tend to fall into distinct social classes, people accentuate the *similarities within similar groups* and the *differences between different groups*:[22] "Tall people are mostly lazy, whereas small people are mostly diligent" or "White people are mostly middle class, whereas colored people are almost all lower class." Second, people often exaggerate the seriousness, and often the significance, of negative events that are infrequently caused by members of minority groups and perceive them in a stereotypical way. For example, when the shooting at San Bernardino occurred on December 2, 2015, Donald Trump, a Republican presidential candidate at that time, instantly reacted and said, "You look at the names, you look at what's happened ... I think it was terrorism."[23] Though it is an "infrequent event with infrequent people"[24] compared to the frequent shootings in the United States, such events often leave permanent marks in people's memory.[25] Third, by degrading the out-group, in-group members enhance their own self-esteem. The idea of the "white man's burden,"[26] for example, differentiated the West from the East and justified the Western colonial enterprise around the globe. The West obtained a positive self-image because it viewed itself as not only more advanced than non-Europeans—*comparison* and *differentiation*—but also as striving to make the countries it colonized more advanced—*justification*.[27]

---

[22] Tajfel, *Human Groups and Social Categories*, 150–1.
[23] John Santucci, "Trump Says San Bernardino Shooting Appears Tied to Terrorism: 'Look at the Names,'" *ABC News*, December 3, 2015, http://abcnews.go.com/Politics/donald-trump-san-bernardino-shooting- appears-tied-terrorism/story?id=35561319. CNN reported on December 4, 2015, that Malik expressed her allegiance to ISIS (Islamic State of Iraq and Levant) leader Abu Bakr al-Baghdadi in a Facebook post. Saeed Ahmed, "Who were Syed Rizwan Farook and Tashfeen Malik?" *CNN*, December 4, 2015, http://www.cnn.com/2015/12/03/us/syed-farook-tashfeen-malik-mass-shooting-profile. CNN also reported that ISIS insisted that the shooters in the San Bernardino shooting, Tashfeen Malik and her husband Syed Rizwan Farook, were "supporters of ISIS." Faith Karimi, Jason Hanna, and Yousuf Basil, "San Bernardino Shooters 'Supporters' of ISIS, Terror Group Says," *CNN*, December 5, 2015, http://www.cnn.com/2015/12/05/us/san-bernardino-shooting. Syed Rizwan Farook was an American citizen born and raised in the United States. His wife Tashfeen Malik acquired U.S. permanent residency through her marriage to Farook.
[24] Tajfel, "Social Stereotypes and Social Groups," 153.
[25] For an up-to-date list of shooting incidents in the United States, see "Last 72 Hours," *Gun Violence Archive*, https://www.gunviolencearchive.org/last-72-hours. For example, the total number of incidents of gun-related violence in the United States on one day, January 1, 2018, was 198, according to the data.
[26] "The White Man's Burden" is a poem written in 1899 by Rudyard Kipling, an English poet, following the U.S. war against Spain in overtaking the Philippines. It portrays the Philippines as the Israelites in Egypt who need to be rescued by the white man, a counterpart of Moses in the Exodus story, and thus justifies the colonial regime.
[27] Victor Kiernan quotes Winwood Reade's reflection on Europe's mission to non-European countries to show how this process takes place: "But those people will never begin to advance ... until they enjoy the rights of men; and these they will never obtain except by means of European conquest." Victor Kiernan, *The Lords of Human Kind: European Attitudes to Other Cultures in the Imperial Age* (London: Weidenfeld & Nicolson, 1969), 24.

Stereotyping is "the process of ascribing characteristics to people on the basis of their group memberships."[28]

(3) *Social Identity and Intergroup Relations*. One's identity emerges from the social arena. Individuals who belong to a certain group and social category not only differentiate themselves from members of an out-group but also internalize their positive distinctiveness to define themselves.[29] Tajfel defines *social identity* as "that *part* of an individual's self-concept which derives from his knowledge of his membership in a social group (or groups) together with the value and emotional significance attached to that membership."[30] His definition stresses three components of social identity: (a) *cognitive*, "I belong to a group"; (b) *evaluative*, "My group is superior (or inferior) to other groups"; and (c) *emotional*, "I (dis)like being a member of the group."[31] Since humans repeat this process of categorization, comparison, and internalization, maintaining positive distinctiveness and thus a positive self-concept is essential.

Tajfel's chief interest, however, was not social identity per se but *intergroup relations*, or how one's self-concept and group memberships influence intergroup behavior.[32] When *social comparison* with out-group(s) leads to realizing *relative deprivation*, one deploys various strategies to restore one's positive self-image, particularly among members of minority groups.[33] "*We* are inferior to *them*. What am *I* to do?" Drawing from a fundamental human desire to resolve cognitive dissonance between who I *want to be* and who I *am*, Tajfel develops two primary strategies to rebuild positive self-image. *Subjective belief structures*—whether one thinks the boundaries between the groups are permeable or not—serve as the dividing line between the two.

A brief summary of Tajfel's theory is helpful here.[34] (1) The first strategy is *social mobility*. When members of the subordinate group agree with the dominant value system, they put aside their own social identity and seek to achieve the social identity of the dominant group. This is the mentality of "I can go up." (2) The second strategy is *social change*. This is based on the "I can't go up" mentality, which brings forth two plans of action: *social creativity* and *social competition*.[35] When subordinated group members

---

[28] Penelope J. Oakes, S. Alexander Haslam, and John C. Turner, *Stereotyping and Social Reality* (Oxford: Blackwell, 1994), 1. Tajfel adopts O. Stallybrass's definition of stereotype: "an over-simplified mental image of (usually) some category of person, institution or event which is shared, in essential features, by large numbers of people." Henri Tajfel, "Social Psychology of Intergroup Relations," *Annual Review of Psychology* 33 (1982): 2. See also O. Stallybrass, "Stereotype," in *The Fontana Dictionary of Modern Thought*, ed. A. Bullock and O. Stallybrass (London: Fontana/Collins, 1977), 601.

[29] Turner, "Henri Tajfel: An Introduction," 16.

[30] Tajfel, *Human Groups & Social Categories*, 255, emphasis in the original.

[31] Tajfel, "Social Psychology of Intergroup Relations," 2.

[32] Irudayaraj, *Violence, Otherness and Identity*, 43.

[33] Philip F. Esler explicates the terms as follows: "groups and individuals know who they are in comparison with other groups," and they experience relative deprivation "when a group considers that it has limited access to various benefits and opportunities, economic and otherwise, compared with other groups." Esler, "An Outline of Social Identity Theory," 19–20. Tajfel provides an extensive discussion of this issue in Tajfel, "Social Categorization, Social Identity, and Social Comparison," in *Human Groups and Social Categories*, 254–67.

[34] See Tajfel, "The Social Psychology of Minorities," in *Human Groups and Social Categories*, 309–43. A graphic illustration of Tajfel's theory of social mobility and social change is found in Philip F. Esler, *Galatians*, NTR (New York: Routledge, 1998), 55.

[35] Hogg and Abrams, *Social Identifications*, 27-9.

cannot see cognitive alternatives within the present social structure that is providing them with a feeling of inferiority, *social change* occurs. Using *social creativity*, they can select a different point of comparison. For example, laborers can overcome their feeling of inferiority by comparing their morality to greedy capitalists, not their material wealth. Similarly, but slightly differently, they can also redefine traditionally negative social identities, such as the use of the slogan "Black is beautiful" by American blacks in the 1960s.[36] A less positive option is available, as well. Members of an out-group can choose to compare themselves to "low-status groups," as occurs in working-class sexism or poor-white racism.[37] In so doing, insecure groups can convince themselves that "We are better than them." In contrast, *social competition* comes into play when an actual change in the social structure occurs by means of resistance, revolution, or war. By replacing the ruling class, the subordinate group is set free from the previously oppressive social structure and the previously dominant value system loses its hegemony.[38]

Insights from SIT are particularly helpful in studying Acts 21:17–23:35. First, the text indicates through Paul's interaction with Jews in Jerusalem that an emerging subgroup, the Way, is desperately seeking the approval of the dominant Jewish group(s). Second, labeling Paul as a threat to the Jewish nation and portraying the Jews as rejecting God's visitation demonstrate that the two sides were fighting each other with the same weapon, *stereotyping*. Third, Paul's speech and self-defense illustrate various attempts to compare the Way with, and differentiate it from, the Jewish out-group(s). In so doing, the text justifies the Way's very existence and constructs its identity, what it *is* and *is not*. Fourth, the character of Paul employs multiple strategies including social creativity to cope with intergroup conflict. In this way, SIT provides the paints for drawing the picture presented in the text.

Yet, some colors still need to be added in order to reflect light and shadow more accurately and produce a more realistic picture of groups not only in the text but also in real life, as well as their relationships with each other. Scholars have pointed out that SIT did not provide reasons for "social identity salience" and failed to explain "*intragroup* processes."[39] Having noted these theoretical loopholes, John C. Turner proposed the self-categorization theory.

2.1.2. Self-categorization Theory (SCT)

Whereas SIT focuses on *intergroup* relationships and the cognitive *motivation* behind intergroup behavior, SCT focuses on *intragroup* processes, "how individuals are able to

---

[36] Hogg and Abrams, *Social Identifications*, 28.
[37] Hogg and Abrams, *Social Identifications*, 29.
[38] The French Revolution (1789–99), the Russian Revolution (1917), and Indian nonviolent resistance to Britain (1930–47) are examples of social competition. As was the case in the Russian Revolution, however, radical social change does not always lead to the demolition of the present social structure. It can simply change dominant groups from one (e.g., the Russian imperial family) to the other (e.g., an oppressive Communist ruling class).
[39] Esler, "An Outline of Social Identity Theory," 22, emphasis in the original. See also Mark Bennett and Fabio Sani, "Introduction: Children and Social Identity," in *The Development of the Social Self*, ed. Mark Bennett and Fabio Sani (New York: Psychology Press, 2004), 11.

act as a group at all"[40] or, simply put, how one identifies oneself with a group.[41] I define the following concepts to aid in the exploration of the text.

(1) *Self-categorization*. Self-concept—the understanding of the self—is created by categorization, which has two innate features.[42] First, it is *situation specific*. Certain social categories are turned on in a particular social context or interaction (e.g., I am a husband, father, or son).[43] One's self-concept is not a fixed attribute, demonstrating one's innate identity in every circumstance, but a flexible entity in which certain facets receive more light than others depending on the circumstances. Categorization, therefore, is a "dynamic, context-dependent process."[44] Second, one's self-concept exists *within a hierarchal system of classification*. The self-concept contains categories that are in a hierarchal relationship with each another. A higher category includes a lower category (e.g., human identity, social identity, and personal identity).[45] When one's social category or group membership becomes internalized and influences self-perception, it plays a vital role in creating one's self-concept.[46]

(2) *Prototypes and Depersonalization*. When categorization occurs in the human psyche, people perceive themselves and others as group prototypes. Prototypes represent social consensus on the "defining attributes (beliefs ... behaviors, etc.) of a

---

[40] Turner, *Rediscovering the Social Group*, 42.
[41] Since SCT delves into the question of how groups come into existence, particularly the categorization process as the cognitive basis of group behavior, its interest encompasses SIT.
[42] John C. Turner defines self-concept as "the set of cognitive representations of self available to a person." Turner, *Rediscovering the Social Group*, 44.
[43] For example, when a Korean American male who is surrounded by whites and blacks sees a few Asians, this circumstance easily activates his Asian self-concept. When he is among Asians and sees a Korean, his Korean self-concept likely ensues. Yet if he is in a jungle full of beasts and danger, he will be drawn to anybody he finds, regardless of his or her ethnicity, because they share one thing in common: *we are humans*.
[44] Oakes, Haslam, and Turner, *Stereotyping and Social Reality*, 95.
[45] Turner, *Rediscovering the Social Group*, 45.
[46] Two basic factors are necessary to make comparison possible and produce certain categories. First, there should be *comparative relations* or *comparative fit*. Sufficiently large differences should be found between the two groups. For example, when comparing birds and fish, the ability to fly and/or survive in water can be a point of contrast. Though hawks and sparrows are different, their differences (e.g., size, color) are *less than* the differences between them and fish (e.g., the ability to live in water). Yet, when birds and fish are compared to plants, the differences between them are *less than* the differences between these two groups and plants. Second, there should be a *social meaning* of differences or a *normative fit*. The subject's behaviors or attributes need to meet the perceiver's knowledge-based expectations. In this case, interactions between *relative accessibility* and *fit* make a self-category more salient. *Relative accessibility* refers to the perceiver's readiness to use certain categories to identify self or others. One's past experience and motive make a more accessible category salient. For example, a veteran who fought for his or her country (past experience) and wants to advocate patriotism in the minds of listeners (motive) will likely use national categories in calling listeners out (e.g., "We *Americans* . . ."). *Fit* refers to the match between a category, which is, in this case, a social norm, and the reality. For example, a person who worships at a mosque every week and prays to Allah five times toward Mecca (reality) will not also be considered a Christian (category). Likewise, in a human group it is not just a person's innate features (e.g., skin color, language) but also his or her social behaviors that differentiate him or her from others and locate that person in a certain social category demanding certain normative behaviors. Turner, *Rediscovering the Social Group*, 47. See also Oakes, Haslam, and Turner, *Stereotyping and Social Reality*, 97.

social category."⁴⁷ The prototypical perception of the self is possible because of depersonalization, which is the "process of 'self-stereotyping.'"⁴⁸ For example, an American soldier during the American Revolutionary War (1775–83) could die honorably at the hands of the British army because he was dying for liberty not just as an individual but as an American. There is no negative implication in depersonalization in and of itself. It refers neither to "dehumanization" nor "deindividuation" but to "a contextual *change* in the level of identity, not to a loss of identity."⁴⁹ Since SCT focuses on cognitive processes behind group formation and behavior, *stereotyping* and *depersonalization* are two of the pillars of SCT.⁵⁰

(3) *Group Cohesion, Social Cooperation, and Social Influence.* After depersonalization, three intragroup processes likely follow. The first is group cohesion, "mutual attraction between in-group members."⁵¹ Attraction is based not simply on physical similarities (e.g., skin color) but on prototypicality, which has positive social meaning and thus can serve as a self-category.⁵² As long as there is attraction between more than two people and such attraction implies the "perception of identity or similarity between oneself and the attractive others," a group comes into existence.⁵³ The second process is social cooperation, which enhances the group's common interest.⁵⁴ Altruism likely ensues because "the goals of other in-group members are perceived as one's own."⁵⁵ Yet, since personalized actions such as seeking personal interests within a group decrease intragroup cooperation and increase interpersonal competition, another process needs

---

47 Hogg, "Intragroup Process, Group Structure and Social Identity," 69. A problem with a prototypical perception of self and others is that it promotes and justifies one's perception of out-group members with non-self-categories. For example, in his speech announcing he would run as a presidential candidate on June 16, 2015, Donald Trump called Mexicans in the United States "rapists" and "people that have lots of problems." Time Staff, "Here's Donald Trump's Presidential Announcement Speech," *Time*, June 16, 2015, http://time.com/3923128/donald-trump-announcement-speech. He was imposing a *non-self*-category, *rapists*, while utilizing a *self*-category, "the best," to describe himself and his supporters. Comments like this likely create a stereotypical image of the out-group in the minds of in-group members that may lead them to view out-group members as having these negative characteristics.

48 Turner, *Rediscovering the Social Group*, 50.

49 Hogg, "Intragroup Process, Group Structure and Social Identity," 69.

50 Dominic Abrams and Michael A. Hogg state, "The concept of depersonalization is fundamentally important for explaining why it is that people act and react in the name of groups to which they belong, and hence why groups are capable of concerted and coordinated actions that bring about social change." Dominic Abrams and Michael A. Hogg, "Social Identity and Self-Categorization," in *The SAGE Handbook of Prejudice, Stereotyping and Discrimination*, ed. John F. Dovidio, Miles Hewstone, Peter Glick, and Victoria M. Esses (London: SAGE, 2010), 182.

51 Turner, *Rediscovering the Social Group*, 57.

52 For example, what strengthens the group solidarity of factory workers during a labor strike is not just the color of their uniform but also the positive work ethic (e.g., diligence, hard work) that they share as a group but greedy capitalists do not possess. The in-group category cannot remain negative because it produces negative self-evaluation and brings down self-esteem. It should be connected to positive values compared to that of the out-group so that it produces a positive self-category and enhances group cohesion.

53 Turner, *Rediscovering the Social Group*, 64.

54 Jenkins, *Social Identity*, 7.

55 Turner, *Rediscovering the Social Group*, 65. For example, various individuals gave their lives to the resistance against Japanese colonialism in Korea (1910–45) because they wanted to live as *Koreans*.

to occur.⁵⁶ This third process is social influence. One's thoughts and behaviors change through interactions with in-group and out-group members.⁵⁷ When group cohesion and social influence are strong enough, group behavior becomes possible.

(4) *Reduction of Intergroup Bias*. Categorization is not only a means through which an in-group increases solidarity but also a seed of intergroup conflict in which an in-group discriminates against an out-group. In order to reduce the conflict, SCT proposes the need to develop common identities that "transform member's cognitive representation of the memberships from two groups to one group."⁵⁸ Since reduction of intergroup bias is one of the key strategies the character of Paul employs in his encounter with the Jewish people, this topic will be discussed in detail later in this chapter (Ch. 2.2).

The insights of SCT are helpful in exploring the text of this study. First, Paul's self-category is multilayered. He is first and foremost a Jew. Under this Jewish umbrella, he places his Pharisaic layer and his Christian layer. When necessary, he places his Roman layer over everything else. Second, the Lukan narrative produces prototypes at the opposite extremes: Torah-abiding, Spirit-led, and sober Paul versus the lawless, emotion-driven, and mobbish Jews. Third, Paul instigates mutual attraction with the Pharisees and makes cooperation possible over against the Sadducees.

2.1.3. Social Identity Approach: Achievements and Problems

Achievements. SIA achieved five milestones.⁵⁹ (1) SIA revived the *collectivistic* nature of human behavior in the study of social psychology. Social phenomena, including interactions between individuals, are the outcomes not simply of interpersonal relations but also of intergroup relations. (2) SIA articulated the *contextual* nature of social identity. One's identity is not only given but also formed through contact with

---

[56] Turner, *Rediscovering the Social Group*, 66. Such conflicts are not a rare phenomenon in a group because not everybody within the same group is attracted to each other. By the same token, not everyone agrees with everything in a given group.

[57] For example, a candidate who presents the United States' ideal as a nation and lives out those prototypes will likely be elected as the president, and this president's supporters will likely attempt to imitate him or her. Negative social influence is also true within in-groups. For example, if a high school student who has just joined a group of drug users and gangs sees every member using cocaine and feels pressured to try it, he or she will likely conform to the in-group's behavior.

[58] Gaertner et al., "Reducing Intergroup Bias," 2. See also Henri Tajfel and John C. Turner, "An Integrative Theory of Intergroup Conflict," in *The Social Psychology of Intergroup Relations*, ed. W. G. Austin and S. Worchel (Monterey: Brooks/Cole, 1971), 33–47. For example, the Second Sino-Japanese War ended a Chinese civil war between the Nationalist Party (Kuomintang) and the Communist Party and created the Second United Front in 1936 against imperial Japan. The greater cause, China's survival as a nation, brought two opposing parties together. Yet, once the Second World War ended, the Nationalist Party (Kuomintang) and the Communist Party resumed the civil war, which ended with the Communist Party's decisive victory in 1949. For details, see Jian Chen, *Mao's China and the Cold War*, The New Cold War History (Chapel Hill: University of North Carolina Press, 2001).

[59] Rupert Brown explicates four significant contributions that SIT made in the analysis of intergroup phenomena: "ingroup bias; responses to status inequality; intragroup homogeneity and stereotyping; changing intergroup attitudes through contact." Rupert Brown, "Social Identity Theory: Past Achievements, Current Problems, and Future Challenges," *European Journal of Social Psychology* 30 (2000): 747–52.

"social structure, social context, and society."[60] (3) SIA revealed the *processual* nature of identity formation. Identity is flexible, not fixed, as categories that define group boundaries can change and one can also switch his or her group membership over time. (4) SIA unveiled the *political* nature of identity construction. Gaining positive in-group bias often accompanies intergroup comparison and out-group hatred.[61] "They" become an object of ridicule by "us" and justify "our" existence: "*We* are different from *them*!" (5) SIA provided *analytical* tools that explain group processes and behaviors. Precise and empirical, SIA continues to attract scholars of social psychology who are eager to explain and evaluate group behaviors and to undertake various studies and experiments regarding such behaviors.[62] Biblical scholars have also recently found SIA useful in analyzing group dynamics and their literary representations in the biblical texts.[63]

[60] S. Alexander Haslam, *Psychology in Organizations: The Social Identity Approach* (London: SAGE, 2004), xix.
[61] In the following statements, Aaron Kuecker aptly captures a dilemma in an individual's social identity: "Social identity is primarily about the ascription of *positive* characteristics to the self and not about a primal disdain for the 'other'; it is primarily an expression of in-group love rather than out-group hate. However, in-group bias is infrequently benign and often forms the seed bed for social tension." Aaron Kuecker, *The Spirit and the "Other": Social Identity, Ethnicity and Intergroup Reconciliation in Luke-Acts*, LNTS 444 (London; New York: T&T Clark, 2011), 30, emphasis in the original.
[62] For example, in conjunction with their research on self-categorization, Dominic Abrams and Michael A. Hogg (1990) produced a study of conformity and group polarization, Penelope J. Oakes and Alexander Haslam (1994) a study of social perception, and Hogg (1992) a study of group solidarity and cohesiveness. Daniel Bar-Tal added a layer of "group beliefs" to SIT and SCT as "a basis of group formation and group maintenance." Others expanded their research into various topics: the correlation between norm violation and positive social identity, the relationship between social identity and contemporary means of communication, and the consequences of group commitment for intergroup behavior. D. Abrams and M. A. Hogg, "Social Identification, Self-Categorization, and Social Influence," *European Review of Social Psychology* 1 (1990): 195–228; P. J. Oakes, S. A. Haslam, and J. C. Turner, *Stereotyping and Social Reality*; M. A. Hogg, *The Social Psychology of Group Cohesiveness: From Attraction to Social Identity* (London: Harvester Wheatsheaf, 1992); Daniel Bar-tal, "Group Beliefs as an Expression of Social Identity," in *Social Identity: International Perspectives*, ed. Stephen Worchel, J. Francisco Morales, Dario Páez, and Jean-Claude Deschamps (London: SAGE, 1998), 93–113; José M. Marques, Dario Páez, and Dominic Abrams, "Social Identity and Intragroup Differentiation as Subjective Social Control," in Worchel et al., *Social Identity*, 124–41; Daniel Wigbodus, Russell Spears, and Gun Semin, "Social Identity, Normative Content and 'Deindividuation' in Computer-Mediated Groups," in *Social Identity*, ed. Naomi Ellemers, Russell Spears, and Bertjan Doosje (Oxford: Blackwell, 1999), 164–83; Bertjan Doosje, Naomi Ellemers, and Russell Spears, "Commitment and Intergroup Behaviour," in Ellemers, Spears, and Doosje, *Social Identity*, 84–106; Naomi Ellemers, Manuela Barreto, and Russell Spears, "Commitment and Strategic Responses to Social Context" in Ellemers, Spears, and Doosje, *Social Identity*, 127–46.
[63] For studies on the Hebrew Bible and the Dead Sea Scrolls, see Jan Petrus Bosman, *Social Identity in Nahum: A Theological-Ethical Enquiry* (Piscataway, NJ: Gorgias, 2008); Peter H. W. Lau, *Identity and Ethics in the Book of Ruth: A Social Identity Approach*, BZAW 416 (Berlin: de Gruyter, 2010); Pong D. Im, "Social Identity in Ancient Israel: An Archaeological and Textual Study of Social Behaviors and Group Identity among Highland Villagers in Iron Age I Palestine" (PhD diss., Graduate Theological Union, 2010); Jutta Jokiranta, *Social Identity and Sectarianism in the Qumran Movement*, ed. Florentino García Martínez, STDJ 105 (Leiden: Brill, 2013); Irudayaraj, *Violence, Otherness and Identity*. For studies in the New Testament and Greco-Roman literature, see Raimo Hakola, "'Friendly' Pharisees and Social Identity in Acts," in *Contemporary Studies in Acts*, ed. Thomas E. Phillips (Macon: Mercer University Press, 2009), 181–200; Matthew J. Marohl, *Faithfulness and the Purpose of Hebrews: A Social Identity Approach* (Cambridge: James Clarke, 2010); Jack Barensten, *Emerging Leadership in the Pauline Mission: A Social Identity Perspective on Local Leadership Development in Corinth and

Problems. Despite the merits mentioned above, SIA has limitations. First, critics target theoretical loopholes within SIA itself. Brown addresses five problematic issues with SIT. (1) *The relationship between group identification and in-group bias.* SIT assumes that "a positive social identity is mainly based on favourable intergroup comparisons."[64] But, empirical data show that the rule is not so much applicable to the "Individualist × Autonomous cell" as it is to the "Collectivist × Relational combination."[65] (2) *The self-esteem hypothesis.* SIT assumes that people discriminate against out-group members to restore "depressed self-esteem."[66] Yet, studies show that self-esteem should be seen as "a by-product of discrimination rather than a direct cause or effect."[67] (3) *The positive-negative asymmetry phenomenon.* SIT argues that in-group solidarity and out-group discrimination increases when a reward is given for so doing. Yet, this rule is only applicable to positive rewards. Studies show that when a negative outcome is promised, such as exposure to a loud noise, "discrimination virtually disappeared."[68] (4) *The effects of intergroup similarity.* SIT argues that (in-)groups are prone to differentiate themselves from out-groups even if there are many similarities between them. Yet, studies show that members of similar groups have "more intergroup attraction and less bias than dissimilar groups."[69] (5) *Choice of identity maintenance strategies by low-status groups.* SIT assumes that members of a minority group will employ strategies,

---

Ephesus, PTMS 168 (Eugene, OR: Pickwick, 2011); Paul Trebilco, *Self-Designations and Group Identity in the New Testament* (Cambridge: Cambridge University Press, 2011); Coleman A. Baker, *Identity, Memory, and Narrative in Early Christianity: Peter, Paul, and Recategorization in the Book of Acts* (Eugene, OR: Pickwick, 2011); Kuecker, *The Spirit and the 'Other'*; V. George Shillington, *James and Paul: The Politics of Identity at the Turn of the Ages* (Minneapolis: Fortress, 2015); Samuel Byrskog, Raimo Hakola, and Jutta Jokiranta, *Social Memory and Social Identity in the Study of Early Judaism and Early Christianity* (Göttingen: Vandenhoeck & Ruprecht, 2016). The publication of Brian Tucker and Coleman A. Baker, *T&T Clark Handbook to Social Identity in the New Testament* (2014), reflects the increasing use of SIA in the study of biblical literature.

[64] Brown, "Social Identity Theory," 753.
[65] Brown, "Social Identity Theory," 753. Brown states that "the level of group identification was high and there was substantial evidence of in-group favoritism … Such data hardly seem consistent with subjectively unimportant category memberships or irrelevant comparative dimensions" (p. 754). The result of the experiment is found in S. Hinkle and R. Brown, "Intergroup Comparisons and Social Identity: Some Links and Lacunae" in *Social Identity Theory: Constructive and Critical Advances*, ed. Dominic Abrams and Michael A. Hogg (Hemel Hempstead: Harvester Wheatsheaf, 1990), 48–70.
[66] Brown, "Social Identity Theory," 755.
[67] Brown, "Social Identity Theory," 756. The studies to which Brown refers are found in M. Hogg and D. Abrams, "Social Motivation, Self-Esteem and Social Identity," in *Social Identity Theory: Constructive and Critical Advances*, ed. D. Abrams and M. Hogg, 28–47; M. Hogg and B. Mullin, "Joining Groups to Reduce Uncertainty: Subjective Uncertainty Reduction and Group Identification," in *Social Identity and Social Cognition*, ed. D. Abrams and M. Hogg (Oxford: Blackwell, 1999), 249–79.
[68] Brown, "Social Identity Theory," 756. See Amélie Mummendey, Bernd Simon, Carsten Dietze, Melanie Grünert, Gabi Haeger, Sabine Kessler, Stephan Lettgen, and Stefanie Schäferhoff, "Categorization is Not Enough: Intergroup Discrimination in Negative Outcome Allocation," *Journal of Experimental Social Psychology* 28 (1992): 125–44.
[69] Brown, "Social Identity Theory," 758. See Rupert J. Brown, "The Role of Similarity in Intergroup Relations," in *The Social Dimension: European Developments in Social Psychology*, ed. Henri Tajfel (Cambridge: Cambridge University Press, 1984), 603–23; Rupert Brown and Dominic Abrams, "The Effects of Intergroup Similarity and Goal Interdependence on Intergroup Attitudes and Task Performance," *Journal of Experimental Social Psychology* 22 (1986): 78–92.

whether social mobility or social creativity, to restore positive self-image. Yet, it is difficult to predict "which strategy will be adopted."[70]

SCT is also not exempt from criticism. Craig McGarty raises two critical points. (1) *Hierarchical categories*. SCT asserts that there are different levels of abstraction in which a higher category encompasses lower categories.[71] Yet, in real life, boundaries are often conflated. For example, "Christians" is a subgroup category including certain "Americans," yet it is also a superordinate category that includes many people throughout the world. (2) *Distinction between impressions of groups and social categories*. SCT asserts that stereotypes explain categories of people. Yet, since categories are often artificial and cannot fully explicate how "they" are perceived by "us," the theory needs to distinguish between what we perceive (impressions) and how we are supposedly perceived (social categories).[72]

The second criticism addresses the theoretical underpinnings of the social scientific approaches under which SIA pitched its tent. Peter H. W. Lau summarizes two key problems with social scientific methods. (1) *Reductionism*. Social scientific approaches narrow down complex causes of social phenomena into a few defined hypotheses.[73] It is equally problematic to apply a social scientific lens to biblical texts that are multidimensional (e.g., literary, theological).[74] (2) *Determinism*. Social scientific approaches apply theories tested elsewhere to a new but similar (con)text and predict a patterned outcome.[75] To avoid the pitfall of oversimplification, Lau suggests using the scientific models as heuristic tools, not as magic formulae to predict what to expect.[76]

In moving forward, thus, two methodological remarks are necessary here. First, keeping in mind the limits of the social scientific approach, this book utilizes SIA not to reduce events that happened in the text to a few hypotheses to bring forth some predicted outcomes. Rather, SIA will be used as a heuristic tool to illuminate nuances of the text while examining theological, literary, and ideological aspects of the text. Second, drawing on the past achievements and problems of SIA, this study will focus on the *contextual*, *processual*, and *political* nature of social identity while paying due attention to the complexities of the interactions between the characters in the story. The goal is not to

---

[70] Brown, "Social Identity Theory," 759. See John C. Turner and Rupert Brown, "Social Status, Cognitive Alternatives, and Intergroup Relations," in *Differentiation Between Social Groups: Studies in the Social Psychology of Intergroup Relations*, ed. Henri Tajfel (London: Academic Press, 1978), 171–99; Rupert J. Brown and Gordon F. Ross, "The Battle for Acceptance: An Exploration into the Dynamics of Intergroup Behavior," in *Social Identity and Intergroup Relations*, ed. Henri Tajfel (Cambridge: Cambridge University Press, 1982), 155–78.

[71] Craig McGarty, *Categorization in Social Psychology* (London: SAGE, 1999), 210–43.

[72] Craig McGarty, "Stereotype Formation as Category Formation," in *Stereotypes as Explanations: The Formation of Meaningful Beliefs about Social Groups*, ed. Craig McGarty, Vincent Y. Yzerbyt, and Russell Spears (Cambridge: Cambridge University Press, 2002), 16–37. Erving Goffman's study on the presentation of self provides helpful insights into impression management and will be taken up in a later section of this chapter.

[73] Lau, *Identity and Ethics in the Book of Ruth*, 7.

[74] Lau, *Identity and Ethics in the Book of Ruth*, 7–8.

[75] Lau, *Identity and Ethics in the Book of Ruth*, 8. For example, see David G. Horrell's critique of Esler's commentary on Galatians in which Esler employs SIA to explore Paul's methods and motives in his writing. David G. Horrell, "Models and Methods in Social Scientific Interpretation: A Response to Philip Esler," *JSNT* 78 (2000): 83–105.

[76] Lau, *Identity and Ethics in the Book of Ruth*, 9; Irudayaraj, *Violence, Otherness and Identity*, 63.

validate the theoretical usefulness of SIA but to underscore the multidimensional nature of the ancient text, its representations, and the discourses it generates.

To apply the chosen methodological framework to Acts 21:17–23:35, one concept from SIA needs further exploration: *dual identity*. Facing various threats from his opponents, Paul constantly discloses common identity markers to them—his devotion to Torah, his Roman citizenship, and his commitment to the Pharisaic tradition. This is a breathtaking drama in which Paul is in great danger, as if he were sitting on a barrel of gunpowder, yet he survives, which not only generates excitement among the Lukan audience but also instills notions of what defines the identity of the Way. The Way is similar to its proximate "other," the Jewish people, in their beliefs and practices, but at the same time it is dissimilar in significant ways. In a word, the text serves as a medium of identity construction through the portrayal of intergroup conflict and Paul's use of his dual identities. The next section is devoted to the study of this specific aspect of SIA.

2.2. Dual Identity and the Proximate "Other"

During the developmental phase of SIA, scholars endeavored to find ways to reduce intergroup conflict.[77] Sherif, Tajfel, and others noted the need to increase intergroup cooperation and decrease in-group bias by setting up superordinate goals that divided groups should work together to achieve. Yet, later studies showed that at the heart of intergroup conflict lies strong in-group bias rather than intergroup bias.[78] For example, "The biases of whites are primarily pro-white rather than anti-black."[79] In other words, reducing intergroup conflict depends, first and foremost, on how we see *ourselves*. Social *categorization* matters. Recently, Samuel L. Gaertner and colleagues proposed two options for "degrading the salience of the two-group categorized representation."[80]

---

[77] Tajfel provides a brief historical survey of the scholarship on intergroup cooperation and superordinate goals in Tajfel, "Social Psychology of Intergroup Relations," 28–9. Muzafer Sherif (1966) concludes from his field study the effectiveness of superordinate goals, which Tajfel (1981) also affirms. Stephen Worchel (1977) discovers from his experimental research that the salience of previously existing group identities decides how successfully intergroup cooperation will work in conflict reduction. Yet, these discoveries apply very little to real-life situations. Y. Amir (1976) and L. N. Diab (1978) find that when there are clear differences in status, power, and resources between groups, efforts to reduce prejudice are often unsuccessful. For more details, see Muzafer Sherif, *In Common Predicament: Social Psychology of Intergroup Conflict and Cooperation* (Boston: Houghton Mifflin, 1966); Tajfel, *Human Groups and Social Categories*; Stephen Worchel, Virginia A. Andreoli, and Roger Folger, "Intergroup Cooperation and Intergroup Attraction: The Effect of Previous Interaction and Outcome of Combined Effort," *Journal of Experimental Social Psychology* 13 (1977): 131–40; L. N. Diab, "Achieving Intergroup Cooperation through Conflict-Produced Superordinate Goals," *Psychological Reports* 43 (1978): 735–41.
[78] Samuel L. Gaertner and John F. Dovidio, "The Aversive Form of Racism," in *Prejudice, Discrimination, and Racism*, ed. John F. Dovidio and Samuel L. Gaertner (Orlando: Academic Press, 1986), 61–89.
[79] Gaertner et al., "The Common Ingroup Identity Model," 5.
[80] Gaertner et al., "The Common Ingroup Identity Model," 5. See also John F. Dovidio, Samuel L. Gaertner, and Gladys Kafati, "Group Identity and Intergroup Relations: The Common In-Group Identity Model," in *Advances in Group Processes*, ed. Shane R. Thye, Edward J. Lawler, Michael W. Macy, and Henry A. Walker (Stamford, CT: JAI, 2000), 1–34.

(1) *Decategorization*.[81] In decategorization, individuals' former group membership is removed. There are two ways to do this. The first is to perceive members of the outgroup via personal interactions that may nullify prior categories.[82] The second is to create new subgroups that include members of both conflicting groups and give cross-memberships. Both strategies aim to blur the former category and have been found useful in laboratory settings but not as much in real-life situations.[83]

(2) *Recategorization*.[84] In recategorization, individuals become members together of a new superordinate group by pursuing a common goal together. There are also two ways to do this. The first is to dissolve the former categories and incorporate the prior identities into a new superordinate identity.[85] For example, the creation of a united Korean team in the 2018 Pyeongchang Winter Olympics evoked a common Korean identity among many Koreans, yet the emotional excitement may diminish in the midst of ever-changing international politics.[86] Scholars have noted that a single common identity is insufficient to diminish "members' fundamental need for distinctiveness" and the seeds of "resistance."[87] The second is to maintain subgroup salience while instilling a superordinate identity. The common goal not only should allow both groups to work together but also should not invalidate previous subgroup identities.[88] For example, the new identity of "Rainbow people" in South Africa gained considerable support in resisting apartheid because blacks and whites were encouraged to keep their own ethnic distinctiveness.[89] This second strategy is not a cure-all for intergroup conflict, as scholars have found that a common identity is insufficient to

---

[81] Gaertner et al., "The Common Ingroup Identity Model," 5.

[82] Miller, "Personalisation and the Promise of Contact Theory," 387– 410. A meeting with a Muslim immigrant serving in the U.S. military may allow a pro-white and anti-Muslim American to set aside his or her former category of Muslims as terrorists against the United States.

[83] For example, Samuel L. Gaertner, Jeffrey Mann, Audrey Murrell, and John F. Dovidio, "Reducing Intergroup Bias: The Benefits of Recategorization," *Journal of Personality and Social Psychology* 57, no. 2 (1989): 239–49. See also David A. Wilder, "Reduction of Intergroup Discrimination through Individuation of the Outgroup," *Journal of Personality and Social Psychology* 36, no. 12 (1978): 1361–74; Barry Commins and John Lockwood, "The Effects on Intergroup Relations of Mixing Roman Catholics and Protestants: An Experimental Investigation," *European Journal of Social Psychology* 8, no. 3 (1978): 383–6.

[84] Gaertner et al., "The Common Ingroup Identity Model," 6.

[85] Kuecker, *The Spirit and the 'Other,'* 33.

[86] There were united North-South Korean teams for the 1991 World Table Tennis Championships in Chiba, Japan, and for the 1991 FIFA U-20 World Cup in Portugal. The Korean team won the championship in the 1991 World Championships and advanced to a quarterfinal in the 1991 U-20 World Cup.

[87] John F. Dovidio, Samuel L. Gaertner, and Tamar Saguy, "Another View of 'We': Majority and Minority Group Perspectives on a Common Ingroup Identity," *European Review of Social Psychology* 18 (2007): 300.

[88] Rupert Brown and Miles Hewstone, "An Integrative Theory of Intergroup Contact," in *Advances in Experimental Social Psychology* 37, ed. M. P. Zanna (San Diego: Academic Press, 2005), 255–343.

[89] Kuecker, *The Spirit and the 'Other,'* 33. For more details, see Desmond Tutu, *The Rainbow People of God: South Africa's Victory over Apartheid* (New York: Doubleday, 1994); *No Future without Forgiveness* (New York: Doubleday, 1999); Helga Dickow and Valerie Møller, "South Africa's 'Rainbow People,' National Pride and Optimism: A Trend Study," *Social Indicators Research* 59 (2002): 175–202; James L. Gibson, "Do Strong Ingroup Identities Fuel Intolerance? Evidence from the South African Case," *Political Psychology* 27, no. 5 (2006): 665–705.

blur persisting categories such as racial and ethnic distinctions.[90] Yet, the appeal of such a dual identity—developing a superordinate identity and retaining a subgroup identity—has led scholars to study it, experiment, and prove its usefulness.[91] The Lukan storyteller is no exception. Paul's shifting of self-(re)presentations bespeaks Luke's endeavor to recategorize a character in the story, seek the cooperation of out-group literary characters, and construct a dual identity for the marginalized Way.

2.2.1. Models of Dual Identity

In order to decrease conflict by employing a superordinate identity, the in-group needs to draw a boundary that will identify its relationship with the out-group. The in-group on a broad scale has three options in identifying its boundary or identity markers, as depicted in Figure 2.1: (1) the in-group is different from the out-group; (2) the in-group is similar to and, at the same time, significantly dissimilar to the out-group; (3) the in-group is what the out-group ought to be but fails to be, and it seeks to fulfill the vision of the greater community that was originally bestowed on the out-group.

Of these three models, model 3 seems to adequately describe the events happening in Acts 21:17–23:35. Paul finds historical roots of the Way in the Torah and seeks to fulfill its vision of bringing Gentiles into God's assembly (e.g., Gen 12:3; Isa 56:1-8). Applying one of these models to the text, however, does more harm than good because the models do not capture the complexities within the text. In fact, all three models illuminate some aspects of Paul's interactions with the Jewish people. Each model will receive particular attention in the following chapters, especially model 1 in chapter 3, model 2 in chapter 5, and model 3 in chapter 4. Furthermore, another critical concept, the proximate "other," needs to be discussed to delineate the ways in which Paul's strategy of claiming his dual identity is played out in the text. From there, three key

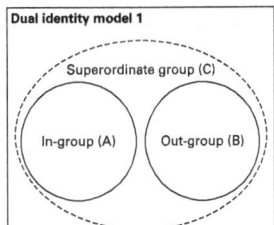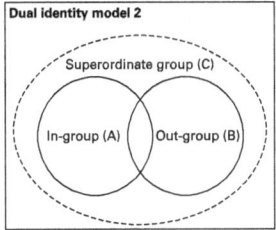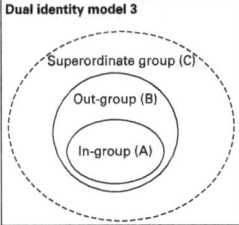

Figure 2.1 Models of Dual Identity.

---

[90] Miles Hewstone, "Contact and Categorization: Social Psychological Interventions to Change Intergroup Relations," in *Stereotypes and Stereotyping*, ed. C. Neil Macrae, Charles Stangor, and Miles Hewstone (New York: Guilford Press, 1996), 323–68.

[91] Gaertner et al., "The Common Ingroup Identity Model"; Michael Wenzel, Amélie Mummendey, and Sven Waldzus, "Superordinate Identities and Intergroup Conflict: The Ingroup Projection Model," *European Review of Social Psychology* 18, no. 1 (2007): 331–72; Linda Argote and Aimée A. Kane, "Superordinate Identity and Knowledge Creation and Transfer in Organizations," in *Knowledge Governance: Processes and Perspectives*, ed. Nicolai J. Foss and Snejina Michailova (New York: Oxford University Press, 2009), 166–90.

methodological elements that contribute to identity construction of the Way will be described: *ambivalence, social creativity,* and *recategorization.*

2.2.2. The Proximate "Other"

The self does not exist in a vacuum. Neither does one's identity. I am who I am in relation to the Other.[92] Therefore, Jonathan Z. Smith declares, "A 'theory of the other' is but another way of phrasing a 'theory of the self.'"[93] In other words, one needs to go beyond traditional binaries of "us" and "them" to think critically about "self" and "the Other." To do so, Smith introduces an intriguing category, the "proximate 'other,'" over against the "radically 'other.'"[94] The radically other is the *remote other* and is not an issue of debate because "absolute 'difference' is not a category for thought, but one that denies the possibility of thought."[95] But, the proximate "other" is near, physically and/or conceptually, and thus "problematic."[96] Smith eloquently expresses the complex relationship the self has with the proximate "other": "While the 'other' may be perceived as being either LIKE-US or NOT-LIKE-US, he is, in fact, most problematic when he is TOO-MUCH-LIKE-US, or when he claims to BE-US."[97]

The proximate "other" is a useful concept for describing the relationship between the Jewish people and the members of the Way. On the one hand, the Way is the proximate "other" to Jews. Paul's assertion of his fidelity to the Torah and the temple claims that the Way is similar and even *identical* to Jewish traditions. Yet, his commitment to the risen Lord and the Gentile mission turns out to be an irreconcilable point of *difference,* as the narrative portrays violent resistance of the Jews against the TOO-MUCH-LIKE-US or the one who claims to BE-US. On the other hand, the Jewish people are also the proximate "other" to the Way. Luke cannot simply leave the Jews alone. Paul and the apostles constantly visit synagogues and preach the gospel there, though they repeatedly face hostility, because their preaching of the risen Messiah can find validity only in the Jewish scripture. Yet, when rejected, persuasion changes to accusation in which those who were formerly called "brothers and fathers" become enemies of God (e.g., Acts 7:2, 51-60). In this agonistic context in which the Way and its Jewish opponents exchange vicious attacks, Luke-Acts presents its own version of the story, creates its proximate "other," and constructs the identity of the Way. The following three elements add complexities to Lukan identity formation.

2.2.3. Ambivalence

The concept of ambivalence originated in the field of psychoanalysis and has recently been widely used among postcolonial theorists, led by Homi K. Bhabha. The term refers

---

[92] Katherine E. Southwood, *Ethnicity and the Mixed Marriage Crisis in Ezra 9–10: An Anthropological Approach* (New York: Oxford University Press, 2012), 24.
[93] Smith, "What a Difference a Difference Makes," 47.
[94] Smith, "What a Difference a Difference Makes," 5.
[95] Smith, "What a Difference a Difference Makes," 46.
[96] Smith, "What a Difference a Difference Makes," 5.
[97] Smith, "What a Difference a Difference Makes," 47.

to "simultaneous *attraction* toward and *repulsion* from an object, person or action."[98] As in colonial discourse, ambivalence allows the self to both comply with *and* resist the Other. The self continually identifies itself with the Other but never gives up its difference because its uniqueness defines who "I" am. The outright anti-Jewish rhetoric of Luke-Acts reflects not just hate but a love-hate relationship with the Jews and a deep yearning for acceptance. This Lukan ambivalence toward its proximate "other" makes the Lukan narrative, as Tyson notes, both profoundly pro-Jewish and anti-Jewish.[99]

Acts 21:17–23:35 is no exception. Paul's purification at the temple, defense before the Jewish crowd, and appeal to Pharisaic tradition elucidate his adherence to Jewishness. Yet, his slanderous remarks against the high priest Ananias illustrate his repulsion toward the Sadducees. The historical turmoil the Jewish nation underwent in the late first century CE may serve as the backdrop of this short episode. The destruction of the Jerusalem temple by the Romans was not only a shock but also a threat to the Jewish people. Before the fall of the temple, they had fixed their eyes intently on another symbol of identity that was still standing, the Torah, and its guardians, the Pharisees. The text also draws lines to identify what the Way is. Luke does this by comparing the Way with other Jewish out-groups and underscoring how "we" are both similar to and different from "them," as a minority group would do with the dominant out-group.[100] This split vision of Luke-Acts toward the "LIKE-US, yet NOT-LIKE-US" paints a picture of the self and the Other in Acts 21:17–23:35.

2.2.4. Social Creativity

As noted earlier, in SIA social creativity refers to a set of strategies a minority group[101] employs to overcome a relative scarcity—of educational opportunities, financial resources, social status, etc.—compared to the dominant out-group when group boundaries are impermeable and overturning the status quo seems infeasible. To maintain positive distinctiveness and thus the positive self-esteem of the in-group, minority group members may (1) compare the in-group with an out-group on a new dimension; (2) re-evaluate and redefine existing comparisons; or (3) compare the in-group with different out-groups.[102] A methodological diversion needs to occur when

---

[98] Bill Ashcroft, Gareth Griffiths, and Helen Tiffin, *Post-Colonial Studies: The Key Concepts* (New York: Routledge, 2000), 12, emphasis added. According to Homi K. Bhabha, colonial ambivalence is expressed both in the colonizer's desire to reproduce *imperfect* replicas of the colonizer and in the colonial subject's desire to mimic and disavow its colonizer. Homi K. Bhabha, *The Location of Culture* (New York: Routledge, 1994), 122: "colonial mimicry is the desire for a reformed recognizable Other, *as a subject of difference that is almost the same, but not quite*," emphasis in the original.

[99] Joseph B. Tyson, *Images of Judaism in Luke-Acts* (Columbia, SC: University of South Carolina Press, 2010).

[100] On the study of how Christianity and Judaism have influenced each other, see Peter Schäfer, *The Jewish Jesus: How Judaism and Christianity Shaped Each Other* (Princeton: Princeton University Press, 2012).

[101] Tajfel makes clear at the outset of his essay "The Social Psychology of Minorities" that his primary concern is not "definitions of social groups (or categories) in terms of the economic, social, cultural or other criteria by which they can be distinguished" but "the psychological effects of these objective factors on the people involved." Tajfel, "The Social Psychology of Minorities," in *Human Groups & Social Categories*, 309.

[102] Esler, *Galatians*, 55.

applying this model. Not only multiple minority groups but also multiple majority groups compete with each other for dominance in society. In this context, comparing one's group with an out-group and drawing a boundary accordingly can keep one group out and, at the same time, keep another in. By placing the in-group together with a former out-group under a superordinate identity, in-group members may claim privileges, status, and resources possessed by the common group.

Acts 21:17–23:35 is an interesting test case for this model because, first, Paul is a member of the Way, a minority and marginalized group in the broader body of Judaism(s). To prove the legitimacy of this new sect, Paul constantly appeals to his commitment to the Law and, thus, to his Jewish identity. How Paul's audience reacts to Paul's claim provides challenges to and insights into theories of intergroup conflict. Second, the Pharisees and the Sadducees are two competing dominant groups in the text. Paul's tug of war between the two illustrates the Way's effort to redefine its identity. Third, Paul had to deal with the Roman authorities as well as Jewish out-groups. In the Roman colonial context, the Way is doubly marginalized by the Jewish majority and the Romans. Does Paul side with one over the other or with both equally? How does he do so? Reading the text in light of social creativity will not only answer these questions but will also illuminate the ambiguities of the Lukan identity construction of the Way.

2.2.5. Recategorization

Taken from Gaertner's common in-group identity model, recategorization refers to the redefining process of a group boundary from "us" and "them" to a more inclusive "we" in order to reduce intergroup bias and conflict.[103] Once cooperative interactions take place between two formerly contested groups, intergroup hostility will likely reduce. Yet, in order for cooperation to occur, a cognitive process needs to take place in the first place. Richard Jenkins calls this process "the internal-external dialectic of individual identification."[104] Relying on Erving Goffman's work, Jenkins argues that in the presentation of the self, individuals present an image of the self that is acceptable to the public (the internal moment), and others decide whether they will receive this image or not (the external moment).[105] Individuals constantly negotiate between their *self-image* (their internal self) and their *public image* (their external self or label) in an effort to make a good impression on others. Identity emerges through the dialectic

---

[103] Gaertner et al., "The Common Ingroup Identity Model," 1.
[104] Jenkins, *Social Identity*, 93. Jenkins's discussion of social identity is drawn from cultural anthropology more than social psychology. "The work of many other authors has been significant—particularly ... Henri Tajfel, Anthony Cohen, Pierre Bourdieu ... but Mead, Goffman and Barth remain my real inspirations." Jenkins, *Social Identity*, 40. SIT and Barthians share similarities and differences in their approaches to identity. Irudayaraj states that although both Fredrik Barth and Henri Tajfel focus on the *relational* and *processual* nature of identity, they differ in their emphasis: "*Similarity* and *difference* form the heart of social identity. But, Barth's emphasis on boundaries is a case of highlighting the difference." Irudayaraj, *Violence, Otherness and Identity*, 63–4, emphasis in the original.
[105] Erving Goffman, *The Presentation of Self in Everyday Life* (Garden City, NY: Doubleday, 1959). See also Erving Goffman, *Stigma: Notes on the Management of Spoiled Identity* (New York: Touchstone, 1986), 2.

between the two and the (re)definition of the boundaries between groups.[106] Katherine Southwood underscores the complexities that arise from Jenkins's discussion of ethnic boundaries:

> Jenkins's argument illustrates the importance not only of appreciating the self-reflective nature of categories, but also the broader contextual considerations and implications such categories have. Decisive questions will therefore be *who* is constructing the categories and, through this, defining the boundaries between groups, who is resisting such imposed identities, and what corollaries are associated with certain groups being forced into particular ethnic categories?[107]

The text illustrates the internal-external dialectic between Paul and his interlocutors and, thus, Luke's search for a common group identity. Facing slander and a discursive labeling by the Jews, Paul constantly *recategorizes* himself to insist that he is not an outsider. An unswerving concern of Acts is how one receives salvation (e.g., Acts 4:12; 13:26, 47; 16:17; 28:28). Can a Gentile join the people of God? Will the Jewish crowd accept faith in Jesus as a new category for being a member of God's people, as Paul argues? Will Paul find a point of reconciliation between his self-image as a devout Jew and his public image as a deviant? Taking these questions into consideration, a social identity reading approaches Paul's interactions from the perspective of the dual identity model. Before delving into the chosen text, the remaining section discusses the categories of membership Luke-Acts sets in place to identify its in-group members.

2.3. Construction of Christian Identity in Luke-Acts

The central concern of Luke-Acts is not only to address God's visitation to Israel but also to expand the boundaries of what constitutes *the people of God*. The primary recipient of the gospel is "the people of Israel" (Lk 1:16, 68; Acts 4:10, 27; 9:15, 10:36; 13:17, 24). Yet, James announces during the Jerusalem council that a new category of "people" (λαός) includes Gentiles: "a *people* for his name" (Acts 15:14). Not all the people of Israel are members of this new "*people*."[108] This people of God is not the new Israel comprised of Gentiles without Jews, as Jack T. Sanders avers.[109] They are instead the "true Israel," which includes repentant Jews and Gentile believers, as Jacob Jervell avers.[110] They are the

---

[106] For Erving Goffman, identity entails the way in which one wants to be treated. Jenkins agrees with Goffman that the external and collective identifications given by others can be internalized and individual identification can result from interactions of individuals. Yet, he criticizes Goffman for failing to acknowledge individuals' capacity to resist external identification at the expense of impression management. Jenkins, *Social Identity*, 93, 97.

[107] Katherine Southwood, "An Ethnic Affair?: Ezra's Intermarriage Crisis against a Context of Self-Ascription and Ascription of Others," in *Mixed Marriages: Intermarriage and Group Identity in the Second Temple Period*, ed. Christian Frevel, LHBOTS 547 (London: T&T Clark, 2011), 50, emphasis in the original.

[108] Jack T. Sanders, *The Jews in Luke-Acts* (Philadelphia: Fortress, 1987), 48. For a discussion of "people," "people of Israel," and "people of God" in Luke-Acts, see especially pp. 48–50.

[109] Sanders, *The Jews in Luke-Acts*, 317.

[110] Jervell, *The Theology of the Acts of the Apostles*, 42.

church, "Christians" who turned to Christ among both Jews and Gentiles (Acts 11:26; 26:28; see also Acts 3:23; 17:30),[111] which Acts also calls ἅγιοι, μαθηταί, and ἀδελφοί.[112] It is a "'church of nations' (Gen 28:3; 35:11; 48:4) from all peoples."[113]

This new category of the people of God is, on the one hand, *Christian*, since it goes beyond the Jewish ethnic category, and, on the other hand, *Jewish*, because it bases its claim on the promise of the God of Israel.[114] The Way is a Jewish sect (Acts 24:5, 14; 28:22). Now the gospel is being delivered to the Gentiles, those who had been outsiders in the past. An entry gate is opened for them. Such joyful news, however, turns out to be a challenge to Jews both inside and outside the Way. Are the categories that kept "us" in and "them" out now ineffective? This is a question generated from within through intra-Jewish interactions as the Lukan Jesus encounters rejection in the synagogue at Nazareth (Lk 4:16-30).[115] Paul's visit to Jerusalem also begins with an intra-Jewish interaction, his meeting with Jewish believers (Acts 21:17-26). What does the Gentiles' acceptance of the gospel mean to the Jewish election, identity, and understanding of God?

To answer this question, Luke-Acts articulates the similarities, not the differences, of the Way with the Jewish tradition. The Way is a Jewish group whose ties to other Jews are undeniable.[116] Here, I will neither enumerate every text in which Luke-Acts speaks of, elucidates, or alludes to the Jewish identity nor compare and contrast the Jewish identity found in Luke-Acts to other Jewish texts in their historical context.[117] Rather, I will focus on Acts 15:1-35, the so-called Council at Jerusalem, and the following relevant texts: Acts 8:26-40, Acts 10:1–11:18, Acts 16:1-5, and Acts 16:11-15.

2.3.1. The Jerusalem Council: Another Way to Join the People of God (Acts 15:1-35)

Martin Dibelius famously called Acts 15 the "Apostolic Council."[118] A decree comes forth after a heated debate over the terms on which the church would include Gentiles.

---

[111] Haenchen, *The Acts of the Apostles*, 209.

[112] David Seccombe, "The New People of God," in *Witness to the Gospel: The Theology of Acts*, ed. I. Howard Marshall and David Peterson (Grand Rapids: Eerdmans, 1998), 372. See also the following references for each term: ἅγιοι (Acts 9:13, 32, 41; 26:10); μαθηταί (Acts 6:1, 2, 7; 9:1, 10, 19, 25, 26, 38; 11:26, 29; 13:52; 14:20, 22, 28; 15:10; 16:1; 18:27; 19:1, 9, 30; 20:1, 30; 21:4, 16); ἀδελφοί (Acts 1:16; 2:29, 37; 6:3; 9:30; 10:23; 11:1, 12, 29; 12:17; 14:2; 15:1, 3, 7, 13, 22, 23, 32, 33, 36, 40; 16:2, 40; 17:6, 10, 14; 18:18, 27; 21:7, 17; 28:14, 15).

[113] Seccombe, "The New People of God," 372.

[114] In a similar vein, Christopher Stroup argues that Acts presents Christians who are not ethnic Jews as Jewish converts through the Holy Spirit. See Christopher Stroup, *The Christians Who Became Jews: Acts of the Apostles and Ethnicity in the Roman City* (New Haven: Yale University Press, 2020).

[115] Mark narrates a similar story after one-third of his Gospel story is already told (Mk 6:1-6). Matthew also places the Markan rejection story in the middle of his Gospel (Mt 13:54-58). Luke locates it early in his Gospel.

[116] Dulcinea Boesenberg, "Negotiating Identity: The Jewishness of the Way in Acts," *JRSSS* 13 (2016): 58–75. According to Boesenberg, Luke articulates ties between the Way and other Jews by (1) using similar familial language, (2) redefining the boundaries of Israel, (3) bringing Gentiles into the community in accord with the law of Moses, and (4) portraying the Way as observing the law of Moses.

[117] For a thorough analysis of Jewishness at the turn of the millennium, see Cohen, *The Beginnings of Jewishness*.

[118] Martin Dibelius, *Studies in the Acts of the Apostles*, trans. M. Ling and Paul Schubert, ed. Heinrich Green (New York: Charles Scribner's Sons, 1956), 93–101.

After the council, there seems to be no disagreement on this issue, at least among the in-group members. The Gentile mission officially begins as readers find Paul busy preaching the gospel to Gentiles in the following chapter. What, then, is the decision that was made? The council's letter to Gentile believers states:

> For it has seemed good to the Holy Spirit and to us to impose on you no further burden than these essentials [ἐπάναγκες]: that you abstain from what has been sacrificed to idols and from blood and from what is strangled [πνικτῶν: "choked"] and from fornication. If you keep yourselves from these, you will do well. Farewell.
> Acts 15:28-29

The four necessary things—ἐπάναγκες—that James, the chair of the council, lists are not a Lukan invention but gleanings from Leviticus 17–18, the so-called Holiness Code.[119] Gentiles should avoid eating food presented to idols (Lev 17:7-9). They should eat neither blood (Lev 17:10-11) nor an animal that died of choking—πνικτός—or was cooked in a certain way.[120] They should also avoid unchastity (Lev 18:6-18).[121] The choice of these four requirements is significant.[122] First, they have nothing to do with Jewish lineage. They are behavioral norms that were expected of proselytes and resident aliens in Israel (Lev 17:8, 10, 13, 15).[123] The Jewish ancestry has lost its stronghold and has given leverage to its sociocultural category. Second, those who keep these norms would be regarded as Jewish and, therefore, would be able to become members of the Way. The

---

[119] Todd Hanneken argues that these four requirements in Acts 15 originated not from the Holiness Code but from Jubilees, which "rewrites the unconditional covenant of the rainbow in Genesis 9 into a conditional covenant binding on all gentiles, all of whom are descended from Noah." Todd R. Hanneken, "Moses Has His Interpreters: Understanding the Legal Exegesis in Acts 15 from the Precedent in Jubilees," *CBQ* 77 (January 2015): 686–706. Hanneken insists that it is difficult to find a verbal correlation suggesting a direct allusion between Lev 17–18 and the four requirements. Yet, his argument cannot be substantiated. First, he himself fails to indicate where exactly Jubilees mentions the prohibition against strangled meat. Second, it is unclear how often and how widely Jubilees was read compared to Leviticus. Third, given the fact that Jubilees is anti-Gentile and pro-separation literature, applying Noachide laws (re)written and (re)interpreted in Jubilees to support the inclusion of the Gentile can be problematic.

[120] Drawing on classical sources, in contrast, Stephen G. Wilson says on πνικτός, "Here it is a culinary term and refers to a particular method of cooking, though precisely what is meant is not clear." Stephen G. Wilson, *Luke and the Law*, SNTSMS 50 (New York: Cambridge University Press, 1983), 89.

[121] Malina and Pilch, *Social-Science Commentary on the Book of Acts*, 109.

[122] Scholars contest two issues related to the apostolic decree (Acts 15:20). First, the decree is at odds with Galatians, in which Paul vehemently criticizes those who compromise and thus comply with the law of Moses. The historical Paul would be dumbfounded to see himself agreeing with and delivering the apostolic decree with joy to his Gentile believers. Second, the text is unstable. Manuscripts vary as to what should and should not be included. There are six forms of the text: "1. Omit 'sexual immorality' (πορνεία) without the golden rule. 2. Four prohibitions, *without* the golden rule. 3. Four prohibitions with the golden rule. 4. Omit 'strangled,' *without* the golden rule. 5. Omit 'strangled,' with the golden rule. 6. Omit 'blood,' *without* the golden rule." Pervo, *Acts*, 377. See also Fitzmyer, *Acts of the Apostles*, 556. Whatever the common ground is in these debates—whether they are historical or textual—the present study looks into how this literary construction of Jewish categories contributes to the formation of Jewish identity in Luke-Acts.

[123] Johnson, *The Acts of the Apostles*, 267; Bruce J. Malina and John J. Pilch, *Social-Science Commentary on the Book of Acts*, 109.

Gentile followers of the Way have a status equal to that of resident aliens living in Palestine and elsewhere (Lev 17:8-9, 10, 15). They are a part of the people of God, though they are required neither to be circumcised nor to observe the laws of Moses (Acts 15:10-11). Third, the four prohibitions have no salvific purpose. The initial conflict arose among those who argued that circumcision was a necessity for salvation: "Unless you are circumcised according to the custom of Moses, you cannot be saved" (Acts 15:1). Peter's speech brings the intense debate to a close: "In cleansing their hearts by *faith* he [God] has made no distinction between them and us" (Acts 15:9). The requirement for salvation is faith in Jesus, not circumcision. Peter continues, "*We* believe that *we* will be saved through the grace of the Lord Jesus, just as *they* will" (Acts 15:11). James accepts this.

This brings us to the heart of the Lukan construction of Christian identity: *how one joins the people of God*. According to Luke-Acts, there are three kinds of people in this group. The first are ethnic Jews who believe in Jesus. Circumcision is a *visible boundary marker* that separates Jews from Gentiles.[124] The second are converts who have been circumcised, keep the entire law, and later believe in Jesus. The third are Gentiles who believe in Jesus and do what is required of resident aliens living among Jews. Circumcision is not necessary for them because, by virtue of their faith in Jesus, they receive membership in the people of God. Luke-Acts is not speaking of completely abandoning the law, whether a believer is of Jewish or Gentile origin, because the Way is in a nutshell a *Jewish* religion. No matter how far from Palestine their gathering is taking place or how many Jewish believers—whether they are native or diaspora Jews—are present in their midst, they are to retain their Jewishness. This is not simply "a *modus vivendi* of Gentile Christians among Jewish Christians," as Joseph A. Fitzmyer argues.[125] Rather, it is the sign of their commitment to the God of Israel. *Jewishness is the heart of Christian identity.*

2.3.2. A Eunuch Joins the People of God (Acts 8:26-40)

Traditionally, scholars approached Acts 8:26-40 from the perspective of geography—(1) demonstrating the spread of the gospel to the ends of the earth (Acts 1:8);[126]

---

[124] Matthew Thiessen argues based on Gen 17, Jubilees, and other Jewish and/or Christian witnesses, that eighth-day circumcision is "a boundary-creating rite between Israel and the circumcised nations surrounding it" for the covenant community in second temple Judaism. Matthew Thiessen, *Contesting Conversion: Genealogy, Circumcision, and Identity in Ancient Judaism and Christianity* (New York: Oxford University Press, 2011), 30. In contrast, some scholars claim that Jews encouraged Gentile conversion during that time. See, for example, Martin Goodman, *Mission and Conversion: Proselytizing in the Religious History of the Roman Empire* (New York: Oxford University Press, 1994) and Cohen, *The Beginnings of Jewishness*, especially part II. Whether one supports Thiessen's position or not, the following statement by Fredrik Barth rings true: "When defined as an ascriptive and exclusive group, the nature of continuity of ethnic units is clear: it depends on the maintenance of a boundary." Fredrik Barth, *Ethnic Groups and Boundaries: The Social Organization of Culture Difference*, ed. Fredrik Barth (London: Allen & Unwin, 1969), 14.

[125] Fitzmyer, *Acts of the Apostles*, 557.

[126] Henry J. Cadbury, *The Book of Acts in History* (New York: Harper & Bros, 1955), 15; Timothy C. G. Thornton, "To the End of the Earth: Acts 1:8," *ExpTim* 89 (1978): 374–5; Brittany E. Wilson, *Unmanly Men: Refigurations of Masculinity in Luke-Acts* (New York: Oxford University Press 2015), 113.

(2) foreshadowing the fulfillment of the mission to the Gentiles;[127] and (3) describing the movement of the gospel out of Jerusalem to the nations[128]—if not as an appendix to Philip's Samaritan mission "separated from the rest of the narrative."[129] Recent scholars focus more on the ambiguities of the eunuch's identity.[130] I argue that this episode answers one of the most significant questions in the narrative scheme of Acts: *Can a Gentile become a full member of the people of God without circumcision?*

The outpouring of the Holy Spirit enabled the apostles to initiate the Jewish mission (Acts 1:1–5:16), and the persecution in Jerusalem drove believers out to the countryside of Judea and Samaria (Acts 5:17–8:3). Readers soon find Philip preaching the gospel in Samaria (Acts 8:4-25). After marking the Samaritan mission as "done,"[131] the narrative introduces a eunuch, a God-fearer, whose devotion to the God of Israel is undoubtedly Jewish.[132] The narrator says he came all the way from Ethiopia to worship and was reading the prophet Isaiah on his way home. Yet he is not a Jew, even if he wishes to be, because his male organ has been castrated (Deut 23:1).[133] He cannot undergo the three mandatory processes—circumcision, proselyte baptism, and an offering in the temple—by which a Gentile is converted to Judaism.[134] This is not even thinkable.[135] To

---

[127] Clarice Jannette Martin, "A Chamberlain's Journey and the Challenge of Interpretation for Liberation," *Semeia* 47 (1989): 117; Scott Shauf, "Locating the Eunuch: Characterization and Narrative Context in Acts 8:26-40," *CBQ* 71 (2009): 762–5.

[128] Samkutty, *The Samaritan Mission in Acts*; Eckhard J. Schnabel, *Early Christian Mission* (Downers Grove, IL: InterVarsity Press, 2004), 1297–9.

[129] Frederick J. Foakes-Jackson, *The Acts of the Apostles*, MNTC 5 (New York: Harper, 1931), 75. See also Tannehill, *The Narrative Unity of Luke-Acts*, 2.107–8; Conzelmann, *Acts of the Apostles*, 67.

[130] For example, Jean-François Racine, "L'hybridité des personnages: Une stratégie d'inclusion des gentils dans les Actes des Apôtres," in *Analyse narrative et Bible: Deuxième colloque international du RRENAB, Louvain-la-Neuve, avril 2004*, ed. Camille Focant and André Wénin, BETL 191 (Leuven: Leuven University Press, 2005), 559–66; Sean D. Burke, *Queering the Ethiopian Eunuch: Strategies of Ambiguity in Acts* (Minneapolis: Fortress, 2013); Wilson, *Unmanly Men*. See also Joshua Seokhyun Yoon, "A Representative Outsider and the Inclusion of the Outsider in Acts 8:26–40" (DMin diss., Duke University, 2016), 7–11.

[131] The status of the Samaritans is debated. Charles K. Barrett sees them as Samaritans, not Gentiles. Jacob Jervell also argues that the Samaritan mission is still a mission to the Jews. The Gentile mission begins in Acts 10. Barrett, *The Acts of the Apostles: A Shorter Commentary*, 118. Jacob Jervell, *Die Apostelgeschichte: Übersetzt und Erklärt*, KEK 3/17 (Göttingen: Vandenhoeck & Ruprecht, 1998), 266. In contrast, Bernd Kollmann sees the Samaritans as apostates from Judaism. Bernd Kollmann, "Philippus der Evangelis und die Anfänge der Heidenmission," *Bib* 81 (2000): 554.

[132] Acts uses a technical term, φοβούμενος τον Θεόν (a God-fearer), to describe "a gentile attracted to Judaism but who has not become a full-fledged proselyte by undergoing circumcision, being immersed in water, and presenting an offering in the temple." Holladay, *Acts*, 229. See Acts 10:2, 22, 35; 13:16, 26.

[133] Deut 23:1 says, "No one whose testicles are crushed or whose penis is cut off shall be admitted to the assembly of the Lord." Jean-François Racine describes a painstaking reality of the eunuch's journey as follows: "In the Temple, he could have accessed the courtyard of the Gentiles, but his physical condition would have prevented him from entering the courtyard of the women, even less the courtyard of the Israelites. He would have therefore made a long journey to end up confined to the first Temple portico." Jean-François Racine, "Hybrid Features in the Acts of the Apostles: A First Exploration" (paper presented at the annual meeting of the Canadian Society of Biblical Studies, Winnipeg, Manitoba, May 30–June 1, 2004).

[134] Holladay, *Acts*, 229.

[135] For full details on conversion to Judaism, see Cohen, *The Beginnings of Jewishness*, 107–238.

this perpetual outsider,[136] Philip preaches the good news about Jesus. At this, the eunuch exclaims, "Look, here is water! What is to *prevent* [κωλύω] me from being baptized?" (Acts 8:36). He is baptized and joins the Way and, thus, the people of God. There is nothing preventing him from doing so. His faith in Jesus substitutes for the ritual of circumcision.[137] It is not a mere coincidence, therefore, that κωλύω appears twice more in Acts to describe the Gentile believers' receiving of the Holy Spirit, their baptism, and their membership within the Way (Acts 10:47; 11:17).[138]

2.3.3. A Gentile Man Joins the People of God (Acts 10:1–11:18)

A eunuch joins the people of God. Does this mean that anyone else whose status is between a eunuch and a Jewish man can do so? Yes, indeed. Acts 10:1–11:18, the story of Peter and Cornelius, describes the crossing of that boundary by a *Gentile male*. It is hard to miss the Jewishness of Cornelius in the narrator's introduction of him: "He was a devout man who feared God with all his household; he gave alms generously to the people and prayed constantly to God" (Acts 10:2; see also Lk 8:40-56).[139] Luke uses the technical term "God-fearer" (φοβούμενος τον Θεόν) to describe this Gentile who sympathizes with the Jewish religion.[140] In spite of Cornelius' devotion to the God of Israel, he is regarded as profane or unclean (Acts 10:14, 15, 28).[141] He is a Gentile because he has not undergone circumcision, a formidable wall separating Jews from Gentiles.[142]

---

[136] Lucian's character Lycinus says, "A eunuch was neither man nor woman but something composite, hybrid, and *monstrously alien to human nature.*" Lucian, "The Eunuch," in *The Works of Lucian*, trans. A. M. Harmon, vol. 5, LCL (Cambridge, MA: Harvard University Press, 1936), 337, emphasis added.

[137] The Western text contains verse 37: "If you believe with all your heart, you may. And he replied, "I believe that Jesus Christ is the Son of God."

[138] Johnson, *The Acts of the Apostles*, 157.

[139] A close look at Luke's description illustrates the Jewishness of Cornelius's action. "He gives alms 'to the people (*tō laō*),' meaning to the Jews, like the centurion of Luke 7:5. His prayer is characterized as *dia pantos*, a term that in the LXX consistently translates the Hebrew *timid* ('continually'), which occurs especially in cultic contexts (Exod 25:29; 27:20; Lev 24:2, 8:2 …)." Johnson, *The Acts of the Apostles*, 182.

[140] There is another term that describes Gentile devotees to the God of Israel: "God-worshiper" (θεοσεβής). God-fearer and God-worshiper refer to basically the same group of people, yet they are different from the full convert or proselyte (προσήλυτος) to Judaism. For a discussion of God-fearers, see David C. Sim, "Gentiles, God-Fearers and Proselytes," in *Attitudes to Gentiles in Ancient Judaism and Early Christianity*, ed. David C. Sim and James S. MacLaren, LNTS 499 (London: Bloomsbury T&T Clark, 2013): 14–18.

[141] Christine E. Hayes insists that "the primary mode of impurity associated with Gentiles in texts of this period [the Second Temple period] is not ritual impurity but moral impurity." Christine E. Hayes, *Gentile Impurities and Jewish Identities: Intermarriage and Conversion from the Bible to the Talmud* (New York: Oxford University Press, 2002), 45. If so, Acts may challenge such negative labeling of Cornelius as "unclean and profane" by mentioning his devotion to the God of Israel.

[142] Why Cornelius did not undergo circumcision is an exegetical red herring. Was it Cornelius' personal preference so that he would not be prevented from serving in the Roman military? It is impossible to know. Jewish soldiers did serve in the Roman military. See Andrew J. Schoenfeld, "Sons of Israel in Caesar's Service: Jewish Soldiers in the Roman Military," *IJJS* 24, no. 3 (2006): 115–26. David C. Sim aptly summarizes the relationship between God-fearers and the Jewish community: "The large numbers of God-fearers compared to the small number of proselytes, implied in Acts and Josephus and corroborated in the Aphrodisias inscription, testifies that most or all Jewish communities were content to accept God-fearers as they were. They perhaps hoped these sympathizers would convert, but they were not obligated to do so." Sim, "Gentiles, God-Fearers and Proselytes," 18.

The geographic location of Cornelius, Caesarea, places him far from Jerusalem where the temple stands. The wall collapses, however, when the Holy Spirit falls on those in Cornelius' house and they begin speaking in tongues. The narrator portrays Peter's Jewish companions, who have so far been almost invisible, as utterly astonished (Acts 10:23, 45). The narrative once again expresses human powerlessness in the face of the divine decision: "Can anyone withhold [κωλύω] the water for baptizing these people who have received the Holy Spirit just as we have?" (Acts 10:47). Surely, no one would dare to obstruct God (see also Acts 28:31). Now Cornelius and his family are undoubtedly saved (Acts 11:14). Circumcised believers in Jerusalem interrogate Peter, who reports God's irrevocable action on behalf of the Gentiles, upon which Peter exclaims, "Who was I that I could hinder [κωλύω] God?" (Acts 11:17). This story marks a turning point in Luke's narrative. The Gentile mission officially begins (Acts 15:7). A Gentile male can join the Way and become a member of God's people without being circumcised.

2.3.4. A Son of a Gentile-Jewish Intermarriage Joins the People of God (Acts 16:1-5)

If the story of Cornelius exemplifies the mission to a Gentile man, as Bonnie J. Flessen rightly asserts,[143] Acts 16:1-5 describes a more complicated case, the circumcision of the son of a Gentile-Jewish intermarriage. Soon after the decree of the Jerusalem council is sent to Antioch, Paul embarks on his mission to the Gentiles, where he meets Timothy, his future traveling companion. Timothy has a unique background. His father is Greek but his mother is Jewish. Is he a Jew or not? He is a Gentile because until the creation of the Mishnah and implementation of the matrilineal principle (e.g., M. Qiddushin 3:12 and M. Yevamot 7:5) in the second to fourth century CE, Jewish ethnicity was determined by the patrilineal principle.[144] Timothy's father is Greek. So, he is Gentile, and his uncircumcised status confirms his lack of Jewish identity.[145] This should not matter anymore, however, since even a Gentile eunuch as well as a Gentile man became full members of the people of God earlier in the narrative. The narrator introduces Timothy as a "disciple," an enduring mark of members of the Way (e.g., Acts 6:7; 9:1, 10) and as "well spoken of by the believers" (ἀδελφῶν; Acts 16:2). His faith in Jesus and adherence to the Jewish law are sufficient to grant him membership within the Way. Yet, surprisingly, Paul has Timothy circumcised.

Two questions arise from this. First, does this mean that circumcision is more important than Timothy's faith in Jesus? By no means. The narrator offers the following rationale behind Timothy's circumcision: "because of the Jews who were in those

---

[143] Bonnie J. Flessen, *An Exemplary Man: Cornelius and Characterization in Acts* (Eugene, OR: Pickwick, 2011).

[144] Cohen, *The Beginnings of Jewishness*, 263–307, esp. 363–77. Shaye J. D. Cohen, "The Origins of the Matrilineal Principle in Rabbinic Law," *AJS Review* 10, no. 1 (1985): 19–53.

[145] Luke T. Johnson argues that Timothy was uncircumcised because his Greek father prevented it. Johnson, *The Acts of the Apostles*, 284. Though this is highly probable, the reason is not indicated in the text.

places, for they all knew that his father was a Greek" (Acts 16:3).[146] Paul did this not for a salvific purpose but to eliminate any confusion that might arise. In the eyes of Jews, Timothy was considered not a Jew, which could make the Jewishness of Paul's mission questionable. With the circumcision, ambiguities in relation to Timothy's Jewish identity disappear. Timothy's Jewish parentage or in-betweenness is not something to be ignored but acknowledged. Since circumcision shifts one's identity "from debatable to certain," Barreto states, "in this one narrative, ethnicity is both concrete and objective as well as negotiable and mutable."[147] Robert W. Wall finds a rationale behind this in the formation of the Pauline church: "Paul wanted Timothy as a traveling companion because he personifies and presumably has a grasp of the tensions between 'being Greek' and 'being Jewish' that will characterize the Pauline church."[148]

Another lingering question is this: How can one resolve the tension between the apostolic decree and Paul's circumcision of Timothy?[149] The Council decreed that there is no need to circumcise Gentiles. This pericope surely adds complexity to and challenges Jerusalem's decision. There will be not only Jewish men and Gentile men but also *in-between* men in the Gentile mission. To those groups of people whom the earlier apostolic decision failed to specify, the story once again reaffirms the basic thread that undergirds the entire narrative: *One's Jewishness should not be abandoned but instead should be respected.* It is necessary for Gentiles to keep the four requirements. For those who have a Jewish mother, it is preferable to be circumcised.[150] Since Acts 16:1-5 forms a prelude to Paul's vision of the man from Macedonia (Acts 16:6-10), the pericope proposes the agenda of Paul's Gentile mission. *The Way is a Jewish movement.*

2.3.5. A Gentile Woman Joins the People of God (Acts 16:11-15)

The last group of people Acts deals with is Gentile women. Moving from his vision of the man from Macedonia, the narrator quickly locates Paul and his companions in Philippi, the central city of Macedonia. The story begins with a group of women listening to the gospel outside the gate by the river and soon zooms in on one woman, Lydia. She listens eagerly to Paul, is baptized with her family, and invites Paul and his

---

[146] Paul's circumcision of Timothy in Acts contradicts Paul's vehement rejection of circumcising Gentile believers in Galatians and Romans (e.g., Gal 2:3-5; Rom 2:25-3:1; 4:11). Paul insists that if circumcision still remains a requirement for Gentiles to become a member of Israel, it nullifies "the salvific effects of the cross (cf. Gal 5:2-6)." Holladay, *Acts*, 314.

[147] Eric D. Barreto, *Ethnic Negotiations: The Function of Race and Ethnicity in Acts 16*, WUNT 2/294 (Tübingen: Mohr Siebeck, 2012), 166.

[148] Wall, "The Acts of the Apostles," 227.

[149] Unlike scholars who read Acts 16:1-5 as embodying the decision at the Jerusalem Council, Eric D. Barreto articulates a tension between the apostolic decree and Paul's mission. Barreto, *Ethnic Negotiations*, 114. Whereas Charles H. Talbert understands Acts 16:1-5 as functioning as a retrospective confirmation of the apostolic council, Joseph A. Fitzmyer sees the passage as a prospective preparation for Paul's efforts to bring the gospel to a greater audience. See Talbert, *Reading Acts*, 136; Fitzmyer, *The Acts of the Apostles*, 570-4.

[150] Acts 16:1-5 is the only passage in Acts that deals with a half-Greek and half-Jewish man. Since the Acts narrative neither revisits nor reinforces the necessity of circumcision for offspring of Jewish-Gentile intermarriages, suffice it to say that circumcision is preferable for members of the Way.

company to her house. The story of Lydia is significant in the discussion of Christian identity in Acts. First, she exemplifies Gentile female devotees to the God of Israel.[151] She is "a worshiper of God" (σεβομένη τὸν θεόν; Acts 16:14; see also Acts 18:7). Her in-betweenness cannot be missed. Like the two preceding male characters, she is ethnically Gentile but religiously Jewish. The narrator does not indicate an ethnic heritage for her to claim except for her devotion to God, and she does not have a male organ to circumcise.[152] Becoming a full member of the people of God is too difficult for her.

Second, the gospel destroys the gendered boundary of circumcision. There are two ways for a woman to be a Jew in first-century Palestine. One is to be born of a Jewish father, and the other is to marry a Jewish man.[153] Considering her occupation as "a dealer in purple cloth," it is not clear whether Lydia is single, married, divorced, or widowed (Acts 16:14). Yet, it is clear that circumcision is not an option for her and that her marital status does not grant her Jewish ethnicity. But, faith in Jesus now replaces circumcision, so there is nothing preventing Lydia from being baptized. She was once an outsider deeply committed to the God of Israel. Now, she is an insider. Peter and his companions stay in her house and eat with her family, which demonstrates not only her hospitality but her changed *identity* (see also Acts 10:48–11:18).[154]

In sum, Acts builds up Christian identity as the narrative progresses. Males can join God's new people through one's faith in Jesus, without circumcision. National and ethnic boundaries that define Jewishness are flung open as Gentiles receive the Holy Spirit, an indisputable mark of salvation (Acts 2:38). They are also the people of God (Acts 2:17-18; Joel 2:28). Would the Jews in Jerusalem accept this? Would they acknowledge that Gentiles have a dual identity as ethnic non-Jews and God's new people? The following chapters investigate how Christian identity is presented and how it at times highlights certain aspects of Jewishness in an effort to create a dual identity in Acts 21:17–23:35.

2.4. Concluding Comments

Beginning with a personal story, this chapter has delved into the enduring nature of a person's social identity and the ways in which dual identity is developed. The chapter first surveyed the social identity approach (SIA) and examined its usefulness as well as its limits in studying the Acts text. Second, three models for developing a dual identity were presented and three methodological elements were highlighted to delineate the complex nature of identity construction of a minority group with its proximate "other":

---

[151] Alexandra Gruca-Macaulay, *Lydia as a Rhetorical Construct in Acts*, ESEC 18 (Atlanta: SBL, 2016).
[152] In the Lukan narrative, Tabitha is a precursor of Lydia. Her Hebrew name, Tabitha, describes her Jewish heritage, while her Greek name, Dorcas, reveals her Hellenic heritage (Acts 9:36). Unlike Tabitha, however, Lydia has no basis for claiming Jewish ancestry.
[153] Cohen, *The Beginnings of Jewishness*, 265.
[154] For literary evidence showing that Jews avoided table fellowship with Gentiles, see Philip F. Esler, *Community and Gospel in Luke-Acts: The Social and Political Motivations of Lucan Theology*, SNTS 57 (Cambridge: Cambridge University Press, 1987), 76–84.

ambivalence, social creativity, and *recategorization*. Lastly, the chapter revealed, through a close reading of five selected pericopes, how Luke-Acts constructs the Christian identity. Drawing on the main methodology and with the Lukan understanding of Christian identity in view, the next chapter explores the first phase of Paul's visit to Jerusalem and how Paul's effort to prove his Jewish identity leads him into not only intragroup conflict but also intergroup conflict.

3

Slander Against Paul and the Labeling of Paul as an Outsider (Acts 21:17-40)[1]

Trouble is inevitable. Paul knew it. The gospel that God bestows salvation and identity as the people of God upon Gentiles through faith in Jesus would be seen as not just *strange* but also *threatening* in the eyes of Jews in Jerusalem. Paul visits Jerusalem to deliver "the good news of God's grace" (Acts 20:22-24) and show that Jews and the Way share the same universe. Two ways of being God's people are truly possible (e.g., Acts 15:1-35). However, in Jerusalem he finds that this is just wishful thinking. He not only faces accusations questioning his Jewish identity but also is dragged out of the temple. Furthermore, he is arrested by a Roman tribune who suspects Paul of being a political agitator. He is doubly excluded as an outsider to the Jewish faith and to Rome.

The present chapter explores this first drama of Paul's stay—his meeting with Jerusalem believers (Acts 21:17-26), his first encounter with the Jewish crowd (Acts 21:27-36), and his first interaction with the Roman tribune (Acts 21:37-40)—which comprise sections (1), (2), and (3) of Paul's roller-coaster ride (see figure 1.1). Paul's missionary journey has finally ended (Acts 13–19). Like his predecessor Jesus, Paul sets his mind on traveling to Jerusalem one last time (Acts 19:21; Lk 9:51). His lengthy farewell trip (Acts 20:1–21:16), emotionally charged addresses to his fellow believers (Acts 20:17-38; 21:11-14),[2] and contested witnesses of the Holy Spirit on his journey to Jerusalem (Acts 20:22 vs. 21:4)[3] increase the suspense within the narrative. Paul will

---

[1] Peter L. Berger and Thomas Luckmann state, "The trouble begins whenever the 'strangeness' is broken through and the deviant universe appears as a possible habitat for one's own people." Peter L. Berger and Thomas Luckmann, *The Social Construction of Reality: A Treatise in the Sociology of Knowledge* (Garden City, NY: Doubleday, 1966), 112–13. Human culture as a whole is a continuum of this process—whether the "strangeness" is accepted or rejected altogether or in part—as in, for example, the Protestant Reformation in the sixteenth century and the rise of contemporary styles of worship in the twentieth century. The text of this study is no exception.

[2] The heart of Paul's speech to the Ephesian elders (Acts 20:17-38) is that "the church's future ... has less to do with its imitation of Paul than with its relationship to the God who calls it into being." Beverly R. Gaventa, "Theology and Ecclesiology in the Miletus Speech: Reflections on Content and Context," *NTS* 50, no. 1 (2004): 36.

[3] In light of ancient Mediterranean practices of oracle reception, particularly as described in Plutarch's work, Devin L. White argues that Paul's rejection of the oracle should not be seen as a sign of impiety. Driven by emotion and grief, Tyrian disciples produce an oracle that seemingly contradicts the Holy Spirit's previous message to Paul (Acts 20:22; 21:4): "The Lukan Paul interprets prophecies based not only on confidence in the divine source of the message, but also his evaluation of the human functionaries who deliver it." Devin L. White, "Confronting Oracular Contradiction in Acts 21:1–14,"

suffer persecution in Jerusalem (e.g., Acts 20:23; 21:11). Paul arrives in Philip's house in Caesarea, a stopping-point on the way to Jerusalem (Acts 21:8), and hears the prophecy of Agabus on Paul's impending suffering.[4] But, nothing prevents Paul from going to Jerusalem because it is not his will but the Lord's (Acts 21:14). His final destination is Rome (Acts 19:21), but his visit to Jerusalem will not be easy.

With this literary context in view, this chapter will pay attention to, first, the accusations that Jewish believers and the Jewish crowd throw at Paul and, second, the label that a Roman tribune imposes on him. Are these accusations and the label true or false? What is the basis of their claim? On the one hand, Paul says nothing in response to the Jewish accusations in this section. On the other, he instantly denies the anti-Roman label. Drawing from insights of SIA, this chapter traces the causes and strategies of Jewish accusations against Paul and investigates the (in)validity of the rebel label the Roman tribune imposes on Paul.

This study argues that the Lukan narrative describes the Jewish accusations and the anti-Roman label as slanderous, although the allegations are not completely groundless. To prove this argument, this chapter first enlists scholarly evaluations of the Jewish accusations against Paul (Acts 21:21, 28). Second, the present inquiry analyzes how the Jews portray Paul in a stereotypical way and produce anti-Way prejudices within the Acts narrative. Third, the chapter unearths the sources of the Jews' accusations against the Way in Luke-Acts. Lastly, Paul's first interaction with the tribune receives due attention to illustrate what this story reveals about the position of the Way vis-à-vis its out-group, Rome.

3.1. Accusations against Paul and Scholarly Approaches

Paul and his companions finally arrive in Jerusalem (Acts 21:17). As on any roller-coaster ride, a sudden drop is preceded by a slow and rather peaceful beginning. A warm breeze touches the faces of those in the train, and a beautiful scene opens up before their eyes. The narrator uses ἀσμένως ("gladly") and ἀποδέχομαι ("to receive, welcome") to express the warm welcome the Jewish believers—ἀδελφοί—provided to their fellow workers.[5] On the following day, upon meeting James and all the elders, Paul explains his ministry in relation to what God has done among the Gentiles (Acts 21:19).[6] They praise God—ἐδόξαζον τὸν Θεόν—just as earlier the circumcised believers

---

NovT 58 (2016): 28. See also Jervell, *Die Apostelgeschichte*, 518. For the importance of the human response to the divine plan in the scheme of Acts, see Kylie Crabbe, "Accepting Prophecy: Paul's Response to Agabus with Insights from Valerius Maximus and Josephus," *JSNT* 39, no. 2 (2016): 188–208.

[4] The sudden appearance of Philip alludes to the geographic movement of not only the protagonist of the story but also of the gospel. Philip brought the gospel beyond the Jewish border until he came to Caesarea (Acts 8:4-40). Now, from Caesarea Paul brings the gospel back to the place from which it sprang (Acts 1:8).

[5] Ἀσμένως occurs only once here in the New Testament. Ἀποδέχομαι expresses hospitality in Luke-Acts (e.g., Lk 8:40; 9:11; Acts 18:27; 28:30). Johnson, *The Acts of the Apostles*, 374.

[6] A literal translation of Acts 21:19 is as follows: "and having greeted them he related one by one the things God had done among the Gentiles through his service" (καὶ ἀσπασάμενος αὐτοὺς ἐξηγεῖτο καθ' ἓν ἕκαστον ὧν ἐποίησεν ὁ θεὸς ἐν τοῖς ἔθνεσιν διὰ τῆς διακονίας αὐτοῦ).

in Jerusalem had responded to Peter's report of Gentiles receiving the Holy Spirit (Acts 21:20; 11:18).

Then, the train hits the hill. Suddenly, it starts to shake, and the people riding inside check their buckles. Leaders in Jerusalem report doubts about the orthodoxy of Paul's ministry circulated among Jewish believers zealous for the law: "that you teach all the Jews living among the Gentiles to forsake Moses [ἀποστασίαν διδάσκεις ἀπὸ Μωϋσέως τοὺς κατὰ ἔθνη πάντας Ἰουδαίους] and that you tell them not to circumcise their children or observe the customs" (Acts 21:21). A warm greeting turns into a cold interrogation: τί οὖν ἐστιν; ("What then is it?").[7] A striking fact that cannot be ignored in this section is that their question is remarkably similar to the accusations Asian Jews will raise against Paul at the temple precincts shortly after: "οὗτός ἐστιν ὁ ἄνθρωπος ὁ κατὰ τοῦ λαοῦ καὶ τοῦ νόμου καὶ τοῦ τόπου τούτου πάντας πανταχῇ διδάσκων" (Acts 21:28). A case is put forward. Paul should defend himself unless he wants to remain condemned.

The microphone, however, stays with the Jerusalem leadership. An order is given— "τοῦτο οὖν ποίησον" (Acts 21:23)—and Paul simply follows their suggestion. He joins four men under a Nazarite vow, paying for the shaving of their heads and thus enabling them together with him to achieve their vow (Acts 18:18; 21:23-24, 26; Num 6:1-21).[8] He completes the seven days of the rite of purification that will secure his entrance to the temple since he is coming from abroad.[9] Though it is unlikely that he has killed a person or touched a corpse, he complies (Num 19:12; 31:19). Paul does all of this for the sake of his Jewish believers.[10] Why, then, are they accusing Paul? What is the basis

---

[7] Richard P. Thompson notes that "the narrative juxtaposes the believers' praise for what God had done and the raising of the accusations against Paul, thereby quickly turning what begins as a hospitable meeting into a rather bewildering one that potentially leaves the reader wondering what the Jerusalem believers were thinking." Richard P. Thompson, "'Say It Ain't So, Paul!': The Accusations against Paul in Acts 21 in Light of His Ministry in Acts 16–20," *BR* 45 (2000): 39.

[8] The narrator never uses the word "Nazarite" (ναζιρ/ναζιραῖος) to describe the vow the four men have made. Yet, drawing from the writings of Josephus (*Ant.* 4.70–2) and Philo (*Spec. Leg.* 1.248), Stuart Chepey argues that the vow is a Nazarite one. Focusing on the timing of Paul's arrival, which is the day of Pentecost (Acts 20:16), he states, "Some Jews made an association between Nazirite vows and the annual giving of First-fruits, the culmination of which took place at Pentecost." Stuart Chepey, "Is the Timing respecting Paul and the Four Men under a Vow in Acts 21:23–27 Plausible?: Possible Implications from Josephus and Philo on the Nazarite Vow and First-Fruits," *CTR* 9, no. 2 (Spring 2012): 71. Num 6:14–15 requires a substantial offering from those who make the Nazarite vow. According to William S. Kurz: "They shall offer their gift to the Lord, one male lamb a year old without blemish as a burnt offering, one ewe lamb a year old without blemish as a sin offering, one ram without blemish as an offering of well-being, and a basket of unleavened bread, cakes of choice flour mixed with oil and unleavened wafers spread with oil, with their grain offering and their drink offerings." Kurz, *Acts of the Apostles*, 322. For the role of the Nazarites in late second temple Judaism and the early Christian era, see Stuart Chepey, *Nazirites in Late Second Temple Judaism: A Survey of Ancient Jewish Writings, the New Testament, Archaeological Evidence, and Other Writings from Late Antiquity*, AJEC 60 (Leiden: Brill, 2005).

[9] Friedrich W. Horn, "Paulus, das Nasiräat, und die Nasiräer," *NovT* 39 (1997): 130. LXX uses ἁγνίζεσθαι in conjunction with a seven-day purification in Num 19:12; 31:19.

[10] Friedrich W. Horn writes, "Ein Heidenchrist hätte nie ein Nasiräat übernehmen können, da ihm zur Auslösung des Nasiräats der Zugang zum Tempel verwehrt war." Horn, "Paulus, das Nasiräat, und die Nasiräer," 136.

of their claim in verse 21 and verse 28? Scholars propose three possible interpretations of the Jewish accusations against Paul in Acts 21.[11]

The accusations are absurd. Jack T. Sanders argues that their charge is not only "baseless" and "devious" but is also designed to "get rid of Paul."[12] Drawing on a (mis) understanding of the Tübingen school, he states that "Jewish Christians ... are here little to be distinguished from non-Christian Jews. Both are hostile to Gentile Christianity."[13] Two contrasting portrayals—Paul as a devout Jew and the Jews as the enemy of divine will—in the Acts account seem to favor this position.[14] Paul did not object when the Jerusalem leadership decided to impose four requirements from the law on Gentile believers. In fact, he circumcised Timothy. Joseph A. Fitzmyer notes that the accusations the Jews make against Paul in Acts 21:28 are similar to those made against Stephen, which the narrator identified as coming from "false witnesses" (Acts 6:13).[15] Paul follows the instructions of the Jewish believers, takes—and surely pays the expenses of—the four men under a Nazarite vow, and completes seven days of purification (Acts 21:26). The Jewish accusations should be viewed as *false*.

In response, Richard P. Thompson points out two problems with this position. First, the narrator's demarcation of "false" regarding Stephen's witnesses is absent in Paul's case when the two incidents are juxtaposed side by side.[16] This validates the accusations made against Paul. The fact that two accusations, one from Jewish believers and the other from the Jewish crowd, are similar alludes to possible allegations that could arise from Paul's missionary activity. Paul in his letters surely speaks of Jewish believers' freedom from the law, which they obtained with their faith in Christ (e.g., Gal 2:15-21; Rom 7:1-6). Has Paul in Acts also preached or acted in such a way? A thorough narrative analysis should be done before accusing Paul's accusers. Second, downplaying the charge put forward by Jews problematizes what meets the eyes of the reader. Thompson states, "Such a reading assumes a major discrepancy between what the reader sees and what the accusers see."[17] It is not only the Jewish crowd but also the whole city—ἡ πόλις ὅλη—that reacted instantly and vehemently to Paul (Acts 21:30). There should be a basis for such turmoil.

---

[11] Here, I follow Richard P. Thompson's survey of the scholarship on the Jewish accusations against Paul in Acts 21, adding more voices from the scholarship from various eras. Thompson, "Say It Ain't So, Paul!" 42–5.

[12] Sanders, *The Jews in Luke-Acts*, 284.

[13] Sanders, *The Jews in Luke-Acts*, 284.

[14] Thompson, "Say It Ain't So, Paul!" 43. For example, see Barrett, *A Critical and Exegetical Commentary on The Acts of the Apostles*, 2.1009; Conzelmann, *Acts of the Apostles*, 180; Fitzmyer, *The Acts of the Apostles*, 693; Haenchen, *The Acts of the Apostles*, 609; Holladay, *Acts*, 411; Johnson, *The Acts of the Apostles*, 375; Keener, *Acts*, 3127; Marguerat, *Les Actes des Apôtres (13–28)*, 260; Parsons, *Acts*, 303; Spencer, *Journey through Acts*, 210–11; Ben Witherington III, *The Acts of the Apostles: A Socio-Rhetorical Commentary* (Grand Rapids: Eerdmans, 1998), 652.

[15] Joseph A. Fitzmyer notes that diaspora Jews identify Stephen as one who is against the law and the temple: "This man never stops saying things against this holy place and the law." Fitzmyer, *The Acts of the Apostles*, 698. See also Acts 6:11-14.

[16] Thompson, "Say It Ain't So, Paul!" 43.

[17] Thompson, "Say It Ain't So, Paul!" 43. Lenski translates κατηχήθησαν in Acts 21:21—"they have been told" (NRSV)—to "[they] have this sound get into the ears," and he considers the accusations "false rumors." Richard C. H. Lenski, *The Interpretation of the Acts of the Apostles* (Minneapolis: Augsburg, 1961), 878.

The accusations are reasonable. F. F. Bruce finds consistency, not discrepancy, in the accusations by comparing them with Paul's letters, not with Paul in Acts. He insists that "Paul's position in such matters is fairly clear from his letters."[18] Paul circumcised Timothy because for him circumcision was "a matter of indifference" (Gal 5:6; 6:15).[19] Even among scholars who refuse to accept Jewish claims at face value, some agree that their charge against Paul could possibly arise in light of Paul's actual writings.[20] Simply put, Paul was behaving himself.

A serious problem with the argument of scholars supporting this position is an *assumption* they make. They assume not only that there is a concrete tie between Paul in Acts and Paul in his letters but also that the Lukan audience knew that connection,[21] that Paul's audience could connect the dots.[22] It is difficult, however, to draw lines between Paul in these two sets of texts and produce a coherent picture of Paul.[23] Differences may originate from the various Pauline traditions or heritages, but the one cannot be forced upon the other.[24] Another obstacle associated with this view is a notable disparity between the Jewish accusations and Paul's self-defense. The Asian Jews indict Paul of teaching against the Jewish people, law, and temple (Acts 21:28). The heart of Paul's speech before the crowd is his zeal for God and the law (e.g., Acts 22:3-5). These two contesting voices are difficult to reconcile.

The accusations are ambiguous. Richard P. Thompson focuses on the presence of these multiple voices in the text. Reading closely the texts concerning Paul's ministry in Corinth and Ephesus—one and a half years in Corinth at the house of Titius next to the synagogue (Acts 18:7) and two years in Ephesus at the lecture hall of Tyrannus (Acts 19:9)—he argues that Paul's teaching outside the Jewish synagogue *could* be seen in the

---

[18] F. F. Bruce, *The Book of the Acts*, NICNT (Grand Rapids: Eerdmans, 1988), 405.
[19] Bruce, *The Book of the Acts*, 405.
[20] Manford G. Gutzke, *Plain Talk on Acts* (Grand Rapids: Zondervan, 1966), 186-7; Krodel, *Acts*, 506; Polhill, *Acts*, 447-8.
[21] Thompson, "Say It Ain't So, Paul!" 44-5.
[22] For example, see William O. Walker, Jr., "Acts and the Pauline Corpus Revisited: Peter's Speech at the Jerusalem Conference," in *Literary Studies in Luke-Acts: Essays in Honor of Joseph B. Tyson*, ed. Richard P. Thompson and Thomas E. Phillips (Macon: Mercer University Press, 1998), 77-86.
[23] Stanley E. Porter, "The Portrait of Paul in Acts," in *The Blackwell Companion to Paul*, ed. Stephen Westerholm (Malden, MA: Wiley-Blackwell, 2011), 124-38. For his previous position, see Porter, *The Paul of Acts*, 187-206.
[24] Daniel Marguerat proposes three types of reception on Paul during his absence between 60 CE and 100 CE to "establish the memory of his life ("biographical" heritage), preserve his writings ("documentary" heritage), institute him as the theological icon who ensures an orthodox interpretation ("doctoral" heritage: cf. Col 2:5)." Daniel Marguerat, *Paul in Acts and Paul in His Letters*, WUNT 310 (Tübingen: Mohr Siebeck, 2013), 7. He argues that all three aspects should be in conversation not to produce a coherent picture but to understand the different trajectories of development of Pauline traditions. His insight is profound: "It is . . . inadequate to measure the Lukan historiographical reliability by a norm constituted by the corpus of Pauline writings, precisely because these writings in and of themselves did not constitute the norm of Pauline tradition" (7). On the contrary, William O. Walker, Jr. argues, "The primary influence of Pauline theology as reflected in the letters is to be seen, not in Luke's portrayal of Paul's message, but rather in his portrayal of Peter's message and activity . . . by portraying Peter as the real founder of the Gentile mission, Luke set the missionary activities of Paul in the larger context of the primitive apostolic mission, thus legitimizing both the work of Paul and the churches founded by him." William O. Walker, Jr., "Acts and the Pauline Corpus Reconsidered," *JSNT* 24 (1985): 23.

eyes of first-century diaspora Jews as apostasy (ἀποστάς. Acts 19:9).[25] Beverly R. Gaventa focuses on the absence of voices. Paul does not speak of "continuing observance of the law" in his preaching, nor does the narrator connect Paul's circumcision of Timothy with "respect for the law."[26] Paul is surely not an apostate Jew, as he risks his life to travel to Jerusalem and defend his Jewish identity. The Acts narrative, at the same time, leaves traces of allegations for readers to decide which voice they should attend to.

The problem with this position is also the *assumption* its adherents make. It is clear that Paul taught outside the synagogue, which *could* be seen as apostasy, but it is not clear whether he taught outside the law. The only potentially problematic statement is in Paul's speech to the Antiochian Jews: "by this Jesus everyone who believes is set free from all those sins from which you could not be freed by the law of Moses" (καὶ ἀπὸ πάντων ὧν οὐκ ἠδυνήθητε ἐν νόμῳ Μωϋσέως δικαιωθῆναι; Acts 13:39). It is debatable, however, whether Paul is speaking of the insufficiency of the law *as a whole* or only *in some cases*.[27] It is also true that Paul never speaks explicitly *for* the observance of the law in his preaching. Yet, the reverse is also true. He never explicitly speaks *against* the law or circumcision. His defense before the Jewish crowd in Jerusalem seems to give more weight to Paul's pro-Jewish side (Acts 22:1-21). With this heated debate not only between Paul and the Jews but also between various scholarly voices as a backdrop, this study turns to the text that is the source of all the trouble.

3.2. Jewish Slander against Paul: Out-Group Stereotyping and Anti-Way Prejudice

"You are not one of us." This is the heart of accusations upon which Jews insist and against which Paul desperately defends himself. After briefly refuting the allegations, this section reads Acts 21:17-36 through the eyes of SIA and analyzes the mechanics of Jewish slander.

3.2.1. Refuting the Allegations

Jewish charges are as follows:

> v. 21: "You teach all the Jews living among the Gentiles to forsake Moses and ... you tell them not to circumcise their children or observe the customs."
>
> v. 28: "This is the man who is teaching everyone everywhere against our people, our law, and this place; more than that, he has actually brought Greeks into the temple and has defiled this holy place."

---

[25] Thompson, "Say It Ain't So, Paul!" 45–9.
[26] Gaventa, *Acts*, 299. Richard I. Pervo notes: "Paul did not generally encourage Jewish believers to have their sons circumcised." Pervo, *Acts*, 544, n. 28. See also Wilson, *Luke and the Law*, 101–2.
[27] Johnson, *The Gospel of Luke*, 236.

These accusations accurately note that Paul's ministry took place in the Gentile territory; that he taught diaspora Jews as well as Gentiles; and that his activity raised suspicion among the Jewish people. Though the two sets of accusations (v. 21 and v. 28) seem to focus on different issues—circumcision, Jewish customs, the people, and temple purity (v. 21b and v. 28b)—the heart of the issue is the same. It is observing the law and, thus, Paul's Jewish identity.[28] Carl R. Holladay notes,

> "Everyone everywhere" (*pantas pantachē*, 21:28) ... signals that Paul is a threat to Jews both in the land of Israel and in the diaspora. Such charges, if true, undermine the rights that Jews have won under the Seleucids and that are ratified by the Romans. These include the right to maintain *their distinct ethnic identity as the Jewish people*, which includes the right to live by the Mosaic law anywhere in the empire and especially the right to honor the Jerusalem temple by collecting money for the annual temple tax and sending it to Jerusalem.[29]

The accusations, however, falsely portray Paul as a threat to Jews, saying that he is hostile to Jewish circumcision or the Jewish law and that he defiled the Jerusalem temple by bringing Trophimus, an Ephesian, into it. The narrative described earlier that Paul circumcised Timothy, ethnically a half-Jew, to make him a full Jew. He also denies in his later defense that he profaned the temple (Acts 24:6, 12-13). Paul insists on his innocence throughout his defense, saying to the Jews in Rome: "Brothers ... I had done nothing against our people or the customs of our ancestors" (Acts 28:17; see also Acts 22:3; 23:2, 5; 24:12-13, 16-20; 25:8, 11; 26:4-8). The Jewish accusations in Acts 21 are Jewish slander against Paul.

Why, then, does the Jewish crowd react immediately and violently to Paul even before validating the charges? Furthermore, why do the Jewish believers not only bring similar charges against Paul but also not help him at all when his life is at stake? Were they scared of the Jewish nonbelievers? The narrative states that the whole city (ἡ πόλις ὅλη; Acts 21:30) was aroused when the accusations were made. This implies that the Jewish believers joined a furious Jewish crowd. How is this possible? Insights from SIA provide one way of answering these questions.

3.2.2. Reading Acts 21:17-36 with SIA

Categorization and Accentuation. In Jerusalem and inside Jewish circles, Jewish ethnic and sociocultural distinctiveness—circumcision and keeping the law—immediately come to the fore. Jerusalem leaders accentuate a Jewish aspect of the Way. They reaffirm the decision previously made at the Jerusalem council. As far as the Gentiles are concerned, they should abstain "from what has been sacrificed to idols and from blood and from what is strangled [πνικτῶν: "choked"] and from fornication" (v. 25; see also Acts 15:20, 29). No further burden is necessary (Acts 15:28). As far as the diaspora Jews

---

[28] It is highly probable, therefore, that the Asian Jews are the source of the information that the Jewish believers share with Paul. Johnson, *The Acts of the Apostles*, 381.
[29] Holladay, *Acts*, 415, emphasis added.

are concerned, however, they should "observe and guard the law" (v. 24). They should be circumcised and observe the customs, as Moses instructed. Paul does not oppose this. Rather, having been informed of four men under a Nazarite vow, he does what a good diaspora Jew would do. He completes the purification rite and pays for it. Paul's self-categorization and the narrator's portrayal of Paul are indisputable. He is a prototypical Jew. Surely, the roller-coaster train has reached the top of a hill. What can better prove Paul's Jewish identity in public than purifying himself and completing the seven days of the purification rite in the temple?

Stereotyping. Then, the train experiences a near free fall. Before the readers figure out what the narrator's warning entails—"When the seven days are almost completed, *the Jews from Asia, who had seen him in the temple*, stirred up the whole crowd" (v. 27a)—they find Paul under arrest and the Jews from Ephesus stirring up the whole crowd and shouting. The slanders they throw at Paul eradicate his Jewish identity, which he had strived to build up. *He is the man against the Jewish people, the law, and the temple* (v. 28a). *He has brought Greeks into the temple* (v. 28b). Deadly labels are induced: *a traitor, heretic, blasphemer,* and *temple defiler*. These labels are negative *stereotypes* built on features the Asian Jews continually found among Paul and the members of the Way. In Ephesus, they saw Paul teaching outside the Jewish synagogue for two years (Acts 19:9-10). In Jerusalem, they saw Trophimus, a Greek, with him in the city. The narrator provides a clue as to how they could identify the Gentile as a defiler. Trophimus is "the Ephesian," as they are (v. 29a; Acts 20:4). They suppose, therefore, that "Paul brought him into the temple" (v. 29b). The narrator previously noted that Jews from Asia along with others argued with Stephen (Acts 6:9) and made similar accusations: "We have heard him speak blasphemous words against Moses and God" (Acts 6:11). He is *a man against the law and the temple* (Acts 6:13). The Jerusalem Jews are aware of these anti-Jewish stereotypes given to the minority group, the Way, as they have heard the charges against Stephen before (Acts 6:12).[30] The ground was fertile for the entire city to perceive Paul in an unfavorable and stereotypical way.

Social Identity and Intergroup Relations. The day of Pentecost is near, and nationalistic feelings are high. As soon as the charges are made, Jerusalem is in an uproar. A riot ensues: "Then all the city was aroused, and the people rushed together" (ἐκινήθη τε ἡ πόλις ὅλη καὶ ἐγένετο συνδρομὴ τοῦ λαοῦ; v. 30). SCT is a useful tool for explicating psychological processes that occur behind the scenes. (1) *Self-categorization*. In this specific situation, differences between groups—the Jerusalem Jews, diaspora Jews, and Jewish believers—disappear. Once again, the highest category, Jew, trumps the lower category, Christian, for the Jewish believers (Acts 11:2-3; 15:1; 21:20-25). (2) *Prototypes and depersonalization*. Everybody perceives each other not only as prototypical Jews but also as in-group members: "We are Jews!" (3) *Group cohesion, social cooperation, and social influence*. With this renewed identity and under the influence of Asian Jews, mutual attraction increases and group cooperation takes place. The whole city is aroused: "He can't be a Jew!" The Asian Jews seize Paul, drag him out of the temple, and

---

[30] The narrator states that the people have seen and heard Stephen being accused: "They stirred up the people as well as the elders and the scribes; then they suddenly confronted him, seized him, and brought him before the council" (Acts 6:12).

try to kill him. In their eyes, he is a trespasser on the Jewish law and a threat to Jewish identity. The narrator's remark is significant: "Immediately the doors were shut" (v. 30). Paul is the ultimate outsider to the Jewish faith. There is no sign of guilt or remorse in committing violence against Paul on the part of Jews because their action does not diminish but instead enhances their self-esteem: "We are the chosen people of God and the keeper of the law and the temple!"

SCT is definitely not a theory that fits perfectly everything that happens in the text. Hierarchical categories between Jews and Gentiles, for instance, become complicated. A higher category, Christian, which potentially includes all Jews and Gentiles, becomes a lower category, and a lower category, Jew, becomes a higher category for Jews in Jerusalem. Yet, SCT presents a compelling case as to how the peaceful crowd suddenly became an angry mob.

Their attempt to kill Paul, however, fails. Having heard the report of the city being in an uproar, Claudius Lysias, the tribune—χιλίαρχος[31]—takes his soldiers and runs down to them from the Antonia Fortress.[32] In the face of this formidable Roman military force, Jews stop beating Paul. Lysias arrests and binds him with two chains (see also Acts 21:10-11). An interrogation follows: "Who are you? What have you done?" This public inquiry bears no fruit due to the multiple voices at odds with each other. Chaos continues within the city. Because he cannot determine what exactly happened, the tribune orders Paul to be led into the barracks (παρεμβολή). Seeing Paul reaching the steps connected to the fortress area, the crowd becomes almost fanatical. The narrator's portrayal of Paul in this scene clearly repeats what happened to Jesus in the Gospel. Paul is carried by the soldiers while the crowd shouts, "Away with him!" (v. 36; Lk 22:54; 23:18).[33] And, there is something more. Their unstoppable violence and crying out demonstrate Paul's status vis-à-vis his fellow Jews. He is not just an outsider but an enemy of Jews.

In other words, Paul is not a radical other who has nothing in common with the Jewish people. He is a *proximate other* who is close to but at the same time different from them. He is teaching the law, yet his teaching is not in accordance with what they consider orthodox. He is jeopardizing their privileged standing with God. He is a deviant. Furthermore, he subverted the Jewish world by breaking the purity law.[34] Now, this deviant has found his "habitat" inside the temple, the heart of the Jewish symbolic universe. Discursive labels are necessary because "negative labels, in fact, are accusations

---

[31] The Roman cohort over which a Roman tribune had control had about three hundred men, one-tenth of a legion, and centurions (v. 32) had about eighty men under their command. Holladay, *Acts*, 417.

[32] The Antonia Fortress that Herod the Great built in honor of Mark Antony was located at the northwestern edge of the Jerusalem temple and provided a bird's-eye view of the temple area to the Roman garrison stationed there. Holladay, *Acts*, 416.

[33] The crowd's shouting is remarkably similar: "Αἶρε τοῦτον" (Lk 23:18); "Αἶρε αὐτόν" (Acts 21:36).

[34] For a discussion of purity, dirt, ordering, and classification in human society, see Mary Douglas, *Purity and Danger: An Analysis of Concepts of Pollution and Taboo* (London: Penguin, 1970), 48. Jerome H. Neyrey states, "'Purity' ... is the orderly system whereby people perceive that certain things belong in certain places at certain times." Jerome H. Neyrey, "The Symbolic Universe of Luke-Acts: They Turn the World Upside Down," in *Social World of Luke-Acts: Models for Interpretation*, ed. Jerome H. Neyrey (Peabody: Hendrickson, 1991) 275.

of *deviance*."³⁵ These labels are fourfold. Paul is teaching against the Jewish (1) law/circumcision, (2) customs, (3) temple, and (4) nation. Commenting on the Jewish perception of Christians in Luke-Acts, Jerome H. Neyrey states:

> They were accused of attacking the major institution of the day, the temple, by rejecting the major symbols of Israel's faith ("this holy place"); they were perceived as dismissing the prerogatives of Israel as a chosen collective ("the people"). They were thought to abrogate the principles by which the faith of this chosen people was structured ("Moses," "the law," "the customs"), and the rituals which symbolize that faith ("circumcision") ... In the eyes of some, then, the Christians appeared to urge a revolution against the traditional values and structures of Israelite faith.³⁶

Thus, the Asian Jews quickly generate anti-Way prejudice from the negative stereotypes they create about the Way³⁷ and trigger fury among the Jews gathered in Jerusalem during a national festival.

One cause of the Jewish slander—from both believers and nonbelievers—is the narrative's double standards or categories regarding how to become beneficiaries of God's salvation. As noted in the earlier discussion of the construction of Christian identity (ch. 2.3), Jews need to be circumcised, keep the law, and believe in Jesus. Gentiles, in contrast, are not circumcised but need to keep the four mandates that the law requires of resident aliens in addition to their faith in Jesus. The Jewish believers confused one with the other by mistakenly assuming that Paul taught the diaspora Jews not to be circumcised and not to observe the law.

This logic seems crystal clear to the implied author, even if it does not to his audience. The accusations are false. Paul is innocent. Yet, the charges are not fully unwarranted. The following section lifts up the voices of the out-group members of the Way, as well as of Paul and his in-group members, to address one of the charges.

3.3. Interrogating Jewish Accusations against the Way

Did Paul or other members of the Way speak or act in a way that justified or strengthened anti-Way prejudices? Of the charges against Paul, this study has so far demonstrated that Luke-Acts never discourages but instead encourages Jews concerning *circumcision* and observing *the law* (chs. 2.3 and 3.2). They are not to abandon but to maintain their Jewish *customs*. The Lukan attitude toward Jews as a nation is ambivalent, which will be discussed later in detail (chs. 5.2 and 6.3). What about the Jewish temple? This section

---

[35] Bruce Malina and Jerome H. Neyrey, "Conflict in Luke-Acts: Labelling and Deviance Theory," in *Social World of Luke-Acts*, 100, emphasis in the original.
[36] Neyrey, "The Symbolic Universe of Luke-Acts," 272.
[37] "Prejudice is typically determined by a process of categorizing others in relation to categories associated with the self: while people and objects associated with ingroup categories are customarily liked, those associated with outgroups are, in certain circumstances, rejected." Oakes, Haslam, and Turner, *Stereotyping and Social Reality*, 30–1.

examines the texts in which Paul and/or other members of the Way are allegedly speaking against the temple.

3.3.1. Accusations Justified: The Temple in Luke-Acts

Paul says, during his speech to the Athenians, "God . . . does not live in shrines made by human hands nor is he served by human hands" (Acts 17:24-25). What about the one in Jerusalem? That is no different (see also Acts 7:44-50). His anti-temple rhetoric later causes a commotion in Ephesus, just as a similar accusation causes another riot in Jerusalem (Acts 21:28-30). Surely, temples are "places of danger for Christians" in Acts, as Jeffrey M. Tripp asserts.[38] Paul's teaching can shake the Jewish symbolic universe in which the temple holds the central place. Paul is not, however, the only person who made anti-temple remarks among the members of the Way.

Stephen also spoke against the temple. The charges made against him are similar to those against Paul: "This man never stops saying things against this holy place and the law" (Acts 6:13; see also Acts 6:11; Acts 21:21, 28).[39] Like Paul, Stephen is labeled as an enemy of Jews. The allegations are twofold: "We have heard him say that this Jesus of Nazareth will destroy this place and will change the customs that Moses handed on to us" (Acts 6:14). Stephen clearly denies the anti-Mosaic charge by insisting that he is an observer of the law, unlike his accusers (Acts 7:53).[40] Against the anti-temple charge, however, he is guilty.[41] Referring to the temple Solomon built, he says, "The Most High does not dwell in houses made with human hands" (Acts 6:48; see also 6:47). He juxtaposes this handmade—χειροποιήτοις (v. 48)—temple with the tent of testimony built in the wilderness according to "an ideal heavenly pattern" (v. 44).[42] He relativizes the significance of the temple—"this place" (Acts 6:13, 14)—by suggesting other holy

---

[38] Jeffrey M. Tripp, "A Tale of Two Riots: The *synkrisis* of the Temples of Ephesus and Jerusalem in Acts 19–23," *JSNT* 37, no. 1 (2014): 86.

[39] The similarities between the two texts, Acts 6:8–8:1 and Acts 21:27–22:23, are striking: (1) the event is taking place in Jerusalem, (2) diaspora Jews are the accusers, (3) the accused is brought before the Jewish council, (4) witnesses testify to anti-Jewish activity, (5) the accused makes a long defense speech, (6) the reaction of the crowd is violent, and (7) the event demonstrates Jewish persecution of the Way. For a brief discussion of the parallels between Stephen and Jesus, see John J. Pilch, *Stephen: Paul and the Hellenist Israelites* (Collegeville: Liturgical Press, 2008), xvii–xx. For a comparative study between the stoning of Stephen and that of Naboth, see Thomas L. Brodie, "The Accusing and Stoning of Naboth (1 Kgs 21:8–13) as One Component of the Stephen Text (Acts 6:9–14; 7:58a)," *CBQ* 45 (1983): 417–32.

[40] The central theme of Stephen's speech is the Jewish rejection of prophets. Their ancestors rejected Joseph, Moses, and God. Just so, his accusers rejected and murdered Jesus, a prophet like Moses, "the Righteous One" (vv. 37-38, 52; see also Lk 23:47; Acts 3:14). Witherington, *The Acts of the Apostles*, 259.

[41] McGarvey argues that during the debate prior to the accusations (vv. 11, 13-14), Stephen might have quoted "the prediction of Jesus that the temple would be destroyed" and his listeners would have thought of that as an end to Jewish customs. McGarvey, *New Commentary on Acts of Apostles*, 114. For scholarly opinions that interpret the accusations against Stephen as entirely false, see Dibelius, *Studies in the Acts of the Apostles*, 167–8; Fitzmyer, *The Acts of the Apostles*, 359; Krodel, *Acts*, 135. For those who find Lukan anti-Jewish slander in Stephen's speech, see Beck, *Mature Christianity*, 220.

[42] Shelly Matthews, *Perfect Martyr: The Stoning of Stephen and the Construction of Christian Identity* (New York: Oxford University Press, 2010), 69. Thomas A. Golding's comment is also noteworthy: "In fact God instructed them to build a σκηνή, a 'tent' (v. 44). Only later did Solomon build an οἶκον, 'house' (v. 47)." Thomas A. Golding, "Pagan Worship in Jerusalem?" *BSac* 170 (2013): 308.

places in Israel's history (Acts 7:7, 33). Lastly, to underscore not only the inferiority but also the inadequacy of the temple, he quotes Isa 66:1-2: "Heaven is my throne, and the earth is my footstool. What kind of house will you build for me, says the Lord, or what is the place of my rest? Did not my hand make all these things?" (Acts 7:49-50). His point is clear. God is not in need of the temple, or, as Shelly Matthews asserts, "It would have been better had the temple never been built."[43]

This anti-temple rhetoric traces back to Jesus (Acts 6:14). The absence of the anti-temple accusation during the trial of Jesus in Luke—"We heard him say, 'I will destroy this temple that is made with hands, and in three days I will build another, not made with hands'" (Mk 14:58)—and the narrator's description of witnesses as "false" (Acts 6:13; Mk 14:57) show that Luke is well aware of the charges made against Jesus in Mark. Furthermore, Jesus' cleansing of the temple, cursing of the fig tree, and prophecy of the destruction of the temple provide substance to their charges (Mk 11:12-21; 13:1-2; 15:29; Mt 26:61; Jn 2:19-22).[44] In other words, the accusations at the narrative level are not completely groundless. Jesus and Stephen speak against the temple. So does Paul.

The Acts narrative reflects such a view, although its overall view of the temple is not entirely negative but ambivalent.[45] First, the tension increases with regard to the Jerusalem temple as the narrative progresses. At first, the apostles and disciples carry out an active ministry in the temple (Acts 2:43–3:36). Then, they are tried and threatened (Acts 4:1-22). In the end, Paul is dragged out, beaten, and excluded from the temple (Acts 21:30, 32). Second, the household emerges as an alternative place of worship. John H. Elliott points out that though Luke's Gospel starts and ends with scenes in the temple (Lk 1:5-23; 24:50-53), Acts does so with scenes in the household (Acts 1:12-14; 28:30-31).[46] The Jerusalem temple loses its importance. Instead, the household becomes the center of the messianic community where people gather, the word of God is proclaimed, the Holy Spirit is poured out, and the people are saved (e.g., Acts 1:12-42; 9:10-18; 10:1–11:18; 12:12-17; 16:15, 30-34; 18:7-11; 20:20-21, 21:8-14; 28:23-31).[47] Third, the Jerusalem temple emerges as an object of worship. The Jerusalem Jews basically replicate

---

[43] Matthews, *Perfect Martyr*, 69.

[44] John R. Donahue and Daniel J. Harrington, *The Gospel of Mark*, SP 2 (Collegeville: Liturgical Press, 2002), 422; Alan Watson, *The Trial of Stephen: The First Christian Martyr* (Athens, GA: University of Georgia Press, 1996), 67. For a different perspective, see Mary A. Beavis, *Mark*, PCNT (Grand Rapids: Baker Academic, 2011), 220–1; M. Eugene Boring, *Mark: A Commentary*, NTL (Louisville: Westminster John Knox, 2006), 412. See also J. Ramsey Michaels, *The Gospel of John*, NICNT (Grand Rapids: Eerdmans, 2010), 164–8.

[45] Esler, *Community and Gospel in Luke-Acts*, 133–5.

[46] John H. Elliott, "Temple versus Household in Luke-Acts: A Contrast in Social Institutions," in *Social World of Luke-Acts*, 215.

[47] John H. Elliott writes, "This system [the temple] proved incapable of mediating the inclusive salvation envisioned by the prophets ... Over against it, Luke contrasts the domestic associations of the movement initiated by Jesus. Here the gospel of a universal salvation is socially embodied in a community of 'brothers and sisters' ... The household, in fact, functions as Luke's prime metaphor for depicting social life in the kingdom of God." Elliott, "Temple versus Household in Luke-Acts," 239. See also Klaus Baltzer, "The Meaning of the Temple in the Lucan Writings," *HTR* 58 (1965): 271–7; Gregory K. Beale, "The Descent of the Eschatological Temple in the Form of the Spirit at Pentecost: Part 2, Corroborating Evidence," *TynBul* 56 (July 2005): 64–90; J. Bradley Chance, *Jerusalem, the Temple, and the New Age in Luke-Acts* (Macon: Mercer University Press, 1988); Nicholas H. Taylor, "The Jerusalem Temple in Luke-Acts," *HvTSt* 60 (2004): 462–70.

the actions of the worshipers of Artemis, as substantial thematic and verbal parallels between the riot in Ephesus and the riot in Jerusalem indicate.[48] Taken together with Stephen's earlier speech on the temple (Acts 7:44-50), the implication of the riot in Jerusalem is clear. They turned from the worship of God to the worship of the temple and thus committed the sin of idolatry as their ancestors had (Acts 7:39-43).[49]

Unveiling both Paul's attitude toward and the Lukan narrative's understanding of the temple leads to the conclusion that Paul and the Way are not completely innocent of the Jewish accusations. The author of Luke-Acts was aware that anti-Way rhetoric was widespread among the Jews in the empire (Acts 21:28; 28:22). Jews recognized Paul and the Way as outside the law and thus as *outsiders* to the Jewish faith. But there is more, as the following episode with the Roman tribune illustrates (Acts 21:37-40). Paul escapes from the hands of the Jews but still finds himself labeled as an outsider.

3.4. Interaction with the Tribune: Paul, an Outsider to the Pax Romana

Leaving behind the Jewish mob shouting with a loud voice, "Away with him!" (v. 36), Paul is getting close to the barracks. The roller-coaster train is slowing down a little bit. Once he is inside the barracks, they could be a safe haven for him. Yet, right before he gets there, he says to the tribune: "May I say something to you?" (v. 37b). Those inside the train wonder what he will say because his request can prolong his time with the angry Jews outside. They hold tight onto their safety bar as the tribune responds, because he is also not in favor of Paul. After examining the question the tribune has for Paul (vv. 37c-38), this section traces sources of anti-Roman allegations against the Way by revisiting the accusations against Jesus (Lk 23:1-5) and Paul (Acts 16:16-24;17:1-9).

3.4.1. The Tribune's Labeling of Paul

Lysias asks:

> vv. 37-38: "Do you know Greek? Then you are not the Egyptian who recently stirred up a revolt and led the four thousand assassins out into the wilderness?"

---

[48] According to Thomas A. Golding, there are two thematic parallels, "the storyline of each narrative" and "the descriptions of the riots," and numerous verbal parallels, for example, "temple" (Acts 19:27; 21:27-30), "Asia" (Acts 19:26-27; 21:27), "Ephesian(s)" (Acts 19:28, 34-35; 21:29), "city" (Acts 19:29; 21:30), "crying out/shouting" (Acts 19:28, 32; 21:28, 36), "confusion/stir up/provoked" (Acts 19:29, 32; 21:27, 30), "crowd" (Acts 19:33, 35; 21:27, 34-35), and "motion with the hand" (Acts 19:33; 21:40). Golding, "Pagan Worship in Jerusalem?" 313–16.

[49] Thomas A. Golding concludes, "Continuing to worship at the temple and venerate the temple while rejecting God's work through Jesus dishonored God." Golding, "Pagan Worship in Jerusalem?" 316. Steve Smith also states, "While the rejection of Jesus is the most significant accusation made, Acts 7 also showed that the destruction of the city was the result of idolatry centered on the temple as a place of false localization of God, and manipulation of God." Steve Smith, *The Fate of the Jerusalem Temple in Luke-Acts: An Intertextual Approach to Jesus' Laments over Jerusalem and Stephen's Speech*, LNTS 553 (London: Bloomsbury T&T Clark, 2017), 192.

The hidden intention of Lysias in capturing Paul is revealed. He seized Paul not to rescue him from the mob per se but to put him under trial and likely to kill him, as the Romans systemically suppressed any attempt to dismantle the Roman peace.[50] "Do you know Greek?" The tribune's question seems at odds with his label of Paul as a Jewish rebel from Egypt because the rebel leader probably spoke some Greek.[51] According to Josephus, this unnamed Egyptian is a false prophet who led thirty thousand "men of Sicarii" (ἄνδρας τῶν σικαρίων; v. 38) to the wilderness and finally to Mount Olive with the intention of bringing down the walls of Jerusalem, although he was thwarted by Roman soldiers led by Felix (Josephus, *War* 2.261–3; *Ant.* 20.169–72).[52] Since the rebel leader escaped from the previous assault, whereas hundreds of his followers were slain and captured, Lysias assumes that he is still around instigating revolt (ἀναστατόω; v. 38; see also Acts 17:6) and conspiring an attack on "upper-class supporters of Rome."[53] Jews were in an uproar in the temple precincts during the Pentecost and had tried to kill a person. 'He must be the one. This is a big catch,' Lysias is probably thinking.

Paul is surely not the one because the risen Lord previously identified the origin of Paul's birth. He is from Tarsus (Acts 9:11, 30; 11;25). Furthermore, Paul has been busy preaching the gospel in the northeastern part of Mediterranean basin. Like Jews in Jerusalem, the tribune is falsely accusing Paul: "This man is a terrorist." This is slander. But, is that all? Is Paul completely innocent? The remaining section visits the political accusations made against the members of the Way in Luke-Acts and tries to answer Rome's suspicions about members of the Way: "Are they political agitators?"

3.4.2. Political Accusations against Jesus (Lk 23:1-5)

By taking Jesus under arrest, the Jewish authorities label Jesus as an enemy of the Jews and of the emperor before Pilate. Their initial charge, "perverting our nation,"[54] is buttressed by the following two charges, "forbidding us to pay taxes to the emperor" and "saying that he himself is the Messiah, a king" (v. 2). The allegation is clear. Jesus is threatening the Roman peace that Pilate has to defend at all costs. Pilate immediately asks him: "Are you the king of the Jews?" (v. 3). Jesus neither acknowledges nor denies the charge. He simply says, "You say so" (v. 3), and does not overtly identify himself as

---

[50] Richard B. Vinson, *Luke*, SHBC (Macon: Smyth & Helwys, 2008), 712.

[51] The use of Greek was a widespread phenomenon among the Jews in Palestine as well as in the diaspora. Jan N. Sevenster, *Do You Know Greek?: How Much Greek Could the First Jewish Christian Have Known?* trans. J. de Bruin, NovTSup 19 (Leiden: Brill, 1968). Richard I. Pervo proposes that the tribune's question may refer to "the quality of Paul's Greek accent." Pervo, *Acts*, 553.

[52] Ardent followers of the Sicarii movement "terrorized Jerusalem, especially during the festivals," with daggers. Holladay, *Acts*, 418. Richard A. Horsley and John S. Hanson note: "The symbolism that shines through Josephus' reports suggests that the movement of the 'Egyptian' understood itself as participating in a new 'conquest' of the promised land. The historical prototype must have been the battle of Jericho led by Joshua." Richard A. Horsley and John S. Hanson, *Bandits, Prophets, and Messiahs: Popular Movements in the Time of Jesus* (Minneapolis: Winston, 1985), 169.

[53] Pervo, *Acts*, 553; Johnson, *The Acts of the Apostles*, 383.

[54] "Leading astray" or "perverting" (διαστρέφω) is an allegation given to Moses and Elijah, with whom Jesus identifies himself in Luke-Acts (e.g., Lk 9:30; Acts 3:22; see also Exod 5:4 and 1 Kgs 18:17). Green, *The Gospel of Luke*, 800. See also J. Severino Croatto, "Jesus, Prophet like Elijah, and Prophet-Teacher like Moses in Luke-Acts," *JBL* 124, no. 3 (2005): 451–65.

a king. Pilate tells the accusers, "I find no basis for an accusation against this man" (v. 4). Having seen that their verbal attack has no effect, the assembly brings another charge: "He stirs up the people by teaching throughout all Judea" (v. 5). He is an agitator. At this time, Pilate does not ask Jesus whether their accusation is true or not. He transfers him to Herod because he has heard that Jesus is from Galilee. Jesus utters no word to Herod and is brought back to Pilate. Pilate says that both he and Herod have found Jesus innocent, not guilty of the charges laid against him. The narrator makes clear that it is the will of the Jewish crowd, not of Pilate, that Jesus be handed over (Lk 23:13-25).

Yet, to understand the case better, one needs to do what any earnest lawyer or jury would do: review the allegations.[55] First, is Jesus a king? Jesus never directly *says* he is, but neither does he ever *deny* it. When some of the Pharisees request him to stop his disciples from saying, "Blessed is the *king* who comes in the name of the Lord!" (Lk 19:38a), Jesus does not comply. Instead, he affirms this royal label: "I tell you, if these were silent, the stones would shout out" (Lk 19:40).[56] Jesus never calls himself the Messiah either (e.g., Lk 9:20; 22:67; 23:3). Yet, the narrator describes him as such (Lk 2:11, 26; 4:41; 9:20; 24:26, 46).[57] Second, is Jesus forbidding Jews to pay taxes to the emperor? He *seems* not to be. When asked whether it is lawful for Jews to pay taxes to the emperor, Jesus avoids choosing one side over the other. His answer is ambiguous: "Give to the emperor the things that are the emperor's, and to God the things that are God's" (Lk 20:25). Yet, the literary context of this story creates a slippage. The Parable of the Wicked Tenants (Lk 20:9-19) makes it clear that the tribute should be paid to God, the owner of the vineyard. Jesus seems to nullify imperial taxes. Third, has Jesus really stirred up the people? He never provokes an anti-Roman resistance, but he constantly speaks of the kingdom of God—βασιλεία του θεού—in Judea (e.g., Lk 4:43; 5:17; 6:17; 7:17). This good news of the kingdom Jesus preaches with his *twelve* disciples could sound politically upsetting: "He has sent me *to proclaim release to the captives* and recovery of sight to the blind, *to let the oppressed go free*" (Lk 4:18; see also Isa 61:1).[58]

---

[55] Scholars are divided into four groups on whether the passage contains (1) no slander, (2) half-truth, (3) Jewish anti-Jesus slander, or (4) Lucan anti-Jewish slander. For the first position, see Alfred Plummer, *A Critical and Exegetical Commentary on the Gospel According to St. Luke*, ICC (New York: Charles Scribner's Sons, 1903), 520; Joel B. Green, *The Gospel of Luke*, NICNT (Grand Rapids: Eerdmans, 1997), 801. For the second position, see Joseph A. Fitzmyer, *The Gospel According to Luke (X–XXIV)*, AB 28A (Garden City, NY: Doubleday, 1985), 1473; John Nolland, *Luke 18:35–24:53*, WBC 35C (Dallas: Word Books, 1993), 1118. For the third position, see George H. P. Thompson, *The Gospel According to Luke in the Revised Standard Version with Introduction and Commentary* (Oxford: Clarendon Press, 1972), 267; Johnson, *The Gospel of Luke*, 368; Christopher F. Evans, *Saint Luke*, TPINTC (London: SCM, 1990), 846; François Bovon, *Luke 3: A Commentary on the Gospel of Luke 19:28–24:53*, Hermeneia, trans. James Crouch (Minneapolis: Fortress, 2012), 254–5. For the fourth position, see Beck, *Mature Christianity*, 178.

[56] Lk 19:38a is taken from Ps 118, which was "used in preexilic Israel as a hymn of royal entry on the occasion of an annual ritual of reenthronement." Green, *The Gospel of Luke*, 686.

[57] Mark A. Powell argues that "salvation in Luke-Acts means participation in the reign of God." Mark A. Powell, "Salvation in Luke-Acts," *WW* 12, no. 1 (1992): 8. When a thief questioned and rebuked him, asking, "Are you not the Messiah? Save yourself and us!" Jesus proves his Messianic identity on the cross—the suffering Messiah (Lk 24:46)—by inviting the other thief to the reign of God and thus saving him: "Truly I tell you, today you will be with me in Paradise" (Lk 23:43).

[58] For Exodus as a literary trope in Acts, see David W. Pao, *Acts and the Isaianic New Exodus*, WUNT 2/130 (Tübingen: Mohr Siebeck, 2000).

On the way to Jerusalem, he is proclaimed to be "the king" by his followers (Lk 19:38). In the end, he is crucified with a sign on the cross reading: "This is the king of the Jews" (Lk 23:38). Jesus was, in the eyes of the Roman authorities, a political criminal.

3.4.3. Political Accusations against the Way (Acts 16:16-41; 17:1-9)

The civic unrest does not die out with the crucifixion of Jesus. His followers constantly cause commotions among the Jews that force the Roman authorities to engage to some degree (Acts 5:17-18; 16:19-24; see also Acts 8:2; 12:1-19; 13:50; 14:19). An anti-Roman label appears in Philippi, where Paul drives out a spirit of divination—πνεῦμα πύθωνα—from an enslaved girl (Acts 16:16-41).[59] Having lost their hope of making money from her fortunetelling, her owners drag Paul and Silas to the forum (ἀγορά; Acts 16:19) and say to the magistrates, "These men are disturbing our city" (v. 20). They are *agitators of the peace*. They lay out specific crimes for that label: "They … are advocating customs that are not lawful for us as Romans to adopt or observe" (v. 21).[60] An uproar follows. The reaction of the crowd in the forum is so great and violent that the magistrates have to intervene, just as is the case with Paul later in Jerusalem. Paul and Silas are stripped, flogged, and thrown into prison. The narrative soon surprises its audience, first by giving a vivid portrayal of God's intervention—their prayer and singing to God, the earthquake, the opening of the prison doors, the unfastening of the chains, and the salvation of the jailer and his household (vv. 25-34). The surprise continues. Second, Paul discloses information that had been hidden so far. He is a Roman citizen (v. 37). Third, the role reverses. It is not Paul but the magistrates who are accused. He says that they unjustly beat the "uncondemned" Roman citizens and threw them into prison (v. 37).[61] Afraid of a counter-punch that could cause more harm than what they had inflicted upon Paul and Silas, the magistrates come, apologize, and free them. The episode concludes with Paul and Silas leaving the prison and arriving at Lydia's house (Acts 16:14-15, 40). Yet, a question still remains. Are they really cleared of all charges? The following episode in Thessalonica reveals the truth.

---

[59] Daniel R. Schwartz argues that the owners of the enslaved girl who accuse Paul and Silas are Jewish for the following reasons. (1) Jews can be Roman citizens just as Paul. Their accusation implies that they are Roman citizens. (2) Paul visits Jewish synagogues during his missionary journey. The enslaved girl's action occurred over many days, which implies that she was also at "the place of prayer" where they regularly went to pray (Acts 16:16, 18-19). Daniel R. Schwartz, "The Accusation and the Accusers at Philippi (Acts 16:20–21)," *Bib* 65, no. 3 (1984): 362. Schwartz further states that "while they must admit that the accused are Jews, they specify that they are teaching non-Jewish and anti-Roman practices. Such a demonstrative Jewish self-distancing from fellow Jews who are now Christians is just what we would expect from Luke-Acts" (362-3).

[60] There is a clear disparity between the action that took place—exorcism and the loss of livelihood—and the accusation made against Paul—civil disobedience. Craig S. de Vos comments: "Since Luke considers magic to have a satanic origin and he presents Christians as opposing magic he cannot allow Paul and Silas to be accused of it. Therefore, he plays down the accusation of magic and presents charges that can easily be refuted." Craig S. de Vos, "Finding a Charge that Fits: The Accusation against Paul and Silas at Philippi (Acts 16.19–21)," *JSNT* 74 (1999): 63.

[61] Cicero's famous line captures the legal status of the Roman citizen: "To bind a Roman citizen is a crime, to flog him is an abomination, to slay him is almost an act of murder" (Cicero, *Verr.* 2.5.66). See also Cicero, *Def. Rabir.* 4.12; Livy, *Hist.* 10.9.3–6.

The uproar continues while Paul and Silas stay in Thessalonica (Acts 17:1-9). Their message in Philippi was indirect, as it came from the mouth of an enslaved girl: "These men are slaves of the Most High God, who proclaim to you/us a way of salvation" (Acts 16:17).[62] But the message is not hidden in Thessalonica. The narrator explains that Paul's preaching in the Jewish synagogue centers around the suffering and resurrection of the Messiah (Acts 17:3a). Paul confirms this: "This is the Messiah, Jesus whom I am proclaiming to you" (Acts 17:3b). The narrator describes *the Jews*—οἱ Ἰουδαῖοι—as having instigated certain wicked men who were hanging out in the marketplace—ἀγορά—to set the city in an uproar out of jealousy when they saw devout Greeks as well as some Jews joining Paul and Silas (Acts 17:4-5). Having failed to find them, *the Jews* drag Jason and some believers—ἀδελφόι—before the city authorities and begin shouting:

> vv. 6-7: "These people who have been turning the world upside down have come here also, and Jason has entertained them as guests. They are all acting contrary to the decrees of the emperor, saying that there is another king named Jesus."

The charges are threefold. The members of the Way turn the empire—οἰκουμένη—upside down (ἀναστατόω; Acts 17:6), act against imperial decrees, and claim another king. The charges become clearer when read as a whole and in reverse, as Kavin C. Rowe suggests: "[B]y proclaiming another king, the Christians act against the decrees of Caesar and thereby turn the world upside down."[63] (1) *They claim another king* (βασιλέα ἕτερον; v. 7c). This is not slander because earlier *the Jews* found Paul calling Jesus the Messiah—Χριστός (v. 3). Previously, the Jewish authorities had accused Jesus of calling himself "the Messiah, *a king*," and had him killed by the Romans (Lk 23:2-3, 25). The political implication is clear as the accusers use ἕτερος instead of ἄλλος and set Jesus in opposition to Caesar (v. 7). The Christian claim that Jesus is "the Lord"—κύριος (e.g., Acts 7:59; see also Acts 25:26)—and "the Lord of all"—πάντων κύριος (Acts 10:36),[64] not the emperor, is troublesome. (2) *They act against the decrees of*

---

[62] The Greek phrase "the Most High God" (Θεός Ὑψίστος), was commonly used by diaspora Jews to signify YHWH. Holladay, *Acts*, 323. Carl R. Holladay continues, "*NewDocs* 3:121 (no. 94) mentions a synagogue built at Alexandria during the second century BCE that was dedicated to *Theos Hypsistos*: 'To the Highest God [the Jews of Alexandria (?)] (dedicated) the sacred precinct and the synagogue and the things belonging to it.'" "The way—ὁδός—of salvation" anticipates the jailer's question—"Sir, what must I do to be saved?"—and the following reply—"Believe on the Lord Jesus" (Acts 16:30-31). Holladay, *Acts*, 324.

[63] Kavin C. Rowe, *World Upside Down: Reading Acts in the Graeco-Roman Age* (New York: Oxford University Press, 2009), 96. Rowe argues that the accusations are verifiable in light of the three core practices that Christians undertook—"confessing Jesus as Lord, engaging in mission to the end of the earth, forming identifiable communities of Jews and gentiles" (135). In contrast to Rowe, Sherwin-White treats the three charges separately. Adrian N. Sherwin-White, *Roman Society and Roman Law in the New Testament* (Oxford: Clarendon Press, 1963), 103.

[64] Kavin C. Rowe provides several examples: "Nero κύριος ... was acclaimed 'the Lord of all the World' (τοῦ παντὸς κόσμου κύριος Νέρων) ... Lucan, who wrote during the reign of Nero, could speak of the victor of the much earlier civil war between Julius Caesar and Pompey as 'the Lord of the world' (*dominus mundi*; Lucan 9.20), as could Cicero (*dominus omnium gentium*).... And Arrian's records of his teacher's discourses speak of the Roman Caesar as the 'Lord of all' (ὁ παντῶν κύριος καῖσαρ; Epictetus, *Disc*, 4.1.12)." Rowe, *World Upside Down*, 106. See also Muñoz-Larrondo, "Living in Two Worlds," 317–18.

Caesar (v. 7b). In a narrow sense, their action refers to claiming the kingship of Jesus (v. 7c). In a broad sense, it may refer to any behavior upsetting the imperial system (Acts 16:21). Raymond Pickett's note on Lk 6:32-36 is helpful in this regard. Jesus says, "If you lend to those from whom you hope to receive, what credit is that to you? ... do good, and lend, expecting nothing in return" (Lk 6:34-35). His teaching is a serious challenge to the Roman patronage system because it not only subverts the "model of reciprocity and power"[65] but also replaces Caesar, its ultimate benefactor, with God, the Most High (Lk 6:35-36).[66] (3) *They turn the world upside down* (v. 6b). A peculiar feature of the Way is its universal mission. It preaches salvation in Jesus to Gentiles as well as Jews (Acts 4:12; 13:26, 47; 16:17; 28:28), which is problematic for Rome. First, the Way posits "a prior problem" that requires salvation.[67] Jesus should intervene to fix the problems, such as economic injustice, that Rome cannot fix (e.g., Lk 4:16-21; Acts 4:23-37) by introducing different patterns of life.[68] Second, it is a supra-ethnic movement whose assembly (ἐκκλησία) is everywhere (Acts 28:22). Its core conviction is "Jesus's universal Lordship" (e.g., Acts 9:15; 26:16-18).[69] No matter how politically innocuous those gatherings are or how theologically, not politically, driven their claims may seem in the eyes of its in-group members, for its out-groups, especially Rome, the members of the Way are agitators against the Roman peace.

3.4.4. Paul's First Defense against the Tribune

Lysias's question (v. 38), though not accurate, reflects political allegations against the Way. Will Paul accept the label of agitator? Is he really a rebel leader? Surely not. Paul replies: "I am a Jew, from Tarsus in Cilicia, a citizen of an important [οὐκ ἀσήμου] city" (v. 39). His Jewish ethnicity may not help him at all because the Egyptian rebel was surely a diaspora Jew, but his Tarsus citizenship will. He is a native of Tarsus, and the phrase οὐκ ἀσήμου—"not insignificant"—is often used in Greco-Roman literature to describe one's native city.[70] Furthermore, Tarsus was both the seat of the Roman governor of Cilicia, a Roman province, and "a renowned cultural and intellectual center" of Hellenism (Strabo, *Geography* 14.5.9–15).[71] The status of Tarsus as a "*municipium*, 'free city*,*' and *civitas libera et immunis*, 'a city free and exempt [from taxation]*,*'"[72] along with the presence of a colony of Jews there, elevates Paul's status from a rebel leader to

---

[65] Pickett, "Luke and Empire," 17.
[66] Rowe, *World Upside Down*, 97: "The practice against the decrees of Caesar is saying that there is a contender for the imperial throne, namely, Jesus." See also Jerome H. Neyrey, "The Symbolic Universe of Luke-Acts," in *Social World of Luke-Acts*, 271. For the Roman patronage system, see John Nicols, *Civic Patronage in the Roman Empire*, MSHACA 365 (Leiden: Brill, 2014).
[67] Rowe, *World Upside Down*, 124.
[68] Pickett, "Luke and Empire," 17. See also Rowe, *World Upside Down*, 103; Sherman E. Johnson, "The Apostle Paul and the Riot in Ephesus," *LTQ* 14, no. 4 (1979): 79–88.
[69] Rowe, *World Upside Down*, 124.
[70] Pervo, *Acts*, 554. For the similar use of "οὐκ ἀσήμου," see, for example, Euripides, *Ion* 8 (Athens) and Strabo, *Geog.* 8.6.15 (Epidaurus).
[71] Fitzmyer, *The Acts of the Apostles*, 427.
[72] Fitzmyer, *The Acts of the Apostles*, 427. See Appian, *Civ. W.* 5.7.

a culturally equipped citizen of οἰκουμένη. Then, he makes a request to speak to the people (v. 39), which the tribune grants him permission to do (v. 40).

Paul's first conversation with the Roman tribune, though brief, elucidates a persistent label imposed on Paul—*an agitator* (e.g., Acts 24:2-5).[73] He is an outsider to the established order for both Jews and Rome. He refutes this double charge by identifying himself as an insider of both groups. He is a Jew and a law-abiding citizen (v. 39). Now, Paul is standing on the steps and waving his hand—κατέσεισε τῇ χειρὶ—to the people for silence (v. 40).[74] The Roman tribune accepted at least temporarily his apology (v. 39). Will the crowd do the same? A great hush follows, yet there is still some noise among the crowd (Acts 22:2). What will he do in this case? As he has done before once he stepped into Jerusalem, he will amplify his Jewishness in his speech. He will categorize himself as a Jew. The first step? Needless to say, he will speak in his native language, Hebrew.[75]

3.5. Concluding Comments

Stephen S. Bush states, "A social practice is a shared pattern of behavior that is conducted according to norms."[76] Paul's purification rite is his statement to the Jewish believers: "I'm willing to conform to the Jewish norms as an insider." The riot that follows states otherwise: "You are not one of us." His first interaction with Lysias implies a similar perception of Paul. "Are you not a threat to the Pax Romana?" Going beyond the confines of the text, Acts 21:17-40, this chapter endeavored to find the traces and strategies of Jewish accusations against Paul and brought forth the following conclusions. (1) The Lukan narrative contains double voices in conflict with each other; the members of the Way say that the charges against Paul are slander, whereas its out-group members say the opposite. (2) The Asian Jews instigate a riot by accentuating the Jewish distinctiveness of the crowd and labeling Paul with negative stereotypes—a man teaching against the Jewish people, law, and temple; the broad Luke-Acts narrative shows that their claims, particularly those regarding the temple, are not empty slurs. (3) Paul's first encounter with the tribune discloses Rome's suspicion that the Way threatens the Roman peace. (4) Though Paul is surely not an Egyptian rebel, the narrative provides evidences that make Rome's hunch plausible.

---

[73] Tertullus accuses Paul before Felix as follows: "Your Excellency, because of you we have long enjoyed peace ... We have, in fact, found this man *a pestilent fellow, an agitator among all the Jews throughout the world*, and *a ringleader of the sect of the Nazarenes*" (Acts 24:2, 5), emphasis added.
[74] For the waving of a hand before making a public speech, see Acts 13:16; 26:1. "That the gesture was part of rhetorical style is suggested by [Apuleius'] *The Golden Ass* 2.21." Johnson, *The Acts of the Apostles*, 384.
[75] Though the text reads literally "in Hebrew"—τῇ Ἑβραΐδι (Acts 21:40)—it refers to Aramaic, "the vernacular language spoken by Jews in Palestine during the Second Temple period." Holladay, *Acts*, 418–19.
[76] Stephen S. Bush, *Visions of Religion: Experience, Meaning, and Power*, Reflection and Theory in the Study of Religion (New York: Oxford University Press, 2014), 3.

Having learned how the Jewish crowd and the tribune see him, Paul is doubly excluded and doubly troubled. Now, a platform is ready for him to speak. In the following two episodes, Acts 21:1-21 and Acts 21:22-29, he will defend his Jewish identity and his Roman identity, respectively. Chapter 4 turns to Paul's public speech to Jews in Jerusalem. The riders on the roller coaster wonder, "Will the silent crowd immediately turn into an angry mob once again and result in another free fall?" What unfolds before their own eyes reveals something different. "Not this time. At least, not so fast. You will experience a spectacle more exciting than you have seen before."

Excursus: Paul's Letters and Jewish Accusations in Acts

An important question that arises from refuting Jewish accusations against the Paul of Acts is what Paul has to say about the contested issues in the letters assigned to him. Since it is not feasible to cover all the instances from which anti-Jewish suspicions could arise, the following passages from Paul's letters explicitly speak of (1) circumcision/the law (Gal 5:2-12; 6:12-16; Rom 2:25–3:2; 4:9-12; 1 Cor 7:17-20; Phil 3:2-11), (2) Jewish customs, particularly related to eating (Gal 2:11-21), and (3) the temple (1 Cor 3:16-17; 2 Cor 6:16) will receive due attention.

To give the conclusion up front, the accusations are not totally groundless. First, the letters' position on *circumcision* is no different from that of the Paul of Acts (Acts 21:21). Circumcision on the eighth day is a distinct mark of Jewish ethnic identity (e.g., Lk 1:59; 2:21; Acts 7:8; Rom 3:1; Phil 3:5). Matthew Thiessen states, "Eighth-day circumcision functioned to weave together Jewish practices with proper genealogical descent."[77] Likewise, when Paul speaks of the inclusion of Gentiles in the descendants of Abraham, he still maintains a clear ethnic boundary between Jews and Gentiles (Rom 11:1-36). The decisive line is circumcision (e.g., Rom 3:1, 30; 4:9, 12; 15:8),[78] which is the sign of Israel's election (Rom 8:33; 9:11; 11:7, 28). In a word, Paul does not undermine the circumcision of Jews.

Yet, he is crystal clear regarding the circumcision of Gentiles; it is a big "no-no." In his eyes, those who wish to be circumcised are not only "foolish" (ἀνόητος; Gal 3:1, 3) but are also cutting themselves off from Christ and have fallen away from grace (Gal 5:4). A person is justified not by the works of the law but through faith in Jesus Christ (Gal 2:16; 3:8, 11, 24). Upon concluding his letter to the Galatians, Paul says, "For neither circumcision nor uncircumcision is anything; but a new creation is everything!" (Gal 6:15). Circumcision has no use because real circumcision is "the matter of the heart," not a matter of the body (Rom 2:29; Phil 3:3). It is not the circumcision but the faith of Abraham that is considered—ἐλογίσθη—to be righteous (Gal 3:6; Rom 4:3; Gen 15:6). It is clear that no one can observe the entire law (Gal 3:10; Rom 3:9-20).[79]

---

[77] Thiessen, *Contesting Conversion*, 143. Thiessen continues, "In theory at least, only the (male) descendants of those who were themselves Jewish would be able to undergo this rite."

[78] In Rom 3:1, Paul uses the words for Jew and circumcision interchangeably: "Then what advantage has *the Jew*? Or what is the value of *circumcision*?"

[79] Thomas R. Schreiner, "Is Perfect Obedience to the Law Possible? A Re-examination of Galatians 3:10," *JETS* 27, no. 2 (1984): 151–60.

Circumcision, one of the works of the law[80] (Gal 2:16; 3:2, 5, 10, 12; Rom 3:20, 28)—along with keeping the Sabbath, Jewish festivals, and dietary laws (Gal 2:11-14; 4:10)—marks someone as distinctively Jewish and separates them from the nations, but circumcision lost its validity with the coming of faith in Christ (Gal 3:23-25).[81] He proclaims: "There is no longer Jew or Greek, there is no longer slave or free, there is no longer male and female; for all of you are one in Christ Jesus" (Gal 3:28; see also 1 Cor 12:13). Therefore, Paul has no agenda to preach circumcision but only Christ to Gentiles (Gal 5:11; 6:12, 14). This seems to coincide with the Paul of Acts.

The second topic is *forsaking Moses or not observing the customs* (Acts 21:21). No specific law or customs are spelled out here. Yet the purification rite that follows implies that the customs are related to Jewish cultural identity or purity that separates the Jews from the Gentiles (vv. 23-26). Paul's comment on keeping the dietary law is helpful in analyzing his stance on this issue.

Though the Mosaic law does not overtly prohibit Jews from eating with Gentiles, by the time Luke-Acts was written, it had become a custom for pious Jews not to eat with Gentiles.[82] Peter's visit to Cornelius' house showcases this. Peter calls the food the Gentiles eat "profane or unclean" (Acts 10:14) and says that "it is improper [ἀθέμιτος] for a Jew to associate with or to visit a Gentile" (Acts 10:28, author's translation). The Jewish believers accuse him of eating with the Gentiles, but he ardently defends his table fellowship (Acts 11:3). In Antioch, however, Peter acts differently, according to Paul. He hurries to escape the scene, before certain people from James arrive (Gal 2:12). Paul condemns him because he acts contrary to "the truth of the Gospel," which implies that Paul sees the Jewish dietary law as no longer valid in Christ (Gal 2:13-21). Gentiles and Jews should all eat together in the church without factions (1 Cor 11:17-34). Paul's inclusive stance could be seen as not only liberal but also threatening in the eyes of Jews who strived to live a Jewish way of life (e.g., Gal 2:14).

The third topic is *teaching against the Jerusalem temple* (Acts 21:28). Paul understands that God's temple is holy and should be well cared for (1 Cor 3:17). The church should follow the model of the temple by being built in an orderly manner with a foundation and other materials (1 Cor 3:12). The temple Paul is describing, however, is not the temple in Jerusalem but the bodies of believers (1 Cor 3:16; 6:19) and the "gathered community of believers" (2 Cor 6:16) in which the Holy Spirit dwells.[83] His spiritualized

---

[80] "The works of the law" (ἔργα νόμου) refers to "a life dedicated to nomistic service," not human deeds to gain salvation or merit in the eyes of God. Joseph B. Tyson, "'Works of Law' in Galatians," *JBL* 92, no. 3 (1973): 431. This position is widely held by scholars supporting the New Perspective on Paul. Ed P. Sanders explains the term *covenantal nomism*, which he himself coined, as follows: "Covenantal nomism is the view that one's place in God's plan is established on the basis of the covenant and that the covenant requires as the proper response of man his obedience to its commandments, while providing means of atonement for transgression." Ed P. Sanders, *Paul and Palestinian Judaism: A Comparison of Patterns of Religion* (Minneapolis: Fortress, 1977), 75. In other words, the law is given to Israel not to *enter into* but to *stay in* the covenant with God. Similarly, James D. G. Dunn insists that the circumcision and the food law in the Greco-Roman world "functioned as identity markers" and "badges of covenant membership" for Jews. James D. G. Dunn, *New Perspective on Paul* (Grand Rapids: Eerdmans, 2008), 109.

[81] Thomas R. Schreiner, "'Works of Law' in Paul," *NovT* 33, no. 3 (1991): 217–44.

[82] See, for example, Daniel 1:8-16; Jubilees 22:16; Letter of Aristeas 142; 4 Maccabees 5; Tobit 1:10-13.

[83] Gordon D. Fee, *The First Epistle to the Corinthians* (Grand Rapids: Eerdmans, 2014), 159.

view of the temple is not unprecedented when compared to Jewish eschatological sources (e.g., Ezek 40–48). Yet, the Jewish roots of his view do not completely annul the charges against him. The suspicion deepens when one looks closely at Paul's teaching and the description of the temple in Luke-Acts. However, readers should not fall into the trap of identifying the Paul of Acts with the Paul of his letters and of validating all of the Jewish accusations against the Paul of Acts on an intertextual basis.

4

Recategorizing Paul as an Insider (Acts 22:1-21)

However detrimental it is, defamation—slander and/or libel—is a part of human life. Violent conflicts, whether they are interpersonal or intergroup, almost always begin with verbal aggression. Distorted information about outsiders fuels the out-group bias of in-group members. When *their* actions correspond to *our* perception, tension intensifies. Misconception can disappear and mutual understanding deepen when opposing parties begin a conversation (e.g., Acts 21:37-40). When discursive rhetoric and hostile speeches turn to friendly remarks, it is a gesture toward peace.[1]

Surrounded by constant accusations and slander within and without, Paul finally replies to the Jewish people, his ultimate interlocutor in Jerusalem. He tries to defend himself by presenting his apology—ἀπολογία (Acts 22:1)—in the hope that the Jewish crowd will change their attitude toward him. His speech (Acts 22:1-21) is significant not only because it takes the central place in "Paul in Jerusalem"—section 4 of Paul's roller-coaster ride (see figure 1.1)—but also because this is Paul's first formal speech in Jerusalem. Paul has visited Jerusalem several times (e.g., Acts 8:1; 15:2-5) and has spoken there before (Acts 9:28), but it was not the character Paul but the narrator who spoke. Paul also remained silent until he reached the steps of Antonia Fortress. Finally, he opens his mouth and reveals why he came to Jerusalem. He defends in his speech his Jewish identity and the Jewishness of his mission.[2] In this sense, Paul's request to the tribune, "May I say something to *you*?" can be rephrased as "May I say something to *my people*?"

Paul's effort to establish in-group membership, however, faces a formidable difficulty. The crowd does not see him as an insider. They identify him as a deviant and, thus, an outsider. What does he do in this situation? How can he maintain his identity as a Jew while asserting the new identity given in Christ? This chapter endeavors to capture Paul's effort to reconcile his dual identity before the Jewish crowd in Jerusalem. I contend that Paul attempts to reduce intergroup bias by articulating common in-group identity and (re)categorizing the Way within the Jewish faith. To demonstrate my

---

[1] For example, see former U.S. president Donald Trump's change in rhetoric toward Kim Jong Un from mocking him as "Little Rocket Man" to calling him "very honorable." Zachary Cohen and Kevin Liptak, "Trump praises Kim Jong Un as honorable, refuses to explain why," *CNN*, April 25, 2018, https://www.cnn.com/2018/04/24/politics/trump-kim-jong-un-honorable/index.html.

[2] Robert C. Tannehill, "The Story of Israel within the Lukan Narrative," in *Jesus and the Heritage of Israel: Luke's Narrative Claim upon Israel's Legacy*, Luke the Interpreter of Israel 1, ed. David P. Moessner (Harrisburg, PA: Trinity Press International, 1999), 337.

argument, this chapter first sketches the structure, rhetorical features, and functions of the given pericope. Second, drawing from insights of Jenkins's internal-external dialectic of individual identification, the study investigates Paul's strategy of mitigating the discrepancy between his self-image and his public image and negotiating the in-group boundaries. Lastly, employing the common in-group identity model, the chapter delineates how Paul's speech attempts to reduce intergroup bias.

4.1. Paul's Speech in Jerusalem: A Literary Analysis

4.1.1. Structure

At the start of Acts 22, Paul is standing on the steps of Antonia Fortress and looking at the Jewish crowd, his fellow countrymen. He opens his speech by calling them "brothers and fathers" and inviting them to "listen," just as Stephen did (v. 1; Acts 7:2; see also Acts 2:22; 15:13). After his introductory remark (v. 1) and the narrator's comment about the crowd becoming silent (v. 2), Paul makes his defense (vv. 3-21). In this speech, Paul describes his Jewish background (v. 3), his past as a persecutor of the Way (vv. 4-5), his first encounter with the risen Lord (vv. 6-11), his meeting with Ananias and hearing of his call (vv. 12-15), and his second encounter with the risen Lord (vv. 17-21). The events in Paul's speech occur in four distinct places—(A) in Jerusalem (vv. 1-5); (B) on the way to Damascus (vv. 6-11); (C) in Damascus (vv. 12-15); and (D) in the Jerusalem temple (vv. 17-21)—and the speech can be divided into four sections accordingly.[3]

Jerusalem (A and D) is Paul's place of origin, where he grew up and was sent from (v. 5; v. 21), but the central place is the *Way* (B and C) where he encounters Jesus and begins following him (vv. 6-10, 14-15). As scholars repeatedly note regarding the chiastic structure of the main body of the speech (vv. 3-21), the center of Paul's speech is Ananias' description of Paul's mission (vv. 14-15).[4] Like a sandwich, the two theophanies (B and D) also place C, particularly Paul's call, at the center of his speech:

---

[3] For example, see Marion L. Soards, *The Speeches in Acts: Their Content, Context, and Concerns* (Louisville: Westminster John Knox, 1994), 111–12; Fitzmyer, *Acts of the Apostles*, 703; Holladay, *Acts*, 419.

[4] The following chiastic pattern is Charles H. Talbert's adaptation of John Bligh's proposal in *Galatians: A Discussion of St. Paul's Epistle* (London: St. Paul's Publications, 1969), 97; Charles H. Talbert, *Reading Acts: A Literary and Theological Commentary*, RNTS (Macon: Smyth & Helwys, 2005), 191. ©Smyth & Helwys. Used with permission.

 A—Paul comes from the Gentile world to Jerusalem (v. 3)
  B—Paul persecuted the Way (vv. 4-5a)
   C—Paul's journey from Jerusalem to Damascus (v. 5b)
    D—Paul's vision on the road to Damascus (vv. 6-11)
     E—Ananias restores Paul's sight (vv. 12-13)
      F—Ananias tells Paul of his mission (vv. 14-15)
     E`—Ananias urges Paul to receive baptism (v. 16)
    D`—Paul's vision in Jerusalem (vv. 17-18a)
   C`—Paul is commanded to leave Jerusalem (v. 18b)
  B`—Paul speaks of his days as a persecutor (vv. 19-20)
 A`—Paul is sent from Jerusalem to the Gentiles (v. 21)

vv. 14-15: "The God of our ancestors has chosen you to know his will, to see the Righteous One and to hear his own voice; for you will be his witness to all the world of what you have seen and heard."

The former persecutor of the Way is called by the God of Israel to the Way in order to become a witness to both Jews and Gentiles (v. 21; Acts 1:8). The Way—ὁδός—is a space where people's lives are changed through their encounter with Jesus (e.g., Lk 17:11-19; 18:35-43; 24:13-35). Paul's calling of his in-group "the Way" (v. 4) in this sense is not only self-indicative but also self-reflective.[5] Carl R. Holladay aptly captures the multiple meanings of "the Way" found in Luke-Acts:

What is remarkable about Luke's usage, which may reflect a much earlier form of Christian self-description, is its metaphorical open-endedness. Depending on the context, it may have a moral connotation, such as the way of righteousness; or it may have a spatial or even temporal connotation, roughly equivalent to "the movement." If the latter, it would be an idea, a vision, sparked by a profound initiating experience, that takes off, moves through time and space, offering people the opportunity to join and even to be transformed by it.[6]

4.1.2. Rhetorical Features

Paul's speech is an ἀπολογία, a term often used in Greco-Roman literature as well as in Hellenistic Jewish literature to refer to a "defense speech" (Plato, *Apol.* 28A; *Phaedr.* 267A; Wis 6:10; Josephus, *Apion* 2.147).[7] The repeated use of the term (Acts 24:10; 25:8; 25:16; 26:1-2, 24) reveals the apologetic purpose of Paul's speeches after his arrest.[8] According to Quintilian and Cicero, Greek forensic speeches are comprised of the following elements:[9] (1) *exordium*, the introduction of a speech (Quintilian, *Orat. Educ.* 4.1); (2) *narratio*, the narrative account of events (Quintilian, *Orat. Educ.* 4.2; Cicero, *Orat.* 1.19.27); (3) *probatio*, the statement of charges or confirmation (Quintilian, *Orat. Educ.* 4.4–5; Cicero, *Orat.* 1.23.34); (4) *refutatio*, answers to charges (Quintilian, *Orat.*

---

[5] Other places where Acts uses the Way (ὁδός) similarly are Acts 9:2; 18:25, 26; 19:9, 23.
[6] Holladay, *Acts*, 194. Paul Trebilco argues that "ἡ ὁδός, 'the Way,' was used as a self-designation in early Jewish Christianity in Palestine. It was used primarily because of Isa 40:3 ... Its use involved the claim that 'the way,' prepared by John, had been undertaken and completed by Jesus. The early Christians were now traveling on that way and their movement could be so designated." Trebilco, *Self-Designation and Group Identity*, 270.
[7] Johnson, *The Acts of the Apostles*, 387.
[8] Holladay, *Acts*, 420. The verbal form, ἀπολογέομαι, is used in Acts 24:10; 25:8; 26:1-2, 24, whereas the noun form, ἀπολογία, is used in Acts 22:1 and 25:16. See also Lk 12:11; 21:14; Acts 19:33.
[9] Troy W. Martin, "Investigating the Pauline Letter Body: Issues, Methods, and Approaches," in *Paul and the Ancient Letter Form*, PS 6, ed. Stanley E. Porter and Sean A. Adams (Leiden: Brill, 2010), 200–1: "Even the ancient rhetorical handbooks disagree about both the number and the names of these parts of speech. Cicero's *De inventione rhetorica* (1.14.19) and the *Rhetorica ad Herennium* (1.3.4) opt for six, Quintilian's *Institutio oratoria* (3.9.1) for five, and Cicero's later works and Aristotle's *Ars rhetorica* (3.13.4) for four or preferably, according to Aristotle (3.13.1), even two. In addition, each rhetorical species requires a different arrangement for a speech."

Educ. 5.13; Cicero, *Orat.* 1.41.77); and (5) *peroratio*, conclusion (Cicero, *Orat.* 1.52.98).[10] Not every element is found in Paul's defense speeches, and the *peroratio* is always missing because of interruptions by his audience (Acts 22:1-21; 24:10-21; 26:2-18).[11]

Paul's first ἀπολογία, his speech in Jerusalem, has two parts. In the *exordium* (v. 1), Paul addresses "the kind and aim of the speech" to which his audience is going to lend their ears (Quintilian, *Orat. Educ.* 4.1.5; Aristotle, *Rhet.* 3.14), and in the *narratio* (vv. 3-21), he then delivers his version of the events.[12] His initial appeal to his Jewish roots, education, and loyalty to the law functions not only as a *captatio benevolentiae*[13] but also as a defense against the charges brought against him.[14] Yet, what is striking is that rather than addressing anti-Jewish charges against him, in particular the defiling of the temple (Acts 21:28), he recounts his encounter with the risen Lord and its aftermath, which have been described earlier and will be repeated later in the narrative (Acts 9:1-30; 26:2-23). Moreover, before he is able to develop his speech further, it ends abruptly (v. 22). Why so? Has the implied author, the ultimate speaker of Luke-Acts, forgotten where he was, as we often do when speaking? In order to put Paul's first defense in perspective, it is necessary to take into account the functions of Acts 22:1-21.

4.1.3. Functions of Paul's Speech in Jerusalem

(1) *Introducing the Trial Narrative.* Speeches in Acts, like those in Greco-Roman historiography, are assumed to be the author's "handiwork."[15] They, first, convey the author's "own point of view" on the events that occurred (e.g., Thucydides, *Hist.* 3.10.52-60; Josephus, *War* 2.345-401; 3.361-91; 7.320-36, 341-88).[16] What is at stake for Paul's immediate audience is the bringing of a Gentile to the temple (Acts 21:28b). For the implied author, the issue is what God's new action in Jesus entails in God's plan for salvation (vv. 14-16).[17] Second, they "often precipitate or cause the action"[18] and switch the direction of (hi)story (e.g., Josephus, *War* 3.472-84). The violence that follows leaves Paul's speech incomplete (vv. 22-24), but it completely prepares him for upcoming trials by revealing his Roman citizenship. Now, he will no longer be in an open courtyard but in closed courtrooms, where he is constantly being tried (Acts 21:30-31a; 22:22-23, 22:30-23:10, 12-15; 24:1-23; 25:6-12; 26:1-32). He will defend the

---

[10] Johnson, *The Acts of the Apostles*, 392-3.
[11] According to Greg H. R. Horsley, the following verses in Acts interrupt speeches: Acts 2:40; 4:1-3; 7:54; 10:44; 13:42; 17:32; 20:36; 22:22; 24:22; 26:24. Kathy R. Maxwell, "The Role of the Audience in Ancient Narrative: Acts as a Case Study," *ResQ* 48, no. 3 (2006): 176.
[12] Witherington, *The Acts of the Apostles*, 668; Craig S. Keener, *The IVP Bible Background Commentary: New Testament* (Downers Grove, IL: InterVarsity Press, 1993), 390. For different views, see George A. Kennedy, *New Testament Interpretation through Rhetorical Criticism*, Studies in Religion (Chapel Hill: University of North Carolina Press, 1984), 134; William R. Long, "The *Paulusbild* in the Trial of Paul in Acts," *SBLSP* (1983): 98.
[13] For *Captatio benevolentiae*, see *BNP* 2.1079.
[14] Acts 21:28a: "Teaching against ... our people, our law."
[15] Johnson, *The Gospel of Luke*, 13.
[16] Holladay, *Acts*, 42.
[17] Dennis Hamm, "Paul's Blindness and Its Healing, Clues to Symbolic Intent (Acts 9, 22 and 26)," *Bib* 71 (1990): 63-72.
[18] Witherington, *The Acts of the Apostles*, 665.

gospel before rulers, authorities, kings, and governors (see also Lk 12:11-12; 21:12-19). He will ultimately travel to Rome and put the gospel under trial not before the emperor but before the Jews in Rome (Acts 23:11; 25:11-12, 21; 26:32; 27:24; 28:14, 16, 19, 23-25a). Therefore, Paul's speech along with the events around it in Acts 21:27–22:29 function as "a programmatic introduction to the trial narrative that follows."[19]

(2) *Disclosing the Blindness of the Jews.* The retelling of Paul's Damascus experience cannot go unnoticed (vv. 6-16; see also Acts 9:1-30; 26:2-23).[20] Scholars have examined Paul's experience from various points of view—soteriological, christological, missiological, doxological, and psychological[21]—and have addressed numerous differences as well as similarities between the three accounts.[22] Paul surely establishes himself to be a Jew, just as his audience is. His recounting, however, brings himself close to his audience and at the same time distant from them.

Paul's account of his Damascus experience (22:6-17a) places his experience of blindness at the center:

Table 4.1 The Chiastic Structure of Acts 22:6-17a

A. Paul is en route to Damascus (v. 6a)
   B. The risen Jesus encounters him and speaks of his call (vv. 7-10)
      C. Paul is blind (v. 11)
   B` Ananias encounters Paul, restores his sight, and speaks of his call (vv. 12-16)
A`. Paul is en route to Jerusalem (v. 17a)

Paul's blindness carries symbolic significance with regard to the characterization of Paul and his Jewish audience. (1) His zeal for God and the law caused him to persecute the Way (vv. 3-5). (2) It is not just his eyes but also his mind that are blinded to the risen Lord (vv. 6-11). (3) The opening of his eyes and his receiving a call lead him to a radical change, from being a persecutor to a "proclaimer" (vv. 12-16).[23] Now, the former

---

[19] Dean P. Béchard, "The Disputed Case Against Paul: A Redaction-Critical Analysis of Acts 21:27–22:29," *CBQ* 65 (2003): 250.

[20] Ronald D. Witherup points out five functions of repeating Paul's conversion/call in Acts: (1) emphasizing that God's will is accomplished in unexpected ways; (2) demonstrating the development of the character of Paul from a persecutor to a proclaimer of faith; (3) explaining the advancement of the plot of Acts presented in Acts 1:8; (4) manifesting the implied author's ideological viewpoint, which is the willingness to suffer for the sake of the name of Jesus; (5) illuminating that Christ is the guiding light in the movement from the Jews to the Gentiles. Ronald D. Witherup, "Functional Redundancy in the Acts of the Apostles: A Case Study," *JSNT* 48 (1992): 85.

[21] A brief history of the interpretation of Paul's Damascus experience in church history is found in Bruce Corley, "Interpreting Paul's Conversion—Then and Now," in *The Road from Damascus: The Impact of Paul's Conversion on His Life, Thought, and Ministry,* ed. Richard N. Longenecker (Grand Rapids: Eerdmans, 1997), 1–17. For a psychological approach to Paul's experience, see John J. Pilch, *Visions and Healing in the Acts of the Apostles: How the Early Believers Experienced God* (Collegeville: Liturgical Press, 2004).

[22] An extensive comparison between the three accounts of Paul's conversion/call in Acts as well as between Luke's version of Paul's conversion/call and Paul's own account is found in Holladay, *Acts*, 203–22.

[23] Witherup, "Functional Redundancy in the Acts of the Apostles," 75. Witherup argues that Paul's Damascus experience is repeatedly presented "to round out the characterization of Paul in his transformation from persecutor to *proclaimer* and persecuted," emphasis added.

persecutor, who was blind but now sees, speaks to the Jews who persecute him. His speech, in this sense, delivers one of the central messages of Luke-Acts, which is that *the Jews are blind* (Lk 4:18; 6:39; 7:21, 22; 14:13, 21; 18:35; 19:42; 22:64; 24:16, 31; Acts 9:8, 18; 26:18; 28:27).[24] The Jews are not correctly perceiving God's will.[25] By revealing his past and the change that occurred in a first-person speech (see also Acts 9:1-30), Paul discloses the blindness of his Jewish audience and invites them to experience the transformation that he underwent.[26]

(3) *Developing the Jewishness of His Message.* A heated debate among scholars centers around how to understand Paul's Damascus experience within Judaism. Is Paul's experience a call or a conversion? The traditional interpretation, led by Augustine and Luther, understands it as a "conversion" of a wretched sinner and his decisive break from Judaism—the religion of works—to Christianity—the religion of grace.[27] Since the publication of Krister Stendahl's pioneering essay *Paul among Jews and Gentiles*, however, a number of scholars began naming Paul's experience "a call," a movement within Judaism.[28]

This study calls it "a conversion/call"[29] because, first, Paul describes the event in the pattern of Old Testament prophets.[30] It is "the God of our ancestors" who has chosen him (v. 14; see also Gen 15:1-6; Exod 3:4-15; Judg 6:11-18; 13:8-20). Jesus not only appears on the road to Damascus but also in the Jerusalem temple to *call* Paul, as God did to Isaiah (vv. 6-8, 17, 18, 21; Isa 6:9). Second, Paul's subsequent radical change in his actions stresses the Jewish aspect of the Way. He immediately proclaims in the synagogue that Jesus is the Son of God, the Jewish Messiah (Acts 9:20, 22). Paul becomes one who is persecuted, no longer a persecutor, for the Jewish hope of resurrection (Acts 23:6; 24:14, 21; Dan 12:2-3; 2 Macc 7:14, 20) and for the need to *turn* to Jesus, as he himself did on the road (Acts 9:23-25; 26:27-29). In short, Paul never abandons but builds up his claims of his Jewish heritage. Paul's speech conveys this double-edged experience—a conversion/call—to his Jewish audience.

---

[24] For a thematic study of blindness as a literary motif in the New Testament, Old Testament, and Greco-Roman literature, see Nils Aksel Røsæg, "The Blinding of Paul: Observations to a Theme," *SEÅ* 71 (2006): 159–85.

[25] Chad Hartsock, *Sight and Blindness in Luke-Acts: The Use of Physical Features in Characterization* (Leiden: Brill, 2008), 184–97.

[26] For an analysis of Paul's self-narration of his past and construction of self from his own letters, see Simon Butticaz, "The Construction of Paul's Self in His Writings: Narrative Identity, Social Memory and Metaphorical Truth," *BibInt* 26 (2018): 244–65.

[27] Corley, "Interpreting Paul's Conversion," 5–13.

[28] Krister Stendahl, *Paul among Jews and Gentiles and Other Essays* (Philadelphia: Fortress, 1976), 7–23. See also Pamela Eisenbaum, *Paul Was Not a Christian: The Original Message of a Misunderstood Apostle* (New York: HarperOne, 2009); Alan F. Segal, *Paul the Convert: The Apostolate and Apostasy of Saul the Pharisee* (New Haven: Yale University Press, 1990), 9.

[29] Holladay, *Acts*, 203.

[30] Segal presents the following parallels between Ezekiel's call and Paul's call: (1) seeing the divine glory (Ezek 1:28; Acts 22:11); (2) hearing a voice (Ezek 1:28–2:8; Acts 22:7-10); (3) falling to the ground (Ezek 1:28; Acts 9:4; 22:7); (4) standing on their feet (Ezek 2:1-2; Acts 22:10-11); and (5) commissioning (Ezek 2:3-7; Acts 22:21). Adapted from Dale C. Allison, Jr., "Acts 9:1–9, 22:6–11, 26:12–18: Paul and Ezekiel," *JBL* 135, no. 4 (2016): 810. Originally from Segal, *Paul the Convert*, 8–11. Mallen finds similarities between Isaiah's call and Paul's second encounter with the risen Lord: (1) theophany in the temple (Isa 6:1-13; Acts 22:17-21) and (2) sending the prophet far away (μακράν; Isa 57:19; Acts 22:21). Peter Mallen, *The Reading and Transformation of Isaiah in Luke-Acts*, LNTS 367 (London: T&T Clark, 2008), 110.

4.2. Paul's Internal-External Dialectic of Individual Identification: A Social Anthropological Analysis

By analyzing the literary features of Paul's speech, this section explores social anthropological aspects of Acts 22:1-21. Will Paul's audience see him as who he says he is? This question brings us back to the central quest of this chapter, which is Paul's efforts to reaffirm his in-group identity in the face of hostility. Paul does this in three ways in Acts 22:1-21 by *explicating* his self-image of a devout Jew, *complicating* his public image as a deviant Jew, and *extending* the in-group boundaries. In order to reconcile the contested images of himself, he introduces his encounter with the risen Lord in a thoroughly Jewish fashion to his audience. Jenkins's theory of the internal-external dialectic of individual identification sheds fresh light on Paul's presentation of self because, as Brittany E. Wilson stresses, Paul is "someone who exercises his ocular agency, but who is also at the mercy of the hostile gaze."[31]

4.2.1. Presentation of Paul's Self-Image: A Devout Jew

Paul's speech follows the rules not only of Hellenistic defense speech but also of everyday human interaction. He tries his best to give a good impression of himself.[32] He saw what happened to Stephen, who broke rule number one of public speaking and was stoned to death—as a result, Paul will never insult his audience. In response to the anti-Jewish slander against him, Paul articulates the Jewish aspects of his life and portrays his self-image as a devout Jew in any way possible.

Paul first identifies himself with his Jewish audience. They are not his opponents but his "brothers and fathers" (v. 1). The defense he makes focuses on his in-group membership (v. 1). The narrator's comment reaffirms his choice of speaking in Hebrew, probably Aramaic, and reinforces his affinity with his own countrymen (v. 2; Acts 21:40). Second, Paul puts forward the thesis statement of his speech: "Ἐγώ εἰμι ἀνὴρ Ἰουδαῖος" (v. 3).[33] This is his self-image, which he will passionately defend. Third, he soon describes his dual identity. He is a diaspora Jew, "born in Tarsus," and at the same time a Jerusalem Jew, "brought up"—ἀνατρέφω— in Jerusalem (v. 3).[34] This brief statement underscores his in-group membership not only with the Asian Jews—diaspora Jews—who were accusing him vehemently but also with the Jerusalem Jews who joined them. The ultimate self-image he attempts to draw, however, is not of a

---

[31] Brittany E. Wilson, "Sight and Spectacle: 'Seeing' Paul in the Book of Acts," in *Characters and Characterization in Luke-Acts*, ed. Frank E. Dicken and Julia A. Snyder (New York: Bloomsbury T&T Clark, 2016), 152.

[32] Erving Goffman, *The Presentation of Self in Everyday Life*, SSRCM 2 (Edinburgh: University of Edinburgh, 1956), 56.

[33] Daniel Marguerat, *La première histoire du christianisme: Les Actes des apôtres*, LD 180 (Paris: Cerf, 1999), 297.

[34] The mention of Paul's sister's son indicates that "he still had family in Jerusalem." Witherington, *The Acts of the Apostles*, 669.

Tarsian citizen but of an orthodox Jew.³⁵ Thus, fourth, he quickly narrates his Jewish education: "at the feet of Gamaliel, educated strictly according to our ancestral law" (v. 3). It is debatable whether ἀνατρέφω refers to his early childhood education or to more advanced education (e.g., Lk 4:16).³⁶ Yet, his statement clearly references his Pharisaic training, which he describes as "according to the exactness [ἀκρίβειαν] of the law of our fathers" (v. 3, author's translation). The narrator introduced Gamaliel earlier in the narrative as "a teacher of the law, respected by all the people" (Acts 5:34), whose recommendations "the elders of Israel" listen to and set the apostles free accordingly (Acts 5:21, 39). This "level-headed Pharisee" is Paul's teacher as well as a member of the Sanhedrin.³⁷ Fifth, Paul concludes his description of his early Jewish life as "being zealous for God just as all of you are today" (v. 3). The consecutive use of participles (v. 3: γεγεννημένος; ἀνατεθραμμένος; πεπαιδευμένος; ὑπάρχων) not only creates "a pleasant, flowing style" but also brings Paul's last description of himself to the center of his self-image.³⁸ He is a zealot—ζηλωτὴς—whose life is committed to defending what is good for the Jewish nation (Josephus, *War* 4.161; 7.268–70).³⁹ His zeal is not in the form of outright anti-Roman resistance but in the strict observance of the law (Acts 26:5; see also 1 Macc 2:20, 24, 26; Josephus, *Ant.* 12. 271).⁴⁰ All of these descriptions of himself

---

35 Surprisingly, neither the character Paul nor the narrator mentions Paul's birthplace, Tarsus, from this point onward. Paul only speaks of his Jewish origin and his fidelity to the Jewish faith. He also never mentions Tarsus in his letters. Fairchild states that "the most logical explanation for this is either that Paul did not consider Tarsus to be his true home town, or that he was not proud of it." Mark R. Fairchild, "Paul's Pre-Christian Zealot Associations: A Re-examination of Gal. 1.14 and Acts 22.3," *NTS* 45 (1999): 515. He continues, "In passages where Paul strongly affirms his Jewish affinities, yet ignores his Diaspora roots (Rom 11:1; 2 Cor 11:22; Gal 1:11–14; Phil 3:5–6), one may detect Paul's embarrassment that his days in Tarsus could be seen as a detriment to his exemplary Jewish credentials" (516).

36 Willem C. van Unnik argues that ἀνατροφή in Acts 22:3 confirms that Paul was brought to Jerusalem early in his childhood and spent most of his youth there. In contrast, Andrie B. du Toit demonstrates through a linguistic, rhetorical, and narratological investigation that Paul came to Jerusalem later, likely in his adolescent years. Willem C. van Unnik, *Tarsus or Jerusalem: The City of Paul's Youth*, trans. George Ogg (London: Epworth, 1962); Andrie B. du Toit, "A Tale of Two Cities: 'Tarsus or Jerusalem' Revisited," *NTS* 46 (2000): 375–402. Τρέφω in Lk 4:16 denotes Jesus's whole life up until his adulthood.

37 Holladay, *Acts*, 421. Luke T. Johnson also points out that "in Luke-Acts the phrase 'at the feet' always symbolizes submission (Luke 7:38; 8:35, 41; 10:39; 17:16; 20:43; Acts 2:35; 4:35, 37; 5:2, 10; 7:58; 10:25)." Johnson, *The Acts of the Apostles*, 388.

38 Du Toit, "A Tale of Two Cities," 384. See also Nigel Turner, *A Grammar of New Testament Greek*, vol. 3 (Edinburgh: T&T Clark, 1963), 158.

39 Mark R. Fairchild writes that Zealot ideology—"Fourth Philosophy" according to Josephus—"transcended sectarian boundaries to the degree that the evidence indicates that Essenes, Pharisees and the unaffiliated masses were attracted to it. This tradition occasionally expressed itself in violent outbursts such as were witnessed during the Maccabean uprising, the days surrounding Herod's ascent to power, Paul's persecution of the Christians and the war with the Romans." Fairchild, "Paul's Pre-Christian Zealot Associations," 526.

40 The term ζηλωτὴς is a noun, not an adjective, even though commentators and interpreters translate it almost always as "zealous." It is not only Paul in Acts but also Paul in Galatians who calls himself "a Zealot" (Gal 1:14). Mark R. Fairchild argues that "the Zealot movement was a powerful influence upon [Paul's] formative Jewish life and theology." Fairchild, "Paul's Pre-Christian Zealot Associations," 514. See also N. T. Wright, *Paul and the Faithfulness of God*, COQG 4 (Minneapolis: Fortress, 2013), esp. 1.80–90. See also "Zealots" in *ABD* 6.1043–54. For opposing views that criticize Paul's direct involvement with the Zealot movement, see Tom Holland, "N. T. Wright and the Identity of Saul of Tarsus," *CTR* 12, no. 2 (2015): 99–118, and Steve Mason, "N. T. Wright on Paul the Pharisee and Ancient Jews in Exile," *SJT* 69, no. 4 (2016): 432–52.

ultimately confirm Paul's in-group membership—καθὼς πάντες ὑμεῖς ἐστε σήμερον (v. 3).[41] He does not stop there. Sixth, he describes his past life as an ardent persecutor of the Way: "I persecuted this Way up to the point of death" (v. 4). This statement discloses not only the past but also the present. His Jewish audience is replicating his past actions against the Way.[42] They are trying to kill him, just as he bound, imprisoned, and approved the killing of Christians (v. 4; Acts 8:1, 3; 21:30, 31, 36).[43] Seventh, he articulates the public nature of his actions: "As the high priest and the whole council of elders can testify about me" (v. 5). This is not a private action taking place backstage but a frontstage, very public performance.[44] Lastly, Paul unveils the activity that his audience has not themselves done: "I also received letters to the brothers in Damascus, and I went there" (v. 5). His attackers found him in Jerusalem, but he had been actively pursuing Christians outside Jerusalem to bring them back for punishment (v. 5).

Paul's self-image is clear. He is a Jew who is zealous for the Jewish faith, just as his audience is and even more so. By conveying his self-image as a devout Jew, Paul seeks to be, and to be seen as, an orthodox Jew, to successfully assume a Jewish identity.[45] This is what Richard Jenkins calls *the internal moment* in which "individuals present an image of themselves—of self—for acceptance by others."[46]

4.2.2. (Re)presentation of Paul's Damascus Experience: Adding Nuances to Paul's Public Image

One's identity, however, is not equivalent to one's self-image. It is, rather, an outcome of negotiation between one's self-image and one's public image. The internal moment is followed by *the external moment* in which one's audience decides whether to accept one's presentation or not.[47] Paul has presented an image of his self (vv. 1-5). The Jewish reaction is absent at this point. Paul continues talking. Yet, since the previous external moment—the crowd's response to the charges against Paul at the temple precincts—

---

[41] Paul's Gentile mission is also a manifestation of his in-group membership. Lappenga says, "In Paul's speech it is Paul's ζῆλος that initiates a strong affinity with his audience (22:3), and it is upon this foundation that Paul details his call to be a witness to the nations (22:6-21). In Luke's narrative, then, the use of the motif of ζῆλος helps to indicate that Paul's conversion was not apostasy but an act of obedience to God." Benjamin J. Lappenga, *Paul's Language of Ζῆλος: Monosemy and the Rhetoric of Identity and Practice*, BIS 137 (Leiden: Brill, 2016), 111.

[42] James A. Kelhoffer, "The Gradual Disclosure of Paul's Violence against Christians in the Acts of the Apostles as an Apology for the Standing of the Lukan Paul," *BR* 54 (2009): 34.

[43] James A. Kelhoffer insists that three descriptions of Paul's violence against the Way—(1) Acts 8:3; 9:1-2; (2) Acts 22:4; (3) Acts 26:9-11—gradually disclose Paul's intention to kill Christians. He states that "the gradual disclosure of Paul's violence is consistent with an agenda of defending the Pauline legacy... as one who suffered for Christ, not as one who had caused suffering for Christ's followers." Kelhoffer, "The Gradual Disclosure of Paul's Violence against Christians," 26. Despite his motivation to punish and kill Christians, the Acts narrative avoids describing Paul's direct engagement in stoning Stephen (Acts 8:1; 10).

[44] Goffman, *The Presentation of Self in Everyday Life*, 69.

[45] Jenkins, *Social Identity*, 42: "An important assumption made by Goffman ... is that individuals consciously pursue goals and interests. They seek to 'be'—and to be 'seen to be'—'something' or 'somebody,' to successfully assume particular identities."

[46] Jenkins, *Social Identity*, 93.

[47] Jenkins, *Social Identity*, 93.

was violent (Acts 21:30-32, 35-36), he tries to change his public image as a deviant Jew to that of an orthodox Jew in his (re)presentation of his Damascus experience (vv. 6-16; Acts 9:1-30). The following observations reveal the ways in which his effort is manifested.

First, his encounter with the risen Lord on the Damascus road echoes Jewish scriptures. (1) *"The people who walked in darkness have seen a great light; those who lived in a land of deep darkness—on them light has shined"* (Isa 9:2). Paul's act of persecution and subsequent loss of sight exemplifies his past status. He was walking and living in darkness. He was in need of light. (2) *"But for your holy ones there was very great light. Their enemies heard their voices but did not see their forms"* (Wis 18:1). The light that shone upon him is "a *great* light from heaven," not just "a light" (vv. 6, 11; Acts 9:3).[48] This light from/of Jesus is all Paul saw, not his face nor his form.[49] But, he heard a voice (v. 7).[50] (3) *The call of Moses* (Exod 3:1-12). In addition to the calls of Ezekiel[51] and Isaiah, parallels between Paul's call and that of Moses, the archetype of Israel's prophets, are noteworthy. They both see a light (v. 6; Exod 3:2-3). They are called twice (v. 7; Exod 3:4). The conversation that follows reveals the identity of the Holy One (v. 8; Exod 3:6, 15). The question of the one who encounters the Lord leads to his commission (v. 10; Exod 3:10, 12).

Second, Jesus's Jewish roots are articulated. (1) Paul adds Jesus's origin: "I am Jesus *the Nazarene*" (v. 8). The Lukan addition previously absent in the first account of Paul's conversion/call emphasizes the Jewishness of the Way (see Acts 9:5).[52] The Lukan material (L)—the infancy narrative and the resurrection narrative—repeatedly identified Nazareth as Jesus' hometown (Lk 1:26; 2:4, 39, 51; 24:19). The (re)location of the rejection of Jesus at Nazareth at the beginning of Luke's Gospel also reinforced this point (Lk 4:16-30; Mk 6:1-5; Mt 13:54-58). The Acts narrative also reminds its audience of Jesus's place of origin by continually calling him "Jesus of Nazareth" (Acts 2:22; 3:6; 4:10; 6:14; 10:38; 22:8; 26:9). (2) Paul publicly identifies Jesus with the God of Israel before the hostile Jewish crowd: "Who are you, *Lord*?" . . . "I am Jesus of Nazareth whom you are persecuting" (v. 8). Earlier in Acts, Jesus is not called "the Lord" in front of an unfriendly Jewish audience except by Stephen (Acts 7:59, 60).[53] His prayer in the

---

[48] Roy A. Harrisville, "Acts 22:6-21," *Int* 42 (1988): 183.
[49] Luke's account of Paul's Damascus experience is different from Paul's own recounting of the same event: "Have I not seen Jesus our Lord?" (1 Cor 9:1); "He [Christ] appeared—ὤφθη [literally, "was seen"]—also to me (1 Cor 15:8)." Røsæg, "The Blinding of Paul," 159.
[50] In the first story of Paul's conversion/call, Paul's companions hear the voice but see no one (Acts 9:7). In contrast, in the second story, they hear no voice but see light (Acts 22:9). The third story does not reconcile this contradicting information but omits it (Acts 26:2-32).
[51] Allison Jr., "Acts 9:1-9, 22:6-11, 26:12-18: Paul and Ezekiel," 807-26.
[52] Witherington, *The Acts of the Apostles*, 671.
[53] "Lord" appears twenty-four times in Acts 1 through 7, chapters in which the disciples are carrying out an active ministry to Jews in Jerusalem. The ministry in Jerusalem is then put on a temporary hold until Acts 22. In Acts 1 through 7, Jesus is called Lord fourteen times in speeches—(1) among the disciples (four times: Acts 1:6, 21, 24; 5:9), (2) to Jewish soon-to-be believers (six times: Acts 2:20, 21, 25, 34, 36, 39), and (3) to a hostile Jewish crowd (two times: Acts 7:59, 60)—as well as in the description of the narrator (two times: Acts 2:47; 4:33). God is called "the Lord" by the narrator (five times: Acts 4:24, 26, 29; 5:14, 19) and by Stephen (three times: Acts 7:31, 33, 49). Yet, when opposition follows, the narrative avoids using Jesus and the Lord interchangeably (two times: Acts 3:20, 22).

middle of the stoning alludes to what is at stake in identifying Jesus in such a way: "*Lord Jesus*, receive my spirit" (Acts 7:59). Now, Paul announces to the Jews in Jerusalem that Jesus is the one in whom they should put their faith. Jews are persecuting their Lord (v. 10: Exod 3:15).[54]

Third, Paul's (re)telling of his meeting with Ananias also strengthens his image as a Jew who adheres to the Jewish faith. Comparison between the first and the second accounts of Paul's conversion/call illustrates this. (1) Ananias is not a disciple, but a devout Jew, "a devout man according to the law" (v. 12; Acts 9:10).[55] He is known not only to Jewish believers but also to all the Jews living in Damascus (v. 12; Acts 9:13-14). He is a respected figure among the Jews there. (2) Paul is identified as a "brother" (v. 13). Ben Witherington aptly captures the nuances ἀδελφός contains in Acts 9:17 and 22:13. He argues that, whereas in the first account in which the implied author speaks to Christian readers "brother" would mean "fellow Christian," in the second account it would mean "fellow Jew."[56] The use of Paul's Hebrew name "Saul" further intensifies the Jewish rendering of ἀδελφός in the context of Acts 22. (3) The divine commissioner changes. Earlier it was "the Lord Jesus" who sent Ananias to cure Paul's blindness and baptize him (Acts 9:10-19). In Acts 22, it is "the God of our ancestors" who sends not only Ananias to Paul but also Paul to "all the world" (vv. 14, 15).[57] The use of the "Mosaic predicate" brings Ananias and Paul closer to the Jewish circle.[58] (4) Jesus is called "the righteous one" (v. 14). Previously used in Jewish contexts of Acts, ὁ δίκαιος is related to the righteous servant who suffers in Jewish scriptures (Acts 3:14; 7:52; Isa 53:11; 1 Enoch 38:2).[59] This christological claim[60] portrays Jesus not only as "morally upright" but also as "an innocent martyr."[61] (5) The mention of Gentiles is omitted. In the first account of Paul's conversion/call, his primary target audience is Gentiles: "to bring my name before *Gentiles* and kings and before the people of Israel" (Acts 9:15). The second account alters it "to all the world" (v. 15; Acts 1:8; 13:47; Isa 18:3), which includes all three categories in one and avoids "offending his hostile audience."[62] (6) Paul's designation takes a prophetic shape. Whereas in the first account he is called to be "an

---

[54] Eric Gans, "Christian Morality and the Pauline Revelation," *Semeia* 33 (1985): 108: "God is he whom one refuses, whom one wishes to extirpate. With Paul, Jesus is converted definitively into Christ; the persecuted man becomes God, or rather already was God."
[55] Johnson, *The Acts of the Apostles*, 389: "It also echoes earlier descriptions of Lukan characters: In the Gospel, Zechariah and Elizabeth (Luke 2:6), Anna (2:37), the centurion with a sick slave (7:5), and Joseph of Arimathea (23:50); in Acts, Tabitha (9:36), and Cornelius (10:2)."
[56] Witherington, *The Acts of the Apostles*, 672.
[57] Still, Paul's use of Κύριος, the name of Israel's deity, in Acts 22:6-21 obscures the identity of the ultimate commissioner of Paul (vv. 8, 10, 14-15, 18, 19, 21). Is it Jesus or God?
[58] Harrisville, "Acts 22:6-21," 183: "The 'Mosaic' predicate (cf. Exod. 3:15-16) appears oftener in Acts than elsewhere in the New Testament (cf. Acts 3:13; 5:30; 7:32; cf. also 13:7)."
[59] Harrisville, "Acts 22:6-21," 183; Johnson, *The Acts of the Apostles*, 68; Witherington, *The Acts of the Apostles*, 672.
[60] For the messianic figure as a righteous one in Enoch, see James A. Waddell, *The Messiah: A Comparative Study of the Enochic Son of Man and the Pauline Kyrios*, JCTS (New York: Bloomsbury T&T Clark, 2011), 69-72.
[61] Holladay, *Acts*, 425.
[62] Witherington, *The Acts of the Apostles*, 672. Earlier in Lk 4:16-30, Jesus's comment on God's visitations to Gentiles alters what is a seemingly favorable or neutral response of his townspeople in Nazareth to a hostile one.

instrument" (Acts 9:15), in the second account he is a "witness"—μάρτυς (v. 15). This new title discloses his prophetic identity. He is the Lord's witness: "You are my witnesses ... and my servant whom I have chosen" (Isa 43:10; see also Isa 43:12; 44:8, 9). The narrative fully develops this Isaianic theme later in Paul's third account of his conversion/call: "to appoint you a servant and a witness" (Acts 26:16).[63] (7) Paul's baptism exemplifies his fidelity to the God of Israel. Earlier, his baptism is one of the many actions that he has taken after regaining his sight (Acts 9:18-19). Now, it is the primary action that follows his prophetic call: "ἀναστὰς βάπτισαι καὶ ἀπόλουσαι τὰς ἁμαρτίας σου" (v. 16).[64] This baptism of repentance is not a break from but a turn to YHWH as it requires praying to YHWH: "calling his name" (e.g., Ps 99:6).[65]

Paul's recounting of his Damascus experience complicates the public image of him held by the Jewish crowd. His experience outside Jerusalem is not what *they* think it is. Members of the Way—Jesus, Paul, and Ananias—are not deviants but orthodox Jews, their in-group members: "just as all of *you* are today" (v. 3).[66] They are all zealous for the law and devoted to the God of Israel. Will Paul's audience accept his version of himself? Will the internal-external dialectic produce a positive outcome for him? His audience remains silent, which hints that his presentation up to this point is well received. The roller-coaster riders find themselves once again going upward as they see Paul's audience is listening to, not interrupting, his speech. The theophany of Jesus in the temple locates the Way at the heart of the Jewish universe. This spectacle is the pinnacle of Paul's speech and also of the roller-coaster ride. Jesus is the Lord. Yet, Paul takes a step further that challenges the Jews and causes the train riders to tremble.

4.2.3. Presentation of Jesus in the Temple: Extending the In-Group Boundary

Having recounted his Damascus experience in a thoroughly Jewish fashion, Paul continues to portray himself as a devout Jew in the remainder of his speech (vv. 17-21). Here, however, Paul endeavors not only to defend but also to extend his Jewish identity. To do so, he first reiterates his Jewish identity. (1) Paul describes himself "praying in the temple" (v. 17).[67] His first encounter with the risen Jesus, his conversion/call, and his new membership in the Way do not go against his fidelity to the Jewish faith (e.g., Acts

---

[63] P. Boyd Mather, "Paul in Acts as 'Servant' and 'Witness,'" *BR* 30 (1985): 24.

[64] The two aorist imperatives in v. 16, βάπτισαι and ἀπόλουσαι, accompanied by two participles, ἀναστὰς and ἐπικαλεσάμενος, on either side, illustrate that the event taking place signifies a radical change of action, a repentance—μετάνοια in Greek and שוב in Hebrew.

[65] Holladay, *Acts*, 425. Jean-François Landolt, "'Be Imitators of me, brothers and sisters' (Philippians 3.17): Paul as an Exemplary Figure in the Pauline Corpus and the Acts of the Apostles," trans. Michael D. Thomas, Eric Gilchrest, and Timothy Brookins, in *Paul and the Heritage of Israel: Paul's Claim upon Israel's Legacy in Luke and Acts in the Light of the Pauline Letters*, LNTS 452, ed. David P. Moessner (London: T&T Clark, 2012), 312: "In 22:16, after the road-to-Damascus event, Paul is baptized; that—we must note—does not prevent him from praying in the Temple (22:17) on his return to Jerusalem, however."

[66] Richard Jenkins accurately notes: "Deviance is very much in the eye of the beholder." Jenkins, *Social Identity*, 97.

[67] Just as Paul does, Peter also falls into a trance, ἔκστασις, during prayer (Acts 10:11; 11:5).

2:46; 3:1; 21:26).⁶⁸ He is a pious Jew who is constantly praying (e.g., Acts 9:11; 13:3; 14:23; 16:13, 16, 25; 20:36; 21:5; 26:29; 27:29; 28;8). (2) He omits his conflict with *the Jews* who caused him to leave Damascus (Acts 9:23-25). His initial encounter with the crowd already put his life in danger. Any negative portrayal of the Jewish people will cause more harm than good to his in-group membership. (3) Jesus's command to leave Jerusalem is based not on the Jewish threat but on their distrust in Paul. In Acts 9:30, the narrator describes that it is *the Jews'* intention to kill Paul that leads to his departure.⁶⁹ In Acts 22:18, it is their rejection: "They will not accept your testimony about me." Paul's past will be a stumbling block for his Jewish audience in accepting his witness because they have been witnesses to Paul as a persecutor of the Way (vv. 19-20). (4) Nonetheless, the Jewish rejection aligns him with Israel's prophets. Paul here uses παραδέχομαι (v. 18), a compound verb of the adverb δεκτός that was earlier used to describe Jesus's prophetic mission and his subsequent rejection (Lk 4:19, 24). Paul will not be accepted, just as Jesus, the prophet, was not accepted.⁷⁰ (5) Paul's commission echoes Isaiah's prophetic call. Both fall into a trance, a visionary experience, in the temple (v. 17; Isa 6:1).⁷¹ They are sent to deliver the word of the Lord (v. 18; Isa 6:8-9). Their words will reach "far away" (v. 21; Isa 6:12). Yet, their messages will not be accepted by their own countrymen (v. 18; Isa 6:9-10). Paul is, as Luke T. Johnson puts it, "a prophet like Isaiah."⁷²

Second, however, Paul's passionate defense of his Jewish roots and experiences are not intended to confirm what constitutes a person's Jewish identity but to conform it to the new rule initiated by the outpouring of the Holy Spirit. God's salvation is extended to Gentiles (e.g., Acts 1:8; 28:28). The Lukan revision of the Isaianic vision illustrates this point. (1) The audience of the prophet's message changes. In Isa 6:9, it is his own countrymen, the people of Judah. In Paul's speech, it is not. Jesus commands: "Go, for I

---

⁶⁸ Johnson, *The Acts of the Apostles*, 390: "Paul's visit to the Temple signifies, as an implicit rebuttal of the charge against him, his long-standing devotion to the ethos of Judaism and in particular to the Temple."
⁶⁹ Based on Paul's letter to Galatians, Edward P. Blair argues that Paul's call to the Gentile mission did not take place during his first visit to Jerusalem after his conversion/call. Paul reports that his message was well received by "the churches of Judea," unlike Acts (Gal 1:22-24; Acts 9:29). The call occurred during his visit to the Jerusalem council after he witnessed to the success of the Gentile mission in Antioch (Gal 2:1-10; Acts 11:27-30; Acts 15:1-29). Edward P. Blair, "Paul's Call to the Gentile Mission," *BR* 10 (1965): 19–33. Although it is tempting to agree, I argue that it is difficult to confirm such a hypothesis. It is more plausible to assume that in Acts 22:17-21 Paul is recounting the first visit that immediately follows his conversion/call. In the same vein, Luke T. Johnson writes that Acts 9:30 and Acts 22:18 "do agree substantially that Paul's message was not accepted in Jerusalem, although Acts 9:29 specifies his opponents as 'Hellenistic' Jews." Johnson, *The Acts of the Apostles*, 390.
⁷⁰ In the Gospel of Luke, Jesus is identified with both Elijah and Moses (e.g., Lk 9:30-33; Acts 3:22). For the prophetic structure of Luke-Acts, see Johnson, *The Gospel of Luke*, 17–21. Another designation that denotes Jesus's role in Luke is "the Messiah of God" (Lk 9:20; 23:35) or "the Lord's Messiah" (Lk 2:26). Carl R. Holladay, *A Critical Introduction to the New Testament: Interpreting the Message and Meaning of Jesus Christ* (Nashville: Abingdon, 2005), 176–8.
⁷¹ Jimmy J. M. Roberts, *First Isaiah: A Commentary*, Hermeneia (Minneapolis: Fortress, 2015), 91–2. See also John N. Oswalt, *The Book of Isaiah: Chapters 1–39*, NICOT (Grand Rapids: Eerdmans, 1986), 177; Donald W. Parry, Jay A. Parry, and Tina M. Peterson, *Understanding Isaiah* (Salt Lake City: Deseret Books, 1998), 64.
⁷² Johnson, *The Gospel of Luke*, 390.

will send you far away to the Gentiles" (v. 21). His speech ends here with an outcry from the crowd (v. 22). Yet, his defense before King Agrippa illustrates what could have been said if he had continued. It is ultimately not his mission but the Messiah's mission "that the Messiah must suffer and that by being the first to rise from the dead, he would proclaim light both to our people and to the Gentiles" (Acts 26:23). (2) The message includes the salvation of Gentiles. Isaiah proclaimed salvation—יֶשַׁע (Isa 12:2, 3; 17:10; 25:9; 33:2, 6; 45:8, 17; 46:13, 49:6, 8; 51:5, 6, 8; 52:7, 10; 56:1, 59:11, 17; 60:18; 61:10, 62:1, 11). The mission of YHWH's servant with whom Paul identifies is found in Isa 49:6: "I will give you as a light to the nations, that my salvation may reach to the end of the earth." The recipients of salvation, however, are not Gentiles but Israelite captives scattered over the face of the earth.[73] This exclusive vision changes in Luke-Acts. Early in the Gospel, Jesus alludes to the inclusion of Gentiles in the people of God in his speech at Nazareth (Lk 4:18-19; 23-27; Isa 61:1-2). It is not Jews but Gentiles who will accept God's visitation. This inclusive vision fully develops later in Acts as the narrator describes the joy that the prophecy of Isaiah brought to Gentile believers (Acts 13:47-48). "A light" is more than a metaphor for salvation, as in Isaiah (Isa 42:6, 49:6).[74] It is a metaphor for the risen Lord who is "a great light" (Acts 9:3; 22:6; 26:13, 18, 23). Jesus is a channel through which God broke the boundary between Jews and Gentiles as corecipients of salvation and life (e.g., Acts 11:18; 15:11). Now, they all can become *the people of God.*

In short, Paul's speech in the city carries out multiple functions with regard to his in-group membership. In a hostile environment, he, first and foremost, defends his Jewish identity as a zealous Jew. Having established his self-image as a devout Jew, he sketches in a Jewish light what seems to be a deviant experience outside Jerusalem. His conversion/call is thoroughly a Jewish experience. This complicated image of himself adds nuances to and challenges his public image as an unorthodox Jew. Finally, by

---

[73] A close look at the Isaiah text demonstrates that Isa 49:6 supports national salvation, not universal salvation. First, Isa 49 specifically concerns the salvation of Israel, not nations: "On a day of salvation I have helped you. I have kept you and given you as a covenant people" (Isa 49:8). Second, in the midst of YHWH's salvation for Israel, the nations cheer rather than participate in it: "Kings shall see and stand up, princes, and they shall prostrate themselves, because of the LORD, who is faithful, the Holy One of Israel, who has chosen you" (Isa 49:7). Third, "the end of the earth"—note the singular form of "end"—is almost always used to indicate a place where Israelite captives are located: "I will say to the north, 'Give them up', and to the south, 'Do not withhold; bring my sons from far away and my daughters from the end of the earth'" (Isa 43:6). Fourth, the nations in Isa 49 are described as though they are humiliated before Israel: "With their faces to the ground they shall bow down to you, and lick the dust of your feet" (Isa 49:23). Second Isaiah says that they will bring captives to Zion (Isa 49:22) and acknowledge that YHWH is the only God who saved Israel (Isa 49:23), but he does not vindicate in any way their salvation. Therefore, it is highly plausible that Isa 49:6 speaks of the salvation of the Israelite captives who are spread out at the end of the earth (Isa 43:6). Joel Kaminsky and Anne Stewart state: "Aside from the puzzling verse 6, chapter 49 overwhelmingly concerns itself with the exilic Israelite community, not the foreign nations. In verse 8, YHWH assigns the servant the task of raising the land and apportioning the desolate inheritances, both of which draw to mind the nation of Israel and the restoration of Zion." Joel Kaminsky and Anne Stewart, "God of All the World: Universalism and Developing Monotheism in Isaiah 40–66," *HTR* 99, no. 2 (2006): 149.

[74] Shalom M. Paul, *Isaiah 40–66: Translation and Commentary*, ECC (Grand Rapids: Eerdmans, 2012), 327.

explaining his call in the temple, he asks his audience to expand the boundary that separates insiders from outsiders. His speech is an invitation for Jews to think critically about Paul's identity and Gentiles' identity in the grand scheme of God's salvation.

4.3. Recategorizing Paul and the Way: A Social Psychological Analysis

This last section revisits Paul's defense in Jerusalem using SIA. Richard Jenkins's theory of the internal-external dialectic of individual identification highlights the processual nature of one's identity. Identity is not simply given. Contested images are presented and re-presented in our interactions with interlocutors. Identity is the outcome of an ongoing negotiation.[75] In order to accomplish his double-edged purpose to affirm his Jewish identity and to attribute Jewishness to Gentiles, Paul (re)categorizes himself and Gentiles in light of his encounters with the risen Lord. He finds common identity markers between his Jewish audience and himself/the Way and places groups in conflict with each other in a superordinate identity, *the people of God*, that includes both. Samuel L. Gaertner's common in-group identity model elucidates the cognitive process behind Paul's presentation of himself.

4.3.1. Recategorization, Not Decategorization, of the People of God

To defend himself, Paul has two options. He can either nullify or ratify his Jewish identity. The ethnic category of being a Jew seems no longer quintessential because God has introduced another way of salvation. Faith in Jesus is necessary for both Jews and Gentiles. Decategorization seems a logical conclusion. Yet, Paul takes a different route. He solidifies not only his Jewish ethnic category but also the Jewishness of his experience. The Way is a *Jewish* religion. He categorizes himself as a Jew and accentuates the Jewish aspects of his life from his upbringing to his conversion/call. The punchline of his speech, however, addresses not Jewish ethnicity per se but a Jewish vision (v. 21; Isa 42:6, 49:6). God will grant salvation to "all people" and make them "a people for his name" (Acts 15:14; 17:30). Gentiles will be also included in *the people of God*. The final remark of his speech—"Go, for I will send you far away to the Gentiles" (v. 21)—is the climax of his speech in Jerusalem.[76]

This statement recategorizes Paul's identity. He is not only an ethnic Jew but also a member of another group, the people of God, a group that God also invites Gentiles to be a part of. This superordinate identity potentially encompasses, but is not limited to, ethnic Jews. Paul does not fully elaborate what is required for membership in this new group in Acts 22:1-21, but the Lukan narrative repeatedly affirms three categories that Jews and Gentiles have in common.

---

[75] Jenkins, *Social Identity*, 93: "Individual identification emerges within the ongoing relationship between self-image and public image."
[76] Dunn, *The Acts of the Apostles*, 292.

The first is a confessional category. A psychological process taking place right after Paul's encounter with the risen Lord is the *recognition* that Jesus is "the Lord" (v. 8) and "the Son of God" (Acts 9:20). This simple but profound revelation along with Jewish rejection of the gospel leads him to realize that God brings salvation to those believing in Jesus regardless of their ethnicity (v. 21; see also Acts 4:12; 13:47; 16:31; 28:28). The ethnic category of being a Jew or an Israelite is no longer the determining factor for acquiring in-group membership in the people of God.[77] Faith is. Anyone who believes in Jesus is an in-group member.[78]

The second category is ritualistic. A ceremonial process that follows Paul's new realization is *baptism* (v. 16). It is the baptism of repentance—μετάνοια—that manifests not the change in one's ethnic identity but the change in one's mind (Lk 3:3). This baptism of Paul does more than forgive his sins, as in John's baptism (v. 16; Lk 3:3, 7-14). It also bestows upon him new membership in the community of faith.[79] Paul's reiteration of his conversion/call before Agrippa alludes to this double function of baptism: "They may receive forgiveness of sins and a place among those who are sanctified by faith in me" (Acts 26:18). The ritual that grants in-group membership in the Messianic community is not circumcision but baptism, as the Acts narrative portrays the baptism of Jews as well as Gentiles as a salvific moment (e.g., Acts 2:38, 41; 8:12, 13, 16, 36, 38; 9:18; 10:37, 47, 48; 13:24; 16:15, 33; 18:8).

The third category is pneumatic. An experiential process that accompanies baptism is *empowerment* by the Holy Spirit (Acts 1:8).[80] (1) The reception of the Holy Spirit is another aspect of the baptismal experience within the Messianic community in Acts. Though Paul does not explicitly describe the outpouring of Holy Spirit in Acts 22, the earlier account alludes to the Spirit's presence in him after baptism: Σαῦλος δὲ μᾶλλον ἐνεδυναμοῦτο—literally, "Saul was all the more *empowered*" (Acts 9:22, author's translation).[81] Peter's speech on the day of Pentecost is programmatic: "*Repent, and be*

---

[77] Luke's Gospel portrays God as primarily the "God of Israel." Israel is, thus, the people of God. For example, Zechariah says, "Blessed be the Lord *God of Israel*, for he has looked favorably on *his people* and redeemed them" (Lk 1:68). See also Lk 1:16; 7:16; 24:19; Acts 4:10; 7:17; 13:17. In particular, Lk 13:29—"Then people will come from east and west, from north and south, and will eat in the kingdom of God"— alludes to "the universality of the kingdom." Evans, *Saint Luke*, 559. A more inclusive vision of the people of God is presented at the end of Luke and fully developed in Acts (e.g., Lk 24:47; Acts 10:45; 11:1, 18; 13:46, 47, 48; 14:27; 15:3, 7, 12, 14, 17, 19, 23; 17:30, 21:19, 25; 22:21; 26:20, 23, 28:28).

[78] Sigurd Grindheim argues that, not unlike Paul in his letters, Luke "saw an antithesis between pursuing righteousness by the law and being accepted by God through faith." Sigurd Grindheim, "Luke, Paul, and the Law," *NovT* 56 (2014): 335–58.

[79] In Luke's Gospel, the primary purpose of baptism is washing away one's sins (Lk 3:3). In Acts, however, it signifies one's joining of the messianic community. Acts 2:41 states: "So those who welcomed his message were baptized, and that day about three thousand persons were *added*" (Acts 2:41).

[80] James F. White includes three elements (italicized) out of the following five chief metaphors of baptismal meaning that he found in the New Testament: (1) *forgiveness of sin*, (2) union with Christ's death and resurrection, (3) *incorporation into the church*, (4) *reception of the Holy Spirit*, and (5) new birth or regeneration. James F. White, *The Sacraments in Protestant Practice and Faith* (Nashville: Abingdon, 1999), 52–72.

[81] Power—δύναμις—is the manifestation of the Holy Spirit in Acts (e.g., Acts 1:8, 6:5, 8, 10; 10:38).

baptized every one of you in the name of Jesus ... and you *will receive* the gift of the Holy Spirit" (Acts 2:38). Sometimes the Spirit falls upon believers before the baptism (Acts 10:44-48). Sometimes the narrator does not describe the receiving of the Spirit at the baptism (e.g., Acts 8:36-39). Yet, it is the presence of the Holy Spirit that separates the baptism of the Way from that of its out-groups (Lk 3:16; Acts 1:5; 8:14-17; 11:16; 18:25; 19:1-7). (2) The Holy Spirit is the source of ministry for the members of the Way. Jesus states at the beginning of his ministry that "the Spirit of the Lord" is what enables him to carry out his mission (Lk 4:18). After his ascension, the Holy Spirit empowers disciples, including Paul, to continue the mission of the Way (e.g., Acts 6:5; 8:39-40; 9:31; 10:19, 38; 13:9). The Holy Spirit is the main actor behind all the drama Acts portrays, as Luke T. Johnson rightly asserts: "Acts can appropriately be called the 'Book of the Holy Spirit.'"[82] Paul's speech in the city is, in this sense, a manifestation of the Holy Spirit, which is the distinct identity marker of the Way (Lk 12:11-12).

Conflict occurs when there is strong intergroup and in-group bias. Jewish prejudice toward Gentiles is direct and overt, unlike contemporary forms of prejudice such as racism, which is often indirect and subtle.[83] Gentiles are impure because of their practices—diet, sexual immorality, eating blood, and idolatry (Acts 10:14, 28; 11:8; 15:20, 29).[84] In the eyes of Jews, they are sinners (e.g., Gal 2:15). This strong out-group hatred is fueled by the in-group bias that Jews are God's chosen (e.g., Lk 2:32; Acts 22:14). Circumcision and observance of the law confirm their election (Acts 7:8; 11:2-3, 15:1, 5; 21:21). In order to reduce intergroup bias, the narrative replaces God's exclusive election of Israel with God's inclusive vision of salvation and circumcision with baptism.[85] Just as Jews ought to believe in Jesus, be baptized, and have their sin washed away, there is no further ritual required for Gentiles to be included in the people of God other than baptism. Then, they will receive the Holy Spirit. Anyone who shares these confessional, ritualistic, and pneumatic categories obtains this new superordinate identity. They are the people of God. The discovery of this common in-group identity and recategorization process changes the Jewish understanding of Gentiles: "*They* are one of *us*!" Gentiles are not "they" but "we." There is clearly a behavioral category of keeping the law that differentiates between Jews and Gentiles, as decided in the Jerusalem Council (Acts 15:19-21, 28-29). Yet, the narrative never brings it to the fore in Paul's missional speeches.[86]

---

[82] Johnson, *The Acts of the Apostles*, 14.
[83] Gaertner et al., "The Common Ingroup Identity Model," 2.
[84] Paul's statement in Gal 2:15 illustrates the Jewish self-image in relation to Gentiles: "We ourselves are Jews by birth and not Gentile sinners."
[85] Dunn, *The Acts of the Apostles*, 296: "As an identity defining ritual in contrast to circumcision it [baptism] was caught up in the tensions of Christian identity.... [I]t was the visible and public character of baptism which gave it the same role and importance within subsequent Christianity that circumcision enjoyed within Judaism at the time of Paul."
[86] Acts 26:20 alludes to the behavioral change that follows after one joins the Way: "[I] ... declared first to those in Damascus, then in Jerusalem and throughout the countryside of Judea, and also to the Gentiles, that they should repent and turn to God and do *deeds consistent with repentance* [ἄξια τῆς μετανοίας ἔργα]." The phrase "works worthy of repentance" does not refer to the four requirements of Gentile converts (Acts 15:20, 29). Rather, it refers to "deeds appropriate to conversion," as in John's preaching (Lk 3:8). Johnson, *The Acts of the Apostles*, 438.

4.3.2. Dual Identity of the People of God

To defend himself, Paul adds another layer to the recategorization process. He maintains the Jewish and Gentile ethnic difference. Ethnic identity neither disappears nor is dissolved into the superordinate identity. The ethnic category is still alive and well, just as SIA notes that a recategorization process is most effective when subgroup salience is maintained, especially "among enduring (i.e. racial and ethnic) groups."[87]

An inclusive vision of God's salvation is laid out: "Go, for I will send you far away to the Gentiles" (v. 21). Paul's proclamation is immediately rejected. The crowd is once again in an uproar, which demonstrates an exclusive understanding of what constitutes God's people: their ethnicity. It is interesting to note, however, that Paul's speech acknowledges a clear ethnic category that separates Jews and Gentiles. The risen Jesus sends Paul to the *Gentiles*, not to make them Jews but to share with them the benefits the God of Israel brought through Jesus (Acts 26:18).[88] The ethnic category is almost impermeable in Luke-Acts, whereas the conceptual category—the people of God—is permeable, except for Timothy in Acts 16:1-4. Gentiles still remain as Gentiles and Jews as Jews after they join the Way. They acquire a new superordinate identity while maintaining their subgroup identity.

Paul's defense before Agrippa (Acts 26:2-29), which provides a more developed version of his speech, also maintains Jewish-Gentile ethnic identities. After narrating his Damascus experience, Paul gives a summary of his ministry (Acts 26:19-23).[89] (1) *Geographic distinction*. His preaching starts in Damascus but immediately follows the roadmap of the gospel introduced in the beginning of Acts (Acts 1:8). He preaches to those in Jerusalem and "throughout the countryside of Judea"[90] and finally "to the Gentiles" (Acts 26:20). Ἔθνος—Gentile—is an ethnic category, but the phrase clearly implies his mission in the Gentile territory reported in chapters 13–14 and 16–20.[91] Moreover, the infinitive phrase, "to repent and to turn to God"—μετανοεῖν καὶ ἐπιστρέφειν ἐπὶ τὸν θεόν (Acts 26:20)—is "standard language describing preaching to Gentiles" in Acts (e.g., Acts 11:18; 17:30; 20:21).[92] (2) *Ethnic distinction*. The summary of his ministry describes not only geographic division but also ethnic division. The first

---

[87] Gaertner et al., "The Common Ingroup Identity Model," 19.
[88] Acts 26:17-18 identifies the benefits that will be bestowed upon the members of the Way: "I will rescue you from your people and from the Gentiles—to whom I am sending you to open their eyes so that they may [1] turn from darkness to light and [2] from the power of Satan to God, so that they may [3] receive forgiveness of sins and [4] a place among those who are sanctified by faith in me."
[89] Paul's temple vision—Acts 22:17-21—is absent in Paul's recounting of his conversion/call before Agrippa in Acts 26.
[90] Besides the grammatical and textual issue pertinent to this phrase—πᾶσάν τε τὴν χώραν τῆς Ἰουδαίας—in which the accusative case coexists with the dative phrase, the report of Paul's ministry in Judea itself is also problematic. After Paul's conversion/call and return to Jerusalem, the narrator reports earlier in Acts 9 his immediate escape to Caesarea and ultimately to Tarsus. Paul surely has contacts with the people from Judea (e.g., Acts 11:25-30; 15:1-4; 21:10-14). Yet, the narrative never describes his mission throughout the countryside of Judea (see also Acts 9:31). Regardless of its historical validity, it is clear that Paul's description of his ministry in Acts 26:19 illustrates the fulfillment of Jesus's promise to his disciples (Acts 1:8). For a grammatical and textual debate on the phrase πᾶσάν τε τὴν χώραν τῆς Ἰουδαίας, see Pervo, *Acts*, 634.
[91] Holladay, *Acts*, 478.
[92] Holladay, *Acts*, 478.

audience of his preaching is the Jews in Damascus, Jerusalem, and Judea (Acts 26:20; 9:20-22, 28-29).[93] The second audience is the Gentiles (Acts 26:20). God's vision of salvation is what Christine Hays termed an "exclusivistic view of Gentile inclusion."[94] This vision does not nullify but instead acknowledges the ethnic distinction. The light should be proclaimed "both to *our people* [the Jews] and to the *Gentiles*" (Acts 26:23). Jews and Gentiles are each the people of God in their own way.

In sum, Paul's defense speech is an attempt to reduce intergroup bias by addressing the common in-group identity he and his audience possibly share. Facing the accusation of being an outsider, he gives up neither his Jewish ethnic identity nor the new identity found in his encounters with the risen Lord. First, he recategorizes himself as a devout Jew by describing his past life and new experiences in a thoroughly Jewish light, just as Luke-Acts articulates Jewishness in any way possible. Second, he recategorizes Gentiles as potential members of the people of God. God has called him to be an apostle to Gentiles.[95] A new confessional, ritualistic, and pneumatic category replaces a hereditary one. The superordinate identity as God's people is a way in which Paul's audience can see Gentiles, a remote Other, no longer as out-group members but as in-group members. Jews and Gentiles can share the same Jewish faith.[96] Third, however, his speech acknowledges subgroup identities. The new people of God, whether they are Jewish or Gentile, still retain their distinct ethnic identities. Their resulting dual identity makes the people of God rich and more diverse.

4.4. Concluding Comments

The following statement from Gerald Izenberg is worth pondering: "Viewed from the outside, identification is what the group continually does; experienced from the inside, identity is what the group continuingly is."[97] *We cannot be defined by them* alone and

---

[93] Acts 26:20a omits the ethnicity of the first group to which Paul preached the gospel, and Acts 26:20b omits the geographic territory of the second group: "But declared first to *those* in Damascus, then in Jerusalem and throughout the countryside of Judea, and also to *the Gentiles*, that they should repent and turn to God . . ."

[94] Christine Hayes, *What's Divine about Divine Law? Early Perspectives* (Princeton: Princeton University Press, 2015), 151. Matthew Thiessen also notes: "Israel's God includes both Jews and gentiles in his eschatological restoration and therefore affirms and eternalizes the ethnic differentiation between Jews and gentiles." Matthew Thiessen, "Gentiles as Impure Animals in the Writings of Early Christ Followers," in *Perceiving the Other in Ancient Judaism and Early Christianity*, ed. Michal Bar-Asher Siegal, Wolfgang Grünstäudl, and Matthew Thiessen, WUNT 394 (Tübingen: Mohr Siebeck, 2017), 32.

[95] According to Caroline J. Hodge, Paul's letter to the Galatians also underlines his identity with regard to his membership and his call: "First, Paul is 'in Christ,' who was revealed to him by God (1:16) . . . Second, as a direct result of this revelation, Paul is called by God to be an apostle to the gentiles (1:16)." Caroline J. Hodge, "Apostle to the Gentiles: Constructions of Paul's Identity," *BibInt* 13, no. 3 (2005): 275–6.

[96] Whether it is Paul the Lukan character or Paul the letter writer, Caroline J. Hodge's comment rings true: "Paul's work as a teacher of gentiles is a part of the larger story of Israel, not a break from it." Hodge, "Apostle to the Gentiles," 276.

[97] Gerald Izenberg, *Identity: The Necessity of a Modern Idea* (Philadelphia: University of Pennsylvania Press, 2016), 365–6.

how they perceive what we are *doing*. *We* have to have our say to explain who we *are*. Paul's speech in Jerusalem is his response to slander against himself and the public's view of the Way. He endeavors to explain to his Jewish audience that he *is* a Jew and that his experience with the risen Lord *is* thoroughly Jewish. This is his defense of his dual identity.

To illustrate this point, this chapter investigated the literary features of Paul's speech. The analysis discovered that the geographic movement within the speech located Paul's Damascus experience and ultimately his call at its center. After noting the nature and rhetorical elements of his speech, the discussion underlined three functions of Acts 22:1-21 in the context of Luke-Acts, proposing that the given text introduces the trial narrative, reveals the blindness of the Jews, and highlights the Jewishness of Paul's message.

With these details in view, the study analyzed Paul's speech through the lens of Jenkins's theory of the internal-external dialectic of individual identification. The deviant whom the Jewish crowd accused, labeled, and attacked is ironically an orthodox Jew, Paul argues. The contest between his self-image and his public image not only adds nuances to who they think he is but also addresses the expansion of in-group membership in God's new vision of salvation.

The chapter then offered a social psychological reading of Paul's speech. Applying Gaertner's common in-group identity model as a vantage point, the analysis uncovered Paul's strategy to reduce intergroup bias and transform Jews' perception of Gentiles from out-group to in-group. By portraying his experiences within the Way in a thoroughly Jewish light, he recategorizes both Jews and Gentiles as potential recipients of a superordinate identity as the people of God while maintaining their distinct subgroup identity. In God's inclusive vision of salvation, ethnic diversity is to be neither ignored or prioritized but is to be acknowledged and celebrated.

5

Ambivalence and the Social Creativity of Paul as an Outsider/insider (Acts 22:22–23:11)[1]

At the temple precincts before a hostile Jewish crowd, Paul proclaimed that Jesus is the Lord and that God's salvation is extended to Gentiles. Certainly, this is one of the most spectacular scenes in Acts. If Peter's speech on the day of Pentecost functions as a paradigmatic scene in which Jews in Jerusalem accept the gospel, Paul's speech in Jerusalem serves as its sequel.[2] There follows a drama. It is not a conversion, but it is still a decisive change of action from silence to violence, from tranquility to hostility. As soon as Paul speaks of Gentiles, the crowd once again becomes furious and raises in unison a murderous voice (v. 22). His ambitious speech turns out to be a total failure. Embracing Gentile outsiders with the superordinate identity of the people of God is too good to be true. The common in-group identity model under the "people of God" is not going to work. If this is not the magic key that can save him, what is left for him?

The present chapter searches for the key that enables Paul to survive in the stories that immediately follow his speech (Acts 22:22–23:11)—sections 5 and 6 of Paul's rollercoaster ride (see figure 1.1). The tribune intervenes a second time, saves Paul, and interrogates him (Acts 22:22-29). The next day, Paul is put on trial before the Sanhedrin (Acts 22:30–23:11). Both pericopes involve violence that was attempted but failed. Divine necessity and protection are surely at work:[3] "You must [δεῖ] bear witness also in Rome" (Acts 23:11). The Lord affirms *why* Paul should survive but not *how* he would survive. The focus of this study, however, is not to gain insights from Paul's maneuvers in agonistic contexts but to explore what Paul's interactions with the tribune and the Sanhedrin reveal with regard to his identity and ultimately the identity of the Way.

---

[1] David Bell argues: "Ethnicity ... is best understood not as primordial phenomenon ... but as a strategic choice by individuals who, in other circumstances, would choose other group memberships as a means of gaining some power and privilege." David Bell, "Ethnicity and Social Change," in *Ethnicity: Theory and Experience*, ed. Nathan Glazer and Daniel P. Moynihan (Cambridge, MA: Harvard University Press, 1975), 171. This claim may sound shocking to many, but for those who have dual identity—for example, a Korean-American or a child whose father is Japanese and mother is German—it can be natural to accentuate a certain ethnicity as leverage in some circumstances. This chapter explores how Paul uses his dual identity to do that.

[2] The timing of Paul's speech close to the day of Pentecost—Acts 20:16—increases the parallelism between Peter's speech on the day of Pentecost in Acts 2 and Paul's speech in Acts 22.

[3] Kenneth Bass, "The Narrative and Rhetorical Use of Divine Necessity in Luke-Acts," *JBPR* 1 (2009): 48–68.

Having been slandered and labeled as an outsider, Paul defended his in-group membership as a respectable citizen of Tarsus (Acts 21:39) and a devout Jew (Acts 22:1-21). Troubles are still ahead. Thankfully, he still has some shields, if not bullets, to protect himself from the spears threatening his life. This chapter demonstrates that Paul's encounter with the tribune and the Sanhedrin discloses that Luke's ambivalence toward Rome and the Jewish people and Paul's social creativity are at play. It begins by delving into Paul's Roman identity. The project first surveys the scholarship on the historicity of Paul's Roman citizenship and looks into its functions in the narrative. Second, the chapter investigates Paul's Pharisaic identity. The study probes the validity of Paul as a Pharisee from a historical point of view and its functions within the narrative. With the Lukan ambivalence in view, this chapter rereads the text with SIA and explicates the mechanics and implications of Paul's social creativity—his claim to have Roman citizenship and Pharisaic identity—in the context of Roman-Christian relations and Jewish-Christian relations.

5.1. Ambivalence toward Rome

The excitement cannot rise too high. The same is true for Paul's speech. The train riders experience another free fall, leaving a marvelous sight behind. When the Jewish crowd hears of Paul's call for the Gentile mission, they become enraged and raise up—ἐπαίρω—their voices: "Banish this fellow from the earth!" (v. 22, author's translation). Their reaction is instant and violent, just as the friendly reception of Jesus's message quickly turned into animosity at Nazareth earlier in the Gospel: "For he should not be allowed to live" (v. 22; Lk 4:16-30).[4] The narrator portrays the ensuing uproar graphically by enlisting three participles in a row—κραυγαζόντων; ῥιπτούντων; βαλλόντων—to illustrate hostility and jealousy (v. 23).[5] Sandwiched between the crowd's eruptions, Paul's speech functions as a climax of the Jewish rejection of the gospel repeated again and again in the narrative (Acts 21:30-36; 22:22-23).

Witnessing another commotion about to break out, Lysias is once again in motion. He quickly arranges for his men to bring Paul to the barracks. Without time to catch their breath from the free fall, roller-coaster riders hold their security bar tightly one more time as the narrator explains why the tribune rescued Paul a second time: "to be examined [ἀνετάζω] by flogging, to find out the reason for this outcry against him"

---

[4] The text reads literally, "For it is not fitting for him to live" (v. 22: οὐ γὰρ καθῆκεν αὐτὸν ζῆν, author's translation).

[5] According to James A. Kelhoffer, "Objections to Paul's preaching to the Gentiles build upon earlier Lukan accusations of the Jews' jealousy (Acts 13:45; 17:5a; cf. 5:17)." Kelhoffer, "The Gradual Disclosure of Paul's Violence against Christians," 32. Earlier, the narrator described the response of the Jewish crowd in an epic manner (Acts 21:30). See also Philo, *Flacc.* 144. Carl R. Holladay notes: "'Throwing off coats' . . . is probably an expression of distrust and rage, as is 'picking dust into the air.' . . . See Plato, *Rep.* 5.474A; cf. Did Chrysostom, *Or.* 7.25." Holladay, *Acts*, 429. The hostile reaction of the crowd in response to Paul's speech has precedents earlier in the narrative: "shouting (Acts 7:57; 14:14); tearing the garments (14:14; 18:6), throwing dust (13:51)." Johnson, *The Acts of the Apostles*, 391.

(v. 24).⁶ Since torturing an individual to obtain evidentiary information is not unusual in Rome's legal system, especially for an alien or a slave, Lysias chooses a violent means to close the case in a decisive manner.⁷ When the soldiers stretch him out with or for the thongs⁸—τοῖς ἱμᾶσιν—however, Paul blurts out to the centurion standing by: "Is it legal for you to flog a Roman citizen who is uncondemned?" (v. 25).

With this statement, Paul gains leverage in this place of interrogation and torture. The operation is immediately put on hold. Bewildered and astonished, the centurion reports to the tribune, "What are you about to do? This man is a Roman citizen" (v. 26). Flogging a Roman citizen who has not been condemned is illegal and can incur censure "not only towards the soldiers, but towards the city in which the event took place"⁹ because it is a violation of his or her basic rights.¹⁰ Paul's Roman citizenship, as the remainder of Acts illustrates, not only protects him and enables him to stand before kings and authorities but also moves the plot forward in the midst of danger that never decreases. Since the entire plot of the trial narrative, also known as Paul's passion narrative, hinges on his Roman citizenship, scholars have undertaken studies to (dis)prove its veracity.

5.1.1. The Historicity of Paul's Roman Citizenship

(1) *Negative*. Those who oppose Paul's Roman citizenship base their arguments on the following rationale. First, it is extremely rare for Jews in Asia Minor to hold Roman citizenship in the first century CE.¹¹ Second, Roman citizenship is obtained in a limited fashion by leading representatives of the provincial aristocracy, whereas Paul's work of making tents locates him at the low end of the social stratum.¹² Third, Paul endured public beatings multiple times (2 Cor 11:25). If he were a Roman citizen, he could have

---

⁶ Ἀνετάζω means to examine someone judicially, often with the aid of torture. See LSJ 135; BDAG 78.
⁷ Johnson, *The Acts of the Apostles*, 391; Witherington, *The Acts of the Apostles*, 677. For the use of torture in a legal inquiry, see, for example, Pliny the Younger, *Ep.* 10:96.
⁸ Ἱμάς denotes a *strap* of a sandal or a strap with which one binds another for flogging. Ἱμάς also means a whip by which one is flogged. Therefore, the dative clause τοῖς ἱμᾶσιν can be translated as either the dative of means—"with the thong" (NRSV)—or the dative of purpose—"for the thong." Holladay, *Acts*, 428.
⁹ Sean A. Adams, "Paul the Roman Citizen: Roman Citizenship in the Ancient World and Its Importance for Understanding Acts 22:22-29," in *Paul: Jew, Greek, and Roman*, PS 5, ed. Stanley E. Porter (Leiden: Brill, 2008), 313 n. 15. See also Cicero, *Def. Rabir.* 12; Adrian N. Sherwin-White, *Roman Society and Roman Law in the New Testament* (Oxford: Clarendon Press, 1963), 71-6.
¹⁰ The rights of a Roman citizen included the right to vote, the right to make legal contracts and hold property, the right to defend oneself in court, the right not to be tortured prior to legal investigation, and the right to be exempted from some taxes or other duties endowed by local governments. Adams, "Paul the Roman Citizen," 313.
¹¹ Wolfgang Stegemann, "War der Apostel Paulus ein Römischer Bürger?" *ZNW* 78 (1987): 216-20.
¹² Stegemann, "War der Apostel Paulus ein Römischer Bürger?" 226, 227; Peter Lampe, "Paulus-Zeltmacher," *BZ* 31 (1987): 256-61. Ronald F. Hock argues that Paul saw his profession as a tentmaker in a not very positive light, whereas Todd D. Still and other scholars disagree with Hock's position. See Ronald F. Hock, *The Social Context of Paul's Ministry: Tentmaking and Apostleship* (Philadelphia: Fortress, 1980), 66-7; "Paul's Tentmaking and the Problem of His Social Class," *JBL* 97 (1978): 555-64; Todd D. Still, "Did Paul Loathe Manual Labor? Revisiting the Work of Ronald F. Hock on the Apostle's Tentmaking and Social Class," *JBL* 125, no. 4 (2006): 781-95.

easily avoided them.¹³ Lastly, Paul's Roman citizenship is an invention of the author of Luke-Acts to allow Christianity to find a place between Judaism and Romanism.¹⁴

(2) *Positive*. Those who support Paul's Roman citizenship present counter-evidence. First, it is probable that Paul's family acquired citizenship when Pompey conquered Tarsus and made it the capital of the Roman province of Cilicia in 67 BCE.¹⁵ Sean A. Adams conjectures that Paul's family was offered citizenship as "part of the upper class of the city" or "through a service to Pompey and/or Rome at this time."¹⁶ Second, there were other ways to obtain Roman citizenship besides birth and service to Rome. Based on Jerome's *Commentary on Philemon*, Mark R. Fairchild proposes that Paul's parents came to Tarsus as slaves when the Romans devastated Judea,¹⁷ either in 63 BCE with the siege or in 37 BCE after the fall of Jerusalem.¹⁸ He argues that they were later manumitted by their Roman owner and thus obtained Roman citizenship.¹⁹ Third, Paul states in his letters that he did not avoid but took beatings "to follow Christ in his suffering" (2 Cor 11:25; Gal 6:17).²⁰ The prohibition against beating a Roman citizen was often violated (e.g., Josephus, *War* 2.308; Plutarch, *Caes.* 29.2).²¹ Martin Hengel insists that Paul hid his Roman citizenship because his citizenship could have hindered his proclamation of Jesus, who was crucified by the Roman authorities.²² Fourth, denying Paul's Roman citizenship is denying the validity of not only Paul's trials but also of Luke-Acts as a whole (Lk 1:1-4; Acts 1:1).²³ Gerd Lüdemann suggests reasons that undergird the argument for Paul's Roman citizenship: his Roman name, his transportation to Rome, his relative freedom during his imprisonment (Phlm 24), and his frequent and wide travel.²⁴ Focusing on Acts, Peter van Minnen also argues that along with Paul's journey

---

[13] Stegemann, "War der Apostel Paulus ein Römischer Bürger?" 224.

[14] Stegemann, "War der Apostel Paulus ein Römischer Bürger?" 229; Walter Schmithals, *Die Apostelgeschichte des Lukas*, ZBNT 3.2 (Zürich: Theologischer Verlag, 1982), 153.

[15] The Roman general Pompey had the authority to confer Roman citizenship to those whom he saw as deserving, as indicated in the *Lex Gellia Cornelia* of 72 BCE. Adams, "Paul the Roman Citizen," 320; F. F. Bruce, *Paul, Apostle of the Heart Set Free* (Grand Rapids: Eerdmans, 1977), 37.

[16] Adams, "Paul the Roman Citizen," 320.

[17] Fairchild, "Paul's Pre-Christian Zealot Associations," 519. Jerome states in his commentary that "they say that the apostle Paul's parents were from the region of Gisela in Judea; and that when the whole province was laid waste by the hands of the Romans, and the Jews were dispersed into the world, they were moved to the city of Tarsus in Cilicia." Jerome, *St. Jerome's Commentaries on Galatians, Titus, and Philemon*, trans. Thomas P. Scheck (Notre Dame, IN: University of Notre Dame Press, 2010), 379.

[18] Adams, "Paul the Roman Citizen," 319.

[19] Fairchild, "Paul's Pre-Christian Zealot Associations," 519.

[20] Martin Hengel, *The Pre-Christian Paul* (Philadelphia: Trinity Press International, 1991), 6; Rainer Riesner, *Paul's Early Period: Chronology, Mission Strategy, Theology*, trans. Doug Stott (Grand Rapids: Eerdmans, 1998), 150.

[21] Hengel, *The Pre-Christian Paul*, 7; Gerd Lüdemann, *Paul, the Founder of Christianity* (Amherst, NY: Prometheus Books, 2002), 133; Lentz, *Luke's Portrait of Paul*, 127; Jerome Murphy-O'Connor, *Paul: A Critical Life* (Oxford: Clarendon Press, 1996), 39; Sherwin-White, *Roman Society and Roman Law in the New Testament*, 73–6.

[22] Hengel, *The Pre-Christian Paul*, 7.

[23] Adams, "Paul the Roman Citizen," 315; Peter van Minnen, "Paul the Roman Citizen," *JSNT* 56 (1994): 43–52.

[24] Lüdemann, *Paul, the founder of Christianity*, 134. For a discussion of Paul's Roman name, see Murphy-O'Connor, *Paul: A Critical Life*, 41–3; Sherwin-White, *Roman Society and Roman Law in the New Testament*, 153.

to Rome, Lysias' rescue of Paul (Acts 23:27) and Paul's connection with the synagogue of Freedmen (Acts 6:9; 7:58) reinforce Paul's Roman citizenship.[25]

(3) *Middle Ground.* Scholars have proposed ways in which Paul's family, probably Paul's father or grandfather, might have obtained Roman citizenship: military service in the legion, manumission from slavery, purchase, or conferring of citizenship by the emperor.[26] Each proposal is feasible to some extent but has its own weakness.[27] Any attempt to (dis)prove the historicity of Paul's Roman citizenship faces a formidable challenge—the lack of hard evidence outside Acts. Wherever one stands in this heated debate, however, it is agreed that Paul's Roman citizenship plays a critical role in the narrative.[28] Carl R. Holladay's statement is fitting to close the debate before turning our attention to the functions of Paul's citizenship in Acts: "Birth in Tarsus of Cilicia to a Roman father, however he might have become so, is the simplest explanation."[29]

5.1.2. Functions of Paul's Roman Citizenship in Acts

Paul mentions his Roman citizenship three times in Acts (Acts 16:37; 22:25, 27). He vocalizes his citizenship in Acts 22 as soldiers are binding him (v. 25). Scholars wonder why Paul waited until this point. Some argue for Paul's lack of pride in his Roman citizenship over against his Tarsuan citizenship[30] or his lack of ability to understand Latin[31] or his preference for appealing to the kindness of the soldier he addresses[32] or the absence of documents proving his citizenship.[33] Whether Paul had in his hand a *diploma civitatis Romane*[34] and why he delayed revealing his citizenship are impossible to (dis)prove. It is clear, however, that revealing his Roman citizenship functions as a game changer for Paul.

---

[25] van Minnen, "Paul the Roman Citizen," 46, 51.
[26] An extensive bibliography of scholars supporting various ways Paul's (grand)parents might have acquired Roman citizenship appears in Adams, "Paul the Roman Citizen," 318–20.
[27] Sean A. Adams criticizes the first three options and proposes the fourth one as a viable option because (1) "prior to Caesar, military service to Rome was not typically rewarded with citizenship"; (2) "[manumitted Jews by Pompey] were likely taken from Jerusalem and the surrounding area in Judea"; (3) "bestowing of citizenship on foreigners ... was strongly resisted during the Republic"; and (4) "It is most likely that citizenship was bestowed upon the family by a general or Emperor, Pompey being the strongest possibility, due to the influence of the family or due to a service rendered to Rome." Adams, "Paul the Roman Citizen," 318–20. Though plausible, the fourth option is speculative due to the lack of hard evidence.
[28] van Minnen, "Paul the Roman Citizen," 43.
[29] Holladay, *Acts*, 430.
[30] *BegC* 4:278; Richard J. Cassidy, *Society and Politics in the Acts of the Apostles* (Maryknoll, NY: Orbis, 1987), 100–3.
[31] Witherington, *The Acts of the Apostles*, 678. Stanley E. Porter concludes from his study of Paul's ability to speak in Latin that "Paul *may* have spoken Latin, but it is far from requiring it, no matter what the circumstances." Stanley E. Porter, "Did Paul Speak Latin?" in *Paul: Jew, Greek, and Roman*, 308, emphasis in the original.
[32] Otto Bauernfeind, *Kommentar und Studien zur Apostelgeschichte*, WUNT 22 (Tübingen: Mohr Siebeck, 1939), 250.
[33] Keener, *Acts*, 3.3249.
[34] Adams, "Paul the Roman Citizen," 326. See also James S. Jeffers, *The Greco-Roman World of the New Testament Era: Exploring the Background of Early Christianity* (Downers Grove, IL: InterVarsity Press, 1999), 201–2; Sherwin-White, *The Roman Citizenship* (Oxford: Clarendon Press, 1973), 247–9.

At the narrative level, three functions of Paul's citizenship are noteworthy. First, it creates tension among his opponents. The narrator's description of the soldiers reacting to Paul's claim is instant and dramatic: "Immediately those who were about to examine him drew back from him" (v. 29). The tribune becomes afraid—φοβέομαι—because he will be liable if he binds a Roman citizen (v. 29). It is not Paul but his interrogators who become nervous. The sudden change in the relationship between the prisoner and the authorities is not unprecedented in the narrative. When Paul reveals his Roman citizenship in the Philippi prison, the pendulum swings back and his opponents shake with fear (Acts 16:37-39). Paul's mention of his Tarsuan citizenship before his speech did its job to annul the misconception of the tribune and resolve the tension.[35] Paul's Roman citizenship places Roman officials once again "in an uncomfortable situation."[36]

Second, Paul's Roman citizenship protects him from danger from *the Jews*. As soon as Paul refers to his citizenship, he is once again placed in custody under the control of Lysias. Matthew L. Skinner avers that Paul's Damascus experience (Acts 9:16),[37] his farewell speech in Miletus (Acts 20:17-38), and Agabus' prophecy in Caesarea (Acts 21:8-14) loom over the imprisonment and suffering of Paul.[38] The place of detention for Paul, however, is a location not of anxiety but of safety. Ever since the appearance of *the Jews* (Acts 9:23ff.), he suffers persecution during his missionary journey as if he is sailing in a pirate-infested ocean. His Roman membership changes the scene once for all. The Lukan audience soon finds the plot to kill Paul thwarted, and those who were once Paul's enemies undertake a nocturnal mission to save Paul from *the Jews* (Acts 23:12-35).

Third, Paul's Roman citizenship allows him more opportunities to proclaim the gospel.[39] Matthew L. Skinner rightly points out that the modus operandi of God in the earlier part of Acts is "to free Jesus' arrested witnesses from their prisons so that ministry might resume."[40] While speaking to the public, disciples have been arrested and put in custody, but they are soon released the next day (Acts 3:1–4:22; 5:17-42; 16:16-40).[41] In Paul's second encounter with the tribune, the setting and audience of Paul's speech quickly change. Now, he speaks to leaders, authorities, and kings in courtrooms, people with whom he had never had a chance to share his proclamation (see Lk 12:11). With the almost invincible ticket of Roman citizenship, Paul finally

---

[35] Haenchen, *The Acts of the Apostles*, 635.
[36] Keener, *Acts*, 3.3249.
[37] Paul suffers in Acts as his call brings to light his fate, if not the specific manner of his death; as Jesus said, "How much he must [δεῖ] suffer [πάσχω] for the sake of my name" (Acts 9:16). Matthew L. Skinner's insight is worth noting here: "It is significant that Jesus uses the word πάσχω in 9:16 as the hallmark of Paul's experience to come. Consistently in Luke-Acts this verb (and its cognitive adjective, παθητός, in Acts 26:23) applies to Jesus' passion. It indicates suffering that is distinct from opposition or rejection (Luke 9:22 and 17:25 reveal a distinction between πάσχω and ἀποδοκιμάζω). The visceral sense of this term for Luke comes across in the observation that in Luke-Acts it almost always refers to the suffering that Jesus endures in his final hours of life through beatings, humiliation, and execution (Luke 22:15; 24:26, 46; Acts 1:3; 3:18; 17:3)." Skinner, *Locating Paul*, 96–7.
[38] Skinner, *Locating Paul*, 94–103.
[39] Skinner, *Locating Paul*, 5.
[40] Skinner, *Locating Paul*, 171.
[41] Παρρησία ("boldness" or "confidence") in Acts is a sign of the Holy Spirit that enables the disciples to carry out their messianic mission in the face of threats (Acts 2:29; 4:29, 31; 28:31).

arrives in Rome and preaches the gospel to the Jews in Rome (Acts 28:16-28). The final scene of Acts, as an epilogue to Luke's epic (hi)story, amplifies the freedom Paul exercises and foreshadows the unhindered proclamation of the gospel that will continue beyond the narrative (Acts 28:30-31).

5.1.3. Rome in Luke-Acts: Ambivalent Portrayals

The discussion leads to an inevitable quest for Luke's attitude toward Rome at the discourse level. It is Paul's Roman citizenship that finally brings Jesus's promise to fruition in a practical sense (Acts 1:8; 28:30-31). Is this indicative of Luke's pro-Roman position? Are there traces of evidence that speak otherwise? A close reading of the text complicates this binary vision and introduces readers to contested images of Rome in Luke-Acts.[42]

(1) *Affirming Rome*. Several texts in Luke-Acts put Rome in a positive light and show that Luke-Acts conveys that Christianity is not a political threat to Rome.[43] In Luke's Gospel, soldiers come forward to John the Baptist and inquire of him how to bear fruits worthy of repentance (Lk 3:8, 14). Centurions are portrayed as men of great faith (Lk 7:1-10)[44] and clear understanding (Lk 23:47). Pilate, the Roman prefect, repeatedly insists on the innocence of Jesus against the Jewish accusers (Lk 23:4, 14, 15, 22).[45] In Acts, Cornelius, a Roman centurion, is not only a devout God-fearer but also allegedly the first Gentile convert (Acts 10:1, 22). Centurions are like saving angels for Paul in places of danger. One defends Paul's right in a place of torture (Acts 22:26). Another reports to the tribune the plot of *the Jews* to kill Paul (Acts 23:17-18). Others show kindness to Paul during his custody and on his way to Rome (Acts 24:23; 27:3, 43). These portrayals of Roman officials together with Rome's protection of Paul in Acts 21–28 seem to consistently generate a positive image of the empire. Rome is like the wind beneath Paul's wings.

(2) *Denouncing Rome*. Another reading of Luke-Acts presents a disturbing image of Rome. Pilate authorized the crucifixion of Jesus (Lk 23:25) as the de facto prefect; he did not act *ex officio*.[46] Jesus is undoubtedly killed by the Romans based on the charge

---

[42] Specifically, there are more than these two extreme views with regard to Luke-Acts and the empire. Walton summarizes previous scholarship into five categories on this issue: (1) political apology for the church to Rome, (2) apology for Rome to the church, (3) providing legitimation for the church's identity, (4) equipping the church to live with the Roman Empire, and (5) not interested in politics at all. Walton, "The State They Were In," 2–12.

[43] Pickett, "Luke and Empire," 5. For example, see Cadbury, *The Making of Luke-Acts*, 299–316; Conzelmann, *The Theology of St. Luke*, 137–49; Bruce, *Commentary on the Book of the Acts*, 17–24.

[44] Compared to its parallel pericope in Matthew (Mt 8:5-13), Luke's Gospel adds a more positive note on the centurion: "He is worthy to have you do this for him, for he loves our nation, and he built us our synagogue" (Lk 7:4).

[45] Joshua Yoder states, "Pilate becomes the foil for Jesus' enemies, insisting on Jesus' innocence while they insist on his guilt." Joshua Yoder, *Representatives of Roman Rule: Roman Provincial Governors in Luke-Acts*, BZNW 209 (Berlin: de Gruyter, 2014), 245.

[46] The narrator laments the coalition of Herod and Pilate, who were once enemies but became friends with each other during this process (Lk 23:12). Steve Walton notes that παραδίδωμι—"hand/give over"—is used in Luke-Acts to describe "persecution, arrest, betrayal or execution" and thus makes Pilate's action "as all the more culpable." Walton, "The State They Were In," 20.

of treason (Lk 23:3, 37, 38). In Acts, Paul and Silas are illegally flogged and put in prison by the magistrates (Acts 16:37). The tribune falsely presumes the identity of Paul and attempts to flog him without the proper legal procedures that a Roman citizen deserves (Acts 21:38; 22:25-29). The narrator discloses the hidden intention of Felix to receive a bribe from Paul in custody (Acts 24:26). Even the centurion Julius, who favors Paul, on one occasion refuses to listen to Paul (Acts 27:11). Considering the fact that the position of the Roman officials steadily strengthens as the narrative progresses in Acts from city officials to governors,[47] their wrongdoings darken the image of Rome. Furthermore, non-Roman characters create subversive discourses. Zechariah's song clearly has a political overtone: "We [Israel] would be saved from *our enemies*" (Lk 1:71). The identity of Israel's enemies is not explicit, yet in the context of Palestine after the Jewish war, the riddle is not difficult to decipher.[48] Jesus in his inaugural address in Nazareth declares a year of jubilee in which the oppressed are set free (Lk 4:18-19). He also challenges the patronage system on which all of Roman society is built by teaching his disciples to practice what Raymond Pickett names "divine generosity," in which one gives without expecting to receive something in return (Lk 6:27-36).[49] Ultimately, "the kingdom/reign of God" (Acts 1:3; 8:12; 14:22; 19:8; 28:23, 31) that the gospel proclaims announces the dawning of such a new society and ironically denounces the reign of Rome.[50]

(3) *Ambivalent Portrayals*. Commenting on Luke's attitude toward Rome, Raymond Pickett states that "Luke-Acts is neither straightforwardly pro nor con."[51] The preceding discussion brings to the fore the contested images of empire that Luke-Acts paints. Paul's second encounter with the tribune intensifies the Lukan ambivalence toward Rome, whose rule Paul both complies with and ridicules if not overtly resists. First, Paul appeals to the Roman legal system that promotes the fair treatment of its citizens. His defense acknowledges that Rome prioritizes justice and order. Proper legal procedures should precede the flogging of a Roman citizen (v. 25). The centurion takes Paul's claim as "a declaration of citizenship," just as Roman law requires (e.g., Livy, *Hist.* 10.9.5-7; Cicero, *Verr.* 2.5.66).[52] Upon hearing that Paul has citizenship from birth, his interrogators immediately draw back (v. 29). Lysias employs a legal measure, no longer a violent measure, to discover what is causing such turbulence among the Jews (v. 30).

---

[47] Muñoz-Larrondo, *Living in Two Worlds*, 280.
[48] Pickett argues, "Zechariah's prophecy ... would more than likely have conjured up for hearers memories of the destruction of Jerusalem and Roman oppression of Jews." Pickett, "Luke and Empire," 14.
[49] Pickett, "Luke and Empire," 17, 18.
[50] Focusing on Luke's use of terms that have imperial connotations—savior, bringer of peace, ascension, and the list of nations—Gary Gilbert argues that Luke-Acts mimics Roman political propaganda and shows that Jesus is the true ruler of the world. Gary Gilbert, "Roman Propaganda and Christian Identity in the Worldview of Luke-Acts," in *Contextualizing Acts: Lukan Narrative and Greco-Roman Discourse*, SBLSymS 20, ed. Todd Penner and Caroline V. Stichele (Atlanta: SBL, 2003), 233–56. For a contrasting view on the interpretation of the kingdom of God, see Jeremy Paterson, "Review-Discussion Responses to Roman Power in Luke-Acts," *Histos* 9 (2015): 61–9.
[51] Pickett, "Luke and Empire," 7.
[52] Adams, "Paul the Roman Citizen," 325. Centurions appear as an agent of protection for Paul during Paul's stay in Jerusalem (Acts 21:32; 22:26; 23:17, 23; see also Acts 24:23; 27:1, 31, 43). The centurion's trust in Paul is contrary to the tribune's mistrust of Paul's claim for citizenship (v. 26 vs. vv. 27-28).

Second, the narrative nevertheless unveils disorder within the Roman system. The tribune misunderstands a Jewish legal matter as a political matter (Acts 21:38; 24:5-8).[53] As Richard Cassidy rightly notes, Lysias arrests Paul not necessarily to rescue him but to prevent disturbance and bring order.[54] Yet, he soon ignores the order and commands his men to flog Paul. The scene at the barracks reveals the irony of Pax Romana. Roman peace is maintained through violence. Anybody who threatens its order is subject to torture and death, as was done to Jesus earlier in the Gospel. Furthermore, the qualitative difference between Paul's citizenship and Lysias' sheds another gray light on the Roman peace. Still suspicious of Paul's claim, Lysias says, "It cost me a large sum of money to get my citizenship" (v. 28). Citizenship, an essential token for climbing up the social ladder, can be obtained through bribery.[55] Paul answers, "But, I was born a citizen" (v. 28).[56] This brief interaction indicts the value system of the Roman aristocracy (e.g., Acts 24:26). Greed trumps all.[57] Paul's meeting with the tribune offers a glimpse of the Roman order eroding in on itself. Steve Walton states, therefore, "Luke presents Roman officialdom 'warts and all,' and does not hesitate to tell of failings and corruption."[58] Paul's interaction in the barracks changes the roles of the examiner and the examined. Rome is on trial and found to be guilty. Luke-Acts is surely not an apologia to Rome.[59] Rather, it encourages its audience to critically (re)examine Rome's rule and (re)locate their position toward Rome in light of the gospel.[60]

5.2. Ambivalence toward the Pharisees

The crowd's shouting and Paul's speech do not explain to the tribune what is causing all the commotion. Flogging and scourging, the (un)usual means of interrogation in the

---

[53] Béchard, "The Disputed Case against Paul," 247–8.
[54] Cassidy, *Society and Politics in the Acts of the Apostles*, 97.
[55] Holladay, *Acts*, 429–30. The selling of Roman citizenship was widespread, especially during the reign of Claudius (41–54 CE). According to Dio Cassius, it was at first only given to those who paid large sums of money but later it became so cheap that a common saying was, "A man could become a citizen by giving the right person some bits of broken glass" (Dio Cassius, *Rom. Hist.* 60.17.4–9).
[56] According to Babu Immanuel, "Citizenship by birth was superior to that procured. In the Roman Empire, proof of citizenship rested on the act of parental recognition." Babu Immanuel, *Acts of the Apostles: An Exegetical and Contextual Commentary*, ICNT 5 (Minneapolis: Fortress, 2017), 242. See also Sherwin-White, *The Roman Citizenship*, 314.
[57] On the contrary, in the kingdom of God the wealth is meant to be redistributed and shared (e.g., Lk 18:18-30; 19:1-10; Acts 2:43-47; 5:1-11).
[58] Walton, "The State They Were In," 23.
[59] According to Loveday Alexander, there are five types of apologetic readings of Acts in New Testament scholarship: (1) apologia as inner-church polemic, (2) apologia as self-defense in relation to Judaism, (3) apologia as propaganda/evangelism, (4) apologia as self-defense in relation to Rome, and (5) apologia as legitimation/self-definition. Loveday C. A. Alexander, "The Acts of the Apostles as an Apologetic Text," in *Acts in Its Ancient Literary Context: A Classicist Looks at the Acts of the Apostles*, LNTS 298 (New York: T&T Clark, 2005), 183–206.
[60] Steve Walton concludes that "Luke offers his readers a strategy of critical distance from the empire." Walton, "The State They Were In," 35. After examining Roman provincial governors in the Lukan narrative, Joshua Yoder concludes, "They vary in integrity from blameless to corrupt. The greater part of Luke's governors falls between these extremes, exhibiting both commendable and blameworthy behavior and characteristics." Yoder, *Representatives of Roman Rule*, 333–4.

Roman legal system, are no longer available. Lysias exploits another legal option to look into the charges brought against Paul. He summons the Sanhedrin so that they may investigate Paul (v. 30).[61] Previously, the council—συνέδριον—has been a place of contest and suffering for the members of the Way—for Jesus (Lk 21:66-71), the apostles (Acts 4:1, 15; 5:21, 27), and Stephen (Acts 6:12, 15).[62] Now, Paul stands before them and delivers his apologia. If Paul wants to stand before Caesar (Acts 23:11; 25:11; 27:24; 28:19), he has to win over the minds of his jury and survive the Jewish council one last time. Inside the barracks, he insisted on his Roman identity. In front of the council, he changes his strategy and articulates, once again, his Jewish identity.

Paul's speech here complicates his attitude toward Jews, just as his encounter with the tribune manifested his split vision toward Rome. Earlier, he articulated his never-ceasing fidelity to the Jewish faith and declared that the Gentile mission is the work of the God of Israel. Acts 22:30–23:11 shows, however, that it is not all Jewish traditions but specifically the Pharisaic tradition that Paul adheres to. Paul comes out of his closet and reveals his Pharisaic identity, and the Pharisees stand with him (vv. 6-9). In this closed ring where he would be expected to stand alone and to be easily knocked out, he finds that one of his opponents is actually his ally. He exploits this advantage, avoids crushing defeat, and is finally taken out alive. This incident is critical because it is a window through which one can understand Luke's complex relationship with Jews and Judaism(s).

5.2.1. The Historicity of Paul's Pharisaic Identity

Like Paul's Roman citizenship, Paul's association with the Pharisaic tradition is also a contested issue among scholars. Paul claims, "I am a Pharisee, a son of Pharisees" (v. 6). Though hidden in the earlier portion of Acts, once brought up, his Pharisaic identity plays a critical role in advancing the plot in Paul's passion/trial narrative, similar to his Roman citizenship. Yet, his Pharisaic membership is not immune to scholarly interrogation.

(1) *Negative.* John C. Lentz raises two critical questions: "(1) Were Pharisees found in the Diaspora? (2) How probable is it that Pharisees would also be citizens of a Greek city?"[63] Quoting Jacob Neusner, first he highlights that Paul is the sole case of someone claiming to be a Pharisee while living outside Palestine.[64] Since it would be practically impossible to maintain cultic purity in the diaspora setting, it is improbable that Paul

---

[61] Carl R. Holladay says, "That the tribune has the power to convene the Sanhedrin to hear Paul's case reflects Rome's ultimate control in political matters." Holladay, *Acts*, 430. The historicity of this event is doubted because the Sanhedrin convenes only when the procurator grants permission (Josephus, *Ant.* 20.202). Gerd Lüdemann, *Early Christianity according to the Traditions in Acts: A Commentary*, trans. John Bowden (Minneapolis: Fortress, 1989), 242. Another proposal is that the meeting in Acts 23:1-10 is possible because it is not a formal trial but a hearing for the benefit of the tribune. Witherington, *The Acts of the Apostles*, 686. Commenting on the physical location of the gathering, Holladay conjectures from Acts 23:10—καταβαίνω—that "the Sanhedrin was meeting downstairs from the Antonia Fortress, somewhere in the temple area." Holladay, *Acts*, 436.

[62] Johnson, *The Acts of the Apostles*, 396.

[63] Lentz, *Luke's Portrait of Paul*, 54.

[64] Lentz, *Luke's Portrait of Paul*, 54.

is a Pharisee.⁶⁵ He also points out that Paul claims his Pharisaic membership only once, in Phil 3:5, but omits it in other places where he lists his credentials (Rom 11:1; 2 Cor 11:22; Gal 1:14).⁶⁶ Regarding the second question, Lentz posits that it is also unlikely for a Pharisee to hold Greek citizenship. The requirements of citizens—"loyalty to the local gods, acceptance of the gymnasium, and assimilation of Hellenistic culture"—are at odds with the "Pharisaic concerns for ancestral law, ritual purity, table fellowship, and strict interpretation of Torah."⁶⁷ Paul's claim of his Pharisaic identity, in this sense, should be seen as "not merely a personal affair, but an ancient family tradition."⁶⁸

(2) *Positive*. Brian Rapske presents counter-evidence. Referring to Jeremias, he argues that Paul's self-identification as "son of a Pharisee" denotes that he was "a pupil of Pharisaic teachers or a member of a Pharisaic association."⁶⁹ Paul's intention here, Rapske suggests, is not to prove the purity of his Pharisaic ancestry but to claim ties to Pharisees since it is probable that his family moved to Jerusalem "in the pursuit of the ideals of Pharisaism."⁷⁰ Furthermore, there existed modified forms of Pharisaic Judaism under Hellenistic culture outside Palestine and diaspora Jews deeply committed to observing the law while possessing Greek and Roman citizenship.⁷¹

(3) *Middle Ground*. (Dis)proving the historicity of Paul's Pharisaic identity is like taking the bait. It looks tempting, but its outcome is not promising. Paul identifies himself as a Pharisee (Phil 3:5). Acts concurs. He not only claims that he is a Pharisee but also defends the Pharisaic belief in the resurrection of the dead (Acts 23:6; 24:15, 21). Reference to his Pharisaic membership is clearly missing in Rom 11:1, 2 Cor 11:22, and Gal 1:14, as Lentz points out. Yet, in Rom 11:1 and 2 Cor 11:22, Paul is speaking of his genealogy, not his sectarian affiliation. Gal 1:14 addresses his fidelity to the law, but the agonistic context in which Paul is arguing against the Judaizers makes it unlikely that he would reveal his Pharisaic identity. His letters contain the traces of rabbinic education, especially in his exegesis of the Scripture, and Pharisaic claims concerning the resurrection give ample evidence of why Paul identifies himself as a Pharisee

---

⁶⁵ Lentz notes that though some Pharisees, such as Hillel, are from the diaspora, their Pharisaic careers begin only after they arrive in the Holy Land. Lentz, *Luke's Portrait of Paul*, 54. See also Jacob Neusner, *The Rabbinic Traditions about the Pharisees before 70 CE.: Part 1: The Masters*, SFSHJ 202 (Atlanta: Scholars Press, 1999).
⁶⁶ Lentz, *Luke's Portrait of Paul*, 54–5.
⁶⁷ Lentz, *Luke's Portrait of Paul*, 56.
⁶⁸ Tajra, *The Trial of St. Paul*, 95.
⁶⁹ Brian Rapske, *The Book of Acts and Paul in Roman Custody*, The Book of Acts in Its First Century Setting 3 (Grand Rapids: Eerdmans, 1994), 96; Joachim Jeremias, *Jerusalem in the Time of Jesus: An Investigation into Economic and Social Conditions during the New Testament Period*, trans. F. H. and C. H. Cave (Philadelphia: Fortress, 1977), 252 n. 26. The text reads literally, "I am a Pharisee, a son of Pharisees" (v. 6: Ἐγὼ Φαρισαῖός εἰμι, υἱὸς Φαρισαίων).
⁷⁰ Rapske, *The Book of Acts and Paul in Roman Custody*, 96. See also Witherington, *The Acts of the Apostles*, 691; Keener, *Acts*, 3.3289.
⁷¹ Rapske, *The Book of Acts and Paul in Roman Custody*, 97. See also Hyam Maccoby, *Judaism in the First Century*, IRS (London: Sheldon Press, 1987), 33; Jacob Neusner, *The Rabbinic Traditions about the Pharisees before 70 CE*, 356–7. Neusner notes that calling the addressees of Gamaliel I's letter (*Tos. Sanh* 2:6) "our brethren" probably does not refer to all the Jews in Palestine and the diaspora but specifically to the Pharisaic brethren.

(e.g., 1 Cor 15:45-49).[72] Yet, in Phil 3:5 he uses "a Pharisee" not to boast about himself but to emphasize the value of knowing Christ (Phil 3:7-11).[73] Even the Pharisees in the Sanhedrin do not seem to know him personally (vv. 6-9). Being able to verify whether he was a member of the Pharisees in the historical sense is not only unlikely but also beyond the scope of this study. Paul's receiving a Pharisaic education under Gamaliel in Jerusalem, however he might have associated himself with the Pharisees, is the simplest explanation.

5.2.2. Functions of Paul's Pharisaic Identity in Acts

Paul identifies himself as a Pharisee several times in Acts. Sometimes he does so explicitly (Acts 23:6; 26:5) and sometimes implicitly (Acts 22:3; 24:15, 21; 26:8, 23). Paul speaks of the resurrection in his missionary speeches (Acts 13:30, 37; 17:18, 32), but he never connects that claim with his identity as a Pharisee until Acts 23:6. Why does he do so at this critical juncture? What are the functions of Paul's Pharisaic membership in his passion narrative?

First, Paul's status as a Pharisee divides the Sanhedrin and saves Paul's life. Standing before the council, the narrator says, Paul looks at them intently (ἀτενίζω; Acts 23:1). This intense gaze is not a sign of "the ability to discern a person's spiritual condition," as Ben Witherington argues.[74] It is a prelude to the spectacles that will immediately follow (Lk 4:20, 22:56; Acts 1:10; 3:4, 12; 6:15; 7:55; 10:4; 11:6; 13:9; 14:9). Paul begins his speech by once again identifying himself to his Jewish audience, whom he calls "brothers" (ἀδελφοί; v. 1; Acts 22:1). His comment on being a good citizen—ἐγὼ πάσῃ συνειδήσει ἀγαθῇ πεπολίτευμαι—though saturated with political overtones, does not amplify on his Roman citizenship that he passionately defended in the previous scene. He is loyal to the God of Israel, not to Caesar (v. 1; see also Phil 1:27).[75] These gestures to gain favor from his audience, however, backfire. The tension only increases (vv. 2-5). In the face of the violence that will likely ensue, he takes out another piece of armor, if not a weapon, with which to defend himself. He appeals to his Pharisaic identity, turns his potential enemy, the Pharisees, into his allies, causes conflict within the Sanhedrin, and survives (vv. 6-10). Just as in the barracks, Paul once again hits the ball to the other side of the court for his own advantage.

---

[72] Menahem Kister, "'First Adam' and 'Second Adam' in 1 Cor 15:45–49 in the Light of Midrashic Exegesis and Hebrew Usage," in *The New Testament and Rabbinic Literature*, JSJSup 136, ed. Reimund Bieringer et al. (Leiden: Brill, 2010), 351–66. For a discussion of the influence of rabbinic hermeneutics on Paul's writings, see Dan Cohn-Sherbok, "Paul and Rabbinic Exegesis," *SJT* 35, no. 2 (1982): 117–32; Anthony J. Saldarini, "Comparing the Traditions: New Testament and Rabbinic Literature," *BBR* 7 (1997): 195–204.

[73] Comparing Phil 3:5 to Acts 23:6, Carl R. Holladay comments, "The main difference is that here Paul's Pharisaic stance is a present reality, whereas in the epistolary autobiographical summary his proud Jewish heritage has been superseded by Christ." Holladay, *Acts*, 434.

[74] Witherington, *The Acts of the Apostles*, 687.

[75] Paul's claim, "Up to this day I have lived my life with a clear conscience before God," seems problematic because Paul was a persecutor of the Way, which the narrative portrays as a sin (Acts 22:4, 5, 16). Paul may be speaking, as Holladay notes, of his full consciousness and moral conviction: "He has acted on his beliefs, fully convinced that his actions are right, especially before God." Holladay, *Acts*, 431.

Second, Paul's identity as a Pharisee distances him from the Sadducees.[76] His conflict with the high priest is presented in a dramatic fashion (vv. 1-5). As soon as he finishes his first utterance, the high priest, Ananias, orders his men to strike him on his mouth (v. 2). Paul punches back not with a fist but with his lips before receiving the first blow. He retorts that Ananias is under a divine curse—"God will strike you"— because he is a "whitewashed wall," a hypocrite (v. 3; see also Deut 28:22; 1 Kgs 22:24; Ezek 13:10-16; Mt 23:27).[77] Ananias sits in the council as a champion of justice, but he himself violates the law by ordering his men to strike Paul before hearing from him (Lev 19:15; Deut 1:6-17; 19:16-19; *m. Sanh.* 3:6-8).[78] The (un)friendly remark of bystanders reiterates the nature of Paul's response. It is an insult to the high priest's face (λοιδορέω; v. 4). Being informed of the identity of Ananias, he immediately apologizes, "I did not realize, brothers, that he was high priest" (v. 5a), but his apology is satirical, if not sarcastic (v. 5b; Exod 22:27). It is difficult to believe that Paul was unaware of who the commander was. The narrator foretold that Paul was looking intently at the council and that the commander was sitting while those nearby were standing (vv. 1, 2). Verse 5 discloses Paul's profound disrespect of the high priest; Ananias' unlawful behavior makes him "unrecognizable"[79] and Paul's insulting him justifiable. All of these wild interactions are a prelude to the violent conflict between the Pharisees and the Sadducees in the next scene, when Paul reveals his Pharisaic identity, and they ultimately illuminate the unbridgeable chasm between Paul and the Sadducees (vv. 6-10).

---

[76] The name "Sadducees" probably originated from the Hebrew term *Zedukim*, which refers to sympathizers with the descendants of Zadok. As a sect—αἵρεσις (Acts 5:17)—within Judaism(s), the Sadducees are closely associated with the high priestly party. They work with the temple functionaries, such as the priests and the captain of the temple, but still remain a distinct entity (Acts 4:1). High priests can be Sadducees, as they occupied the high priesthood in the first century CE (e.g., Josephus, *Ant.* 20.9.1), but not all high priests are Sadducees. Two designations, Boethusians and Sadducees, are used interchangeably to refer to them in the Talmudic literature. Mansoor, "Sadducees," 654–55. Because of this ambiguity, Robert L. Brawley suggests that Boethusians were probably one of the groups within the sect of the Sadducees. From the time of Herod the Great to the destruction of the temple, eight high priests had a connection with the family of Boethus. Furthermore, the Sadducees' concerns were far broader than the priesthood and issues related to the temple. Menahem Mansoor, "Sadducees," *Encyclopaedia Judaica*, ed. Michael Berenbaum and Fred Skolnik, 2nd ed., vol. 17 (New York: Macmillan Reference USA, 2007), 654–55, *Gale Virtual Reference Library*, http://link.galegroup.com/apps/doc/CX2587517261/GVRL?u=gradtul&sid=GVRL&xid=4ae7e20c; Brawley, *Luke-Acts and the Jews*, 107–11.

[77] C. M. du Veil, *A Commentary on the Acts of the Apostles*, ed. Hanserd Knollys Society with an historical introduction by F. A. Cox, trans. Acta Sanctorum Apostolorum ad literam explicata (London: printed for the Society by J. Haddon, 1851), 469. The negative portrayal of Ananias in Acts coincides with Josephus' report of his greed as well as his wealth (Josephus, *Ant.* 20.103, 205–7). Given the fact that Ananias was assassinated on the eve of the first Jewish Revolt and that Paul's words in v. 3 agree with this, Carl R. Holladay notes, "If Luke knew of Ananias' death and its circumstances, this may establish 66 CE as the *terminus post quem* [the earliest possible date] for dating Acts." Holladay, *Acts*, 432.

[78] Holladay, *Acts*, 432; Johnson, *The Acts of the Apostles*, 397; Witherington, *The Acts of the Apostles*, 689. Paul's charge against the high priest in v. 3 proves that Stephen's charge against his Jewish audience was right: "You are the ones that received the law as ordained by angels, and yet you have not kept it" (Acts 7:53).

[79] Johnson, *The Acts of the Apostles*, 397.

Third, Paul's identity as a Pharisee not only situates Paul on the side of the Pharisaic tradition but also highlights the continuity between the Way and Pharisaism.[80] After escaping the first punch, he takes the initiative as if he knows the next blow could be fatal. Noticing the presence of Pharisees as well as of Sadducees in the Sanhedrin, he exclaims—κράζω—"Brothers, I am a Pharisee, a son of Pharisees" (v. 6). His claim is based on a Pharisaic belief that is irreconcilable with that of the Sadducees: "I am on trial concerning the hope of the resurrection of the dead" (v. 6; περὶ ἐλπίδος καὶ ἀναστάσεως νεκρῶν κρίνομαι; see also Lk 20:27-40; Acts 4:1-4).[81] The belief in the resurrection might not be the central dividing line between these two dominant groups.[82] Yet, the impact of his outcry is decisive. His opponents begin fighting among themselves, and the Pharisees side with Paul (vv. 7, 9). Some read Paul's claim as an "adroit move"[83] or "the apple of discord."[84] Some point out his use of the military principle of *divide et impera*, "divide and conquer,"[85] which allows him to survive, if not win, the battle. The point of this story is not Paul's cleverness but the position of the Way vis-à-vis Judaism(s). The narrator's comment makes explicit what separates the Way from the Sadducees and brings it close to the Pharisees: "The Sadducees say that there is no resurrection, or angel, or spirit; but the Pharisees acknowledge all three" (v. 8).[86] The following outcry illustrates

---

[80] The word "Pharisee" likely derives from the Hebrew stem *parash*—"to be separated"—and, thus, the Pharisees mean "the separated ones" or "the separatists." Like the Sadducees, they are a sect— αἵρεσις—within Judaism(s) (Acts 15:5; 26:5). They are associated with the scribes whom the narrator also calls "the teachers of the law" or "lawyers" (e.g., Lk 5:17, 21, 30; 6:7; 7:30; 11:37, 45; 14:3). Some of them are the scribes themselves (Acts 23:9). They are experts in Jewish law, as they are constantly involved in disputes with Jesus concerning the strict observance of the law (e.g., Lk 6:1-11). Menahem Mansoor, "Pharisees," *Encyclopaedia Judaica*, ed. Michael Berenbaum and Fred Skolnik, 2nd ed., vol. 16 (New York: Macmillan Reference USA, 2007), 30–2, *Gale Virtual Reference Library*, http://link.galegroup.com/apps/doc/CX2587515688/GVRL?u=gradtul&sid=GVRL&xid=c142beb6.

[81] "Περὶ ἐλπίδος καὶ ἀναστάσεως νεκρῶν" reads literally "concerning [the] hope and resurrection of [the] dead" (author's translation). Luke T. Johnson notes, "It should be understood as a *hendiadys*, two phrases joining in a single concept." Johnson, *The Acts of the Apostles*, 398. See also Conzelmann, *Acts of the Apostles*, 192; Fitzmyer, *Acts of the Apostles*, 718.

[82] The main difference between the Pharisees and Sadducees revolves around how to construct the sociocultural reality for the Jewish people. Eyal Regev writes, "The Sadducees' cultural construction of reality is built upon that of the so-called priestly Code: the priestly system and the Temple cult are the main means of linkage between Israel and God. The priests maintain and lead this system. The Rabbinic cultural construction of reality (already established by the Pharisees) is built upon a broader concept of Torah and commandments, a system of interpretation that is led by the sage ... Thus, the Pharisaic-Rabbinic social system is individualistic in comparison to the hierarchic one of the Sadducees." Eyal Regev, "The Sadducees, the Pharisees, and the Sacred: Meaning and Ideology in the Halakhic Controversies between the Sadducees and Pharisees," *RRJ* 9, no. 1 (2006): 139–40. See also "Pharisees" and "Sadducees," *ABD* 5.289–303, 892–5.

[83] Witherington, *The Acts of the Apostles*, 691.

[84] Bruce, *The Book of the Acts*, 453; Haenchen, *The Acts of the Apostles*, 641.

[85] Fitzmyer, *Acts of the Apostles*, 718.

[86] The Lukan narrative underscores two topics as points of contention between the Sadducees and the Way. The Sadducees deny the resurrection of the dead and reject God's engagement in human affairs.

The resurrection. Early in the Gospel (Lk 20:27-40), the narrator identifies the Sadducees as "those who say there is no resurrection" (Lk 20:27). This is attested by outside sources (e.g., Josephus, *War* 2.163–5; *Ant.* 13.297–8; 18.16–17; *bT San* 90b; *bT RoshHaShan* 16b–17a). They ask what will happen in the case of multiple marriages if there is a resurrection of the dead (Lk 20:33). Whose wife will a woman be who has married multiple men? Jesus retorts that their inquiry is fundamentally flawed

a newly formed coalition between Paul and the Pharisees: "We find nothing wrong with this man. What if a spirit or an angel has spoken to him?" (v. 9) Verse 11 immediately confirms the continuity between the positions of Paul and the Pharisees. The risen Jesus who was dead but is now alive in spirit speaks to Paul and directs his way (v. 11).

Fourth, Paul's Pharisaic identity introduces the central topic of the dispute that will be developed in the course of his trial. The real issue of Paul's trial is the resurrection of the dead (v. 6; see also Acts 24:21).[87] Previously, the core of his proclamation was the identity of Jesus as the Messiah (Acts 17:3; 18:5, 28). He referred to the resurrection then, but it was secondary and focused on the resurrection of Jesus (Acts 17:18, 32; 13:30, 37; 17:3). From this time onward, however, the resurrection not only includes all of humanity but also is the primary subject that Paul passionately defends. Its outcome is both decisive and divisive. Fierce dissension ensues, and the Sanhedrin is divided (v. 7).[88] Nevertheless, Paul continues to proclaim this message because he believes that it is the hope that the Jewish people are awaiting (Acts 24:15). He later pleads before the governor Felix, "There will be a resurrection of both the righteous and the unrighteous" (Acts 24:15). He reiterates this at his defense before King Agrippa (Acts 26:8, 23). The resurrection of the dead is what is at stake in his trial because it is "the fulfillment of the Jewish hope" that the prophets have foretold, and this is where Paul, the prophet, finds

---

because although there surely *will be* the resurrection, as the patriarchs are still alive, not abandoned in Sheol, there will be no marriage after death. The resurrection of the dead is a recurring theme that causes quarrels between the Sadducees and the Way in Acts as well (Acts 4:2, 10; 5:30; 23:6, 8).

God's involvement in human affairs. Two subjects are at the heart of this theological debate. The first subject is the existence of an angel or spirit. The narrator states in Acts 23:8 that the Sadducees do not believe in the existence of "angel or spirit"—μήτε ἄγγελον μήτε πνεῦμα. Some scholars see this as "an anomaly" because the Sadducees' denial of celestial beings is not reported elsewhere, and the Pentateuch—the written law that they recognize authoritative over against the oral law—is full of stories with angelic interventions. Holladay, *Acts*, 435; Parsons, *Acts*, 315. Floyd Parker provides a brief summary of the positions scholars take with regard to the Sadducees' views of angels and spirits. Floyd Parker, "The Terms 'Angel' and 'Spirit' in Acts 23:8," *Bib* 84, no. 3 (2003): 344–59. Others understand that these terms refer to an angel or spirit of the deceased in the interim state between death and resurrection. David Daube, "On Acts 23: Sadducees and Angels," *JBL* 109, no. 3 (1990): 494; Parsons, *Acts*, 315–16; Witherington, *The Acts of the Apostles*, 692. I argue that the key to understanding this issue is v. 11. The Pharisees' vociferous response reiterates the narrator's remark (v. 9). Regardless of its form or name—angel or spirit—Paul argues that God intervenes in human affairs, which the Sadducees deny. This point leads to the second subject of debate. The Sadducees deny determinism and emphasize free will, whereas the Pharisees acknowledge both fate and free will (Josephus, *Ant.* 13.171–3; 18.13; *War* 2.162–5). Parsons, *Acts*, 315. See especially Jonathan Klawans, "Josephus on Fate, Free Will, and Ancient Jewish Types of Compatibilism," *Numen* 56, no. 1 (2009): 44–90. The Sadducees cherish human free will so much that they regard divine providence, predestination, and supernatural beings as interfering with free will. Such theological positions are, needless to say, incompatible with the Way whose message is deeply rooted in belief in the resurrection and divine providence.

[87] Tannehill, *The Narrative Unity of Luke-Acts*, 2.288.
[88] The dissension between the Pharisees and the Sadducees exemplifies the opposition in Israel that Simeon foretold with regard to Jesus in the beginning of Luke-Acts (Lk 2:34-35). Peter Mallen comments: "Division within Israel over the person of Jesus becomes a device that advances the plot from the beginning of Jesus' public ministry (Lk. 4.22–30) to the end of Paul's ministry (Acts 28.23–28)." Mallen, *The Reading and Transformation of Isaiah in Luke-Acts*, 68.

common ground with the Pharisees, beyond the controversy over Jesus's identity (Acts 24:21; 26:26-29; 28:20).[89]

5.2.3. Pharisees in Luke-Acts: Ambivalent Portrayals

The preceding discussion opens up another important issue in Lukan studies. If Paul claims to be a Pharisee and his Pharisaic identity is pivotal in the development of the plot, is this in harmony with the portrayal of the Pharisees in Luke-Acts? Is there a coherent picture of the Pharisees in Luke-Acts? Or does Acts 23:6-10 present contradictory images within the narrative itself? A critical reading of the text leads to ambiguity, not certainty, and ambivalence, not assurance.

(1) *Denouncing the Pharisees*. In the Gospel, the Pharisees are one of the opponents of Jesus. They complain about Jesus's ministry, challenge his teaching, watch over him to accuse him, and even ridicule him (Lk 5:21, 30; 6:2, 7; 7:39; 11:53; 14:1, 3; 15:2; 16:14; 19:39). Jesus's aggressive rhetoric against them dramatizes the gulf between himself and the Pharisees. He labels them as "fools" (Lk 11:40),[90] "unmarked graves" (Lk 11:44), and "hypocrites" (Lk 12:1).[91] The narrator adds a couple more. They are "the lovers of money" (Lk 16:14),[92] the self-righteous (Lk 16:15; 18:9), and those "having contempt for others" (Lk 18:9).[93] They invite Jesus to table fellowship, which implies a certain level of relationship between them (Lk 7:36-50; 11:37-54; 14:1-24).[94] Yet, even these encounters do not end on favorable terms.[95]

(2) *Affirming Pharisees*. Acts, however, presents quite a different picture of the Pharisees. Gamaliel, a Pharisee, stops the Sanhedrin from killing Peter and the apostles and indirectly protects them (Acts 5:33-40). Some of the Pharisees belong to the Way (Acts 15:5). Paul identifies himself as a Pharisee without reservation (Acts 23:6; 26:5). Furthermore, the Pharisees defend Paul from the Sadducees in the Sanhedrin (Acts 23:7-9).

---

[89] Tannehill, *The Narrative Unity of Luke-Acts*, 2.288.
[90] Here, the word "fools" has a strong moral connotation rather than an intellectual overtone. Jesus calls the Pharisees "fools" not because they are ignorant but because their heart is "full of greed and wickedness" (Lk 11:39; see also Lk 12:16-21). For a socioeconomic reading of the parable of the Rich Fool, see James A. Metzger, *Consumption and Wealth in Luke's Travel Narrative*, BIS 88 (Leiden: Brill, 2007), 63-84.
[91] The parable of the Pharisee and the Tax Collector (Lk 18:9-14) reiterates the Lukan theme of great reversal. The Pharisee who exalted himself is brought down, whereas the tax collector who acknowledged his status as a sinner and humbled himself before God is lifted up (see also Lk 1:51-53). In this sense, the negative labels the Pharisee gives to sinners in the pericope ironically apply to himself: "thieves, rogues, adulterers" (Lk 17:11).
[92] The Lukan designation of the Pharisees, in this case, is not to be generalized: "The Pharisees are chosen only because of Luke's need to explain ongoing Pharisaic hostility to the Christian movement in his own context of concern." Nolland, *Luke 9:21-18:34*, 810. Chapter 6 of this study explores how Luke's negative portrayals of the Jews reflect ongoing Christian ambivalence toward the Jewish people.
[93] Levine, "Luke's Pharisees," 129.
[94] For example, Simon, the Pharisee who invited Jesus to his house, holds a banquet in honor of him because he considers Jesus a prophet (Lk 7:36-50). Suppogu Joseph, *Table Fellowship of Jesus: According to Luke* (Delhi: ISPCK, 2009), 14.
[95] Jack T. Sanders, "The Pharisees in Luke-Acts," in *The Living Text: Essays in Honor of Ernest W. Saunders* (Lanham, MD: University Press of America, 1985), 174-6.

(3) *Ambivalent Portrayals.* Such mixed portrayals lead scholars to various appraisals on the depictions of the Pharisees in Luke-Acts. Some argue that Luke-Acts consistently maintains a negative view toward the Pharisees.[96] Others insist that the Lukan narrative portrays them fairly positively.[97] It is fair to say, however, that this Lukan ambiguity is present both in Luke and Acts. In Luke, the Pharisees are bad guys overall. Yet, the Lukan redaction of Mark and Q in which Pharisees appear either tempers the hostility between the Pharisees and Jesus or changes the view of the audience.[98] They glorify God when they see the healing of the paralytic (Lk 5:17-26; see also Mk 2:1-12; Mt 9:1-8).[99] Some scribes, presumably belonging to the Pharisees, acknowledge Jesus's teaching (Lk 20:39).[100] In Acts, the Pharisees seem to be good guys, but only in a limited way. Some of them are believers, but even nonbelieving Pharisees protect the members of the Way (Acts 5:33-40; 15:5; 23:6-9). Yet, they are either wary of the way in which the

---

[96] Jack T. Sanders states: "Luke consistently draws … ultimate doom for the Pharisees." Sanders, *The Jews in Luke-Acts*, 110. See also Albertus F. J. Klijn, "Scribes, Pharisees, Highpriests, and Elders in the New Testament," *NovT* 3, no. 4 (1959): 266. The Pharisees refuse to be contrite and repent, while holding onto the Law of Moses for salvation (Lk 7:29-30). Because of their exclusivist behavior, Sanders points out, the labels "hypocrites" and "bad yeast" should be attached to the Christian Pharisees (Lk 7:36-50; 18:9-14; Acts 15:5). Sanders, *The Jews in Luke-Acts*, 111-12. Similarly, Robert C. Tannehill states that the Pharisees "did not join the 'people prepared' through repentance for 'the stronger one' who has come after John" (Lk 1:17; 11:22). Robert C. Tannehill, *The Narrative Unity of Luke-Acts*, 1.176. According to Luke T. Johnson, the biggest problem of the Pharisees is that their hearts are closed to God's new action. Gamaliel's recommendation to "wait and see" (Acts 5:34-39), the Christian Pharisees' claim to circumcise the Gentile believers (Acts 15:1, 5), and the Pharisees' support for the "hope of resurrection" while not actually following the Way (Acts 23:6-9) represent the Pharisees' disobedience to God. Johnson, *The Acts of the Apostles*, 401-2.

[97] John T. Carroll asserts that, although the hostility between Jesus and the Pharisees in Luke shows two conflicting understandings of the kingdom of God, the Pharisees' defense of the Way in Acts ultimately legitimates the Christian faith as the authentic expression of the Jewish faith. John T. Carroll, "Luke's Portrayal of the Pharisees," *CBQ* 50 (1988): 604-21. Robert F. O'Toole goes even further and says that "in spite of the ambiguities, … according to Luke, Christians are the true Pharisees (cf. Acts 26:4-8)." Robert F. O'Toole, "Luke's Position on Politics and Society," in *Political Issues in Luke-Acts*, ed. Richard J. Cassidy and Philip J. Scharper (Maryknoll, NY: Orbis, 1983), 5.

[98] For example, in Lk 6:11, Luke changes Mark's direct reference to the Pharisees and their conspiracy against Jesus to the general anger that Jesus caused (Mk 3:6). Luke changes the addressees to whom Jesus speaks in Lk 11:37-12:1 from the Pharisees to the lawyers so that the Pharisees receive only half of the woes, in contrast to Matthew (Mt 23:1-36). Robert L. Brawley argues that "the Gospel already tends to present the Pharisees in comparatively favorable light and anticipate their posture in Acts." Brawley, *Luke-Acts and the Jews*, 84.

[99] In Mark, it is only the scribes who criticize Jesus's healing and forgiveness of sins (Mk 2:5-7). The narrator says, "They were all amazed and glorified God" (Mk 2:12). The identity of "they" is somewhat ambiguous. Are the scribes included in "they"? In Matthew and Luke, there is no such confusion. In Matthew, the scribes who accuse Jesus of blasphemy are different from the crowd who glorify God (Mt 9:3, 8). In contrast, in Luke, the Pharisees belong to the group—"all of them"—who glorify God because they saw Jesus heal the paralytic (Lk 5:26). The Lukan insertion of the Pharisees, in this sense, has not only a negative connotation—criticizing Jesus's ministry—but also positive implications—being filled with awe at the sight of Jesus's healing.

[100] The identity of the scribes who agree with Jesus's teaching on the resurrection is not clear. Yet, Acts 23:6-9, as well as other instances where the scribes appear with the Pharisees, increases the likelihood of the scribes in Lk 20:39 being Pharisees. See also I. Howard Marshall, *The Gospel of Luke: A Commentary on the Greek Text*, NIGTC 3 (Grand Rapids: Eerdmans, 1978), 743.

Gentiles are being included in the people of God or reluctant to join the Way. In a word, Lukan ambivalence toward the Pharisees is undeniable.[101]

5.3. Social Creativity of Paul

The Lukan ambivalence toward Rome and the Pharisees presents more than what meets the eye, namely the rescue of Paul, the story of which continues in the following episode (Acts 23:12-35).[102] His second encounter with Lysias and the subsequent contest in the Sanhedrin reflects the multilayered process of the formation of the identity of the Way, the group he represents. Since the audience of Luke's story is most likely its in-group members, Paul's interactions with his interlocutors are indicative and a reflection of intergroup relations between the Way and its out-groups, which are Rome and the Jewish people in a broad sense. How Paul switches the point of comparison with out-group members (re)presents the identity of the Way in a dramatic way (see Table 5.1).

5.3.1. An SIA (Re)reading of Acts 22:22-29

Paul's ambitious proposal to bestow the superordinate identity of the people of God on Gentiles is not accepted. The once-silent crowd quickly breathes threats and murder toward Paul. He cannot be an insider; he is an apostate deserving of death (vv. 22-23). The Jewish opposition makes it clear to Paul that the members of the Way cannot remain even on the periphery of the Jewish circle or at the bottom of the Jewish social

Table 5.1 Paul's Social Creativity

	In the Antonia Fortress	In the Sanhedrin
In-group vs. out-group	Paul vs. the tribune/soldiers	Paul/the Pharisees vs. the Sadducees
Criteria of comparison	Ethnicity and political affiliation	Ethnicity and doctrinal position
Existing evaluation	A Jew and an agitator of Rome	A Gentile-inviter and a law-breaker
New evaluation	A Roman and a law-abiding citizen	A devout Jew and a defender of the Jewish faith

---

[101] Mary Marshall argues that the following three themes are pertinent to the portrayals of the Pharisees in Luke-Acts: (1) the Pharisees have no place in the kingdom of God; (2) they are respected by the general population; and (3) they have an affinity with Jesus and/or early Christianity. She points out that, whereas the first theme applies almost exclusively to the Gospel, the second and third apply to both Luke and Acts. Mary Marshall, *The Portrayals of the Pharisees in the Gospels and Acts*, FRLANT 254 (Göttingen: Vandenhoeck & Ruprecht, 2015), 128–87. For a discussion of the Pharisees' respectable position and authority in Luke-Acts, see Brawley, *Luke-Acts and the Jews*, 91–105.

[102] After being brought to the barracks, in all three occasions in which Paul is in danger but later saved, Paul is an active participant, not a passive receiver, in his own rescue (Acts 22:24-29; 22:30-23:11; 23:12-35).

stratum. The Jewish ethnic boundary is not permeable. Any attempt to change or challenge the established Jewish sociocultural system will do more harm than good. Similarly, his Tarsuan citizenship and, thus, his Greek sociocultural identity are useless in the Roman (il)legal system. Resisting the Roman soldiers with violent means is not a possibility. Although doubly marginalized, however, Paul does not remain in a position of relative scarcity but claims positive distinctiveness as he compares himself to his interrogators in new dimensions.

(1) *From an Agitator to a Law-abiding Citizen.* Paul's passionate speech is a resounding gong in Lysias' ears because he speaks in Hebrew, not in Greek. Even his Jewish ethnic identity, which he described earlier, is "a mere category" for a Roman tribune (Acts 21:39). Though "the Jew" is "a distinct category" that forms a social group with its own rights and duties of membership in the Roman imperial system, the benefits and privileges of the Jews are no use in the context of a criminal investigation.[103] The violent measure soon to be employed with Paul provides a glimpse of Lysias' perception of Paul: "He may not be an Egyptian, but he is another agitator!" To the tribune, Paul was and is, now, in an out-group category.[104] Surely, the psychological reality of Paul—who Lysias thinks Paul is—is "a matter of judgments, abstractions, [and] categories."[105] He is also subjected to torture (v. 25).

Yet, the roller-coaster train that is rapidly going downhill with the Jewish commotion and the binding of Paul reaches bottom and then quickly moves uphill. Confronting a Roman tribune, Paul compares his status not within a Jewish circle but within a Roman circle. He accentuates his Roman citizenship, a positive distinctiveness inside the Antonia Fortress, and puts himself in a better position. Clearly, his identity is *situation specific*, and his self-concept is *within a hierarchal system of classification*, as SCT delineates the process of self-categorization. His ethnicity and political affiliation are still at stake, but the comparison produces quite a different outcome. Previously, Paul was considered a Jew and an agitator in Rome. Now, he is claiming to be a Roman and a law-abiding citizen, unlike his lawbreaking examiners. The tribune's interrogation only makes Paul feel better. He insists that his Roman citizenship is not a property right, which he gained with money like the tribune did, but a birthright (v. 28). The benefits and privileges that come with its membership should be protected; he should not be deprived of them.

(2) *Paul's Superordinate Roman Identity.* It is interesting to note that Paul employs another superordinate identity to defend himself. It is *the people of Rome*. Roman citizenship, though highly limited and granted to a selected few, is not completely exclusive. Those who wished to join *and* were able to join could become citizens, at

---

[103] For a discussion of a "social group" and a "social category" in conjunction with ethnic groups, see H. S. Morris, "Ethnic Groups," in *International Encyclopedia of the Social Sciences*, vol. 5 (New York: Macmillan Co., 1968), 167–72. See also Tajfel, "The Social Psychology of Minorities," 310.

[104] Jerome S. Brunner argues: "All perception is necessarily the end product of a categorization process." Jerome S. Brunner, "On Perceptual Readiness," *Psychological Review* 64 (1957): 124.

[105] This sentence is adapted from the following statement: "The *psychological reality* of the person is a matter of judgments, abstractions, categories." Oakes, Haslam, and Turner, *Stereotyping and Social Reality*, 115, emphasis in the original.

least in theory if not in practice.¹⁰⁶ The members of the Way *could* be under the bigger umbrella of the Romans.

Though it is an ethnic category, Roman citizenship, however, is not an enduring category for Paul; it is simply a category that is at his disposal to exploit. He knows and makes use of Roman law¹⁰⁷ but is loyal only to the God of Israel (Acts 23:2). In this sense, his decisive move, the presentation of his Roman citizenship, is not a strategy for social mobility. He is striving neither to join the dominant group, Roman citizens, nor to exit the subordinate group, the Way. It is, rather, a strategy of social creativity. His public image changes, whereas his self-image in terms of what he values most stays the same.¹⁰⁸ Paul's divided allegiance is in accord with the Lukan ambivalence toward Rome. Roman law is a safety net and even a springboard that allows Paul to accomplish what he desires to do in the face of opposition. He is, however, neither at the service of Caesar nor a promoter of the Roman superordinate identity. He is at the service of God and is promoting the ultimate superordinate identity, *the people of God*, through the proclamation of the gospel.

5.3.2. An SIA (Re)reading of Acts 22:30–23:11

The following episode also implicates Paul's use of social creativity. Standing in front of the Sanhedrin, Paul first addresses the ethnic dimension, as he did previously inside the Antonia Fortress. Yet, he presents a different card. He identifies himself as a devout Jew since the players at the table have changed. He accentuates his fidelity to God in defense of the accusations previously brought against him (v. 1; Acts 21:28; 22:3).¹⁰⁹ History repeats itself. So does Paul's experience with his own people. As soon as he claims his Jewish identity, he becomes once again the object of violence (v. 2). The violent interchange between Paul and his interlocutors illuminates that the high priest is informed of the crimes Paul allegedly committed and probably has heard of Paul's speech in the temple precinct (vv. 2-3; Acts 21:28). Paul's defense in verses 3 and 5 articulates his knowledge of the law, yet it does not secure either his membership in the Jewish nation or his life. In the eyes of his opponents, he is a defiler not only of the temple but also of his Jewish ethnicity. He has invited Gentiles to be members of God's people, which could be seen by Jews as taking away the benefits and privileges that

---

¹⁰⁶ For a discussion of Roman plural ethnicity, see David L. Balch, "The Contested Movements in Rome, Athens, and Jerusalem toward Citizenships/Memberships of Multiple Ethnicities (Introducing Chapters 2–11)," in Balch, *Contested Ethnicities and Images: Studies in Acts and Art*, WUNT 345 (Tübingen: Mohr Siebeck, 2015), 17–35.

¹⁰⁷ The following verses demonstrate Paul's knowledge of the Roman law and its usage: Acts 16:37; 22:25; 23:17; 25:11, 21; 26:32; 28:19.

¹⁰⁸ Charles Taylor's insight into one's self is helpful at this point. He observes that the sources of the self are inescapable moral frameworks that give meaning to one's life: "Our identity is what allows us to define *what is important to us* and what is not." Taylor, *Sources of the Self*, 30, emphasis added.

¹⁰⁹ The multifaceted label previously given to Paul is "the one against the Jewish nation, law, and temple." Paul's statement in v. 1, though brief, makes a clear case that he has committed none of these crimes in opposition to God.

come with being God's elect.[110] Furthermore, they have heard of his teachings and actions that are contrary to the law. The odds are against Paul. The more he appeals to the law, the more he will be perceived as a liar, a hypocrite.

As his appeal to his Jewish ethnic identity fails, Paul next employs the same strategy, social creativity, that he used inside the barracks, but he exploits a different point of comparison. Yet, this time, it is not his political affiliation with Rome but a doctrinal position that changes his intergroup relations. The narrator's mention of a Pharisaic group puts once-hidden characters inside the Sanhedrin and on the front stage (v. 6; Acts 22:30).[111] He brings to the fore his Pharisaic identity by accentuating his belief in the resurrection of the dead and categorizes himself with this former out-group (v. 6). The narrator introduces the Sadducees to the scene, and dissension occurs (v. 7). Sandwiched between the Pharisees and the Sadducees, Paul takes advantage of the intergroup conflict between the two dominant groups.

(1) *From a Lawbreaker to a Defender of the Jewish Faith*. Paul's outcry is a wake-up call for the Pharisees. Their belief in the resurrection of the dead is not "a mere category" but "a distinct category" that makes them "a social group," according to the narrator, who labors to underscore the different belief systems between the Pharisees and the Sadducees (v. 8). A coalition is quickly formed, and the Pharisees become Paul's supporters. In contrast, the Sadducees oppose Paul; they appear to be a consistent enemy of the Way. Earlier, they attempted to trap Jesus (Lk 20:27-40).[112] They persecuted his disciples (Acts 4:1-4; 5:17-41). Now, they try to kill Paul (v. 10). Unlike the priests, whose attitude to Jesus and his followers is either neutral or turning positive,[113] together

---

[110] For Julius Caesar's favoring of the Jews, see Josephus, *Ant.* 14.186–285. Harry W. Tajra summarizes: "The Jews were able to form legally-cognized religious corporations around their synagogues, enjoy freedom of worship and assembly for the synagogal communities and create special tribunals to settle their differences." Harry W. Tajra, *The Trial of St. Paul: A Juridical Exegesis of the Second Half of the Acts of the Apostles*, WUNT 2/35 (Tübingen: Mohr Siebeck, 1989), 15 (see esp. 14–21).

[111] Acts 22:30 intensifies the tension in the air as the narrator introduces the chief priest and the Sanhedrin, who acted as the opponents of the Way, to be Paul's main interrogators. Neither the Pharisees nor the Sadducees are mentioned at this point. Συνέδριον appears fourteen times in Acts. Yet, on only one occasion out of seven occurrences—Acts 4:15; 5:21, 27, 34, 41; 6:12, 15—prior to Acts 22:30 does a Pharisee vocalizes his opinion (Acts 5:34-39).

[112] The Sadducees appear to be one of the three groups that question and challenge Jesus after his entry to Jerusalem—"the chief priests and the scribes ... with the elders" (Lk 20:1), their "spies" (Lk 20:20), and "some Sadducees" (Lk 20:27). David L. Tiede, *Luke*, ACNT (Minneapolis: Augsburg, 1988), 347.

[113] (1) *Positive*. Luke-Acts opens with the story of Zechariah, a priest, and Elizabeth, who also has a priestly origin. The narrator describes them in an extremely favorable light: "Both of them were righteous before God, living blamelessly according to all the commandments and regulations of the Lord" (Lk 1:6). Their old age and barrenness echo the story of Abraham and Sarah, whose faith, in the end, is rewarded with a son (Gen 18:11; 21:1-7). François Bovon, *Luke 1: A Commentary on the Gospel of Luke 1:1—9:50*, Hermeneia, trans. Christine M. Thomas (Minneapolis: Fortress, 2002), 34; Danker, *Jesus and the New Age*, 28; Tiede, *Luke*, 41. The narrator also reports on priests who join the Way early in Acts: "A great many of the priests became obedient to the faith" (Acts 6:7). (2) *Neutral*. Jesus tells lepers to show themselves to the priests (Lk 5:14; 17:14). He affirms the role of priests legitimizing their cure (Lev 14:2-3). In the parable of the Good Samaritan, a priest ignores the suffering of a victim of robbery and passes him by (Lk 10:31). But, Robert L. Brawley points out, "Inasmuch as for Luke the parable answers the captious lawyer, it is he who appears in bad light." Brawley, *Luke-Acts and the Jews*, 110. (3) *From Negative to Positive*. In Acts 4:1-3, the priests join the Sadducees and the captain of the temple and persecute Peter and John. "The priests," however, quickly disappear in the following scene in which those of the high priestly family begin

with the chief priests and high priests they maintain a negative attitude toward the Way throughout the narrative. Paul is accused of teaching against the Jewish establishment—the law, the temple, and the Jewish people—over which the Sadducees exercise their religious authority and enjoy privileges. Making it worse, now he insists on the resurrection of the dead and God's engagement in human affairs, which they cannot accept (v. 8).[114] He is surely an enemy of Jews and should not be allowed to live.

The descending train once again hits the bottom, but then it goes back uphill. As soon as Paul vocalizes his belief in the resurrection, a defining attribute of being a Pharisee, the Pharisees perceive him in a prototypical way. Paul's uniqueness, particularly his faith in Jesus, is forgotten, though it has not disappeared, and he is now seen as an interchangeable member of the Pharisaic group. Verse 9 implies that Paul's depersonalization is complete and an "ideological social identity" has been created:[115] "We find nothing wrong with this man. What if a spirit or an angel has spoken to him?" They recategorize Paul as a member of their in-group. Mutual attraction takes place. So does social cooperation. They join a tug of war against their out-group, the Sadducees, to protect their newly joined in-group member. With this new point of comparison, Paul's public image changes for the Pharisees from a lawbreaker to a devout Jew and a defender of the Jewish faith.

(2) *Paul's Subgroup Pharisaic Identity*. This story illustrates another aspect of Luke's creative genius. Whereas Paul utilizes his superordinate Roman identity before the tribune, he articulates his subgroup identity in front of the Sanhedrin. He is a Jew, yet more specifically a Pharisee. He is a member of the people of God, yet he belongs with those who wait for the resurrection of the dead. This recategorization process illustrates, once again, not social mobility but social creativity. He articulates the Pharisaic aspect of his identity yet remains a member of the Way. Given the Lukan ambivalence toward the Pharisees and Paul's dual identity as a Pharisee and a Christian, Paul's subgroup Pharisaic identity bespeaks his split self-image.

---

interrogations (Acts 4:5-7). After the narrator reports that many priests have joined the Way, only the high priest and chief priests appear to be opponents of the Way (Acts 6:7; see also Acts 4:6, 23; 5:17, 21, 24, 27; 7:1; 9:1, 14, 21; 22:5, 30; 23:2, 4, 5, 14; 24:1; 25:2, 15; 26:10, 12). Drawn from Luke's portrayals of priests, priestly interests, and the use of hymns, Rick Strelan proposes that the author of Luke-Acts is a priest. Rick Strelan, *Luke the Priest: The Authority of the Author of the Third Gospel* (Burlington, VT: Ashgate, 2008).

[114] Brawley, *Luke-Acts and the Jews*, 114–15. Although Luke-Acts brings to the fore these two topics, Josephus in his discussion of Jewish philosophies and the leading Jewish sects (Josephus, *War* 2.119-66; *Ant.* 18.11–25) points out two additional significant issues in comparing the Sadducees to the Pharisees. (3) The Sadducees differ in their notion of the afterlife. Whereas the Pharisees believe that the soul lives on after death—virtuous souls in another body and wicked souls in eternal suffering—the Sadducees believe that the soul ceases to exist with the death of the body. Daube, "On Acts 23: Sadducees and Angels," 494; Holladay, *Acts*, 435. (4) The Sadducees recognize only the written law—Pentateuch—while rejecting the oral law that the Pharisees see as authoritative. In speaking of levirate marriage, they specifically state, "Moses wrote for us" (Lk 20:28; Deut 25:5; see also Gen 38:6-11; Ruth 3:9–4:10). "For us" is emphatic. It designates Israel as *the* recipient of the written law. Bovon, *Luke 3*, 65; Green, *The Gospel of Luke*, 719.

[115] Ideological Social Identity (ISI) is "designed to capture feelings of psychological attachment to an ideological in-group." Christopher J. Devine, "Ideological Social Identity: Psychological Attachment to Ideological In-Groups as a Political Phenomenon and a Behavioral Influence," *Political Behavior* 37 (2015): 509.

Yet, Paul's subgroup identity is not meant to narrow down the in-group he envisions. Rather, it gives away a ticket to a stadium that is large enough to hold all people. It is not an ethnic category but a confessional category that allows anybody to come in and see the spectacle of God's salvation. To illustrate his point, Paul articulates, as he always does, the Jewishness of his belief. The resurrection of the dead is deeply rooted in Pharisaic hope (v. 6). It is the hope, he insists, that all Jewish people share and for which they all await (Acts 24:15).[116] This hope is based on the Jewish Scripture. Paul's last question to King Agrippa dramatically illustrates this point: "King Agrippa, do you believe the prophets? I know that you believe" (Acts 26:27).[117] For this "hope of Israel," he is being held in chains (Acts 28:20). He is surely the defender of the Jewish faith.[118]

5.3.3. Implications of Paul's Social Creativity

A story is meant to be read by its readers. So is Luke-Acts. Though hidden behind the Lukan theater, the Lukan audience is an active participant in the story in their imagination if not in action. Paul's interactions with his interrogators not only inform the readers of what happened between them but also provide insights into their relationship with their out-groups. Paul's identity is inextricably connected with his interlocutors, and his chameleon-like presentation of his self reflects the process of the identity formation of the Way.

(1) *Rome Shelters Yet Has No Rights over the Way (Acts 22:22-29).* The event that took place inside the barracks alludes to the fact that the Way is in conflict with Rome. Rome is an out-group trying to get rid of Paul. Paul later comes under the protection of Rome, yet he does not hesitate to reveal its wrongdoings. The Lukan audience was probably comprised of Jews and Gentiles, including some Romans.[119] Luke's positive portrayals of Roman soldiers, particularly centurions, may reassure Romans in the

---

[116] Daniel Marguerat notes: "The Christian faith, expounded by Paul, represents the best that Judaism has to offer; and, for Luke, the best it offers is surely the Pharisaic piety. There are Pharisees in Jerusalem, Luke writes, who agree with this idea." Daniel Marguerat, *The First Christian Historian: Writing the 'Acts of the Apostles,'* SNTSMS 121, trans. Ken McKinney, Gregory J. Laughery, and Richard Bauckham (New York: Cambridge University Press, 2002), 148–9.
[117] Robert C. Tannehill comments: "One who shares the Jewish belief in the prophets might well be moved by Paul's message of the fulfillment of the Jewish hope (26:26–29)." Tannehill, *The Narrative Unity of Luke-Acts*, 2.288.
[118] Luke T. Johnson eloquently underscores what the last episode of Acts, Acts 28:30-31, demonstrates: "God's fidelity to his people and to his own word. And that point concluded, the ending of Acts is truly an opening to the continuing life of the messianic people." Johnson, *The Acts of the Apostles*, 476.
[119] For example, Paul mentions in Phil 4:22 a greeting from all the saints—πάντες οἱ ἅγιοι—who belong to "the household of Caesar." According to Wayne A. Meeks, the following references show that Luke-Acts is "interested in portraying the Christian sect as one that obtained favor from well-placed, substantial citizens": Lk 8:3; Acts 13:7-12; 16:14-15, 40; 17:5-9, 12, 34; 18:7; 24:26; 26:2-31; 28:7-10. Wayne A. Meeks, *The First Urban Christians: The Social World of the Apostle Paul* (New Haven: Yale University Press, 1983), 61–3. See also Bruce W. Longenecker, "Socio-Economic Profiling of the First Urban Christians," in *After the First Urban Christians: The Social-Scientific Study of Pauline Christianity Twenty-Five Years Later*, ed. Todd D. Still and David G. Horrell (New York: Continuum, 2009), 36–59. Commenting on Paul's defense before Felix, Robert C. Tannehill rightly notes: "Thus the Jewish audience is still in mind, even though Paul is speaking before a Roman governor." Tannehill, *The Narrative Unity of Luke-Acts*, 2.288.

church that "their allegiance to the empire and Christian faith are quite compatible."[120] Yet, it is the Way, not Rome, that the story ultimately legitimates. Rome may protect the members of the Way with Roman citizenship and even support them in their proclamation of the gospel, but it does not have final authority over them. Their Lord is Christ, not Caesar (see Lk 20:20-26). The members of the Way *can* be in-group members of Rome, just like Paul, but even if they are not, it does not really matter. Deep inside, they are all outsiders to Rome, even if they live within the bounds of Rome. They are either outsiders/insiders or outsiders to Rome. Their true membership belongs to the kingdom of God. It is this ambivalence upon which the identity of the Way is formed and its in-group solidarity is intensified.

(2) *The Way Is the Ultimate Insider of the Jewish Faith (Acts 22:30–23:11).* Intergroup conflict and coalition in the Sanhedrin reveal both divergence and convergence. The Way is surely an out-group to the Sadducees, but to the Pharisees, its in-group/out-group boundary is not clear-cut. Paul's claim regarding the resurrection illustrates not only the continuity between Judaism and Christianity but also the conviction that "Christianity fulfills Judaism and the hope of the twelve tribes of Israel."[121] Especially in the post-Jewish War context in which the chief priests and the Sadducees have lost their dominance and the Pharisees have gained the upper hand over the sociocultural life of Jews in Palestine, it is crucial for the Way to articulate the Jewish faith that they share with the Pharisees. The Way's members are either outsider/insiders or insiders to the Pharisees. Just as with Rome, the identity of the Way is constructed "for its identity-affirming strands even amidst its unsettling ambivalences."[122] Mary Marshall's comment is worth restating to explain what Paul's encounter with the Sanhedrin entails with regard to Jewish-Christian relations:

> Christians are therefore the legitimate heirs of God's promises to Israel. Christianity is not at odds with but has its roots in Judaism. This continuity validates the Christian claim to the Jewish scriptures and the promises made to Israel.[123]

5.4. Concluding Comments

Peter L. Berger and Thomas Luckmann argue: "Every group engaged in social conflict requires solidarity. Ideologies generate solidarity."[124] Thus, Paul's pleas to his Roman

---

[120] This is Seyoon Kim's summary of those who find the legitimation of Rome in Luke-Acts. Seyoon Kim, *Christ and Caesar: The Gospel and the Roman Empire in the Writings of Paul and Luke* (Grand Rapids: Eerdmans, 2008), 173. For this view, see Esler, *Community and Gospel in Luke-Acts*, 201–19; Christopher Bryan, *Render to Caesar: Jesus, the Early Church, and the Roman Superpower* (New York: Oxford University Press, 2005), 96.

[121] Marshall, *The Portrayals of the Pharisees in the Gospels and Acts*, 181.

[122] Irudayaraj, *Violence, Otherness, and Identity*, 87. The historical context of Judahite returnees from the Babylonian exile that Irudayaraj discusses and the context of the Way that this study focuses on are different. Yet, a similar process of identity construction takes place over against the proximate "other," the Edomites, on the one hand, and the Jewish people, on the other.

[123] Marshall, *The Portrayals of the Pharisees in the Gospels and Acts*, 182.

[124] Berger and Luckmann, *The Social Construction of Reality*, 114.

citizenship and Pharisaic membership illustrate the artificial and even somewhat arbitrary nature of social reality. Ethnicity, though it seems innate, can be a matter of choice, especially for those with dual ethnic identity, a means to gain power in the context of intergroup conflict. Common beliefs can also turn old enemies into close allies and provide privileges that come with the formation of group solidarity. Paul's defense before the tribune and the Sanhedrin reflects the Way's efforts to situate itself and construct its identity in the first-century Roman-Palestine sociopolitical milieu.

The proposed reading articulated that Paul's ever-switching self-presentation originated in Lukan ambivalence toward Rome and the Pharisees. By delving into the validity of Paul's Roman citizenship and Pharisaic identity in the narrative context, the discussion highlighted not only the key approach, social creativity, that enabled Paul to survive in agonistic contexts but also the process of identity construction of the Way. As Paul changes the measuring stick and elevates himself above his interrogators, the narrative degrades them and, at the same time, demonstrates the Way's mixed attitudes toward its out-groups. It is within this complex dynamic of intergroup relations that the identity of the Way is passionately situated, pursued, and constructed.

6

Challenging the Vicious Cycle of Slander, Labeling, and Violence (Acts 23:12-35)[1]

Jerusalem is a locus of conflict. If earlier incidents from Paul's arrest at the temple precincts to his contest at the Sanhedrin failed to underline it, the last day of his stay will reaffirm that it would be better for him to leave sooner rather than later. Following the dissension between the Pharisees and the Sadducees, the tribune comes to Paul's rescue for a third time, not realizing that there will be another more urgent and difficult challenge. Now, *the Jews*—οἱ Ἰουδαῖοι—devise a plot to kill him (v. 12). Paul's membership in the Pharisaic group will be of no use anymore because he will be dead before he has a chance to speak at the Sanhedrin (v. 15). Will he face death like his predecessor, Jesus, as he made his last trip to Jerusalem in the face of impending death? Or will his life be spared to face Rome, as the risen Lord told him in a vision (v. 11)? What is the plan of Lysias, which will sabotage the plot of *the Jews* and save Paul from this recurring violence?[2]

The aim of this chapter is not simply to analyze how the violent attack of *the Jews* is thwarted in the last episode of our study (Acts 23:12-35), which is section 7 of Paul's roller-coaster ride (see figure 1.1). On the one hand, the chapter explores, at the narrative level, the mechanics of how Jewish opposition and violence reached its climax in the given pericope.[3] Once Paul is out of Jerusalem, the deadly threat of *the Jews* is also out the window. His defense continues with Jewish interlocutors (Acts 24–26, 28). His life is once again in danger at the hands of Roman officers (Acts 27). Yet, mention of the murderous attack of *the Jews* is found no more in the ensuing narrative, which poses a question in view of the narrative scheme of Luke-Acts: "If the passion of Paul

---

[1] Aziz Esmail asserts: "Religious violence is invariably accompanied by religious discourse, whatever we may think of the objective quality of its claim to be regarded as religious." Aziz Esmail, "Religion, Identity, and Violence: Some Theoretical Reflections," in *The Blackwell Companion to Religion and Violence*, ed. Andrew R. Murphy (Malden, MA: Wiley-Blackwell, 2011), 51. It is not surprising that "You shall not make wrongful use of the name of the Lord your God" is part of the Decalogue (Exod 20:7). Evoking the name of God, whether it is direct or indirect, is often intended to evoke a passionate response, including a violent one, as this chapter delves into.

[2] In his commentary, Ben Witherington entitles Acts 23:12-35 "The Plot and the Plan." Witherington, *The Acts of the Apostles*, 694.

[3] Luke T. Johnson rightly notes: "The gathering resistance to Paul's mission among Diaspora Jews (Acts 13:45; 14:2-5; 14:19; 17:5-9; 18:12-16; 19:9; 20:3) which reached a riot pitch at the instigation of Asian Jews in the Temple precincts (21:28-36; 22:22) is now hardened into a deadly resolve to ambush and assassinate Paul." Johnson, *The Acts of the Apostles*, 407.

mimics that of Jesus, what does this narrative dissonance, Paul's so-called survival, mean for understanding Luke's two-volume work?" On the other hand, at the discourse level the chapter looks into the consequences of the dramatic presentation of Jewish hostility against the Way. The narrative describes Jewish people slandering and labeling Paul to justify their violence against him (Acts 21:17-40); Paul defends his Jewish identity and the new identity given to the Gentiles based on their faith in Jesus (Acts 22:1-21); he experiences attempted violence on the part of the Jewish crowd, Roman soldiers, and the Sanhedrin (Acts 22:22–23:11). What are the impacts of such a negative portrayal of the Jewish people? What kinds of images does the narrative generate with regard to the identity of Jews, as well as of the Way?

The focus of this chapter is, therefore, not only the event in Acts 23:12-35 but also its ramifications on the narrative structure of Luke-Acts and its implications for the construction of Christian identity. By synthesizing the previous discussions and the SIA reading of Acts 21:17–23:35, this chapter underscores the main argument of this study. Acts 21:17–23:32 constructs the Jewish people caught in a vicious cycle of slandering, labeling, and inflicting violence and attempts to break this cycle by presenting Paul's multiple subgroup and/or superordinate identities (e.g., a Jew, a Roman, a Pharisee), yet the passage falls into the same cycle at another level in the construction of Christian identity. To prove the argument, the discussion first traces the pattern of opposition in which the Jews slander, label, and commit violence against the Way in Luke-Acts. Second, the project inquires how the counter-pattern of deliverance emerges and discusses the ramifications of the Lukan literary asymmetry between the passion of Jesus and that of Paul. Lastly, the chapter problematizes the discursive portrayal of the Jews as the proximate "other" at the cost of the identity construction of the Way. The study not only explores Paul's use of his dual identity to break free from the vicious cycle of violence but also challenges the politics of group identity that the narrative both criticizes and advocates.

6.1. A Pattern of Jewish Opposition in Luke-Acts

During his brief stay in Jerusalem, Paul encounters diverse groups of Jews. Jewish believers cast doubt on his mission, Asian Jews throw charges against him, the Jewish crowd joins in the commotion, and the Sanhedrin fall into dissension among themselves because of him. In the end, *the Jews*—οἱ Ἰουδαῖοι—will carry out a plot to give Paul an ultimatum: "You are not welcome here." The Jewish reaction to the gospel in Luke-Acts is multilayered, ranging from heartwarming acceptance to heartbreaking rejection (e.g., Acts 2:37-47; Acts 7:57-58).[4] Yet, Acts 21:17–23:35 dilutes this complexity and

---

[4] Luke-Acts presents a complex picture of the Jewish people, as it does of Rome. The difficulty with grasping Luke's attitude toward the Jews is threefold. (1) *The Jewish people are comprised of multiple groups*: the Jewish populace, the chief priests, the Pharisees, the Sadducees, Jewish believers, *the Jews*—οἱ Ἰουδαῖοι—and so on. Robert L. Brawley investigates the characterization of the Jews under the following headings: (a) the Pharisees, (b) Sadducees, priests, and temple, and (c) the Jewish populace. Brawley, *Luke-Acts and the Jews*, 84–154. Jack T. Sanders's range of categories is more extensive: (a) the Jewish leaders, (b) Jerusalem, (c) the Jewish people, (d) the Pharisees, and (e) the

ambiguity while increasing the certainty. The Jewish opposition reaches its height in Jerusalem. *The Jews* place themselves under a curse—ἀνεθεμάτισαν ἑαυτοὺς—"neither to eat nor drink until they had killed Paul" (v. 12).[5] Their profile is hidden, but the narrative sequence alludes to their being "some of the Jewish crowd that had previously tried to do away with Paul in the temple precincts."[6] The Jews from Asia slandered Paul as *a man against the Jewish nation, law, and temple* and labeled him as a *traitor, heretic, blasphemer,* and *temple defiler* (Acts 21:28). The crowd joined the attack and cried out, "Away with him!" (Acts 21:36; see Acts 21:30; 22:22, 23) Now, *the Jews* are attempting to carry out the unfinished business of killing Paul (v. 12; Acts 21:30b). This vicious cycle of slander, labeling, and violence is most vividly manifested in Acts 21:17–23:35, but it is not unprecedented in Luke-Acts.

6.1.1. The Pattern of Slander, Labeling, and Violence against the Way

The Acts of the Apostles opens with Peter's address on the day of Pentecost to "devout Jews from every nation under heaven living in Jerusalem" (Acts 2:5).[7] The narrative presents the conversion of these diaspora Jews in a dramatic fashion: "They were cut to the heart and said . . . 'Brothers, what should we do?'" (Acts 2:37). About three thousand persons—ψυχαὶ—repent, welcome his message, and are baptized (Acts 2:41). The opposition, however, soon arises and complicates the Jewish response toward the Way. The Jewish violence against the Way increases as the narrative progresses.

(1) *Initial Strategy: Shut Their Mouths (Acts 4:1-23a; 5:17-40).* In the first conflict (Acts 4:1-23a) the priests, the captain of the temple, and the Sadducees arrest Peter and John and put them in custody (v. 3). They are annoyed by Peter's message, whereas about five thousand Jews believed the word (vv. 2, 4). Annas the high priest and his entourage interrogate the apostles but do not inflict violence on them. They simply order them not to speak or teach in the name of Jesus, and they threaten the apostles (vv. 18, 21). The

---

periphery: outcasts, Samaritans, proselytes, and God-fearers. Sanders, *The Jews in Luke-Acts*, 3–299. (2) *Some maintain a positive stance, while others remain hostile to the members of the Way.* For example, Luke portrays the outcasts of Jewish society, such as tax collectors and sinners, in a positive light (Lk 3:12; 5:27, 29, 30, 32; 7:29, 34, 37, 39; 15:1-7, 8-10; 18:9-14; 19:1-10). In contrast, the chief priests, leaders, and elders of the people remain consistently antagonistic to Jesus and his disciples (Lk 9:22; 19:47; 20:1, 19; 22:2, 4, 52, 66; 23:4, 10, 13, 35; 24:20; Acts 4:23; 5:21, 24; 6:12; 9:14, 21; 22:5, 30; 23:14; 24:1; 25:2, 15; 26:10, 12). (3) *Some change their view, at particular times or over time, vis-à-vis Jesus and his followers.* For instance, the people—λαός, πλῆθος, ὄχλος—sometimes follow Jesus and listen to his teaching but sometimes reject him and his followers (e.g., Lk 8:4, 35, 37; 6:12). The scribes appear to be one of the main opponents of Jesus, and Jesus openly denounces them in Luke's Gospel (Lk 5:21, 30; 6:7; 9:22; 11:53; 15:2; 19:47; 20:19, 46, 47; 22:2, 66; 23:10). Yet, one time they do acknowledge Jesus's teaching (Lk 20:39). Later, in Acts, the narrator reports that "certain scribes of the Pharisees' group" defend Paul (Acts 23:9).

[5] The same verb, ἀναθεματίζω, is used in LXX Num 21:2 and 3 to convey "'placing something under the ban (*herem*),' that is, utterly destroying it (Deut 13:15; 20:17; Josh 6:21; Judg 1:17; 21:11; 1 Sam 15:3)." Johnson, *The Acts of the Apostles*, 403–4; BDAG 63.

[6] Witherington, *The Acts of the Apostles*, 694.

[7] These Jews speak of their places of origin in the following verses: "Parthians, Medes, Elamites, and residents of Mesopotamia, Judea and Cappadocia, Pontus and Asia, Phrygia and Pamphylia, Egypt and the parts of Libya belonging to Cyrene, and visitors from Rome, both Jews and proselytes, Cretans and Arabs" (Acts 2:7-11).

narrator indicates their stumbling block: "They let them go, finding no way to punish them *because of the people*" (v. 21). People—λαός—in Jerusalem already knew about Peter's healing of the crippled beggar and were glorifying God (vv. 16, 21). Thus, even after a heated verbal exchange, Peter and John are released unharmed (v. 23).

The second conflict (Acts 5:17-40) is both similar to and different from the first. The high priest and the Sadducaic group (re)arrest the apostles and put them in prison (vv. 17-18). Though they escape from the prison, the captain and his entourage bring them to the Sanhedrin without violence because "they were afraid of being stoned by the people" (v. 26). The high priest reminds them of the gag order that had been previously given (v. 28). The council (re)orders them not to speak in the name of Jesus (v. 40). Yet, the story also shows points of difference. The level of violence increases from a verbal warning to a flogging (v. 40). Moreover, the narrator reveals that the members of the Sanhedrin want to kill them (v. 33). (Un)fortunately, Gamaliel, a Pharisee, intervenes, places limits on how the followers of the Way are to be treated, and causes them to be released a second time (vv. 34-39). The initial approach of Jewish authorities is clear. *As long as the members of the Way remain silent, there will be no killing.* The following story, however, contains significant changes concerning both the agents and the mechanics of Jewish opposition.

(2) *Testing a New Strategy: Stir up the Crowd (Acts 6:8-15).* Two earlier incidents had made it clear that, in order to punish the members of the Way, it is critical to win the minds of the people. The opponents of the Way should never make the people their enemy; the people should be their ally. The disciples are not going to stop talking and manifesting the power of the Holy Spirit and gaining support from people. The arrest of Stephen demonstrates a strategic turn in the Jewish opposition to the Way. Stephen does "great wonders and signs among the people" (v. 8). So, his opponents devise a great scheme.

(a) *Slander.* The diaspora Jews from the synagogue of the Freedmen instigate or prompt—ὑποβάλλω—men to say, "We have heard him [Stephen] speak blasphemous words against Moses and God" (v. 11). The narrator makes clear this slander originated from "false witnesses" (v. 13). The Jewish opponents earlier were dealing with "a notable sign" everybody *saw*, one that they themselves cannot deny (Acts 4:16; see also Acts 5:12-16). Now, they are dealing with "blasphemous words" that some men insist they *heard* (vv. 11, 14). The people are stirred up (v. 12).

(b) *Label.* Slander surely works. What makes their slander so effective, stirs up the people, and turns the direction of their stones,[8] however, is the discursive label that comes out of the slanders. Stephen is a *blasphemer* who speaks against the Jewish law and the temple (vv. 11, 14). The people are ready to stone anyone acting against the will of God (Acts 5:26). They have heard that Stephen has spoken evil of their sacred symbols.[9] His temple speech showed them that the accusation is not completely

---

[8] The narrator says earlier that the captain of the temple could have been stoned by the people if he had brought Peter and the apostles using violence (Acts 5:26). The death of Stephen indicates where their stones finally landed (Acts 7:54-60).
[9] Leonard W. Levy defines blasphemy as "speaking evil of sacred matters." Leonard W. Levy, *Blasphemy: Verbal Offense against the Sacred, From Moses to Salman Rushdie* (New York: Alfred A. Knopf, 1993), 3.

baseless (Acts 7:44-50; see chapter 3 of this book). Moreover, he called his addressees enemies of the Holy Spirit, betrayers and murderers of the Righteous One, and lawbreakers (vv. 51-53). Their stones have finally found its target and will not miss it.

(c) *Violence.* The final step is the killing of Stephen. They are enraged—διαπρίω— and are grinding their teeth—βρύχω—at Stephen (v. 54).[10] Nothing hinders them because the people are on their side. The narrator depicts what the madness and fury turn the people into: "But they covered their ears, and with a loud shout all rushed together against him. Then they dragged him out of the city and began to stone him" (vv. 57-58). The people have become a *mob* able to carry out a murder that could not be done earlier (Acts 5:33).[11]

(3) *Replicating the Strategy: Slander, Labeling, and Inflicting Violence.* Once they have succeeded, the new action plan is vigorously employed, especially by *the Jews*—οἱ Ἰουδαῖοι. From their first appearance to their last, what they intend to do with Paul is clear (Acts 9:23-24; 23:12-15). They want to kill him. Death threats and killings continue by different groups (e.g., the Hellenists—Acts 9:29; Herod—Acts 12:1-4).[12] Yet, it is *the Jews* who repeatedly use this new model, if not in whole then in part.

(a) *In Antioch of Pisidia (Acts 13:13-52).* The Jews find that the crowds are eager to hear Paul (vv. 42-45). They *slander*—βλασφημέω—him out of jealousy by speaking against what he says (v. 45; see also Lk 12:10).[13] When Paul and Barnabas win the minds of many, especially of Gentiles, they incite—παροτρύνω—"the devout women of high standing and the leading men of the city" (v. 50). Verse 44 reads: "*Almost* the whole city gathered" (σχεδὸν πᾶσα ἡ πόλις συνήχθη). *The Jews* once again win the favor of many and bring forth *violence*. They stir up—ἐπεγείρω—persecution and drive Paul and Barnabas out of their region (v. 50; see also Acts 14:2). The story ends with the disciples leaving the city but remaining joyful (v. 52).

(b) *In Iconium (Acts 14:1-7).* The ensuing story notifies readers that the pattern is set: "The same thing occurred in Iconium" (v. 1). The narrator (re)uses ἐπεγείρω to describe the reaction of *the Jews* when they see a great number of Jews and Greeks

---

[10] Διεπρίοντο ταῖς καρδίαις αὐτῶνreads literally "their hearts were torn apart" (author's translation). Luke T. Johnson translates the phrase as "they were ripped through their hearts" and comments that βρύχω, "grinding the teeth," is "a sign of hostility and rage, especially of the wicked against the righteous, see LXX Job 16:9; Pss 34:16; 36:12; 111:10; Lam 2:16." Johnson, *The Acts of the Apostles*, 139; BDAG 184. The narrator earlier uses διαπρίωto express the rage that the high priest and his men had against Peter and the apostles (Acts 5:33).

[11] Commenting on the death of Stephen, Shelly Matthews states: "In Acts' story, Stephen is the originary martyr. The particular details of the deaths of all other apostolic martyrs—including Paul, Peter, and James the brother of Jesus—need no elaboration; they are all superceded by/folded into the type." Matthews, *Perfect Martyr*, 77.

[12] Unlike *the Jews* and Herod, the Hellenists—αἱ Ἑλληνιστάι—are not a flat character whose characteristics are entirely negative. They are Greek Jews. In their three appearances in Acts, they belong to different groups—the disciples who complain against the Hebrew believers (Acts 6:1), those who attempt to kill Paul (Acts 9:29), and those who believe and turn to the Lord (Acts 11:20).

[13] The narrative context explains what βλασφημέωhas to do with. It is "the things spoken by Paul" (Acts 13:45: τοῖς ὑπὸ Παύλου λαλουμένοις). Luke T. Johnson comments: "Since Paul's words have to do with the message from God about Jesus, and are considered by Luke to be, in fact, 'The Word of the Lord,' slander here comes very close to the properly religious sense of 'blasphemy' (compare Luke 5:21; 22:65; 23:39)." Johnson, *The Acts of the Apostles*, 240. See also Witherington, *The Acts of the Apostles*, 415; Johnson, *The Gospel According to Luke*, 195.

becoming believers (v. 2; Acts 13:50). Though not explicit, the narrator's comment that "they poisoned the minds of the Gentiles against the brothers" implicates *slander* as a cause of the sudden turn of their minds.[14] *The Jews* again gain support from many— "both Gentiles and Jews, with their rulers"—who in the end attempt to use *violence* to mistreat and to stone them (v. 5). The narrator closes the story with the disciples fleeing Iconium but still proclaiming the good news (v. 7).

(c) *In Lystra (Acts 14:8-20)*. The story begins with a man lame from birth—χωλὸς ἐκ κοιλίας μητρὸς αὐτοῦ (v. 8; Acts 3:2). Paul's healing of the crippled man resembles the earlier incident with Peter.[15] The healing brings forth wonder and enthusiasm from the crowd, though the one praised is not God but the miracle workers Paul and Barnabas (vv. 11-12; Acts 3:9-10). The crowds even offer sacrifice to them (vv. 13, 18). Their passionate, almost fanatical, support, which Paul's speech about serving the living God does not overturn, however, quickly disappears when *the Jews* from Antioch and Iconium appear (v. 19a). The crowds join them, stone Paul, and drag him out of the city (v. 19b). How does this happen? The narrator's comment, "having persuaded the crowds"—πείσαντες τοὺς ὄχλους—though indirect, gives a clue as to what turned their support to hatred. It is the *words* of the Jews from Antioch and Iconium. They once again *slander* Paul and inflict *violence* on him. Yet, he gets up and continues traveling on his next mission (v. 20).

(d) *In Philippi (Acts 16:11-40)*. The baptism of Lydia's household and Paul's exorcism of an enslaved girl illustrate that Paul's ministry in Philippi is successful at first. Opposition, however, soon arises. The owners of the enslaved girl accuse Paul and Silas of disturbing the city and advocating customs contrary to Roman law (vv. 20-21). The charges are invalid because Paul pacified rather than disturbed the city by silencing the civic annoyance the girl created (v. 18). Paul's identification as "uncondemned," and his immediate release after confronting the magistrates imply that he and Silas are innocent of the charges from a legal standpoint (vv. 37-39). But, the public seizing/dragging and the *slander* are enough to persuade the public. *Violence* ensues. The crowd joins in attacking Paul and Silas (v. 22). The magistrates have them stripped, beaten, and imprisoned (vv. 22-24) but later apologize and release them from prison (v. 39). After encouraging their brothers and sisters, Paul and Silas depart for their next destination (v. 40).

---

[14] The narrator's introductory comment makes the use of slander all the more probable (v. 1). The Greek κακόω in v. 2 likely means "make angry" or "embitter" (Josephus, *Ant*. 16.10; 205; 262; Ps 105:32). BDAG 502. In other instances in Acts, κακόω denotes "to harm," "oppress," or "mistreat" (Acts 7:6, 19; 12:1; 18:10).

[15] Just like Peter, Paul heals the man, and his healing demonstrates that the same power that used to work in Peter and Jesus is now with him. Both Paul's healing of the crippled man (Acts 14:8-20) and Peter's healing of the crippled beggar (Acts 3:1-4:22) resemble Jesus's healing of the paralytic (Lk 5:17-26). All three miracle stories ultimately implicate that the Holy Spirit is the source of power, a power that remains consistent. Robert C. Tannehill observes the following four common elements in Paul's and Peter's healings: (1) the location of the stories: they are both the first healing stories of Peter and Paul; (2) the ensuing opposition: the healing causes resistance in the end; (3) the rebuke: the missionaries rebuke the crowd by saying, "Men … why?"; and (4) the confusion: the people mistakenly think that the healing power came from the missionaries themselves, not from God. Tannehill, *The Narrative Unity of Luke-Acts*, 2.178.

(e) *In Thessalonica (Acts 17:1-9).* Paul's initial teaching in the synagogue is well received. Some are persuaded—πείθω—and join—προσκληρόω—Paul and Silas (v. 4). Once again, the people's reaction—a large crowd of devout Greeks and a few important women begin following them—causes the jealousy of *the Jews* (v. 5). The narrator's description of those who help them to set the city in an uproar—ἄνδρας τινὰς πονηροὺς: "certain wicked men"—implies that the crowd will be swayed by *false witnesses* and join their *violence* (v. 5). Their accusations are saturated with a political overtone that seems not altogether slanderous and immediately disturbs the city (vv. 6-8; see chapter 3.4.3 in this book). The anti-Way *label* is clear. They are *traitors* (v. 7; Lk 23:2). The ending of the story, however, complicates the issue. The city officials, after taking bail from Jason and the others, let them go (v. 9). They could not have been freed if they had been found guilty of treason. The incident reveals Rome's changing view toward the Way as well as the change in its treatment of members of the Way from violence to nonviolence (Acts 16:22-24). The accusers' claims are not so much political as religious, which will become more explicit in Corinth (Acts 18:14-15).

(f) *In Beroea (Acts 17:10-15).* Sent to Beroea, Paul and Silas are welcomed first at the synagogue, in which they find believers not only among the Jews but also among the leading Greeks of the city (vv. 10-12). Then, *the Jews* come from Thessalonica, and they stir up and incite the crowds (v. 13). The possible *slander* and *labels* they employ to create a mob are unclear, yet their *violence* is fierce enough for the believers—ἀδελφοὶ—to send Paul as far away as Athens (v. 15). The story ends with Paul's request for Silas and Timothy to join him on the unfinished mission (v. 15).

(g) *In Athens (Acts 17:16-34).* Paul's unintended visit to Athens deviates from the proposed pattern yet conveys a message. The setting is initially the Jewish synagogue and then changes to the marketplace and ultimately to the Areopagus (vv. 17, 19). His message leads to a disturbance among Epicurean and Stoic philosophers at first yet ultimately to acceptance from some (vv. 18, 19, 34).[16] His stay at Athens illustrates that without slanderous attacks from *the Jews*, Paul is able to not only persuade some but also to remain safe (vv. 32, 34).

(h) *In Corinth (Acts 18:1-17).* In Corinth, *the Jews* reappear and the cycle repeats itself. Paul's ministry starts with preaching both to Jews and Greeks at the synagogue, yet it quickly becomes an apology against *the Jews* (vv. 4-5). Though brief, the narrator's comment on what happened between Paul and *the Jews*—"they opposed and reviled him"—is self-explanatory (v. 6). Their opposition is collective—ἀντιτάσσομαι[17]—and their words are *slanderous*—βλασφημέω(v. 6; Acts 13:45). Violence is absent, as no report of converts is found. However, when Paul later makes many converts—Crispus, his household, and many of the Corinthians—the situation changes (v. 8). *The Jews* rise

---

[16] Surely, Paul's success is modest in Athens. Yet, the names of the converts show that he continues to gain support among leading men and devout women of the city. Luke T. Johnson notes that the male convert, Dionysius, Ἀρεοπαγίτης, is likely "a member of Athenian council and therefore of high social rank (Aristotle, *Politics* 1273B–1274A)" and that Damaris is a woman whose conversion likely led to "the foundation of a community." Johnson, *The Acts of the Apostles*, 317–18.

[17] "This is Luke's only use of *antitassomai* ('oppose'), which has the connotation of an organized front of resistance (see Herodotus, *Hist.* 4.134)." Johnson, *The Acts of the Apostles*, 323.

up together against Paul and bring him to the tribunal—βῆμα (v. 12).[18] They say to Gallio, "This man is persuading people to worship God in ways that are contrary to the law" (v. 13). The charge is similar to those given against Stephen (Acts 6:11, 13). But, in the narrative context, the accusation is vague and even slanderous because the heart of Paul's message in Corinth is that Jesus is the Messiah (v. 5). Rather than investigating the allegation, Gallio refuses to be involved. He says, "It is a matter of questions about words and names and your own law" (v. 15). Upon Gallio's order of dismissal—ἀπελαύνω—the victim shifts from Paul to Sosthenes, the official of the synagogue, and the violence continues (v. 17). The text is unclear as to why *the Jews* beat Sosthenes. Is he a member of the Way? The narrative does not say. But, it is clear that *the Jews* are programmed to carry out violence after defamation.

(i) *In Ephesus (Acts 19:8-41)*. The story begins with Paul meeting some disciples and baptizing them (vv. 1-7).[19] His successful ministry first encounters resistance at the synagogue (v. 8). Some not only harden—σκληρύνω[20]—their hearts and refuse to believe but also speak evil of—κακολογέω—the Way before the congregation (v. 9). This "public reviling," Luke T. Johnson rightly notes, "corresponds to blaspheming (*blasphemein*) Paul experienced in 18:6" (see Herodotus, *Hist.* 7.237).[21] It is their *slander*, malicious words designed to destroy—κακολογέω—that causes him to leave the synagogue (v. 9). Violence is not involved because Paul's ministry has gained no popularity at this point. Yet, as he begins teaching outside the synagogue, the situation changes. Paul's preaching, healing, and exorcism shake the entire city (vv. 10-12). Its residents praise the name of Jesus, many become believers, and those who practiced magic burn their books publicly (vv. 13-20).

His success, arguably "the climax of Paul's ministry and missionary work as a free man,"[22] however, causes the vicious cycle to begin. Demetrius, a silversmith of Artemis, stirs up those in his guild and puts the city in confusion (vv. 23-29). The initial *charge*—that Paul was telling many that "gods made with hands are not gods"—seems valid, as Paul repeatedly underscores this point (v. 26; Acts 14:15-17; 17:24-25; see also Acts 7:48-50). The shouting—"Great is Artemis of the Ephesians!"—implies that Paul was *labeled* "a blasphemer" who was profaning what was considered sacred (vv. 28, 34). *Violence* follows. The crowd drags Gaius and Aristarchus to the theater (v. 29). The

---

[18] The D-text emphasizes the opposition of *the Jews*: "the Jews, having talked together among themselves against Paul . . ." βῆμα, "the tribunal," denotes a physical space in which judicial matters are discussed and decided or an official person or body before whom the hearing is presented. BDAG 175. Carl R. Holladay notes: "*Bēma* as the site of court appearances occurs in Acts 12:21; 18:12, 16-17; 25:6, 10, 17." Holladay, *Acts*, 353.

[19] The narrator reports that the disciples were not yet baptized in the name of Jesus, and, when Paul baptized them, they received the Holy Spirit (vv. 5-8).

[20] The use of the term σκληρύνω should not be overlooked. "The language of 'hardening,' of course, recalls the biblical characterization of Pharaoh (LXX Exod 4:21; 7:3; 8:19; 13:15), and of the people of Israel in its turning from the Lord (Deut 2:30; 10:16; Ps 94:8; Isa 63:17; Jer 7:26; 17:23; 19:15). It signifies a stubborn resistance in the face of God's visitation." Johnson, *The Acts of the Apostles*, 339.

[21] Johnson, *The Acts of the Apostles*, 339.

[22] Witherington, *The Acts of the Apostles*, 572. Robert C. Tannehill also notes that Ephesus is "the place where Paul most fully realizes his calling to be Jesus' 'witness to all persons' (22:15)." Tannehill, *The Narrative Unity of Luke-Acts*, 2.236.

ensuing scene complicates who causes the commotion in the city. The narrator's report of the crowd's reaction—"The assembly was in confusion, and most of them did not know why they had come together"—shows that Demetrius' words turned a crowd into a mob ready to cause trouble (vv. 32, 40). The city clerk—γραμματεὺς—intervenes, like Gallio did in Corinth, and dismisses the assembly (vv. 35-41).

Unlike the riot in Corinth, however, violence of *the Jews* is absent because the crowd does not favor them (v. 34). The city clerk's speech is significant in several ways. First, he argues that Paul and his co-workers are not blasphemers of Artemis, which illustrates that the Way, just as one stream in the Jewish tradition, does not advocate deriding or blaspheming pagan deities (v. 37; Josephus, *Ant.* 4.207; *Apion* 2.237).[23] Second, complaints against the Way should be made at the court according to the legal process, not in a public space where there is danger of a riot (vv. 38-39). The matter should not be done rashly—προπετής(v. 36). Third, falsely accusing the Way and causing a commotion are subject to civil justice (v. 40). Lastly, the speech foreshadows what will happen next (v. 38). There will be a commotion, but Paul will be at the court defending himself (Acts 23–26).[24]

(j) *In Jerusalem (Acts 21:27–23:11)*. The cycle repeats when Paul is in Jerusalem. *The Jews* from Asia *slander* Paul as a man who is against the Jewish nation, law, and temple and *label* him a *traitor, heretic, blasphemer,* and *temple defiler* (Acts 21:27-29). The people quickly respond, and the city is in an uproar (vv. 30-31). After arresting and dragging him, the beating begins (vv. 30, 32). The tribune intervenes and saves him from the *violence* (vv. 33-36). Unlike Gallio and the city clerk in Ephesus, he neither speaks to nor dismisses the crowd. Rather, he allows Paul to defend himself (vv. 37-40). His defense ends, however, with another commotion (Acts 22:1-23). Following the crowd's outcry, the tribune attempts to flog Paul but fails to do so because of his Roman citizenship (vv. 24-29). He is handed over to the Sanhedrin, and the violence persists (vv. 30–23:5). Yet, this time the instigator of the crowd is not his opponents but Paul himself (vv. 6-9). Violent dissension rises, and the tribune rescues Paul one more time (v. 10).

(4) *Summary*. Richard P. Thompson rightly identifies a typical pattern in the Pauline ministry in Acts: (a) Paul's visit to the synagogue, (b) Paul's proclamation of the gospel, (c) a positive response from the audience, and (d) Jewish opposition.[25] This study tackles the last piece of this puzzle by exploring how the (Jewish) rejection unfolds in public spaces. Section 6.1.1 in this chapter argued that the opposition typically starts with *slander*, making false statements about someone. The crowd reacts vehemently when the slander generates *labels* that threaten the very foundation of society, particularly the sociopolitical and religious symbols upon which Roman/Jewish society is built. *Violence* ensues to eliminate the threat, which is the Way, and to maintain the status quo. The Jewish opposition in Jerusalem (Acts 21:17–23:35), in this sense, is a replication (and even amplification!) of the vicious cycle of slander, labeling, and

---

[23] Holladay, *Acts*, 386.
[24] *The Jews*—οἱ Ἰουδαῖοι—appear in Acts 20:3, in which they devise a plot against Paul, but their plan fails as he leaves Greece (see also Acts 20:19).
[25] Thompson, "Say It Ain't So, Paul!" 46.

violence. Now, the risen Lord tells Paul, "You must bear witness also in Rome" (Acts 23:11). How can Paul leave Jerusalem, go to Rome, and proclaim the gospel there while he is in chains? The key to this mystery is ironically found in the last piece of the vicious cycle. It is the undying determination of *the Jews* to kill Paul that ultimately saves Paul and enables him to embark on his journey to Rome.

6.1.2. The Final Cycle of Violence (Acts 23:12-15)

(1) *The New Plot Devised: "Fool the Romans!"* Acts of violence are constantly being attempted in Jerusalem by the Jewish crowd (Acts 21:31-36; 22:22-24a), by the tribune (Acts 22:24b-29), and by the Sanhedrin (Acts 23:1-10). None is successful. Paul's defense speech and almost miraculous survival, however, "serves only to consolidate Jewish opposition to him."[26] *The Jews* join a conspiracy—ποιήσαντες συστροφὴν[27]— and place themselves under a curse—ἀναθεματίζω(vv. 12, 14).[28] Their oath to neither eat nor drink not only shows their fanaticism[29] but also makes it clear that the vicious cycle will continue until Paul ceases to exist. Earlier, Paul had fasted to discern God's plan (Acts 9:9). Now, *the Jews* fast to defy it (v. 11).

A formidable difficulty is that Paul is under the tribune's care. Inciting the crowd will no longer work. Thus, a new plot is devised. This time, *the Jews* will deceive the Romans, not the crowd, by taking advantage of the Roman legal process under which Paul has found a safe haven.[30] They will pretend to respect Roman judicial law but will ultimately break it. The murderous scheme is as follows. The chief priests and elders make a request for the tribune to bring Paul down to them for a more thorough investigation (v. 15b). On his way to the Sanhedrin, *the Jews* will do away with him (v. 15c). The invitation to a courtroom is, in fact, a summons to the guillotine. They— "more than forty men"—will act with the help of the chief priests and elders (v. 13). The tribune and his entourage, when they find out, will be stunned. The roller coaster drops, and there seems to be neither brakes nor an exit, just a dead end.

(2) *Replicating the Death Plot*. The conspiracy (vv. 12-15) is significant in two ways. First, it shows the new pattern of violence *the Jews* have developed: "Deceive the Romans and kill Paul in an ambush." After Festus replaces Felix, they make a similar

---

[26] Fitzmyer, *The Acts of the Apostles*, 722.

[27] Συστροφήgenerally means "a meeting," but here it refers to "a protest meeting." Fitzmyer, *The Acts of the Apostles*, 722. According to BDAG, it means a "disorderly or seditious gathering." BDAG 795. Three roughly synonymous terms are used to refer to the plan of the Jews in this pericope: συστροφή, "a seditious gathering" (v. 12); συνωμοσία, "a league bound by oath" (v. 13); and ἐπιβουλή, "a plan against" (v. 30). Similarly, ἀναθεματίζωappears three times (vv. 12, 14, 21). Johnson, *The Acts of the Apostles*, 403–4. It is interesting to note that the narrative uses ἀπαγγέλλω—"to report"— three times also in disclosing the plot of *the Jews* (vv. 16, 17, 19).

[28] Some manuscripts, such as Papyrus 48, read "some [τίνες] Jews" and thus soften the Jewish opposition. Carl R. Holladay further comments: "This revision was likely prompted by the mention in 13 of forty conspirators, thus indicating that they were a subset of the larger Jewish population." Holladay, *Acts*, 437.

[29] Pervo, *Acts*, 582.

[30] Verse 21—"They are ready now and are waiting for your consent"—implies that the demand for the second investigation is finally made by the council to the tribune. Witherington, *The Acts of the Apostles*, 695.

request for their new governor to transfer Paul from Caesarea to Jerusalem so that they may kill him on the way (Acts 25:1-3). Second, the plot of *the Jews*, when juxtaposed against the plot to kill Jesus (Lk 22:1-6), shows an interesting Lukan characterization. In both stories, three groups of characters appear—authorities, conspirators, and the victim. In Luke, *the chief priests* with the scribes and officers of the temple police seek the life of *Jesus*, the victim. In like manner, in Acts, *the chief priests* with the elders set the stage to stab Paul from behind. In Luke, *Judas* discusses with—συλλαλέω—the authorities how to betray Jesus. In Acts, it is *the Jews* who devise a joint plan—συστροφή—to kill Paul. Are *the Jews* the parallel to Judas? It seems so, but there is more.

(3) *Satan Replaced by the Jews.* The ultimate conspirator seeking Jesus's life in Luke is neither the Jewish authorities nor Judas but Satan (Lk 22:3, 53).[31] As soon as Jesus begins his ministry, Satan/the Devil *tests*—πειράζω—Jesus (Lk 4:2, 12, 13). Though he withdraws from Jesus temporarily,[32] Satan's presence in the narrative is alive and well as the archenemy of Jesus behind the scenes (Lk 8:12; 10:18; 11:18; 13:16). Satan (re)enters the narrative when Jesus is in Jerusalem and successfully carries out the murderous plot (Lk 22:3, 31, 53; 23:44-46).[33]

Early in Acts, Satan deceives Ananias and leads Ananias as well as his wife to death (Acts 5:1-11). Though Satan's appearance is brief, the story aptly captures Satan's character. Satan is to "speak falsely" or "willfully misrepresent"—ψεύδομαι—to the Holy Spirit and to "put the Spirit of the Lord to the test"—πειράζω(Acts 5:3, 9). Satan falsely encourages Jesus to turn the stone into a loaf of bread; worship Satan, not God; and prove that God is protecting Jesus (Lk 4:3, 6-7, 9-11). These misrepresentations ultimately aim to "put the Lord your God to the test" (Lk 5:12; Acts 5:9).[34] Satan/the Devil, particularly its activity, is almost absent in the rest of Acts, including the passion of Paul. But, the test of God's plan of salvation continues with the emergence of *the Jews* who engage in slander, labeling, and violence.

---

[31] "Darkness" in Luke represents the area in which Satan's energy is manifest (Lk 1:79; 11:34, 35, 36; 22:53; 23:44).

[32] From Lk 4:13, Hans Conzelmann argues that the end of the Temptation is the beginning of the "Satan-free" era: "The Temptation is finished decisively (πάντα), and the devil departs ... where Jesus is from now on, there Satan is no more." Conzelmann, *The Theology of St Luke*, 28. See also Schuyler Brown, *Apostasy and Perseverance in the Theology of Luke* (Rome: Pontifical Biblical Institute, 1969), 5.

[33] Jesus calls out at his arrest, "This is your hour, and the power of darkness" (Lk 22:53). The narrator portrays at the crucifixion *who* is behind Jesus's death: "It was now about noon, and *darkness came over the whole land*" (Lk 23:44).

[34] The three temptations of the devil contain misrepresentations in certain aspects. (1) *Turning the stone into a loaf of bread* (Lk 4:1-4). This miracle is not unprecedented. God provided manna to the Israelites in the wilderness and fed them (Exod 16:1-36). By rejecting the miracle, however, Jesus chooses to be obedient to the word of God. (2) *Worshiping Satan* (Lk 4:5-8). Satan's claim that he has the power and glory of all the kingdoms of the earth is a lie. Satan surely oppresses people (e.g., Lk 13:16; Acts 26:18). But, it is God who has the final victory over Satan, as Jesus demonstrates in his ministry. (3) *Throwing himself down from the pinnacle of the temple* (Lk 4:9-12). Satan specifically quotes Psalm 91(LXX, Ps 90):11-12 to justify his request on a scriptural basis. Jesus refuses because that would be tempting God, just as the Israelites tempted God by demanding water in the wilderness (Exod 17:1-7). Bovon, *Luke 1*, 142–5.

The Jews first appear as soon as Paul converts to the Way and begins proclaiming the gospel, just as Satan intervenes at the beginning of Jesus's ministry (Acts 9:20-25; Lk 3:21–4:15). *The Jews* are present in almost every corner where Paul preaches the gospel, and they stir up opposition to him (e.g., Acts 9:23, 24; 13:45, 50, 14:2, 4, 5, 19; 17:5, 13; 18:12; 20:3, 19). Acts is full of what Gonzalo Haya-Prats calls *"invasive irruptions"* and the *"complementary influence"* of the Holy Spirit.[35] Since the Holy Spirit, as "a distinct narrative character,"[36] initiates, orchestrates, and participates in the mission of the Way, this slandering of Paul and resisting his proclamation ultimately put the Spirit to the test.[37] The united attack of *the Jews* in vv. 12-15 marks not only the penultimate attempt to murder Paul but also the distinct Lukan characterization.[38] *The Jews* are destined to kill Paul (Acts 9:23; 23:12-15). Paul is in Jerusalem. Just as Satan plotted against and killed Jesus, *the Jews* plan to make Jerusalem Paul's graveyard (vv. 12-15; Lk 22:1-6). Their *Satan-like* role continues and becomes clearer in the passion of Paul when they are called οἱ κατήγοροί—"the accusers" (Acts 23:30, 35; 24:8; 25:16, 18); the singular form refers to Satan (הַשָּׂטָן: *the accuser*).[39]

6.2. Breaking the Vicious Cycle

History does not repeat itself, however. Paul's last day in Jerusalem arguably provides one of the most dramatic scenes in Acts. The person who seems destined to be the ultimate victim escapes Jerusalem, not on his own but with the help of Roman soldiers who had previously attempted to flog him. What happens thereafter and how it transpires are breathtaking. The rescue mission takes place in secret, whereas the story

---

[35] "Invasive irruptions" refer to the mode of action in which the Holy Spirit directs human decisions by means of speech or action like a boss (e.g., Acts 8:29, 39; 10:19; 11:12, 28; 13:2, 4; 16:6-7; 20:22, 23, 28; 21:4, 11). A "complementary influence" refers to the mode of action in which the Holy Spirit provides the impulse so that the person acts (e.g., Acts 2:4; 4:8, 13, 20, 31; 6:3, 5, 10; 7:55; 11:24; 13:9-10; 19:21). Gonzalo Haya-Prats, *Empowered Believers: The Holy Spirit in the Book of Acts*, ed. Paul Elbert, trans. Scott A. Ellington (Eugene, OR: Cascade Books, 2011), 72–6.

[36] Christos Karakolis, "The Holy Spirit in Luke-Acts: Personal Entity or Impersonal Power?" in *The Holy Spirit and the Church according to the New Testament: Sixth International East-West Symposium of New Testament Scholars, Belgrade, August 25 to 31, 2013*, ed. Predrag Dragutinovic, Karl-Wilhelm Niebuhr, and James Buchanan Wallace in co-operation with Christos Karakolis, WUNT 354 (Tübingen: Mohr Siebeck, 2016), 87–109.

[37] Commenting on the Spirit and the work of the prophetic figures in Luke-Acts, William H. Shepherd states: "It is clear that behind many human conflicts there stands a cosmic battle (Luke 4:1–14; Acts 5:1–11; 6:1—7:55; 8:4–25; 13:4–12). The spirit is characterized by contrast with the forces which work against the fulfillment of God's purposes." William H. Shepherd Jr., *The Narrative Function of the Holy Spirit as a Character in Luke-Acts*, SBLDS 147 (Atlanta: Scholars Press, 1994), 249.

[38] *The Jews* make one last attempt to kill Paul when he is in Felix's care (Acts 25:1-3).

[39] Κατήγορoς is a literal transcription of the Hebrew קָטֵיגוֹר, a name the rabbis gave to the devil. Satan with the definite article appears thirteen times in the Old Testament to convey the meaning of "adversary" or "accuser" (Job 1:6, 7, 8, 9, 12; 2:1, 2, 3, 4, 6, 7; Zech 3:1, 2). BDAG 533; BDB 966; LSJ 926–7; *Strong's* 1508. The portrayal of Jews in John's Gospel is no different from that of *the Jews* in Acts. David Nirenberg comments: "John's Jews are as close as canonical scripture ever comes to the embodiment—Satan aside—of *a purely negative principle* . . . [The author of Acts] presents the Jews as *enemies not only of God but also of all other prophets including Paul*." Nirenberg, *Anti-Judaism*, 83, emphasis added.

provides a sequence vivid, swift, and exciting enough to create a spectacle before the eyes of its audience. Yet, there is more to what this anecdote entails for the grand narrative of Luke-Acts.

6.2.1. The Pattern of Deliverance: Discovery, Development, and Destruction

Not only the pattern of Jewish opposition but also the pattern of deliverance begins emerging in the narrative. Just as *the Jews* slander, label, and inflict violence to frustrate the efforts and expansion of the Way, the Way discovers the conspiracy, develops a counterplan, and defeats the attempt of *the Jews* by departing the area. Furthermore, with the ever-increasing presence of Rome, Acts gradually changes the attitude of the Roman officials toward both *the Jews* and the Way and portrays them ultimately as the last piece of the puzzle and essential for the deliverance of Paul.

(1) *The Counter-Pattern Introduced (Acts 9:23-30)*. The first encounter between Paul and *the Jews* in Damascus is a programmatic passage, just as Jesus's inaugural address exemplifies the Jewish rejection that will be repeated in Luke-Acts (Lk 4:16-30).[40] Paul's bold preaching leads to "plots on his life."[41] *The Jews* devise, for the first time, a plot to kill Paul (v. 23). Paul finds out that they are looking for a chance to ambush him (v. 24). His disciples develop a counterplan. They take him by night and let him down through the wall in a basket (v. 25). The conspiracy fails, and Paul is out of Damascus (v. 26). The same pattern appears during his first stay in Jerusalem after his conversion/call. Paul's preaching results in another attempt to kill him by the Jewish Hellenists (v. 29). The believers learn of it, bring Paul down to Caesarea, and send him away to Tarsus (v. 30). The plot is disclosed first, the counterplan is devised upon learning of the plot, and the conspiracy falls apart. This passage surely links Paul to Jesus, the apostles, and Stephen by portraying "plots to do away with him" (ἀναιρέω, v. 29; Acts 2:23; 5:33; 10:39; 13:28; 8:1; 22:20).[42] Yet, there is another connection/pattern that the passage generates.

(2) *The Counter-Pattern Replicated (Acts 14:1-7)*. A similar event occurs in Iconium. Here, Paul's audience is not limited to Jewish people only, as in the previous incidents, but encompasses Gentiles as well (v. 1). His bold preaching once again triggers opposition. The vicious cycle is initiated. Unbelieving Jews slander Paul and Barnabas and stir up Gentiles, poisoning their minds (v. 2). Eventually, a violent reaction takes place. This time, both Jews and Gentiles join the plot to mistreat and stone Paul and Barnabas (v. 5). A counter-cycle also starts spinning to nullify their attempt. Paul and Barnabas discover the plot and develop a counterplan. They flee to Lystra and Derbe and destroy the plot by continuing their efforts to proclaim the gospel (vv. 6-7). The pattern fades out until it is fully (re)introduced in Acts 23. In the meantime, the Way finds a new form of protection in the midst of the ever-increasing opposition.

(3) *The Counter-Pattern Reinforced: Rome in Favor of the Way*. The portrayal of Rome in Luke-Acts is ambivalent. The narrative does not hesitate to disclose both the

---

[40] Bovon, *Luke 1*, 157.
[41] Tannehill, *The Narrative Unity of Luke-Acts*, 2.122.
[42] Tannehill, *The Narrative Unity of Luke-Acts*, 2.123.

corruption and the folly of the Roman officials. Yet, at the same time, the growing Roman presence increases the resources of the Way in this fierce battle with its opponents.

The Roman protection of the Way comes relatively late in the narrative. Early in Acts, the Jewish authorities arrest, threaten, and flog the apostles (Acts 4:18, 21; 5:17, 18, 40). Stephen is killed, and severe persecution breaks out (Acts 7:58–8:3; 9:1-2). The Roman officials, despite the turbulence these conflicts may have caused, are not found in these episodes. It is the same with Paul's early ministry. Paul's proclamation of the gospel leads to public commotion and violence, but Roman law enforcement is virtually missing (Acts 13:50; 14:4-5, 19).

After the Jerusalem council and the official beginning of the Gentile mission, however, Roman officials intrude on the narrative. Rome's change in attitude is worth noting. At first, the Romans are in support of the mobbish crowd and in opposition to the Way (16:19-22; 17:5-8, 13). Gradually, they cast doubt on the reckless attacks of the crowd (18:12-17; 19:28-41). The final episode of this study—Acts 23:12-35—highlights not only the increased status of the Roman officials but also the change in how Romans are represented in the narrative. By the end, Rome is no longer an opponent of the Way—it has become its protector. The vicious cycle will continue and even be notched up later on, but the counter-cycle will also fully develop with Rome's legal protection, defy the murdering plot of *the Jews*, and deliver Paul to safety.

6.2.2. The Final Cycle of Deliverance (Acts 23:16-35)

In view of these two cycles—one vicious and the other benevolent—developed so far, Paul's escape from Jerusalem more than heightens "the sense of danger encompassing Paul."[43] As the vicious cycle reaches its height, the counter-cycle fully discloses its shape. The episode is both the climax and amplification of the violent struggle between *the Jews* and the Way.

(1) *The Plot Discovered*. In Jerusalem, the vicious cycle is reactivated. Paul's bold defense and proclamation incite anger among his audience, especially *the Jews* (vv. 12, 14). Then, there comes a hero who reveals their plan and helps save Paul.[44] Paul's nephew hears about the ambush, goes to the barracks, and unveils the plot to Paul (v. 16). His adventure does not end there.[45] Paul calls a centurion and asks him to take the young man[46]—νεανίας—to the tribune to make a report to him (v. 17). His request is accepted, and the young man finally encounters the head of the cohort (v. 18).[47]

---

[43] Gaventa, *Acts*, 318.
[44] The boy is "an ad hoc character who disappears as soon as he has fulfilled his function," as Richard I. Pervo argues. Pervo, *Acts*, 582. Yet, he is also a critical character necessary for the plot development.
[45] Commenting on Acts 23:16-35, Luke T. Johnson notes: "Regarded simply as a story, this section has the intrinsic charm of a boy's adventure." Johnson, *The Acts of the Apostles*, 407.
[46] The narrative uses νεανίαςin v. 17 and νεανίσκοςin v. 18 and v. 22 to refer to Paul's nephew. LXX translates the Hebrew נער in Gen 41:12 to νεανίσκοςto signify a young man between twenty and forty years old.
[47] The term "prisoner"—δέσμιος—is problematic since Paul, though in the barracks, is not a prisoner in the technical sense. Carl R. Holladay states: "By the time Luke wrote, Pauline imprisonments had become a well-established feature of his legendary profile, which included 'prisoner' as a form of self-description." Holladay, *Acts*, 439.

This meeting is critical in several aspects. First, the event takes a central place in the episode (Acts 23:12-35).[48] Second, the young man's conversation brings the suspense, which has been building up to this point, to its climax. The narrative time slows down as the camera focuses on detailed movements: "The tribune *took him by the hand, drew him aside privately*, and *asked*" (v. 19). The open conversation between two military personnel suddenly becomes a private report of a secret emissary to the tribune (vv. 18-22). Third, the young man's last comment—"They are *ready now* and are *waiting* for your consent"—demands decisive action from the tribune (v. 21). The matter is urgent and in need of immediate action. Fourth, Lysias' final words—"Tell no one that you have informed me of this"—foreshadow another plan that will soon develop and will upset the plot of *the Jews* (v. 22). The ambush will be ambushed, and the oath of *the Jews* will be obliterated.

(2) *The Counterplan Developed*. Strangely enough, the tribune neither doubts nor further investigates the young man's report. He quickly summons two centurions and orders them to take Paul and leave Jerusalem by nine o'clock that night (v. 23).[49] Four hundred and seventy Roman military personnel—"two hundred soldiers, seventy horsemen, and two hundred spearmen/archers"[50]—are to undertake the last mission to rescue Paul (v. 23). How the mission is carried out is not just fanciful and fantastic but unrealistic and even unnecessary. These men are almost half of the cohort stationed at Antonia Fortress. These trained, armed soldiers outnumber the Jews lying in the ambush by twelve to one.

The story, however, successfully conveys its message, "the sense of security guaranteed to Paul,"[51] as Lysias reiterates at the end of his command: "take him safely [διασώζω] to Felix the governor" (v. 24; Acts 27:43, 44; 28:1, 4).[52] Although he normally

---

[48] The chiastic structure of Acts 23:12-35 is as follows:

    A.   vv. 12-15: *The Jews* devise and develop the plan to kill Paul
    B.   vv. 16-21: The plan is disclosed
    A`.   vv. 22-35: Lysias designs and directs the plan to save Paul

[49] The text reads literally "from the third hour of the night" (v. 23: ἀπὸ τρίτης ὥρας τῆς νυκτός, author's translation), which means "three hours after sunset." Fitzmyer, *The Acts of the Apostles*, 726.

[50] The Greek δεξιόλαβος means literally "to grasp with the right hand." Scholars propose several translations. For example, Ben Witherington reads "those who led horses (with the right hand)." Witherington, *The Acts of the Apostles*, 696. Carl R. Holladay reads "archers." Holladay, *Acts*, 440. Luke T. Johnson gives multiple options, "from 'guard,' to 'spearman,' to 'swordsman.'" Johnson, *The Acts of the Apostles*, 405 (NRSV: "a spearman"). Joseph A. Fitzmyer's suggestion probably captures the ambiguity of the term at its best: "light-armed auxiliaries." Fitzmyer, *The Acts of the Apostles*, 727.

[51] Fitzmyer, *The Acts of the Apostles*, 726-7.

[52] Some suggest that "mounts for Paul to ride" in v. 24 shows that Paul's companions are present at the scene. They argue, first, that the plural form κτήνη—"beasts of burden"—is used, which infers that those with Paul are also provided with mounts. Second, Acts 24:23 implies that Paul's friends accompanied Paul to Caesarea. Third, "we" picks up when Paul enters Jerusalem and leaves Caesarea (Acts 21:17; 27:1). David J. Williams, *Acts* (San Francisco: Harper, 1985), 390; Witherington, *The Acts of the Apostles*, 697-8.

Although the narrative calls Felix's office ἡγεμών, "governor" (23:24, 26, 33; 24:1, 10), he was in a technical sense a procurator, ἐπίτροπος or ἐπιτροπεία, "the name by which these Roman appointees were known after the death of Agrippa I in 44 CE (12:23), when Judea was restored to direct Roman rule." Holladay, *Acts*, 441. A solution to this dilemma is the Lukan literary technic, "prophecy and fulfillment." Earlier in the Gospel, Jesus foretold to his disciples that they would be "brought before

would have waited until Felix next visited Jerusalem on his judicial tour of duty, he cannot afford such leisure at this point. He writes a letter to Felix, which the narrator describes as "having this form [ἔχουσαν τὸν τύπον τοῦτον]" (v. 25, author's translation; NRSV: "to this effect").[53] Scholars are divided over how reliable this letter can be and who actually wrote it. The debate is "a tempest in a teapot,"[54] as Richard I. Pervo puts it, since the letter is clearly a Lukan creation. The letter has none of the proper mentions of the prisoner's "parentage, place of birth, and the charges against him" that a *libellus dimissoriae* should have (Justinianus, *Dig. Just.* 49.6.1).[55] Even Paul's name is missing!

(3) *The Plot Destroyed*. Nevertheless, Lysias' letter (vv. 26-30) plays a critical role in Acts. It breaks the vicious cycle of Jewish violence in several ways. First, it gives Paul a ticket to Caesarea without cost to him. He will be out of Jerusalem, the place of Jewish violence, and will be transferred to the governor's care (v. 30). Second, the letter upgrades the resources with which Paul is provided. Previously, he was treated harshly by the soldiers, who threatened him with thongs. Now, he will have plenty of space for his luggage and will have travel attendants to assist him (vv. 23-25). Third, the letter states that this is Paul's right. As a Roman citizen, he has the right not only to defend himself at the court but also to have the protection of Rome (vv. 27-30).[56] Fourth, the document reports to Felix the wrong treatment Paul received during his stay in Jerusalem. *The Jews* are blamed for their murderous plot as well as the commotion they created (vv. 27, 30). Fifth, the letter allows Paul to stand on the high ground before the investigation begins. His accusers brought charges against him, but they are not serious crimes deserving death or imprisonment (v. 29). Finally, but most importantly, the correspondence changes the setting of the dispute once and for all. Formerly, Paul was mistreated both inside and outside Jerusalem and by both Jews and Gentiles. It was relatively easy for the opposing party to lay hands on him. From this time on, Paul is under Rome's legal protection, and *the Jews* cannot throw him into the vicious cycle designed to cut him into pieces. They can neither drag him out to public spaces nor stir

---

kings and governors," prominent rulers of the empire (Lk 21:12; see also Lk 20:20). Now, Paul defends both himself and the gospel before the governor, Felix. Commenting on his procuratorship over Judea, which lasted from 52/53-59/60, Tacitus says that Felix "practiced every kind of cruelty and lust, wielding the power of king with all the instincts of a slave" (Tacitus, *Hist.* 5.9; *Ann.* 12.54; see also Josephus, *War* 2.12.8; *Ant.* 20.7.1-2).

[53] Some think that the letter is an actual copy of Lysias' letter (e.g., Witherington), that it derives from Paul (e.g., Hemer), or that it was a Lukan composition (e.g., Fitzmyer). *NewDocs* 1 (1981), 77-8; Witherington, *The Acts of the Apostles*, 698-9; Colin J. Hemer, *The Book of Acts in the Setting of Hellenistic History*, WUNT 49 (Tübingen: J. C. B. Mohr, 1989), 348; Fitzmyer, *The Acts of the Apostles*, 726.

[54] Pervo, *Acts*, 584.

[55] Pervo, *Acts*, 586. See also Fitzmyer, *The Acts of the Apostles*, 726; Sherwin-White, *Roman Society*, 54-5. Upon meeting Paul, Felix inquires of his origin and states that he will hear the case against Paul (vv. 34-35).

[56] The tribune's report in v. 27—"when I had learned that he was a Roman citizen, I came with the guard and rescued him"—is far from what actually happened. Lysias intervened not to rescue Paul but to restore order. By bending the truth, Ben Witherington comments, Lysias accomplishes two goals, one "face-saving" and the other "self-serving." Witherington, *The Acts of the Apostles*, 700-1. Lysias covers up the wrongs he has done to Paul and, at the same time, conveys a positive impression to Felix as to how he handled the case. See also Cassidy, *Society and Politics*, 100; Tannehill, *The Narrative Unity*, 295.

up crowds with slander and labeling. In order to kill him, they need to persuade the judge with reason and good conscience, which they have failed to do so far against Paul (v. 30; Acts 21:27-36; 22:22-23; 23:1-5, 10, 12-15).

Now, the rescue team takes action. They move Paul at night and bring him to Antipatris, about halfway between Jerusalem and Caesarea (v. 31).[57] When Paul has traveled far enough to be off the radar of *the Jews*, the soldiers return to the barracks the next day and the horsemen continue on their mission (v. 32). Paul finally arrives in Caesarea and is presented to Felix (v. 33). Upon reading the letter, Felix asks Paul which province he belongs to and learns that he is from Cilicia (v. 34). As the governor of Judea, Felix could have sent Paul away to the governor of the double province Syria-Cilicia, according to Roman custom—*forum domicili*—but decides instead to put Paul under his care.[58] Why he does so is an issue of debate. Joseph A. Fitzmyer proposes *forum delicti*.[59] The crime took place in Judea, of which Felix is the governor. Luke T. Johnson points to geographic distance as the main issue: "Paul could not face his accusers if he were extradited so far away."[60] Yet, a clue is given in Lysias' letter. Paul's accusers are already on the way, which Felix himself (re)affirms at the end of his comments (vv. 30, 35). Now, the new stage is set. Paul will defend himself and the gospel in the courtrooms in the following narrative (Acts 24–26).

6.2.3. Breaking Free from the Second Vicious Cycle

Paul's transportation from Jerusalem to Caesarea entails more than a change of scene from marketplace to courthouse. When juxtaposing Acts with Luke, readers find that another chain of the vicious cycle is beginning to deteriorate. Though Acts has endeavored so far to replicate what Jesus did in the ministry of the apostles and disciples, the parallel breaks with the person who is arguably the most Jesus-like character, Paul, and with the most characteristic of Jesus's stories, his passion.[61]

(1) *Reconstructing the Passion of Jesus*. The resemblance between these two characters and these two passion narratives is so striking that it is impossible to ignore. Long before his passion, Jesus predicts multiple times the impending suffering he will endure in Jerusalem (Lk 9:18-22, 44; 18:31-33). Paul also speaks of and is spoken to about the suffering he will face in the city (e.g., Acts 20:22-23; 21:11). Just as Jesus is handed over to the Gentiles there, so it will be with Paul (Lk 18:32; Acts 21:11). After speaking of the passion, Jesus asks his disciples to follow his example (Lk 9:23).

---

[57] Antipatris is a city Herod the Great founded in memory of his father, Antipater II (Josephus, *Ant.* 16.5.2; *War* 1.21.9). It is about 40 miles (65 kilometers) from Jerusalem and 25 miles from Caesarea. The overnight journey might have taken about 14 hours for a Roman army marching 3.6 miles per hour and making two to three stops in between. Fitzmyer, *The Acts of the Apostles*, 729; Holladay, *Acts*, 442; Witherington, *The Acts of the Apostles*, 697.
[58] Fitzmyer, *The Acts of the Apostles*, 729.
[59] Fitzmyer, *The Acts of the Apostles*, 729.
[60] Johnson, *The Acts of the Apostles*, 406.
[61] For an extensive parallel reading of Luke-Acts. see James R. Edwards, "Parallels and Patterns between Luke and Acts," *BBR* 27, no. 4 (2017): 485–501. Charles H. Talbert focuses on intra-Luke and intra-Acts parallels. Talbert, *Literary Patterns*.

Likewise, before his departure to Jerusalem, Paul encourages the Ephesian elders to imitate his life (Acts 20:33-35). Before his entry into Jerusalem, people follow Jesus near the city (Lk 19:36-40). Some disciples also escort Paul before he arrives at the city (Acts 21:15-16). In both Luke and Acts, weeping and intense prayers precede the passion (Lk 19:41-44; 22:39-46; Acts 20:36-38; 20:36; 21:5). Both protagonists almost immediately visit the temple after entering Jerusalem (Lk 19:28-40, 45-48; Acts 21:21-26). Both spend some days in the temple (Lk 19:47; 21:37–22:1, 7, 53; Acts 21:27). Jewish authorities, particularly the chief priests, are involved in murder plots against the two intruders (Lk 22:2; Acts 23:14-15). After their arrests, beatings follow (Lk 22:63-65; Acts 21:32). Both are involved in a series of defenses. They both defend themselves first before the Sanhedrin (Luke 22:66-71; Acts 23:1-10). Afterward, they meet with rulers from the Roman side and the Jewish side (Lk 23:1-25; Acts 23:33–26:32). The charges are both political and religious. They are accused of violating Roman law and Jewish law (Lk 22:66-71; 23:2, 5; Acts 21:28; 23:5-6; 24:5-9). The Roman authorities repeatedly assure them of their innocence (Lk 23:4, 14-16, 22; Acts 23:29; 25:18, 25; 26:31-32). So do Herod Antipas and Herod Agrippa (Lk 23:14; Acts 26:31-32). Paul is a foil character for Jesus, and his passion is a reconstruction of Jesus's last days in Jerusalem in the Gospel. As James R. Edwards states, surely "the Lukan master-disciple paradigm" is at work.[62]

(2) *Deconstructing the Passion of Jesus.* Despite the similarities, the dissimilarities between the two passion narratives are also indisputable. In Luke, none of the disciples urges Jesus to avoid the suffering (Lk 9:18-22). Compare this to the parallel passage in Mark (8:32-33). In contrast, Paul's final journey to Jerusalem causes resistance among his in-group members (Acts 21:12). Whereas Jesus's disciples have no clue as to his passion prediction, Paul's fellow believers understand what he will face (Acts 21:12-14). As soon as Jesus enters Jerusalem, he begins teaching people in the temple, and he does so until his arrest (Lk 19:47; 21:37-38). In contrast, Paul addresses the general public only once, and it is in the form of a defense (Acts 22:1-21). Whereas the passion of Jesus occurs around the Passover, the passion of Paul takes place around the day of Pentecost (Lk 22:1, 7-20; Acts 20:16). Jesus's disciples cannot pray for him because of their grief in the face of his coming suffering (Lk 22:45). Yet, Paul's fellow believers pray for him in spite of their great sorrow (Acts 20:36; 21:5). Jesus is arrested outside the temple by the Jewish people, but Paul is arrested within the temple by the Roman military (Lk 22:52-54; Acts 21:33). Unlike Jesus's defense, which is brief and ambiguous, Paul's defense is lengthy and direct (Lk 22:67-69; 23:3; Acts 22:1-21, 25, 27-28; 23:1, 3, 5, 6).

The more one looks closely into the parallels, the more asymmetry emerges. Parallel material to Lk 20–21, in particular, is virtually missing in Acts. Yet, the most striking dissonance has to do with the ending of the passion narratives. Jesus dies, but Paul survives (Lk 23:46; Acts 28:30-31). Whereas Jesus suffers from Jewish slander and becomes a victim of anti-Jewish/Roman labels and deadly violence, Paul escapes the plot to murder him.

---

[62] Edwards, "Parallels and Patterns between Luke and Acts," 485.

(3) *Rethinking the Passion of Paul.* The decisive reversal of Paul's fortune has prompted scholars to propose various interpretations of the suffering/survival of Paul and ultimately the ending of Acts. Some focus on the need to decrease the tension between the Way and its out-group. For example, Ernst Haenchen argues that Luke intends not "to equip the Christians for martyrdom, but rather to spare the church martyrdom as far as possible."[63] Robert Maddox, in a similar fashion, states: "The Christian business is not to play the hero, but to bear witness in humility."[64] Others, however, pay attention to the enduring tension. Charles K. Barrett says, "Luke is caught between two motivations, on the one hand to show how much Paul was prepared to suffer for Christ, on the other to show the power of God to deliver him from suffering."[65] Mikeal C. Parsons, in the same vein, explains that Paul in Acts "must plunge into the depth of suffering and *there* experience the help of Christ."[66]

This study claims that the passion of Paul illustrates violent conflicts with and miraculous deliverance from *the Jews*. As long as the gospel is proclaimed, the opposition, particularly from the Jewish side, will rise, and, at the same time, God will continue to save the disciples from the danger. The two cycles this project brings to the fore—one vicious and the other benevolent—convey a message within the purview of Lukan literary (dis)symmetry. *The record of violence is meant to be broken.* The Jews have been trapped in this cycle. Their ancestors rejected and killed the prophets (e.g., Lk 4:24; Acts 7:52). The vicious cycle was so viral that it did not spare the long-awaited Messiah, the Righteous One (Acts 2:22-23, 36; 7:52). Slanders and false labels will be thrown at the members of the Way; their accusers constantly appear at the courts later in Acts (Acts 23:30, 35; 25:16, 18). The Jewish people, for the most part, will continue to reject the gospel (e.g., Acts 28:23-27). Yet, they will not be able to lay violent hands on the disciples any longer. As long as the dispute with *the Jews* is carried out within the Roman legal system and the members of the Way are under its care, not handed over to their accusers, no innocent people will die.

(4) *Reconsidering the Significance of Acts 21:17–23:35.* The literary exploration this study has undertaken up to this point demands a new perspective on Paul's last visit to Jerusalem. Transitions definitely take place in and through Paul's experience there.[67] Paul's status changes from a freeman to a prisoner. The setting of the story moves from public disputes to private defenses. Paul's audience changes the Jewish public to governors and kings. But, the most important event that takes place in the most contested city is the disappearance of violence from the Lukan theater. Even though an attempt is made, the actual attack will not be carried out (Acts 25:1-5).

This reading of Acts provides an answer to the long and heated debate on the ending of Acts. Paul does not die but proclaims the kingdom of God and teaches about the Lord Jesus "with all boldness and without hindrance" (Acts 28:30-31). How is this possible? *It is possible because the chain of violence is already broken.* In the grand

---

[63] Haenchen, *The Acts of the Apostles*, 732.
[64] Maddox, *The Purpose of Luke-Acts*, 81.
[65] Barrett, *A Critical and Exegetical Commentary on The Acts of the Apostles*, 1:457.
[66] Parsons, *Acts*, 322, emphasis in the original.
[67] Johnson, *The Acts of the Apostles*, 407.

scheme of Luke-Acts, there is no way for Paul to die at this point. As long as the narrative continues, his life and the proclamation of the gospel will go on.

6.3. Challenging the Portrayal of Intergroup Conflict and Identity Construction in Acts: An SIA (Re)reading of Acts 21:17–23:35

In the end, however, the vicious cycle is not broken and history does repeat itself. Unlike his model-master, Jesus, Paul breaks free of the vicious cycle. But, the narrative is not free from violence. The present chapter has explored up to this point two interlocking cycles at play at the narrative level: how the pattern of opposition and deliverance emerges and how the benevolent cycle ultimately gains the upper hand as the narrative unfolds. This last section undertakes an SIA (re)reading of Acts 21:17–23:35 and inquires into what the Lukan presentation of intergroup conflict reveals regarding the identity construction of the Way at the discourse level.

6.3.1. Literary Construction of the Jews: Discursive Portrayal of the Proximate "Other"

The literary analysis of *the Jews* makes it clear that the conflict between the Way and its opponents is, borrowing John D. Crossan's term, more "prophecy historicized" than "history remembered."[68] Jesus foretold his disciples of the persecution, and Paul fulfills that prophecy (Lk 21:12-19). The historical basis of the recurring opposition is undeniable. Otherwise, such a hard-fought battle between the two groups would not have appeared in the narrative in the first place. The pattern of the opposition, however, elucidates that these conflicts are more likely what Luke T. Johnson calls "realistic ('history-like') narratives" than historical reports.[69] Acts embellishes Paul's life with literary imagination and imitation both within and without the narrative itself (e.g., Acts 14:8-18 and Ovid, *Metam.* 8.613–738; Acts 17:16-34 and Lucian, *The Eunuch*; Acts 28:1-6 and Dio Chrysostom, *Or.* 7).[70] In contrast, Acts denigrates the acts of *the Jews*. Contrasting and contesting images of Paul and *the Jews* demonstrate a Lukan view of who "*they*" are.

---

[68] Commenting on Raymond Brown, who leans more toward the historicity of the passion narrative found in the Gospels, John D. Crossan says, "Ray Brown is 80 percent in the direction of history remembered. I'm 80 percent in the opposite direction." Peter Steinfels, "Scholar Sees 4 Views of Jesus in Accounts of Death," *New York Times*, March 27, 1994, https://www.nytimes.com/1994/03/27/us/scholar-sees-4-views-of-jesus-in-accounts-of-death.html. See also John D. Crossan, *Who Killed Jesus? Exposing the Roots of Anti-Semitism in the Gospel Story of the Death of Jesus* (San Francisco: HarperSanFrancisco, 1995); Raymond E. Brown, *The Death of the Messiah: From Gethsemane to the Grave: A Commentary on the Passion Narratives in the Four Gospels*, ABRL (New York: Doubleday, 1994).

[69] "Realistic ('history-like') narratives are authorial constructions that contain both fact and *fiction* . . . [T]he author is in charge of plot, but to an even greater extent—because it is less publicly known and therefore more malleable—*characterization*." Luke T. Johnson, "Anti-Judaism and the New Testament," in *Contested Issues in Christian Origins and the New Testament: Collected Essays*, 550, emphasis added.

[70] Johnson, *The Acts of the Apostles*, 5.

(1) *The Jews in the Vicious Cycle*. At the level of discourse, from these intergroup conflicts emerges a portrait of *the Jews* caught in a cycle of slander, labeling, and violence. The narrative creates this image in two ways. First, as discussed above, once their attempt to kill Stephen succeeds, the cycle replicates itself. Almost everywhere the gospel gains popularity among the crowds, *the Jews* intervene and stir up opposition. The recurring mobbish violence shows that the implied author is in control of, not controlled by, the narrative.[71] Second, Paul is portrayed in a radically different way. Unlike *the Jews*, who are prone to act maliciously and riotously, Paul appears to be "a decent, law-observant Jew dedicated to the welfare of other Jews."[72] His constant efforts to bring the gospel first to his fellow Jews in spite of their violent reactions illustrates that it is not Paul but *the Jews* who are trapped in a vicious cycle.

(2) *The Lukan Identity Construction of Jews*. Such a (re)presentation of *the Jews* incurs in the minds of the Lukan audience two *categorization* processes. First is the creation of in-group and out-group categories: "*The Jews* are not of us." Acts *accentuates* their repeated acts of instigating, stirring, and inciting the crowds—Acts 6:11, 12; 13:50; 14:2; 17:13; 21:27—and produces *prejudices* and negative *stereotypes*: "Jews are ignorant, stubborn, violent, and above all against God" (e.g., Acts 7:51-53; 28:25-28). Though *the Jews* quickly create, through their persecution against the Way, *intergroup relations* (e.g., "us" vs. "them") and the *social identity* that stems from it (e.g., "We are the defenders of the Jewish faith against *those* heretics"), in the eyes of the beholder they are in fact whoever they "blame" and "claim" to stand against.

Second is the blurring of the boundary between *the Jews* and other Jewish groups. It has already been noted that the absence of help from Jewish believers during the commotion in Jerusalem points to *prototypes* and *depersonalization* at work (see chapter 3.2.2). Acts 21:30 alludes to the dilution of the in-group and out-group categories as if all Jerusalemites are defending Jewish symbols and in opposition to Paul.[73] It is clear that οἱ Ἰουδαῖοuς a literary character referring to a Jewish faction attempting to murder Paul, and the narrative takes an ambivalent attitude toward the Jewish people. Yet, Acts repeatedly confirms the Jewish rejection of the gospel and the gospel's inevitable turn from Jews to Gentiles (Acts 13:46; 18:6; 28:28). Paul's final declaration to the Jews in Rome is particularly symbolic. As much as Paul will continue to proclaim the hope of Israel without hindrance, Jews will continue to hinder him and reject the message as their ancestors did (Acts 28:24-31). Some scholars see this last episode as "a call to repentance."[74] Yet, the ending of Luke-Acts is so tragic and ironic[75]

---

[71] Against Ernst Haenchen, who insists that "Luke by mentioning witnesses ... attempts to steer his account back into the paths of juridical procedure," Shelly Matthews points out that the sudden change is the key to the Lukan reconstruction of the scene: "Jewish juridical process is so base that it cannot but result in riotous behavior." Matthews, *Perfect Martyr*, 76; Haenchen, *The Acts of the Apostles*, 296.

[72] Dixon Slingerland, "'The Jews' in the Pauline Portion of Acts," *JAAR* 54, no. 2 (1986): 314.

[73] Similarly, see Jon A. Weatherly, *Jewish Responsibility for the Death of Jesus in Luke-Acts*, JSNTSup 106 (Sheffield: Sheffield Academic Press, 1994), esp. chap. 2, "Jerusalem's Responsibility for the Death of Jesus in Luke-Acts," 50–98.

[74] Lee, *Luke-Acts and 'Tragic History,'* 278. See also David L. Tiede, *Prophecy and History in Luke-Acts* (Philadelphia: Fortress, 1980), 93; Johnson, *The Acts of the Apostles*, 475.

[75] Tannehill, *The Narrative Unity of Luke-Acts*, 2:345.

that it easily trumps any positive characterizations of Jews in Acts and leads to a *stereotypical perception* of Jews as having negative traits—ignorant, stubborn, violent, etc.[76]

(3) *Jews as the Proximate "Other."* The Lukan downplay of Jews demonstrates not only the inevitable chasm but also the undeniable closeness between the two groups. This project highlights that the narrative articulates the Jewishness of the Way in any way possible (see chapter 2.3). Paul's purification rite in the temple (Acts 21:26), his appeal to his Jewish lineage and education (Acts 22:3), his career as a persecutor of the Way (Acts 22:4-5), and the reconstruction of his encounter with the risen Lord in light of Isaiah's call (Acts 22:6-21) underline that the Way is a Jewish sect (see chapters 3 and 4 of this book). Yet, at the same time, the resistance of Jews shows that they are not ready to accept Gentiles joining the people of God through their faith in Jesus instead of through circumcision and observing the Torah (Acts 21:20-25, 27-31, 36; 22:22; 23:1-5), and the resurrection of the dead still remains an issue of heated debate within the Jewish circle (see chapter 5 of this book).

In other words, the Way in the eyes of Jews is a proximate "other" because for them the Way, a minority group, looks too much like them or claims to be them. Its emergence, presence, and growth are problematic. Its claim undermines the Jewish ethnic category and relativizes the centrality of Jewish law and the Jewish temple in be(com)ing God's chosen people (Acts 21:28). The violent reaction is unavoidable. Yet, since the Jewish tradition is the soil out of which the Way grew, the narrative is saturated with *ambivalence* toward Jews.[77] They are depicted as prone to mobbish violence (Acts 21:30-31, 36; 22:22-23). Their leaders, especially the temple authorities, are hypocrites who act contrary to Jewish and Roman law and are ignorant of God's action in the resurrection of Jesus (Acts 22:2-3, 7-10; 23:12-15, 30). In contrast, Paul constantly categorizes himself as a devout Jew whose fidelity to the law is unquestionable (Acts 21:26; 22:3; 23:1). It is the hope of the resurrection/Israel for which Paul is on trial (Acts 23:6; see also Acts 24:15; 26:6, 7; 28:20). Above all, Paul's recurring visits to synagogues in spite of constant rejection and his final return to Jerusalem in the face of the impending persecution show that the Jewish people are not the remote or radical "other" but the proximate "other" to whom the Way *must* speak and compare itself. The more the narrative exposes the fallacy of Jews, the more it delineates its affinity with the Way. Violent rejection of the Jews is necessary because it proves the validity of the disciples and the apostles. They are the prophets whom God commissioned (e.g., Lk 4:16-30; Acts 6:8–7:60; 21:17–23:35). In a word, discursive portrayals of the Jews reveal not only how wicked and unfaithful "they" are but also how virtuous and devoted "we"

---

[76] Commenting on the Jews in this passage, Hans Conzelmann says "hopeless" and Haenchen "obdurate." Conzelmann, *Acts of the Apostles*, 227; Haenchen, *Acts of the Apostles*, 729. Robert Maddox's evaluation implies how powerful an impression this ending can convey: "Its burden is entirely negative." Maddox, *The Purpose of Luke-Acts*, 43.

[77] The Fourth Gospel is another example of ambivalence toward the Jews and Jewishness in the New Testament. See Raimo Hakola, *Identity Matters: John, the Jews and Jewishness*, NovTSup 118 (Leiden: Brill, 2005).

are.[78] Daniel Boyarin's comment on heresiology rings true here: "*Orthodoxy* and *heresy* must, of necessity, come into the world of discourse together. *Orthodoxy* and *heresy* are decidedly not things, but notions that must always be defined in each other's context."[79]

6.3.2. Identity Construction of Paul and the Way: Dual Identity and Victimization

As much as the narrative endeavors to generate discursive images of the Jews, positive images of the Way emerge out of Paul's interactions with his out-group members: "decent," "devout," "determined," etc. Such a literary construction produces not only images saturated with ethical connotations but also identities mixed with sociocultural categories. The plot of *the Jews* is destroyed by its discovery and the development of the counterplan. Paul's Roman citizenship is a difference that makes all the difference. Yet, his other identities also save him from recurring violence at the hands of the Jews and the Romans. Exploring Paul's dual identity provides insights into the construction of Christian identity and, at the same time, reveals the dilemma of this identity.

(1) *Dual Identity of Paul*. The first tool the narrative utilizes is dual identity. The following observations are drawn from Paul's multiple self-representations. First, Christian identity is a *superordinate identity* that trumps *political boundaries*. Arrested by a tribune who misunderstood him to be an Egyptian rebel, Paul describes himself as "a citizen of an important city," Tarsus (Acts 21:39). Standing before his Jewish countrymen, he articulates his membership in the Jerusalem community (Acts 22:3). Confronted with the threat of thongs by soldiers, he discloses his Roman citizenship (Acts 22:25-29). Yet, whatever political affiliations he may disclose—as a Greek, a Jew, or a Roman—his Christian identity endures. He is a member of the *people of God*. Second, Christian identity is also a *subgroup identity* that stays within Jewish *socioreligious boundaries*. Facing the tribune, he introduces himself as a diaspora Jew (Acts 21:39). Before the Jewish crowd, he says that he received legal training in Jerusalem (Acts 22:3). At the council, he cries out that he is a Pharisee waiting for the resurrection of the dead (Acts 23:6). The Christian faith is thoroughly a Jewish faith based on the Jewish law and beliefs. Third, Christian identity does not nullify, but it is also not bound by, *ethnic boundaries*. Paul is a Greek, a Roman, and a Jew (e.g., Acts 21:39; 22:25-29; 23:1). His ethnic identity persists before and after his joining the Way. Yet, he flexibly uses these ethnic categories to defend himself. In short, Christian identity can be bestowed on diverse political entities and ethnic groups, as long as they share a Jewish faith.[80]

---

[78] In the same vein, commenting on John's Gospel, Tobias Nicklas observes: "While we do not know very much about the concrete circumstances of what John means with the *aposynagogos*, the Gospel of John does not just witness that 'the Jews' create a 'borderline,' throwing out followers of Jesus from their community. It is even more directly, a witness for the other side of the movement: with his image of 'the Jews,' John itself creates a 'borderline.'" Tobias Nicklas, "The 'Jews' in the Gospel of John: Past and Future Lines of Scholarship," in *Perceiving the Other in Ancient Judaism and Early Christianity*, ed. Michal Bar-Asher Siegal, Wolfgang Grünstäudl, and Matthew Thiessen, WUNT 394 (Tübingen: Mohr Siebeck, 2017), 62.
[79] Boyarin, *Border Lines*, 3, emphasis in the original.
[80] According to Acts, in order to gain membership within the Way, one is to believe in Jesus, be baptized, and receive the Holy Spirit (see chapter 4.3.1 of this book).

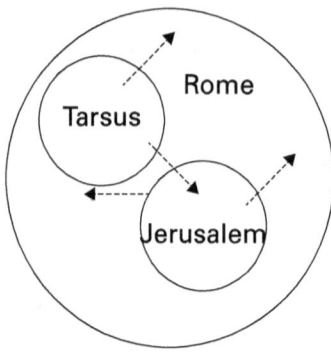 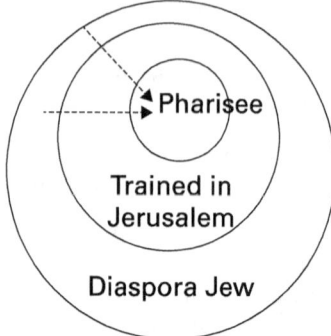

The zooming out of political affiliation of Paul, a Christian

The zooming in of religious affiliation of Paul, a Jew

Figure 6.1 The Interplay of Paul's Dual Identity.

(2) *Victimization*. The second tool is victimization. Marginalization is often a social reality of minorities in intergroup relations. This study has described how Paul endeavored to overcome the Way's relative deprivation by recategorizing Gentiles within *the people of God* and employing social creativity when facing threats from Romans and Jews. Failure to gain membership within the Jewish (out-)group, however, does not grant a negative social identity to the Way. Rather, it generates and amplifies a positive social identity for them. The more suffering Paul endures, the more he becomes a prophet. The more severe the rejection he experiences from the Jews, the more legitimation his Gentile mission gains. Above all, the more the Jews act wickedly and faithlessly, the more the Way becomes righteous and faithful.[81] In other words, negative (re)constructions of an out-group almost always construct and verify the identity of an in-group: "Although at first glance it may appear that the attention is on the delineation of one's outgroup, there are nevertheless traces that speak of the ingroup's plea for its own identity construction."[82]

The violence Paul endures in Jerusalem reflects to some extent the historical reality the Way faced with the local synagogues in 50–90 CE.[83] Nascent Christianity was marginalized, persecuted, and victimized by the Jewish (out-)group to some degree. Yet, in this agonistic context, by breaking the vicious cycle of slander, labeling, and violence and generating a mobbish and even devilish image of Jews, its in-group

---

[81] On the Lukan construction of charismatics, the Jews, and women, Mitzi J. Smith states: "Stereotypical images of proximate others are weaved into the fabric of Acts." Mitzi J. Smith, *The Literary Construction of the Other in the Acts of the Apostles*, PTMS 154 (Eugene, OR: Pickwick, 2011), 7.

[82] Dominic Irudayaraj's comment on the identity construction of the returned Judahite community over against its proximate "other," the Edomite community living in their previous territory, rings true for Acts 21:17–23:35. Irudayaraj, *Violence, Otherness, and Identity*, 141.

[83] Johnson, "Anti-Judaism and the New Testament," 546.

members find themselves no longer *victims* but instead *victors*. This process of identity construction is not just a "looking glass self"[84] but a "looking (stained) glass self." The identity of the Way is constructed through intergroup interactions: "How do we *want* to appear to others?" The members of the Way do not passively internalize self-images imposed on them. An internal-external dialect of individual identification takes place. To make the case more complicated and sometimes worse, these images in the mirror are *stained*—Christianized on one level and distorted on the other. In the story, the members of the Way are victors as well as victims. In history, their successors often turned to be the persecutors, not the persecuted, of their proximate "other."

6.3.3. Inbreaking and Outbreaking of the Vicious Cycle: Beyond Lukan Anti-Jewish Slander, Labeling, and Violence

The discussion thus far has highlighted two interlocking cycles that emerge in the narrative, the kinds of images that are generated with regard to intergroup conflicts, and how the identity of the Way, as well as of the Jews, is constructed. The effort to break the vicious cycle is unsuccessful because Paul's miraculous escape leads to a new vicious cycle.

(1) *Enduring Cycle*. Paul's escape from Jerusalem implies that the chain of violence is broken. Anti-Way slander, labeling, and violence no longer work. Acts is surely a fierce defense of the Way, its mission, and its Jewish identity. Yet, its armor is actually a deadly spear, as if the best defense is a good offense. Luke-Acts shows that "Jewish opposition to Jesus and his followers was total, consistent, and violent."[85] Such negative portrayals of Jews give rise to anti-Jewish *slander*. Jews are "ignorant," "stubborn," "unfaithful," "violent," etc. Certain *labels* are induced from these out-group qualities: "Christ-killers," "enemy of God," "legalists," "exclusivists," etc.[86] These slanders and labels that the narrative (in)directly prompts often justify *violence* against Jews. History has proved how effective anti-Jewish rhetoric can be, from the expulsion of Jews from certain countries in medieval Europe to the Holocaust of the twentieth century. In a word, in an effort to break the vicious cycle Acts falls into another cycle that is even more devastating.

---

[84] Charles H. Cooley, *Human Nature and the Social Order* (New York: Schocken Books, 1964). According to Cooley, our view of self is created in three ways: (1) asking, "How do I appear to others?" (2) asking, "What must others think of me?" and (3) revising how we think about ourselves.

[85] Johnson, *Anti-Judaism and the New Testament*, 549.

[86] "The image of Jews as Christ-killers meant that Jews were not merely people who rejected Jesus; they rejected God and, as a result, God had rejected them. The mutual enmity between God and Jews consequently led to the perception that Jews were the agents and allies of Satan." Pamela Eisenbaum, "Anti-Semitism," *NIDB* 1.184. See, in particular, Mt 27:25, Jn 8:44, and Gal 3:10. "Demonization of enemies," Amy-Jill Levine and Ben Witherington note, "can only have tragic repercussions." Amy-Jill Levine and Ben Witherington III, *The Gospel of Luke*, NCBC (Cambridge: Cambridge University Press, 2018), 124.

(2) *A New Hermeneutical Cycle: A Proposal.* This study calls for new ways of interpreting Acts and understanding Jewish-Christian relations. (1) *Approval Instead of Slander.* First and foremost, readers need to acknowledge the Jewishness of the Christian gospel as well as of Acts. Once they understand this connection, they will realize that the anti-Jewish slander that Luke-Acts generates is an expression of ambivalence toward the Jews and an appeal to be a part of the Jewish faith. What ultimately needs to take place is not an *escape from* but an *encounter with* Jerusalem, with a confirmation of and appreciation for the Jewish roots of Christian traditions. (2) *Investigation Instead of Labeling.* Based on this new attitude, readers need to undertake a critical (re)evaluation of the history-like narrative the text presents and the anti-Jewish labels that they themselves have unwittingly bought into. To do so, readers should be aware of the danger of "mirror reading."[87] Acts is not an objective (re)presentation of historical events but a literary construction that is subjective and biased. They also should be reminded of the mutual "othering"[88] reflected in the text. Not only the Jews but also the members of the Way attack in order "to stigmatize the 'other' and to depict the 'other' as peripheral, non-essential and less than human."[89] As Luke T. Johnson notes, "through historical, social, and rhetorical analysis," the New Testament can be liberated from anti-Jewish polemic.[90] (3) *Peace Instead of Violence.* Finally, readers need to seek the common ground and, at the same time, the distinct voices attested among groups represented within the text and groups present within their own context. Once positive labels are developed (e.g., "*unique*, not deviant," "*friends*, not enemy"), mutual appreciation can take place. Then, "those who were closest, but still different" are no longer "the greatest threat" but are the greatest asset in the construction of one's identity.[91]

---

[87] Luke T. Johnson explains "mirror reading" as follows: "The literary compositions are read as windows to the historical situation they address, and the reconstructed historical situation then provides the key to the meaning of the composition." Luke T. Johnson, *The Real Jesus: The Misguided Quest for the Historical Jesus and the Truth of the Traditional Gospels* (San Francisco: HarperSanFrancisco, 1996), 91. William M. Wright observes that "the reasoning implicit in this kind of approach is patently circular." William M. Wright, *Rhetoric and Theology: Figural Reading of John 9*, BZNW 165 (Berlin: de Gruyter, 2009), 96.

[88] Coined by Gayatri Spivak, "othering describes the various ways in which colonial discourse produces its subjects ... [O]thering is a dialectical process because the colonizing *Other* is established at the same time as its colonized *others* are produced as subjects." Ashcroft, Griffiths, and Tiffin, *Post-Colonial Studies: The Key Concepts*, 171.

[89] Raj Nadella, *Dialogue Not Dogma: Many Voices in the Gospel of Luke*, LNTS 431 (New York: T&T Clark, 2011), 63.

[90] Johnson, "Anti-Judaism and the New Testament," 568. Stephen L. Franzoi, *Social Psychology*, 5th ed. (New York: McGraw-Hill, 2009), 235: "People can circumvent stereotypical thinking if they make a conscious effort to use more rational, inductive strategies." See also Patricia G. Devine and Margo J. Monteith, "Automaticity and Control in Stereotyping," in *Dual Process Theories in Social Psychology*, ed. Shelly Chaiken and Yaacov Trope (New York: Guilford Press, 1999), 339–60.

[91] Discussing the belief in the resurrection of the dead and boundary formation within Christian traditions, Outi Lehtipuu states: "In the struggle for Christian identity, those who were closest, but still different, formed the greatest threat. Labeling them as false and counterfeit strengthened the boundaries around that which was deemed true and normative." Outi Lehtipuu, "How to Expose a Deviant? Resurrection Belief and Boundary Creation in Early Christianity," in *Others and the Construction of Early Christian Identities*, ed. Raimo Hakola, Nina Nikki, and Ulla Tervahauta, PFES 106 (Helsinki: Finnish Exegetical Society 2013), 189.

6.4. Concluding Comments

Commenting on anti-Jewish slander in the New Testament, Luke T. Johnson avers: "Not historical evidence but rhetoric shapes the reader."[92] This is precisely what has frequently happened with readers' perceptions of the Jews in their reading of Luke-Acts. Jewish rejection and persecution of the Way has led to acceptance and affirmation of the fate of Jews. Though anti-Jewish polemic and slander are designed for "internal consumption,"[93] distorted and despicable images of Jews have dominated both scholarly debates and public discourses about Jews and Jewish-Christian relations for centuries.[94] Its impact, once David became Goliath and vice versa, has been fatal to millions of Jews.

In order to expose, problematize, and challenge such a misreading and such a misleading interpretation, the present chapter analyzed the cycles spinning within and without the Lukan narrative. Tracing the conflicts between Paul and his opponents throughout Acts unveiled the pattern of Jewish opposition replicated again and again in the narrative. The subsequent narrative analysis also revealed the counter-scheme that emerged in response. Against the plot of the Jews, through which they slander, label, and afflict violence against Paul, the members of the Way discover the plot, develop a counterplan, and destroy the scheme. The rise of the benevolent cycle over against the vicious one is interesting since it creates a literary asymmetry in Paul's reenactment of the passion of Jesus. The broken chain has no power over Paul, who protects himself with multiple identities. Yet, the inquiry did not stop there, because in actuality the problem remains. Discursive images of the Jews that the narrative creates were brought to the fore, and the problems resulting from the construction of the identity of the Way through slandering, labeling, and attacking the Jews were narrated. In the end, an effort to develop a hermeneutical counter-cycle was made to restore and rectify Jewish-Christian relationships as well as to reread and reinterpret this text that many cherish and admire.

---

[92] Johnson, *Anti-Jewish Slander*, 518.
[93] Johnson, *Anti-Jewish Slander*, 530.
[94] See, in particular, Paula Fredriksen and Adele Reinhartz, *Jesus, Judaism, and Christian Anti-Judaism: Reading the New Testament after the Holocaust* (Louisville: Westminster John Knox, 2002); Tod Linafelt, *A Shadow of Glory: Reading the New Testament after the Holocaust* (New York: Routledge, 2002).

Conclusion

Why do we hate and fight with each other, more often than not? Why do those in power so frequently use divisive rhetoric and people so easily take the bait even while bleeding from the fight? Why do individuals who are normally quite gentle, nice, and compassionate suddenly become violent, unpleasant, or indifferent in a group setting? Why do faith traditions, when involved in these conflicts, oftentimes do more harm than good? These questions of mine are interwoven with the existential inquiry I pursued after immigrating to, and later becoming a citizen of, the United States. Who am I? Am I Korean or American? Am I an insider or outsider in the eyes of the beholder in this increasingly diverse and multilayered American society? What can I do as a Christian, pastor, and biblical scholar to reduce conflicts among people?

The search for answers to these questions became not only an impetus of this book but also one of the lenses through which I read and interpreted Acts 21:17–23:35. My initial questions listed above elicited in me an eagerness to explore Paul's multilayered and multifaceted identity. My yearning to maintain my roots and also to adapt myself in the rapidly evolving American society prompted me to rethink, reanalyze, and reevaluate Paul's interactions with his interrogators. My wrestling with the entire text of Acts, as well as the chosen passage, led me to the discovery of two cycles that rise and fall in the text and to a discussion of Lukan literary asymmetry and identity construction.

Intergroup conflict and identity construction remain central concerns of this book as Paul swings back and forth, reveals his diverse memberships, and escapes the deadly snares of violence. All these efforts manifest not just his creative genius as an orator and apologist but also his mission and its ramifications. God has *recategorized* who the insiders and outsiders of the people of God are, and the significance of this is indicated by the title of this book: *Intergroup Conflict, Recategorization, and Identity Construction in Acts*.

To illustrate these central threads of the study, this book used the analogy of a roller coaster. This conclusion begins by recalling the ups and downs of the ride so far. The first section reiterates the intriguing scenes our eyes have seen at each curve. Taking our learnings thus far as guideposts, the following section discusses where our journey will take us next, first in our interpretation of other biblical texts and second in our understanding of contemporary society. In this section, I focus on my two sociocultural contexts—the United States and South Korea—and suggest final thoughts on how we are to live in peace in a diverse and multilayered society.

Summary

Chapter 1 began by presenting an aerial view of the text as well as directions and precautions for the upcoming adventure. Three common threads—locus, content, and cause—of the text made it clear that Acts 21:17–23:35 is a distinct literary unit in which Paul's Jewish identity is interrogated and explained through his conflicts with the Jews in Jerusalem. The image of the roller coaster alerted readers to the hidden dangers present as soon as Paul enters Jerusalem and encounters different interlocutors. The survey of the scholarship on Paul in Jerusalem showed that the majority of scholars are apologetic in their purpose, but there seems to be no consensus on the essence of his defense. Some scholars focus their argument on Paul's long custody or the legitimacy of Christianity in relation to Judaism or the legitimacy of the Gentile mission. Others highlight Paul's proclamation or Christianity's political inclination vis-à-vis Rome. Aided by the group of scholars who focus on Paul's Jewish identity, this book paid special attention to identity construction and mimesis in Acts 21:17–23:35. Then, unmistakable and notable parallels between the passion of Jesus in Luke and the passion of Paul in Acts were brought up that left readers wondering what Paul's survival entailed in the narrative scheme of Luke-Acts. A brief discussion of the historical background and the function of the chosen text helped to focus on Luke's discursive rhetoric against the Jews.

Chapter 2 outlined the social identity approach (SIA), the main methodology of this study. A personal story of the author offered cues to the important topic to be discussed later in the chapter: *dual identity*. The basic tenets of SIA were delineated, first with social identity theory—(1) categorization and accentuation; (2) stereotyping; (3) social identity and intergroup relations—and second with self-categorization theory—(1) self-categorization; (2) prototypes and depersonalization; (3) group cohesion, social cooperation, and social influence; and (4) reduction of intergroup bias. Informed by scholarly debates on SIA's achievements and limits, the discussion delved into the latter aspect of SIA via a particular intergroup relationship: *recategorizing the in-group membership and reducing intergroup bias with the proximate "other."* Three methodological elements helped to articulate the manifold aspects of identity construction in the text: *ambivalence, social creativity,* and *recategorization.* Guided by discussions on dual identity, Luke's new category, *the people of God,* helped identify critical moments in Acts in which those formerly regarded as outsiders have become insiders, regardless of their gender, ethnicity, or circumcision status, through their faith in Jesus.

Chapter 3 examined Paul's first meeting with Jewish believers, the Jewish crowd, and the Roman tribune in which Paul is constantly accused by his interlocutors (Acts 21:17-40). Three scholarly positions were presented—that the accusations were *absurd, reasonable,* or *ambiguous.* A close look at the Jewish accusations revealed that the charges against Paul were mostly false. The SIA reading helped delineate the psychological process that led the Jews in Jerusalem to the intergroup behavior of committing violence against Paul. After tracing the anti-temple rhetoric in Luke-Acts, the labels the tribune imposed on Paul were examined. He had nothing to do with those labels. Yet, an analysis of the political accusations against Jesus, Paul, and his companions demonstrated that the Way did act in a way that destabilized the Roman peace.

Chapter 4 engaged Paul's speech in Jerusalem using three different approaches (Acts 22:1-21). First, a literary analysis provided the following information. Paul's call/conversion on his way—ὁδός—to Damascus is the center of his speech. Paul's apologia, though incomplete and with an abrupt ending, introduces the trial narrative, reveals the blindness of the Jews, and develops the Jewishness of his message. Second, a social anthropological analysis brought to the fore what Jenkins calls *the internal-external dialectic of individual identification*. Facing the Jewish crowd, whose public image of Paul is that of a deviant and/or Jewish apostate, Paul presents his self-image as a devout Jew and challenges their perception by delivering a speech saturated with Jewish scriptural echoes, traces, and connotations. In the end, standing in the temple precinct, he makes what is arguably the most exciting and dangerous claim: *Now, Gentiles can become full members of the people of God*. Third, a social psychological analysis disclosed the process of recategorization in which three categories of identity emerged as an alternative to Jewish ethnicity—confessional, ritualistic, and pneumatic. Yet, the discussion on dual identity made it clear that even in the midst of this recategorization, the Jewish-Gentile ethnic distinction persisted, not in order to discriminate against each other but to acknowledge and celebrate the presence of one another.

Chapter 5 dealt with Paul's ambivalent relationship with Rome and the Jewish people (Acts 22:22–23:11). First, a survey of the scholarship unraveled the complexity and uncertainty of the historical basis of Paul's Roman citizenship. The discussion on the functions of Paul's Roman citizenship proved the significance of Paul's Roman identity for the development of the plot. Scholarly debates on Luke's attitude toward Rome have made clear the Lukan ambivalence toward the empire. Second, scholarly discussions of the historicity of Paul's Pharisaic identity have noted that any historical guesswork is untenable. Then, the functions of Paul's Pharisaic membership were put forward. His status as a Pharisee not only saves him but also alludes to the continuity between the Way and Pharisaism. The Lukan portrayals of the Pharisees, however, are thoroughly ambivalent, just as are Luke's portraits of Rome. Third, an SIA reading captured social creativity at work in how Paul switches the point of comparison to Rome and the Jewish people and, thus, articulates his in-group membership. In so doing, Paul (re)presents himself as a law-abiding citizen, not an agitator, and as a defender of the Jewish faith, not a lawbreaker. His superordinate identity as a Roman citizen and his subgroup identity as a Pharisee reflect the identity of the Way that has found shelter under Rome but owes its fidelity only to the God of Israel.

Chapter 6 brought the discussion so far to a close. It analyzed Paul's last stay in and escape from Jerusalem and problematized Luke's negative portrayals of the Jewish people (Acts 23:12-35). The chapter provided a flashback to the conflicts between the Jews and the Way and identified the pattern of Jewish opposition in Luke-Acts: *slander*, *labeling*, and *violence*. The mechanics of the new death plot of *the Jews*, along with the discussion of the Lukan characterization of *the Jews*, were delineated. Another flashback in the reading of Acts elicited a counter-cycle: *discovery*, *development*, and *destruction*. The emergence of these two cycles at play—one vicious and the other benevolent—not only in Acts alone but also in the entire Luke-Acts finally revealed one of the implications of this Lukan asymmetry: *the chain of violence will be broken.* The SIA reading of Acts, however, problematized Luke's rhetoric that described its proximate "other," the Jewish people, in a negative way in order to confer a positive group identity on the Way. A new hermeneutical cycle was presented for reducing intergroup conflict and better understanding one's in-group as well as one's out-group. We should *approve*, not slander, *them*. We should *investigate* (dis)similarities between *us* and *them* before labeling them out of ignorance. We should encourage *peace* rather than violence among *ourselves*.

Avenues for Further Research

The focus of this study has been the identity construction of the Way and challenging the vicious cycle of slander, labeling, and violence that the Lukan narrative fights against and, at the same time, utilizes. There are journeys yet to be taken. Some sites still remain unvisited and require scholarly exploration. I suggest three topics for further research.

First, one could undertake an SIA reading of Paul's ensuing defenses in Acts 24–26 to find out which aspects of his identity Paul continued to intensify in relation to the Jewish faith and Rome. In addition, what implications do the speeches of out-group members—Tertullus (Acts 24:2-8), Felix (Acts 25:13-22, 23-27), and Agrippa (Acts 26:24, 28, 30-32)—have with regard to the identity of Paul and the Way?

Second, one could explore the pattern of the escape-from-prison scenes in Acts (e.g., Acts 5:17-21; 12:1-19; 16:16-40; 27:1–28:10). Assuming Paul's voyage and shipwreck to be the climax of this type of scene, what does the shift from "escape" to "voluntary imprisonment" signify regarding to the Way's self-definition in relation to Rome? It would also be interesting to compare and contrast the roles that each character plays, such as the angels, Roman guards, and members of the Way, in these scenes.

Third, one could investigate Paul's letters to see whether the vicious cycle of slander, labeling, and violence in Luke-Acts is also found in the letters. For example, his letter to the Galatians not only defends his gospel but also accuses his opponents (e.g., Gal 1:6-10; 2:1-14; 3:10-14; 4:8-20, 28–5:21). The more discursively he portrays them, the more orthodox he sounds. Furthermore, a close reading of the Pauline epistles in which the writer condemns false teachers would provide both insights into the identity construction of Pauline Christianity and comparisons, if not parallels, to Lukan slander against its opponents.

Implications of This Study

Fratricide has been an intrinsic part of human history; Cain's killing of Abel describes the first homicide in primeval history. Humans' search for orthodoxy and their thirst for power often result in attacks on their closest kinspeople or their own nation or those from a similar sociocultural and/or religious background. From endless civil wars to religious conflicts to genocides, history is filled with stories of internal violence intended to create internal solidarity and suppress dissenting voices. The present study illustrates that the Christian identity presented in Luke-Acts is not free from the mechanics of the first homicide. Intergroup conflicts around religion are at the extreme end of the spectrum because the annihilation of the Other, who is considered to be too *close* yet *different*, proves one's righteousness before one's deity and one's rightful position in society.

The findings from this study have implications for my first sociocultural milieu, South Korea, whose politics are driven by the vicious cycle of slander, labeling, and violence. Due to the Korean War (1950–3), those in power have frequently used the rhetoric of falsely accusing dissenters, mostly progressives, of being communists as a way to attack and eliminate their political enemies.[1] From the People's Revolutionary Party Incident in 1975[2] to the slandering of the victims of the *Sewol* ferry incident in 2014,[3] this dark legacy of polarizing and instigating hatred and violence among South Koreans—often the progressives versus the conservatives—remains alive and well.[4] With the emergence of the internet and social media, cyberspace has become a hard-fought battleground where fierce slander, labeling/libel, and verbal violence are employed because people who are anonymous recognize each other through their group membership as either progressives or conservatives.

In American society, which is my second sociocultural milieu, the stories are no different. With the constant influx of immigrants, the United States is becoming more and more diverse and multilayered—racially, ethnically, culturally, religiously, and socioeconomically. Yet, increasingly divisive rhetoric turns the political discourse to the singular and exclusive around issues such as migration, homeland security, and the economy. The question ultimately becomes who is in and who is out. Such speeches, more often than not, label noncitizens of the United States not simply as outsiders but as threats to U.S. citizens. When the politics of group identity and/or ideology is combined with resource allocation, situations tend to become dire for the marginalized and those viewed as "outsiders" in the political discourse. For example, the Trump administration's public-charge rule to penalize immigrants for their use of government benefits forced many to choose not just between a green card and food stamps but

---

[1] For the use of North Korean sympathizer rhetoric, see Junghoon Kim, "The Stealthy Rise of North Korean Sympathizer Rhetoric in Opposition to the Anti-THAAD Sentiment," *Nocut News*, July 11, 2016, http://www.nocutnews.co.kr/news/4620885.
[2] Choe, "In Seoul, marking a somber anniversary of executions."
[3] For the causes of and the theological responses to the sinking of the *Sewol* ferry, see Hyun Ho Park, "Minjung in the Sinking of the Sewol Ferry: A Reading of Luke 10:25–42 from Minjung Theology's Perspective," *Korea Presbyterian Journal of Theology* 48, no. 3 (2016): 59–79.
[4] The 2016–17 Candlelight Revolution marks the end of another chapter of South Korean politics. The South Korean populace overthrew a corrupted and oppressive government through a peaceful demonstration. Hyun Ho Park, "Unmasking the Injustice: The Korean Candlelight Revolution and the Parable of the Pounds," paper presented at the annual meeting of the Society of Biblical Literature, Boston, Massachusetts, November 18–21, 2017.

between their right to stay and their right to survive.[5] Can those at the opposite ends of the spectrum be brought together and find a (re)solution?

The present study asks us, first, to remember that there are superordinate identities and/or common ground that everybody shares. For Koreans, these are fidelity to their nation and concern for the well-being of their country. Korean identity, not differing political views, should be where the conversation begins. For those in the United States, the superordinate identities and/or common ground are the humanity of everyone and their love for *this* land, and these should be put forward first. God's inclusive vision of salvation invites Gentiles, formerly the outsiders, into the new category of *the people of God*. This challenges us to go beyond the racial, ethnic, and political binaries and boundaries that we think are impermeable. In God's plan of salvation, *everyone* is welcome.

Second, this study encourages us to celebrate various subgroup identities among ourselves. The presence of diverse political views and different racial, ethnic, cultural, and religious groups makes a society rich and dynamic. Any attempt to suppress contrasting voices other than one's own makes the society not only exclusive but also totalitarian. We ought to acknowledge and celebrate our diversity in unity and our unity in diversity.

Finally, this book asks us to be critical listeners, readers, and thinkers regarding the divisive rhetoric coming from politicians, the media, and daily conversations. These speeches are often designed to blind, disguise, and divide us. Unless we examine those inputs not only from *their* side but also from *our* side, we easily become the victims, not the victors, in the politics of group identity. It is our duty as responsible citizens to investigate these speeches and to engage in conversations with those who have different ideas from ours.

The present work, therefore, is a challenge and an invitation. It challenges us to critically (re)examine the biblical texts and our own identity so that we may identify our premises or prejudices that have blocked the influx of new ideas, understandings, and people. It also invites us to embrace God's vision of salvation in Jesus Christ in which peace trumps violence and difference is celebrated because *everyone* can belong to *the people of God*.

---

[5] According to Palm Fessler and Joel Rose, for example, "13.7%—1 in 7—of adults in immigrant families say that they or a family member did not participate in a benefit program last year [2018] 'out of fear of risking future green card status.'" "Trump Administration Rule Would Penalize Immigrants For Needing Benefits," *NPR*, August 12, 2019, https://www.npr.org/2019/08/12/748328652/trump-administration-rule-would-penalize-immigrants-for-using-benefits. This rule was revoked by the Biden-Harris administration in 2022. See HHS Press Office, "New Rule Makes Clear that Noncitizens Who Receive Health or Other Benefits to Which They Are Entitled Will Not Suffer Harmful Immigration Consequences," *U.S. Department of Health and Human Services*, September 8, 2022, https://www.hhs.gov/about/news/2022/09/08/new-rule-makes-clear-noncitizens-who-receive-health-or-other-benefits-which-they-are-entitled-will-not-suffer-harmful-immigration-consequences.html.

Bibliography

A. Social Identity

Abrams, Dominic and Michael A. Hogg. "Social Identification, Self-Categorization, and Social Influence." *European Review of Social Psychology* 1 (1990): 195–228.

Abrams, Dominic and Michael A. Hogg. "Social Identity and Self-Categorization." Pages 179–93 in *The SAGE Handbook of Prejudice, Stereotyping and Discrimination*. Edited by John F. Dovidio, Miles Hewstone, Peter Glick, and Victoria M. Esses. London: SAGE, 2010.

Allport, Floyd. *Social Psychology*. Boston, MA: Houghton Mifflin, 1924.

Argote, Linda and Aimée A. Kane. "Superordinate Identity and Knowledge Creation and Transfer in Organizations." Pages 166–90 in *Knowledge Governance: Processes and Perspectives*. Edited by Nicolai J. Foss and Snejina Michailova. New York: Oxford University Press, 2009.

Baker, Coleman A. *Identity, Memory, and Narrative in Early Christianity: Peter, Paul, and Recategorization in the Book of Acts*. Eugene, OR: Pickwick, 2011.

Barensten, Jack. *Emerging Leadership in the Pauline Mission: A Social Identity Perspective on Local Leadership Development in Corinth and Ephesus*. PTMS 168. Eugene, OR: Pickwick, 2011.

Bar-tal, Daniel. "Group Beliefs as an Expression of Social Identity." Pages 93–113 in *Social Identity: International Perspectives*. Edited by Stephen Worchel, J. Francisco Morales, Dario Páez, and Jean-Claude Deschamps. London: SAGE, 1998.

Barth, Fredrik. *Ethnic Groups and Boundaries: The Social Organization of Culture Difference*. Edited by Fredrik Barth. London: Allen & Unwin, 1969.

Bell, David. "Ethnicity and Social Change." Pages 141–74 in *Ethnicity: Theory and Experience*. Edited by Nathan Glazer and Daniel P. Moynihan. Cambridge, MA: Harvard University Press, 1975.

Bennett, Mark and Fabio Sani, "Introduction: Children and Social Identity." Pages 1–26 in *The Development of the Social Self*. Edited by Mark Bennett and Fabio Sani. New York: Psychology Press, 2004.

Berger, Peter L. and Thomas Luckmann, *The Social Construction of Reality: A Treatise in the Sociology of Knowledge*. Garden City, NY: Doubleday, 1966.

Bosman, Jan Petrus. *Social Identity in Nahum: A Theological-Ethical Enquiry*. Piscataway, NJ: Gorgias, 2008.

Brown, Rupert J. "Social Identity Theory: Past Achievements, Current Problems, and Future Challenges." *European Journal of Social Psychology* 30 (2000): 747–52.

Brown, Rupert J. "The Role of Similarity in Intergroup Relations." Pages 603–23 in *The Social Dimension: European Developments in Social Psychology*. Edited by Henri Tajfel. Cambridge: Cambridge University Press, 1984.

Brown, Rupert J. and Dominic Abrams. "The Effects of Intergroup Similarity and Goal Interdependence on Intergroup Attitudes and Task Performance." *Journal of Experimental Social Psychology* 22 (1986): 78–92.

Brown, Rupert J. and Gordon F. Ross. "The Battle for Acceptance: An Exploration into the Dynamics of Intergroup Behavior." Pages 155–78 in *Social Identity and Intergroup Relations*. Edited by Henri Tajfel. Cambridge: Cambridge University Press, 1982.

Brown, Rupert J. and Miles Hewstone. "An Integrative Theory of Intergroup Contact." Pages 255–343 in *Advances in Experimental Social Psychology* 37. Edited by M. P. Zanna. San Diego: Academic Press, 2005.

Brunner, Jerome S. "On Perceptual Readiness." *Psychological Review* 64 (1957): 123–52.

Byrskog, Samuel, Raimo Hakola, and Jutta Jokiranta. *Social Memory and Social Identity in the Study of Early Judaism and Early Christianity*. Göttingen: Vandenhoeck & Ruprecht, 2016.

Commins, Barry and John Lockwood. "The Effects on Intergroup Relations of Mixing Roman Catholics and Protestants: An Experimental Investigation." *European Journal of Social Psychology* 8, no. 3 (1978): 383–86.

Cooley, Charles H. *Human Nature and the Social Order*. New York: Schocken Books, 1964.

Devine, Christopher J. "Ideological Social Identity: Psychological Attachment to Ideological In-Groups as a Political Phenomenon and a Behavioral Influence." *Political Behavior* 37 (2015): 509–35.

Devine, Patricia G. and Margo J. Monteith. "Automaticity and Control in Stereotyping." Pages 339–60 in *Dual Process Theories in Social Psychology*. Edited by Shelly Chaiken and Yaacov Trope. New York: Guilford Press, 1999.

Diab, L. N. "Achieving Intergroup Cooperation through Conflict-Produced Superordinate Goals." *Psychological Reports* 43 (1978): 735–41.

Dickow, Helga and Valerie Møller. "South Africa's 'Rainbow People,' National Pride and Optimism: A Trend Study." *Social Indicators Research* 59 (2002): 175–202.

Doosje, Bertjan, Naomi Ellemers, and Russell Spears. "Commitment and Intergroup Behaviour." Pages 84–106 in *Social Identity*. Edited by Naomi Ellemers, Russell Spears, and Bertjan Doosje. Oxford: Blackwell, 1999.

Dovidio, John F., Samuel L. Gaertner, and Gladys Kafati. "Group Identity and Intergroup Relations: The Common In-Group Identity Model." Pages 1–34 in *Advances in Group Processes*. Edited by Shane R. Thye, Edward J. Lawler, Michael W. Macy, and Henry A. Walker. Stamford, CT: JAI, 2000.

Dovidio, John F., Samuel L. Gaertner, and Tamar Saguy. "Another View of 'We': Majority and Minority Group Perspectives on a Common Ingroup Identity." *European Review of Social Psychology* 18 (2007): 296–330.

Ellemers, Naomi, Manuela Barreto, and Russell Spears. "Commitment and Strategic Responses to Social Context." Pages 127–46 in *Social Identity*. Edited by Naomi Ellemers, Russell Spears, and Bertjan Doosje. Oxford: Blackwell, 1999.

Esler, Philip F. "An Outline of Social Identity Theory." Pages 13–40 in *T&T Clark Handbook to Social Identity in the New Testament*. Edited by J. Brian Tucker and Coleman A. Baker. London: Bloomsbury T&T Clark, 2016.

Esler, Philip F. *Galatians*. NTR. New York: Routledge, 1998.

Esmail, Aziz. "Religion, Identity, and Violence: Some Theoretical Reflections." Pages 50–65 in *The Blackwell Companion to Religion and Violence*. Edited by Andrew R. Murphy. Malden, MA: Wiley-Blackwell, 2011.

Franzoi, Stephen L. *Social Psychology*. 5th ed. New York: McGraw-Hill, 2009.

Freud, Sigmund. *Group Psychology and the Analysis of the Ego*. London: Hogarth Press, 1921.

Gaertner, Samuel L., Jeffrey Mann, Audrey Murrell, and John F. Dovidio. "Reducing Intergroup Bias: The Benefits of Recategorization." *Journal of Personality and Social Psychology* 57, no. 2 (1989): 239–49.
Gaertner, Samuel L. and John F. Dovidio, "The Aversive Form of Racism." Pages 61–89 in *Prejudice, Discrimination, and Racism*. Edited by John F. Dovidio and Samuel L. Gaertner Orlando, FL: Academic, 1986.
Gaertner, Samuel L., John F. Dovidio, Phyllis A. Anastasio, Betty A. Bachman and Mary C. Rust. "The Common Ingroup Identity Model: Recategorization and the Reduction of Intergroup Bias." *European Review of Social Psychology* 4, no. 1 (1993): 1–26.
Gibson, James L. "Do Strong Ingroup Identities Fuel Intolerance? Evidence from the South African Case." *Political Psychology* 27, no. 5 (2006): 665–705.
Goffman, Erving. *The Presentation of Self in Everyday Life*. Garden City, NY: Doubleday, 1959.
Goffman, Erving. *The Presentation of Self in Everyday Life*. SSRCM 2. Edinburgh: University of Edinburgh Press, 1956.
Goffman, Erving. *Stigma: Notes on the Management of Spoiled Identity*. New York: Touchstone Books, 1986.
Hakola, Raimo. "'Friendly' Pharisees and Social Identity in Acts." Pages 181–200 in *Contemporary Studies in Acts*. Edited by Thomas E. Phillips. Macon: Mercer University Press, 2009.
Haslam, S. Alexander. *Psychology in Organizations: The Social Identity Approach*. London: SAGE, 2004.
Herriot, Peter. *Religious Fundamentalism and Social Identity*. London: Routledge, 2007.
Hewstone, Miles. "Contact and Categorization: Social Psychological Interventions to Change Intergroup Relations." Pages 323–68 in *Stereotypes and Stereotyping*. Edited by C. Neil Macrae, Charles Stangor, and Miles Hewstone. New York: Guilford Press, 1996.
Hinkle, S. and R. Brown, "Intergroup Comparisons and Social Identity: Some Links and Lacunae." Pages 48–70 in *Social Identity Theory: Constructive and Critical Advances*. Edited by D. Abrams and M. Hogg. Hemel Hempstead: Harvester Wheatsheaf, 1990.
Hogg, Michael A. *The Social Psychology of Group Cohesiveness: From Attraction to Social Identity*. London: Harvester Wheatsheaf, 1992.
Hogg, M. and B. Mullin. "Joining Groups to Reduce Uncertainty: Subjective Uncertainty Reduction and Group Identification." Pages 249–79 in *Social Identity and Social Cognition*. Edited by D. Abrams and M. Hogg. Oxford: Blackwell, 1999.
Hogg, Michael A. and Dominic Abrams. *Social Identifications: A Social Psychology of Intergroup Relations and Group Process*. London: Routledge, 1998.
Hogg, Michael A. and Dominic Abrams. "Social Motivation, Self-Esteem and Social Identity." Pages 28–47 in *Social Identity Theory: Constructive and Critical Advances*. Edited by D. Abrams and M. Hogg. Hemel Hempstead: Harvester Wheatsheaf, 1990.
Horrell, David G. "Models and Methods in Social Scientific Interpretation: A Response to Philip Esler." *JSNT* 78 (2000): 83–105.
Im, Pong D. "Social Identity in Ancient Israel: An Archaeological and Textual Study of Social Behaviors and Group Identity among Highland Villagers in Iron Age I Palestine." PhD diss., Graduate Theological Union, 2010.
Izenberg, Gerald. *Identity: The Necessity of a Modern Idea*. Philadelphia: University of Pennsylvania Press, 2016.
Jenkins, Richard. *Social Identity*. 3rd ed. New York: Routledge, 2008.
Jokiranta, Jutta. *Social Identity and Sectarianism in the Qumran Movement*. Edited by Florentino García Martínez. STDJ 105. Leiden: Brill, 2013.

Kiernan, Victor. *The Lords of Human Kind: European Attitudes to Other Cultures in the Imperial Age*. London: Weidenfeld & Nicolson, 1969.

Kuecker, Aaron. *The Spirit and the "Other": Social Identity, Ethnicity and Intergroup Reconciliation in Luke-Acts*. LNTS 444. London: Bloomsbury T&T Clark, 2011.

Lau, Peter H. W. *Identity and Ethics in the Book of Ruth: A Social Identity Approach*. BZAW 416. Berlin: de Gruyter, 2010.

Le Bon, Gustave. *The Crowd: A Study of the Popular Mind*. Anonymous Translation. London: T. Fisher Unwin, 1921.

Marohl, Matthew J. *Faithfulness and the Purpose of Hebrews: A Social Identity Approach*. Cambridge: James Clarke, 2010.

Marques, José M., Dario Páez, and Dominic Abrams. "Social Identity and Intragroup Differentiation as Subjective Social Control." Pages 124–41 in *Social Identity: International Perspectives*. Edited by Stephen Worchel, J. Francisco Morales, Dario Páez, and Jean-Claude Deschamps. London: SAGE, 1998.

McDougall, William. *Ethics and Some Modern World Problems*. New York: G. P. Putnam's Sons, 1924.

McGarty, Craig. *Categorization in Social Psychology*. London: SAGE, 1999.

McGarty, Craig. "Stereotype Formation as Category Formation." Pages 16–37 in *Stereotypes as Explanations: The Formation of Meaningful Beliefs about Social Groups*. Edited by Craig McGarty, Vincent Y. Yzerbyt, and Russell Spears. Cambridge: Cambridge University Press, 2002.

Miller, Norman. "Personalisation and the Promise of Contact Theory." *Journal of Social Issues* 58 (2002): 387–410.

Morris, H. S. "Ethnic Groups." Pages 167–72 in *International Encyclopedia of the Social Sciences*. Vol. 5. New York: Macmillan Co., 1968.

Mummendey, Amélie, Bernd Simon, Carsten Dietze, Melanie Grünert, Gabi Haeger, Sabine Kessler, Stephan Lettgen, and Stefanie Schäferhoff. "Categorization is Not Enough: Intergroup Discrimination in Negative Outcome Allocation." *Journal of Experimental Social Psychology* 28 (1992): 125–44.

Oakes, Penelope J., S. Alexander Haslam, and John C. Turner. *Stereotyping and Social Reality*. Oxford: Blackwell, 1994.

Sherif, Muzafer. *In Common Predicament: Social Psychology of Intergroup Conflict and Cooperation*. Boston, MA: Houghton Mifflin, 1966.

Sherif, Muzafer, O. J. Harvey, B. Jack White, William R. Hood, and Carolyn W. Sherif. *Intergroup Conflict and Cooperation: The Robbers Cave Experiment*. Norman, OK: University of Oklahoma Press, 1961.

Shillington, V. George. *James and Paul: The Politics of Identity at the Turn of the Ages*. Minneapolis: Fortress, 2015.

Smith, Jonathan Z. "What a Difference a Difference Makes." Pages 3–48 in *"To See Ourselves as Others See Us": Christians, Jews, 'Others' in Late Antiquity*. Edited by Jacob Neusner, Ernest S. Frerichs, and Caroline McCracken-Flesher. Chico, CA: Scholars Press, 1985.

Southwood, Katherine E. "An Ethnic Affair?: Ezra's Intermarriage Crisis against a Context of Self-Ascription and Ascription of Others." Pages 46–59 in *Mixed Marriages: Intermarriage and Group Identity in the Second Temple Period*. Edited by Christian Frevel. LHBOTS 547. London: Bloomsbury T&T Clark, 2011.

Southwood, Katherine E. *Ethnicity and the Mixed Marriage Crisis in Ezra 9–10: An Anthropological Approach*. New York: Oxford University Press, 2012.

Stallybrass, O. "Stereotype." Page 601 in *The Fontana Dictionary of Modern Thought*. Edited by A. Bullock and O. Stallybrass. London: Fontana/Collins, 1977.

Tajfel, Henri. *Human Groups and Social Categories: Studies in Social Psychology.* Cambridge: Cambridge University Press, 1981.
Tajfel, Henri. "Social Psychology of Intergroup Relations." *Annual Review of Psychology* 33 (1982): 1–39.
Tajfel, Henri and A. L. Wilkes, "Classification and Quantitative Judgment," *British Journal of Psychology* 54, no. 2 (1963): 101–14.
Tajfel, Henri and John C. Turner. "An Integrative Theory of Intergroup Conflict." Pages 33–47 in *The Social Psychology of Intergroup Relations.* Edited by W. G. Austin and S. Worchel. Monterey: Brooks/Cole, 1971.
Tajfel, Henri, M. G. Billig, R. P. Bundy, and Claude Flament. "Social Categorization and Intergroup Behaviour." *European Journal of Social Psychology* 1, no. 2 (1971): 149–78.
Taylor, Charles. *Sources of the Self: The Making of the Modern Identity.* Cambridge, MA: Harvard University Press, 1989.
Trebilco, Paul. *Self-Designations and Group Identity in the New Testament.* Cambridge: Cambridge University Press, 2011.
Turner, John C. "Henri Tajfel: An Introduction." Pages 1–23 in *Social Groups & Identities: Developing the Legacy of Henri Tajfel.* International Series in Social Psychology. Edited by W. Peter Robinson. Oxford: Butterworth-Heinemann, 1996.
Turner, John C. *Rediscovering the Social Group: A Self-Categorization Theory.* New York: Basil Blackwell, 1987.
Turner, John C. and Rupert Brown. "Social Status, Cognitive Alternatives, and Intergroup Relations." Pages 171–99 in *Differentiation Between Social Groups: Studies in the Social Psychology of Intergroup Relations.* Edited by Henri Tajfel. London: Academic Press, 1978.
Tutu, Desmond. *No Future without Forgiveness.* New York: Doubleday, 1999.
Tutu, Desmond. *The Rainbow People of God: South Africa's Victory over Apartheid.* New York: Doubleday, 1994.
Wenzel, Michael, Amélie Mummendey, and Sven Waldzus. "Superordinate Identities and Intergroup Conflict: The Ingroup Projection Model." *European Review of Social Psychology* 18, no. 1 (2007): 331–72.
Wigbodus, Daniel, Russell Spears, and Gun Semin. "Social Identity, Normative Content and 'Deindividuation' in Computer-Mediated Groups." Pages 164–83 in *Social Identity.* Edited by Naomi Ellemers, Russell Spears, and Bertjan Doosje. Oxford: Blackwell, 1999.
Wilder, David A. "Reduction of Intergroup Discrimination through Individuation of the Outgroup." *Journal of Personality and Social Psychology* 36, no. 12 (1978): 1361–74.
Worchel, Stephen, Virginia A. Andreoli, and Roger Folger. "Intergroup Cooperation and Intergroup Attraction: The Effect of Previous Interaction and Outcome of Combined Effort." *Journal of Experimental Social Psychology* 13 (1977): 131–40.

B. Luke-Acts and Other Sources

Adams, Sean A. "Paul the Roman Citizen: Roman Citizenship in the Ancient World and its Importance for Understanding Acts 22:22–29." Pages 309–26 in *Paul: Jew, Greek, and Roman.* PS 5. Edited by Stanley E. Porter. Leiden: Brill, 2008.
Alexander, Loveday C. A. "The Acts of the Apostles as an Apologetic Text." Pages 183–206 in *Acts in its Ancient Literary Context: A Classicist Looks at the Acts of the Apostles.* LNTS 298. New York: T&T Clark, 2005.

Allison Jr., Dale C. "Acts 9:1–9, 22:6–11, 26:12–18: Paul and Ezekiel." *JBL* 135, no. 4 (2016): 807–26.

Anh, Yong-Sung. *The Reign of God and Rome in Luke's Passion Narrative: An East Asian Global Perspective*, BIS 80. Leiden: Brill, 2006.

Ashcroft, Bill, Gareth Griffiths, and Helen Tiffin. *Post-Colonial Studies: The Key Concepts*. New York: Routledge, 2000.

Aune, David E. *The New Testament in its Literary Environment*. Philadelphia: Westminster, 1989.

Balch, David L. "Comments on the Genre and a Political Theme of Luke-Acts: A Preliminary Comparison of Two Hellenistic Historians." Pages 343–61 in *SBL 1989 Seminar Papers*. Edited by David J. Lull. Atlanta: Scholars Press, 1989.

Balch, David L. "ΜΕΤΑΒΟΛΗ ΠΟΛΙΤΕΙΩΝ—Jesus as Founder of the Church in Luke-Acts: Form and Function." Pages 139–88 in *Contextualizing Acts: Lukan Narrative and Greco-Roman Discourse*. Edited by Todd C. Penner and Caroline V. Stichele. Atlanta: Scholars Press, 2003.

Balch, David L. "The Contested Movements in Rome, Athens, and Jerusalem toward Citizenships/Memberships of Multiple Ethnicities (Introducing Chapters 2–11)." Pages 17–35 in David L. Balch, *Contested Ethnicities and Images: Studies in Acts and Art*. WUNT 345. Tübingen: Mohr Siebeck, 2015.

Baltzer, Klaus. "The Meaning of the Temple in the Lucan Writings." *HTR* 58 (1965): 263–77.

Barreto, Eric D. *Ethnic Negotiations: The Function of Race and Ethnicity in Acts 16*. WUNT 2/294. Tübingen: Mohr Siebeck, 2012.

Barrett, C. K. *A Critical and Exegetical Commentary on the Acts of the Apostles: Vol. 2*. ICC. Edinburgh: T. & T. Clark, 1994.

Barrett, C. K. *Luke the Historian in Recent Study*. London: Epworth, 1961.

Barrett, C. K. *The Acts of the Apostles: A Shorter Commentary*. Edinburgh: T&T Clark, 2002.

Bass, Kenneth. "The Narrative & Rhetorical Use of Divine Necessity in Luke-Acts." *JBPR* 1 (2009): 48–68.

Bauernfeind, Otto. *Kommentar und Studien zur Apostelgeschichte*. WUNT 22. Tübingen: Mohr Siebeck, 1939.

Beale, Gregory K. "The Descent of the Eschatological Temple in the Form of the Spirit at Pentecost: Part 2, Corroborating Evidence." *TynBul* 56 (2005): 64–90.

Beavis, Mary A. *Mark*. PCNT. Grand Rapids: Baker Academic, 2011.

Béchard, Dean P. "The Disputed Case Against Paul: A Redaction-Critical Analysis of Acts 21:27–22:29." *CBQ* 65 (2003): 232–50.

Beck, Norman A. *Mature Christianity: The Recognition and Repudiation of the Anti-Jewish Polemic of the New Testament*. Cranbury, NJ: Associated University Press, 1985.

Bhabha, Homi. *The Location of Culture*. New York: Routledge, 1994.

Blair, Edward P. "Paul's Call to the Gentile Mission." *BR* 10 (1965): 19–33.

Bligh, John. *Galatians: A Discussion of St Paul's Epistle*. London: St. Paul's Publications, 1969.

Bock, Darrell L. *Acts*, BECNT. Grand Rapids: Baker Academic, 2007.

Bock, Darrell L. *A Theology of Luke and Acts: God's Promised Program, Realized for All Nations*. BTNT. Grand Rapids: Zondervan, 2012.

Boesenberg, Dulcinea. "Negotiating Identity: The Jewishness of the Way in Acts." *JRSSS* 13 (2016): 58–75.

Bonz, Marianne P. *The Past as Legacy: Luke-Acts and Ancient Epic*. Minneapolis: Fortress, 2000.

Boring, M. Eugene. *Mark: A Commentary*. NTL. Louisville: Westminster John Knox, 2006.
Bovon, François. *Luke 1: A Commentary on the Gospel of Luke 1:1–9:50*. Hermeneia. Translated by Christine M. Thomas. Minneapolis: Fortress, 2002.
Bovon, François. *Luke 3: A Commentary on the Gospel of Luke 19:28–24:53*. Hermeneia. Translated by James Crouch. Minneapolis: Fortress, 2012.
Boyarin, Daniel. *Border Lines: The Partition of Judaeo-Christianity*. Philadelphia: University of Pennsylvania Press, 2004.
Brawley, Robert L. *Luke-Acts and the Jews: Conflict, Apology, and Conciliation*. SBLMS 33. Atlanta: Scholars Press, 1987.
Brenner, Michael. *A Short History of the Jews*. Translated by Jeremiah Riemer. Princeton: Princeton University Press, 2010.
Brodie, Thomas L. *Luke the Literary Interpreter: Luke-Acts as a Systematic Rewriting and Updating of the Elijah-Elisha Narrative in 1 and 2 Kings*. STD diss., Pontificia Universita S. Tommaso d'Aquino, Vatican City, 1981.
Brodie, Thomas L. "The Accusing and Stoning of Naboth (1 Kgs 21:8–13) as One Component of the Stephen Text (Acts 6:9–14; 7:58a)." *CBQ* 45 (1983): 417–32.
Brown, Raymond E. *The Death of the Messiah: From Gethsemane to the Grave: A Commentary on the Passion Narratives in the Four Gospels*. ABRL. New York: Doubleday, 1994.
Brown, Schuyler. *Apostasy and Perseverance in the Theology of Luke*. Rome: Pontifical Biblical Institute, 1969.
Bruce, F. F. *Commentary on the Book of Acts*. Grand Rapids: Eerdmans, 1976.
Bruce, F. F. *Paul, Apostle of the Heart Set Free*. Grand Rapids: Eerdmans, 1977.
Bruce, F. F. *The Acts of the Apostles: The Greek Text with an Introduction and Commentary*. Grand Rapids: Eerdmans, 1973.
Bruce, F. F. *The Book of the Acts*, NICNT. Grand Rapids: Eerdmans, 1988.
Bryan, Christopher. *Render to Caesar: Jesus, the Early Church, and the Roman Superpower*. New York: Oxford University Press, 2005.
Burke, Sean D. *Queering the Ethiopian Eunuch: Strategies of Ambiguity in Acts*. Minneapolis: Fortress, 2013.
Burridge, Richard. *What Are the Gospels? A Comparison with Greco-Roman Biography*. Grand Rapids: Eerdmans, 2004.
Burrus, Virginia. "The Making of a Heresy: Authority, Gender, and the Priscillianist Controversy." PhD diss., Graduate Theological Union, 1991.
Bush, Stephen S. *Visions of Religion: Experience, Meaning, and Power*. Reflection and Theory in the Study of Religion. New York: Oxford University Press, 2014.
Butticaz, Simon. *The Book of Acts in History*. New York: Harper & Brothers, 1955.
Butticaz, Simon. "The Construction of Paul's Self in His Writings: Narrative Identity, Social Memory and Metaphorical Truth." *BibInt* 26 (2018): 244–65.
Cadbury, Henry J. *The Making of Luke-Acts*. London: Macmillan, 1927.
Cassidy, Richard. *Jesus, Politics, and Society: A Study of Luke's Gospel*. Maryknoll, NY: Orbis, 1978.
Cassidy, Richard. *Society and Politics in the Acts of the Apostles*. Maryknoll, NY: Orbis, 1987.
Chance, J. Bradley. *Jerusalem, the Temple, and the New Age in Luke-Acts*. Macon: Mercer University Press, 1988.
Chen, Jian. *Mao's China and the Cold War*. The New Cold War History. Chapel Hill: University of North Carolina Press, 2001.
Chepey, Stuart. "Is the Timing respecting Paul and the Four Men under a Vow in Acts 21:23–27 Plausible? Possible Implications from Josephus and Philo on the Nazarite Vow and First-Fruits." *CTR* 9, no. 2 (2012): 69–75.

Chepey, Stuart. *Nazirites in Late Second Temple Judaism: A Survey of Ancient Jewish Writings, the New Testament, Archaeological Evidence, and Other Writings from Late Antiquity.* AJEC 60. Leiden: Brill, 2005.

Cohen, Shaye J. D. *The Beginnings of Jewishness: Boundaries, Varieties, Uncertainties.* HCS 31. Berkeley: University of California Press, 1999.

Cohen, Shaye J. D. "The Origins of the Matrilineal Principle in Rabbinic Law." *AJS Review* 10, no. 1 (1985): 19–53.

Cohn-Sherbok, Dan. "Paul and Rabbinic Exegesis." *SJT* 35, no. 2 (1982): 117–32.

Conzelmann, Hans. *Acts of the Apostles: A Commentary on the Acts of the Apostles.* Hermeneia. Translated by James Limburg, A. Thomas Kraabel, and Donald H. Juel. Philadelphia: Fortress, 1987.

Conzelmann, Hans. *Theology of St. Luke.* Translated by Geoffrey Buswell. 2nd ed. New York: Harper & Row, 1961.

Corley, Bruce. "Interpreting Paul's Conversion—Then and Now." Pages 1–17 in *The Road from Damascus: The Impact of Paul's Conversion on His Life, Thought, and Ministry.* Edited by Richard N. Longenecker. Grand Rapids: Eerdmans, 1997.

Crabbe, Kylie. "Accepting Prophecy: Paul's Response to Agabus with Insights from Valerius Maximus and Josephus." *JSNT* 39, no. 2 (2016): 188–208.

Croatto, J. Severino. "Jesus, Prophet like Elijah, and Prophet-Teacher like Moses in Luke-Acts." *JBL* 124, no. 3 (2005): 451–65.

Crossan, John D. *Who Killed Jesus? Exposing the Roots of Anti-Semitism in the Gospel Story of the Death of Jesus.* San Francisco: HarperSanFrancisco, 1995.

Daube, David. "On Acts 23: Sadducees and Angels." *JBL* 109, no. 3 (1990): 493–7.

de Vos, Craig S. "Finding a Charge that Fits: The Accusation against Paul and Silas at Philippi (Acts 16.19–21)." *JSNT* 74 (1999): 51–63.

Dibelius, Martin. *Studies in the Acts of the Apostles.* Translated by M. Ling and Paul Schubert. Edited by Heinrich Green. New York: Charles Scribner's Sons, 1956.

Dinkler, Michal Beth. "The Acts of the Apostles." Pages 327–64 in *The Gospels and Acts: Fortress Commentary on the Bible Study Edition.* Edited by Margaret Aymer, Cynthia Briggs Kittredge, and David A. Sánchez. Minneapolis: Fortress, 2016.

Donahue, John R. and Daniel J. Harrington. *The Gospel of Mark.* SP 2. Collegeville, MN: Liturgical Press, 2002.

Douglas, Mary. *Purity and Danger: An Analysis of Concepts of Pollution and Taboo.* London: Penguin, 1970.

Dunn, James D. G. *New Perspective on Paul.* Grand Rapids: Eerdmans, 2008.

Dunn, James D. G. *The Acts of the Apostles.* NC. Valley Forge, PA: Trinity Press International, 1996.

du Toit, Andrie B. "A Tale of Two Cities: 'Tarsus or Jerusalem' Revisited." *NTS* 46 (2000): 375–402.

du Veil, C. M. *A Commentary on the Acts of the Apostles.* Edited by Hanserd Knollys Society with an historical introduction by F. A. Cox. Translated by Acta Sanctorum Apostolorum ad literam explicata. London: Printed for the Society by J. Haddon, 1851.

Easton, Burton S. *Early Christianity: The Purpose of Acts, and Other Papers.* Edited by Frederick C. Grant. Greenwich, CT: Seabury, 1954.

Edwards, James R. "Parallels and Patterns between Luke and Acts." *BBR* 27, no. 4 (2017): 485–501.

Eisenbaum, Pamela. "Anti-Semitism." *NIDB* 1.184–85.

Eisenbaum, Pamela. *Paul Was Not a Christian: The Original Message of a Misunderstood Apostle.* New York: HarperOne, 2009.

Elliott, John H. "Temple versus Household in Luke-Acts: A Contrast in Social Institutions." Pages 211–40 in *Social World of Luke-Acts: Models for Interpretation*. Edited by Jerome H. Neyrey. Peabody, MA: Hendrickson, 1991.

Esler, Philip F. *Community and Gospel in Luke-Acts: The Social and Political Motivations of Lucan Theology*. SNTS 57. Cambridge: Cambridge University Press, 1987.

Evans, Christopher F. *Saint Luke*, TPI New Testament Commentaries. London: SCM, 1990.

Fairchild, Mark R. "Paul's Pre-Christian Zealot Associations: A Re-examination of Gal. 1.14 and Acts 22.3." *NTS* 45 (1999): 514–32.

Fee, Gordon D. *The First Epistle to the Corinthians*. Grand Rapids: Eerdmans, 2014.

Fitzmyer, Joseph A. *The Acts of the Apostles: A New Translation with Introduction and Commentary*. AB 31. New York: Doubleday, 1998.

Fitzmyer, Joseph A. *The Gospel According to Luke (X–XXIV)*. AB 28A. Garden City, NY: Doubleday, 1985.

Flessen, Bonnie J. *An Exemplary Man: Cornelius and Characterization in Acts*. Eugene, OR: Pickwick, 2011.

Foakes-Jackson, F. J., Kirsopp Lake, Henry J. Cadbury, and James H. Ropes. *The Beginnings of Christianity*. London: Macmillan, 1920–33. See BegC.

Foakes-Jackson, F. J. *The Acts of the Apostles*. MNTC 5. New York: Harper, 1931.

Foxhall, Lin. *The Trojan War: Its Historicity and Context*. Bristol: Bristol Classical Press, 1984.

Fredriksen, Paula and Adele Reinhartz. *Jesus, Judaism, and Christian Anti-Judaism: Reading the New Testament after the Holocaust*. Louisville: Westminster John Knox, 2002.

Gans, Eric. "Christian Morality and the Pauline Revelation," *Semeia* 33 (1985): 97–108.

Gaventa, Beverly R. *The Acts of the Apostles*, ANTC. Nashville: Abingdon, 2003.

Gaventa, Beverly R. "Theology and Ecclesiology in the Miletus Speech: Reflections on Content and Context." *NTS* 50, no. 1 (2004): 36–52.

Gilbert, Gary. "Roman Propaganda and Christian Identity in the Worldview of Luke-Acts." Pages 233–56 in *Contextualizing Acts: Lukan Narrative and Greco-Roman Discourse*. SBLSymS 20. Edited by Todd Penner and Caroline V. Stichele. Atlanta: SBL, 2003.

Golding, Thomas A. "Pagan Worship in Jerusalem?" *BSac* 170 (2013): 304–16.

Gonzalez, Justo L. *The Story Luke Tells: Luke's Unique Witness to the Gospel*. Grand Rapids: Eerdmans, 2015.

Goodman, Martin. *Mission and Conversion: Proselytizing in the Religious History of the Roman Empire*. New York: Oxford University Press, 1994.

Green, Joel B. *The Gospel of Luke*. NICNT. Grand Rapids: Eerdmans, 1997.

Grindheim, Sigurd. "Luke, Paul, and the Law." *NovT* 56 (2014): 335–58.

Gruca-Macaulay, Alexandra. *Lydia as a Rhetorical Construct in Acts*. ESEC 18. Atlanta: SBL, 2016.

Gruen, Erich S. Review of *The Beginnings of Jewishness: Boundaries, Varieties, Uncertainties*, by Shaye J. D. Cohen. *JQR* 92, nos. 3–4 (2002): 594–7.

Gutzke, Manford G. *Plain Talk on Acts*. Grand Rapids: Zondervan, 1966.

Haenchen, Ernst. *The Acts of the Apostles: A Commentary*. Oxford: Basil Blackwell, 1982.

Hakola, Raimo. *Identity Matters: John, the Jews and Jewishness*. NovTSup 118. Leiden: Brill, 2005.

Hamm, Dennis. "Paul's Blindness and its Healing, Clues to Symbolic Intent (Acts 9, 22 and 26)." *Bib* 71 (1990): 63–72.

Hanneken, Todd R. "Moses Has His Interpreters: Understanding the Legal Exegesis in Acts 15 from the Precedent in Jubilees." *CBQ* 77 (2015): 686–706.

Harrisville, Roy A. "Acts 22:6–21." *Int* 42 (1988): 181–5.
Hartsock, Chad. *Sight and Blindness in Luke-Acts: The Use of Physical Features in Characterization*. Leiden: Brill, 2008.
Haya-Prats, Gonzalo. *Empowered Believers: The Holy Spirit in the Book of Acts*. Edited by Paul Elbert. Translated by Scott A. Ellington. Eugene, OR: Cascade Books, 2011.
Hayes, Christine E. *Gentile Impurities and Jewish Identities: Intermarriage and Conversion from the Bible to the Talmud*. New York: Oxford University Press, 2002.
Hayes, Christine E. *What's Divine about Divine Law? Early Perspectives*. Princeton: Princeton University Press, 2015.
Hemer, Colin J. *The Book of Acts in the Setting of Hellenistic History*. WUNT 49. Tübingen: J. C. B. Mohr, 1989.
Hengel, Martin. *Acts and the History of Earliest Christianity*. London: SCM, 1979.
Hengel, Martin. *The Pre-Christian Paul*. Philadelphia: Trinity Press International, 1991.
Hock, Ronald F. "Homer in Greco-Roman Education." Pages 56–77 in *Mimesis and Intertextuality in Antiquity and Christianity*. SAC. Edited by Dennis R. MacDonald. Harrisburg, PA: Trinity Press International, 2001.
Hock, Ronald F. "Paul's Tentmaking and the Problem of His Social Class." *JBL* 97 (1978): 555–64.
Hock, Ronald F. *The Social Context of Paul's Ministry: Tentmaking and Apostleship*. Philadelphia: Fortress, 1980.
Hodge, Caroline J. "Apostle to the Gentiles: Constructions of Paul's Identity." *BibInt* 13, no. 3 (2005): 270–88.
Holladay, Carl R. *A Critical Introduction to the New Testament: Interpreting the Message and Meaning of Jesus Christ*. Nashville: Abingdon, 2005.
Holladay, Carl R. *Acts: A Commentary*. NTL. Louisville: Westminster John Knox, 2016.
Holland, Tom. "N. T. Wright and the Identity of Saul of Tarsus." *CTR* 12, no. 2 (2015): 99–118.
Horn, Friedrich W. "Paulus, das Nasiräat, und die Nasiräer." *NovT* 39 (1997): 117–37.
Horsley, Richard A. and John S. Hanson, *Bandits, Prophets, and Messiahs: Popular Movements in the Time of Jesus*. Minneapolis: Winston, 1985.
Immanuel, Babu. *Acts of the Apostles: An Exegetical and Contextual Commentary*. ICNT 5. Minneapolis: Fortress, 2017.
Irudayaraj, Dominic S. *Violence, Otherness and Identity in Isaiah 63:1–6*. LHBOTS 633. London: Bloomsbury T&T Clark, 2017.
Janowitz, Naomi. "Rethinking Jewish Identity in Late Antiquity." Pages 205–19 in *Ethnicity and Culture in Late Antiquity*. Edited by Stephen Mitchell and Geoffrey Greatrex. London: Duckworth, 2000.
Jeffers, James S. *The Greco-Roman World of the New Testament Era: Exploring the Background of Early Christianity*. Downers Grove, IL: InterVarsity Press, 1999.
Jeremias, Joachim. *Jerusalem in the Time of Jesus: An Investigation into Economic and Social Conditions during the New Testament Period*. Translated by F. H. and C. H. Cave. Philadelphia: Fortress, 1977.
Jerome, St. *Jerome's Commentaries on Galatians, Titus, and Philemon*. Translated by Thomas P. Scheck. Notre Dame: University of Notre Dame Press, 2010.
Jervell, Jacob. *Die Apostelgeschichte: Übersetzt und Erklärt*. KEK 3/17. Göttingen: Vandenhoeck & Ruprecht, 1998.
Jervell, Jacob. *Luke and the People of God: A New Look at Luke-Acts*. Minneapolis: Augsburg, 1972.

Jervell, Jacob. *The Theology of the Acts of the Apostles*. Cambridge: Cambridge University Press, 1996.

Johnson, Luke T. "Anti-Judaism and the New Testament." Pages 541-68 in *Contested Issues in Christian Origins and the New Testament: Collected Essays*. NovTSup 146. Edited by Luke T. Johnson. Leiden: Brill, 2013.

Johnson, Luke T. "On Finding the Lukan Community: A Cautious Cautionary Essay." Pages 129-44 in *Contested Issues in Christian Origins and the New Testament Collected Essays*. NovTSup 146. Edited by Luke T. Johnson. Leiden: Brill, 2013.

Johnson, Luke T. *The Acts of the Apostles*. SP 5. Collegeville, MN: Liturgical Press, 1992.

Johnson, Luke T. *The Gospel of Luke*. SP 3. Collegeville, MN: Liturgical Press, 1991.

Johnson, Luke T. *The Real Jesus: The Misguided Quest for the Historical Jesus and the Truth of the Traditional Gospels*. San Francisco: HarperSanFrancisco, 1996.

Johnson, Sherman E. "The Apostle Paul and the Riot in Ephesus." *LTQ* 14, no. 4 (1979): 79-88.

Joseph, Suppogu. *Table Fellowship of Jesus: According to Luke*. Delhi: ISPCK, 2009.

Kaminsky, Joel and Anne Stewart. "God of All the World: Universalism and Developing Monotheism in Isaiah 40-66." *HTR* 99, no 2 (2006): 139-63.

Kang, Wi Jo. *Christ and Caesar in Modern Korea: A History of Christianity and Politics*. Albany, NY: State University of New York Press, 1997.

Karakolis, Christos. "The Holy Spirit in Luke-Acts: Personal Entity or Impersonal Power?" Pages 87-109 in *The Holy Spirit and the Church according to the New Testament: Sixth International East-West Symposium of New Testament Scholars, Belgrade, August 25 to 31, 2013*. Edited by Predrag Dragutinovic, Karl-Wilhelm Niebuhr, and James Buchanan Wallace in Co-operation with Christos Karakolis. WUNT 354. Tübingen: Mohr Siebeck, 2016.

Keener, Craig S. *Acts: An Exegetical Commentary*. Grand Rapids: Baker Academic, 2014.

Keener, Craig S. *The IVP Bible Background Commentary: New Testament*. Downers Grove, IL: InterVarsity Press, 1993.

Kelhoffer, James A. "The Gradual Disclosure of Paul's Violence against Christians in the Acts of the Apostles as an Apology for the Standing of the Lukan Paul." *BR* 54 (2009): 25-35.

Kennedy, George A. *New Testament Interpretation through Rhetorical Criticism*. Studies in Religion. Chapel Hill: University of North Carolina Press, 1984.

Kim, Seyoon. *Christ and Caesar: The Gospel and the Roman Empire in the Writings of Paul and Luke*. Grand Rapids: Eerdmans, 2008.

Kister, Menahem. "'First Adam' and 'Second Adam' in 1 Cor 15:45-49 in the Light of Midrashic Exegesis and Hebrew Usage." Pages 351-66 in *The New Testament and Rabbinic Literature*. JSJSup 136. Edited by Reimund Bieringer, Florentino García Martínez, Didier Pollefeyt and Peter Tomson. Leiden: Brill, 2010.

Klawans, Jonathan. "Josephus on Fate, Free Will, and Ancient Jewish Types of Compatibilism." *Numen* 56, no. 1 (2009): 44-90.

Klijn, Albertus F. J. "Scribes, Pharisees, Highpriests, and Elders in the New Testament." *NovT* 3, no. 4 (1959): 259-67.

Kollmann, Bernd. "Philippus der Evangelis und die Anfänge der Heidenmission." *Bib* 81 (2000): 551-65.

Krodel, Gerhard A. *Acts*. ACNT. Minneapolis: Augsburg, 1986.

Kurz, William S. *Acts of the Apostles*. CCSS. Grand Rapids: Baker Academic, 2013.

Lampe, Peter. "Paulus-Zeltmacher." *BZ* 31 (1987): 256-61.

Landolt, Jean-François. "'Be imitators of me, brothers and sisters' (Philippians 3.17): Paul as an Exemplary Figure in the Pauline Corpus and the Acts of the Apostles." Translated by Michael D. Thomas, Eric Gilchrest, and Timothy Brookins. Pages 290–317 in *Paul and the Heritage of Israel: Paul's Claim upon Israel's Legacy in Luke and Acts in the Light of the Pauline Letters*. Edited by David P. Moessner, Daniel Marguerat, Mikeal C. Parsons, and Michael Wolter. LNTS 452. London: T&T Clark, 2012.

Lappenga, Benjamin J. *Paul's Language of Ζῆλος: Monosemy and the Rhetoric of Identity and Practice*. BIS 137. Leiden: Brill, 2016.

Lee, Doohee. *Luke-Acts and "Tragic history": Communicating Gospel with the World*. WUNT 2/346. Tübingen: Mohr Siebeck, 2013.

Lehtipuu, Outi. "How to Expose a Deviant? Resurrection Belief and Boundary Creation in Early Christianity." Pages 165–94 in *Others and the Construction of Early Christian Identities*. Edited by Raimo Hakola, Nina Nikki, and Ulla Tervahauta. PFES 106. Helsinki: Finnish Exegetical Society 2013.

Lenski, Richard C. H. *The Interpretation of the Acts of the Apostles*. Minneapolis: Augsburg, 1961.

Lentz, John C., Jr. *Luke's Portrait of Paul*. SNTSMS 77. Cambridge: Cambridge University Press, 1993.

Levine, Amy-Jill and Ben Witherington III. *The Gospel of Luke*. NCBC. Cambridge: Cambridge University Press, 2018.

Levy, Leonard W. *Blasphemy: Verbal Offense Against the Sacred, From Moses to Salman Rushdie*. New York: Alfred A. Knopf, 1993.

Linafelt, Tod. *A Shadow of Glory: Reading the New Testament after the Holocaust*. New York: Routledge, 2002.

Long, William R. "The *Paulusbild* in the Trial of Paul in Acts." *SBLSP* (1983): 87–105.

Longenecker, Bruce W. "Socio-Economic Profiling of the First Urban Christians." Pages 36–59 in *After the First Urban Christians: The Social-Scientific Study of Pauline Christianity Twenty-Five Years Later*. Edited by Todd D. Still and David G. Horrell. New York: Continuum, 2009.

Lucian, "The Eunuch." *The Works of Lucian*. Translated by A. M. Harmon. Vol. 5. LCL. Cambridge, MA: Harvard University Press, 1936.

Lüdemann, Gerd. *Early Christianity According to the Traditions in Acts: A Commentary*. Translated by John Bowden. Minneapolis: Fortress, 1989.

Lüdemann, Gerd. *Paul, Apostle to the Gentiles: Studies in Chronology*. Philadelphia: Fortress, 1984.

Lüdemann, Gerd. *Paul, the Founder of Christianity*. Amherst, NY: Prometheus Books, 2002.

Maccoby, Hyam. *Judaism in the First Century*. IRS. London: Sheldon Press, 1987.

MacCulloch, Diarmaid. *Christianity: The First Three Thousand Years*. New York: Penguin Books, 2009.

MacDonald, Dennis R. *Does the New Testament Imitate Homer?: Four Cases from the Acts of the Apostles*. New Haven: Yale University Press, 2003.

MacDonald, Dennis R. *Luke and Vergil: Imitations of Classical Greek Literature*. NTGL 2. Lanham, MD: Rowman & Littlefield, 2015.

MacDonald, Dennis R. *The Gospels and Homer: Imitations of Greek Epic in Mark and Luke-Acts*. NTGL 1. Lanham, MD: Rowman & Littlefield, 2015.

Maddox, Robert. *The Purpose of Luke-Acts*. FRLANT 126. Göttingen: Vandenhoeck & Ruprecht, 1982.

Malamat, Abraham. *A History of the Jewish People*. Cambridge, MA: Harvard University Press, 1976.

Malina, Bruce and Jerome H. Neyrey. "Conflict in Luke-Acts: Labelling and Deviance Theory." Pages 97–122 in *Social World of Luke-Acts: Models for Interpretation*. Edited by Jerome H. Neyrey. Peabody, MA: Hendrickson, 1991.
Malina, Bruce J. and John J. Pilch. *Social-Science Commentary on the Book of Acts*. Minneapolis: Fortress, 2008.
Mallen, Peter. *The Reading and Transformation of Isaiah in Luke-Acts*. LNTS 367. London: T&T Clark, 2008.
Mandell, Sara. "Who Paid the Temple Tax When the Jews Were under Roman Rule?" *HTR* 77, no. 2 (1984): 223–32.
Mansoor, Menahem. "Pharisees." *Encyclopaedia Judaica*. Edited by Michael Berenbaum and Fred Skolnik, 2nd ed. Vol. 16. New York: Macmillan Reference USA, 2007, 30–32.
Mansoor, Menahem. "Sadducees." *Encyclopaedia Judaica*. Edited by Michael Berenbaum and Fred Skolnik. 2nd ed. Vol. 17. New York: Macmillan Reference USA, 2007, 654–55.
Marguerat, Daniel. *La première histoire du christianisme: Les Actes des apôtres*. LD 180. Paris: Cerf, 1999.
Marguerat, Daniel. *Les Actes des apôtres (13–28)*. CNT 5b. Geneva: Labor et fides, 2015.
Marguerat, Daniel. *Paul in Acts and Paul in His Letters*. WUNT 310. Tübingen: Mohr Siebeck, 2013.
Marguerat, Daniel. *The First Christian Historian: Writing the 'Acts of the Apostles.'* SNTSMS 121. Translated by Ken McKinney, Gregory J. Laughery, and Richard Bauckham. New York: Cambridge University Press, 2002.
Marshall, I. Howard. *The Acts of the Apostles: An Introduction and Commentary*. Grand Rapids: Eerdmans, 1980.
Marshall, I. Howard. *The Gospel of Luke: A Commentary on the Greek Text*. NIGTC 3. Grand Rapids: Eerdmans, 1978.
Marshall, Mary. *The Portrayals of the Pharisees in the Gospels and Acts*. FRLANT 254. Göttingen: Vandenhoeck & Ruprecht, 2015.
Martin, Clarice Jannette. "A Chamberlain's Journey and the Challenge of Interpretation for Liberation." *Semeia* 47 (1989): 105–35.
Martin, Troy W. "Investigating the Pauline Letter Body: Issues, Methods, and Approaches." Pages 185–212 in *Paul and the Ancient Letter Form*. PS 6. Edited by Stanley E. Porter and Sean A. Adams. Leiden: Brill, 2010.
Mason, Steve. "N. T. Wright on Paul the Pharisee and Ancient Jews in Exile." *SJT* 69, no. 4 (2016): 432–52.
Mather, P. Boyd. "Paul in Acts as 'Servant' and 'Witness.'" *BR* 30 (1985): 23–44.
Matthews, Shelly. *Perfect Martyr: The Stoning of Stephen and the Construction of Christian Identity*. New York: Oxford University Press, 2010.
Maxwell, Kathy R. "The Role of the Audience in Ancient Narrative: Acts as A Case Study." *ResQ* 48, no. 3 (2006): 171–80.
McGarvey, John W. *New Commentary on Acts of Apostles: Vol. 1*. Delight, AR: Gospel Light Publishing, 1892.
Meeks, Wayne A. *The First Urban Christians: The Social World of the Apostle Paul*. New Haven: Yale University Press, 1983.
Metzger, James A. *Consumption and Wealth in Luke's Travel Narrative*. BIS 88. Leiden: Brill, 2007.
Michaels, J. Ramsey. *The Gospel of John*. NICNT. Grand Rapids: Eerdmans, 2010.
Muñoz-Larrondo, Rubén. *A Postcolonial Reading of the Acts of the Apostles*. Studies in Biblical Literature 147. New York: Peter Lang, 2012.
Murphy-O'Connor, Jerome. *Paul: A Critical Life*. Oxford: Clarendon Press, 1996.

Nadella, Raj. *Dialogue Not Dogma: Many Voices in the Gospel of Luke.* LNTS 431. New York: T&T Clark, 2011.

Neagoe, Alexandru. *The Trial of the Gospel: An Apologetic Reading of Luke's Trial Narratives.* SNTSMS 116. Cambridge: Cambridge University Press, 2002.

Neusner, Jacob. *The Rabbinic Traditions about the Pharisees before 70 CE.: Part 1: The Masters.* SFSHJ 202. Atlanta: Scholars Press, 1999.

Neyrey, Jerome H. "The Symbolic Universe of Luke-Acts: They Turn the World Upside Down." Pages 271–304 in *Social World of Luke-Acts: Models for Interpretation*, Edited by Jerome H. Neyrey. Peabody, MA: Hendrickson, 1991.

Nicklas, Tobias. "The 'Jews' in the Gospel of John: Past and Future Lines of Scholarship." Pages 49–66 in *Perceiving the Other in Ancient Judaism and Early Christianity*. Edited by Michal Bar-Asher Siegal, Wolfgang Grünstäudl, and Matthew Thiessen. WUNT 394. Tübingen: Mohr Siebeck, 2017.

Nicols, John. *Civic Patronage in the Roman Empire*, MSHACA 365. Leiden: Brill, 2014.

Nirenberg, David. *Anti-Judaism: The Western Tradition.* New York: W. W. Norton & Co., 2013.

Nolland, John. *Luke 18:35–24:53.* WBC 35C. Dallas: Word Books, 1993.

Oswalt, John N. *The Book of Isaiah: Chapters 1–39.* NICOT. Grand Rapids: Eerdmans, 1986.

O'Toole, Robert F. "Luke's Position on Politics and Society." Pages 1–17 in *Political Issues in Luke-Acts*. Edited by Richard J. Cassidy and Philip J. Scharper. Maryknoll, NY: Orbis, 1983.

Pao, David W. *Acts and the Isaianic New Exodus.* WUNT 2/130. Tübingen: Mohr Siebeck, 2000.

Park, Hyun Ho. "From Jewish Mission to Gentile Mission: Triple Stories of Peter and the Border Crossing in Acts 9:32–10:48." Paper presented at the annual meeting of the Society of Biblical Literature, San Antonio, Texas, November 19–22, 2016.

Park, Hyun Ho. "Minjung in the Sinking of the Sewol Ferry: A Reading of Luke 10:25–42 from Minjung Theology's Perspective." *KPJT* 48, no. 3 (2016): 59–79.

Park, Hyun Ho. "Unmasking the injustice: The Korean Candlelight Revolution and the parable of the Pounds." Paper presented at the annual meeting of the Society of Biblical Literature, Boston, Massachusetts, November 18–21, 2017.

Parry, Donald W., Jay A. Parry, and Tina M. Peterson, *Understanding Isaiah*. Salt Lake City: Deseret Books, 1998.

Parsons, Mikeal C. *Acts.* Grand Rapids: Baker Academic, 2008.

Paterson, Jeremy. "Review-Discussion Responses to Roman Power in Luke-Acts." *Histos* 9 (2015): 61–9.

Paul, Shalom M. *Isaiah 40–66: Translation and Commentary.* ECC. Grand Rapids: Eerdmans, 2012.

Penner, Todd C. *In Praise of Christian Origins: Stephen and the Hellenists in Lukan Apologetic Historiography.* ESEC 10. New York: T&T Clark, 2004.

Pervo, Richard I. *Acts: A Commentary.* Hermeneia. Minneapolis: Fortress, 2009.

Pervo, Richard I. *Dating Acts: Between the Evangelists and the Apologists.* Santa Rosa, CA: Polebridge, 2006.

Pervo, Richard I. *Profit with Delight: The Literary Genre of the Acts of the Apostles.* Philadelphia: Fortress, 1987.

Phillips, Thomas E. *Acts Within Diverse Frames of Reference.* Macon: Mercer University Press, 2009.

Pickett, Raymond. "Luke and Empire." Pages 1–22 in *Luke-Acts and Empire: Essays in Honor of Robert L. Brawley*. Edited by David Rhoads, David Esterline, and Jae Won Lee. PTMS 151. Eugene, OR: Pickwick, 2011.

Pilch, John J. *Stephen: Paul and the Hellenist Israelites*. Collegeville, MN: Liturgical Press, 2008.
Pilch, John J. *Visions and Healing in the Acts of the Apostles: How the Early Believers Experienced God*. Collegeville, MN: Liturgical Press, 2004.
Plummer, Alfred. *A Critical and Exegetical Commentary on the Gospel According to St. Luke*. ICC. New York: Charles Scribner's Sons, 1903.
Polhill, John B. *Acts*, NAC 26. Nashville: Broadman, 1992.
Porter, Stanley E. "Did Paul Speak Latin?" Pages 289–308 in *Paul: Jew, Greek, and Roman*. PS 5. Edited by Stanley E. Porter. Leiden: Brill, 2008.
Porter, Stanley E. *The Paul of Acts: Essays in Literary Criticism, Rhetoric, and Theology*. WUNT 115. Tübingen: Mohr Siebeck, 1999.
Porter, Stanley E. "The Portrait of Paul in Acts." Pages 124–38 in *The Blackwell Companion to Paul*. Edited by Stephen Westerholm. Malden, MA: Wiley-Blackwell, 2011.
Powell, Mark A. "Salvation in Luke-Acts." *Word & World* 12, no. 1 (1992): 5–10.
Quintilian. *The Institutio Oratoria of Quintilian*. LCL. Translated by Harold E. Butler. Cambridge, MA: Harvard University Press, 1953.
Racine, Jean-François. "Hybrid Features in the Acts of the Apostles: A First Exploration." Paper presented at the annual meeting for the Canadian Society of Biblical Studies, Winnipeg, Manitoba, May 30–June 1, 2004.
Racine, Jean-François. "L'hybridité des personnages: Une stratégie d'inclusion des gentils dans les Actes des Apôtres." Pages 559–66 in *Analyse narrative et Bible: Deuxième colloque international du RRENAB, Louvain-la-Neuve, avril 2004*. Edited by Camille Focant and André Wénin. BETL 191. Leuven: Leuven University Press, 2005.
Rackham, Richard B. *The Acts of the Apostles: An Exposition*. London: Methuen, 1957.
Rapske, Brian. *The Book of Acts and Paul in Roman Custody*. The Book of Acts in Its First Century Setting 3. Grand Rapids: Eerdmans, 1994.
Regev, Eyal. "The Sadducees, the Pharisees, and the Sacred: Meaning and Ideology in the Halakhic Controversies between the Sadducees and Pharisees." *RRJ* 9, no. 1 (2006): 126–40.
Riesner, Rainer. *Paul's Early Period: Chronology, Mission Strategy, Theology*. Translated by Doug Stott. Grand Rapids: Eerdmans, 1998.
Roberts, Jimmy J. M. *First Isaiah: A Commentary*. Hermeneia. Minneapolis: Fortress, 2015.
Røsæg, Nils Aksel. "The Blinding of Paul: Observations to a Theme." *SEÅ* 71 (2006): 159–85.
Rosenblatt, Marie-Eloise. *Paul the Accused: His Portrait in the Acts of the Apostles*. ZSNT. Collegeville, MN: Liturgical Press, 1995.
Roskam, Hendrika N. *The Purpose of the Gospel of Mark in Its Historical and Social Context*. NovTSup 114. Leiden: Brill, 2004.
Rothschild, Clare K. *Luke-Acts and the Rhetoric of History: An Investigation of Early Christian Historiography*. WUNT 2/175. Tübingen: Mohr Siebeck, 2004.
Rowe, Kavin C. *World Upside Down: Reading Acts in the Graeco-Roman Age*. New York: Oxford University Press, 2009.
Saldarini, Anthony J. "Comparing the Traditions: New Testament and Rabbinic Literature." *BBR* 7 (1997): 195–204.
Samkutty, V. J. *The Samaritan Mission in Acts*. LNTS 328. London: T&T Clark, 2006.
Sanders, E. P. *Paul and Palestinian Judaism: A Comparison of Patterns of Religion*. Minneapolis: Fortress, 1977.
Sanders, Jack T. *The Jews in Luke-Acts*. Philadelphia: Fortress, 1987.
Sanders, Jack T. "The Pharisees in Luke-Acts." Pages 141–88 in *The Living Text: Essays in Honor of Ernest W Saunders*. Lanham, MD: University Press of America, 1985.

Scaer, Peter J. *The Lukan Passion and the Praiseworthy Death*. NTM 10. Sheffield: Sheffield Phoenix, 2005.

Schäfer, Peter. *The Jewish Jesus: How Judaism and Christianity Shaped Each Other*. Princeton: Princeton University Press, 2012.

Schmithals, Walter. *Die Apostelgeschichte des Lukas*. ZBNT 3.2. Zürich: Theologischer Verlag, 1982.

Schnabel, Eckhard J. *Early Christian Mission*. Downers Grove, IL: InterVarsity Press, 2004.

Schoenfeld, Andrew J. "Sons of Israel in Caesar's Service: Jewish Soldiers in the Roman Military." *IJJS* 24, no. 3 (2006): 115–26.

Schreiner, Thomas R. "Is Perfect Obedience to the Law Possible? A Re-examination of Galatians 3:10." *JETS* 27, no. 2 (1984): 151–60.

Schreiner, Thomas R. "'Works of Law' in Paul." *NovT* 33, no. 3 (1991): 217–44.

Schwartz, Daniel R. "The Accusation and the Accusers at Philippi (Acts 16:20–21)." *Bib* 65, no. 3 (1984): 357–63.

Schwartz, Daniel R. *Theology as History, History as Theology: Paul in Ephesus in Acts 19*. BZNW 133. Berlin: de Gruyter, 2005.

Seccombe, David. "The New People of God." Pages 349–72 in *Witness to the Gospel: The Theology of Acts*. Edited by I. Howard Marshall and David Peterson. Grand Rapids: Eerdmans, 1998.

Seesengood, Robert P. *Paul: A Brief History*. Blackwell Brief Histories of Religion Series. Chichester: Wiley-Blackwell, 2010.

Segal, Alan F. *Paul the Convert: The Apostolate and Apostasy of Saul the Pharisee*. New Haven: Yale University Press, 1990.

Sevenster, Jan N. *Do You Know Greek? How Much Greek Could the First Jewish Christian Have Known?* Translated by J. de Bruin. NovTSup 19. Leiden: Brill, 1968.

Shauf, Scott. "Locating the Eunuch: Characterization and Narrative Context in Acts 8:26–40." *CBQ* 71 (2009): 762–75.

Shepherd, William H., Jr. *The Narrative Function of the Holy Spirit as a Character in Luke-Acts*. SBLDS 147. Atlanta: Scholars Press, 1994.

Sherwin-White, Adrian N. *Roman Society and Roman Law in the New Testament*. Oxford: Clarendon Press, 1963.

Sherwin-White, Adrian N. *The Roman Citizenship*. Oxford: Clarendon Press, 1973.

Sim, David C. "Gentiles, God-Fearers and Proselytes." Pages 9–27 in *Attitudes to Gentiles in Ancient Judaism and Early Christianity*. Edited by David C. Sim and James S. MacLaren. LNTS 499. London: Bloomsbury T&T Clark, 2013.

Skinner, Matthew L. *Locating Paul: Places of Custody as Narrative Settings in Acts 21–28*. SBLAB 13. Atlanta: SBL, 2003.

Skinner, Matthew L. *The Trial Narratives: Conflict, Power, and Identity in the New Testament*. Louisville: Westminster John Knox, 2010.

Slingerland, Dixon. "'The Jews' in the Pauline Portion of Acts." *JAAR* 54, no. 2 (1986): 305–21.

Smith, Mitzi J. *The Literary Construction of the Other in the Acts of the Apostles*. PTMS 154. Eugene, OR: Pickwick, 2011.

Smith, Steve. *The Fate of the Jerusalem Temple in Luke-Acts: An Intertextual Approach to Jesus' Laments over Jerusalem and Stephen's Speech*. LNTS 553. London: Bloomsbury T&T Clark, 2017.

Soards, Marion L. *The Speeches in Acts: Their Content, Context, and Concerns*. Louisville: Westminster/John Knox, 1994.

Songer, Harold S. "Paul's Mission to Jerusalem: Acts 20–28." *RevExp* 71, no. 4 (1974): 499–510.
Spencer, F. Scott. *Journeying Through Acts: A Literary-Cultural Reading*. Peabody, MA: Hendrickson, 2004.
Squires, John T. *The Plan of God in Luke-Acts*. SNTSMS 76. Cambridge: Cambridge University, 1993.
Stegemann, Wolfgang. "War der Apostel Paulus ein Römischer Bürger?" *ZNW* 78 (1987): 200–29.
Stendahl, Krister. *Paul among Jews and Gentiles and Other Essays*. Philadelphia: Fortress, 1976.
Sterling, Gregory E. *Historiography and Self-Definition: Josephos, Luke-Acts, and Apologetic Historiography*. NovTSup 64. Leiden: Brill, 1992.
Sterling, Gregory E. "Mors Philosophi: The Death of Jesus in Luke." *HTR* 94 (2001): 383–402.
Still, Todd D. "Did Paul Loathe Manual Labor? Revisiting the Work of Ronald F. Hock on the Apostle's Tentmaking and Social Class." *JBL* 125, no. 4 (2006): 781–95.
Strauss, Barry. *The Trojan War: A New History*. New York: Simon & Schuster, 2007.
Strauss, Stephen J. "The Purpose of Acts and the Mission of God." *BSac* 169 (2012): 443–64.
Strelan, Rick. *Luke the Priest: The Authority of the Author of the Third Gospel*. Burlington, VT: Ashgate, 2008.
Stroup, Christopher. *The Christians Who Became Jews: Acts of the Apostles and Ethnicity in the Roman City*. New Haven: Yale University Press, 2020.
Tajra, Harry W. *The Trial of St. Paul: A Juridical Exegesis of the Second Half of the Acts of the Apostles*. WUNT 2/35. Tübingen: Mohr Siebeck, 1989.
Talbert, Charles H. *Literary Patterns, Theological Themes, and the Genre of Luke-Acts*. Cambridge, MA: SBL and Scholars Press, 1975.
Talbert, Charles H. *Reading Acts: A Literary and Theological Commentary*. RNTS. Macon: Smyth & Helwys, 2005.
Tannehill, Robert C. *The Narrative Unity of Luke-Acts: A Literary Interpretation*. 2 Vols. Minneapolis: Fortress, 1986–90.
Tannehill, Robert C. *The Shape of Luke's Story: Essays on Luke-Acts*. Eugene, OR: Cascade, 2005.
Tannehill, Robert C. "The Story of Israel within the Lukan Narrative." Pages 325–39 in *Jesus and the Heritage of Israel: Luke's Narrative Claim upon Israel's Legacy*, Luke the Interpreter of Israel 1. Edited by David P. Moessner. Harrisburg, PA: Trinity Press International, 1999.
Taylor, Nicholas H. "The Jerusalem Temple in Luke-Acts." *HvTSt* 60 (2004): 462–70.
Thiessen, Matthew. *Contesting Conversion: Genealogy, Circumcision, and Identity in Ancient Judaism and Christianity*. New York: Oxford University Press, 2011.
Thiessen, Matthew. "Gentiles as Impure Animals in the Writings of Early Christ Followers." Pages 19–32 in *Perceiving the Other in Ancient Judaism and Early Christianity*. Edited by Michal Bar-Asher Siegal, Wolfgang Grünstäudl, and Matthew Thiessen. WUNT 394. Tübingen: Mohr Siebeck, 2017.
Thompson, George H. P. *The Gospel According to Luke in the Revised Standard Version with Introduction and Commentary*. Oxford: Clarendon Press, 1972.
Thompson, Richard P. "'Say It Ain't So, Paul!' The Accusations against Paul in Acts 21 in Light of His Ministry in Acts 16–20." *BR* 45 (2000): 34–50.
Thornton, Timothy C. G. "To the End of the Earth: Acts 1:8." *ExpTim* 89 (1978): 374–5.
Tiede, David L. *Luke*, ACNT. Minneapolis: Augsburg, 1988.

Tiede, David L. *Prophecy and History in Luke-Acts*. Philadelphia: Fortress, 1980.
Tripp, Jeffrey M. "A Tale of Two Riots: The *synkrisis* of the Temples of Ephesus and Jerusalem in Acts 19–23." *JSNT* 37, no. 1 (2014): 86–111.
Turner, Nigel. *A Grammar of New Testament Greek*. Vol. 3. Edinburgh: Clark, 1963.
Tyson, Joseph B. *Images of Judaism in Luke-Acts*. Columbia, SC: University of South Carolina Press, 2010.
Tyson, Joseph B. "'Works of Law' in Galatians." *JBL* 92, no. 3 (1973): 423–31.
van Minnen, Peter. "Paul the Roman Citizen." *JSNT* 56 (1994): 43–52.
van Unnik, Willem C. *Tarsus or Jerusalem: The City of Paul's Youth*. Translated by George Ogg. London: Epworth, 1962.
Verheyden, Joseph. "The Unity of Luke-Acts: One Work, One Author, One Purpose?" Pages 43–66 in *Issues in Luke-Acts: Selected Essays*. Edited by Sean A. Adams and Michael Pahl. GH 26. Piscataway, NJ: Gorgias, 2012.
Vielhauer, Philipp. "On the 'Paulinism' of Acts." Pages 3–17 in *Paul and the Heritage of Israel: Paul's Claim Upon Israel's Legacy in Luke and Acts in the Light of the Pauline Letters*. Edited by David P. Moessner, Daniel Marguerat, Mikeal C. Parsons, and Michael Wolter. LNTS 452. London: T&T Clark, 2012.
Waddell, James A. *The Messiah: A Comparative Study of the Enochic Son of Man and the Pauline Kyrios*. JCTS. New York: Bloomsbury T&T Clark, 2011.
Walaskay, Paul. *And So We Came to Rome: The Political Perspective of St Luke*. SNTSMS 49. Cambridge: Cambridge University Press, 1983.
Walker, William O., Jr. "Acts and the Pauline Corpus Reconsidered." *JSNT* 24 (1985): 3–23.
Walker, William O., Jr. "Acts and the Pauline Corpus Revisited: Peter's Speech at the Jerusalem Conference." Pages 77–86 in *Literary Studies in Luke-Acts: Essays in Honor of Joseph B. Tyson*. Edited by Richard P. Thompson and Thomas E. Phillips. Macon: Mercer University Press, 1998.
Wall, Robert W. "The Acts of the Apostles: Introduction, Commentary, and Reflections." Pages 1–368 in *Acts, Introduction to Epistolary Literature, Romans, 1 Corinthians*. NIB 10. Edited by Leander E. Keck. Nashville: Abingdon, 2002.
Walton, Steve. "The State They Were In: Luke's View of the Roman Empire." Pages 1–41 in *Rome in the Bible and the Early Church*. Edited by Peter Oakes. Grand Rapids: Baker Academic, 2002.
Watson, Alan. *The Trial of Stephen: The First Christian Martyr*. Athens, GA: University of Georgia Press, 1996.
Weatherly, Jon A. *Jewish Responsibility for the Death of Jesus in Luke-Acts*. JSNTSup 106. Sheffield: Sheffield Academic Press, 1994.
White, Devin L. "Confronting Oracular Contradiction in Acts 21:1–14." *NovT* 58 (2016): 27–46.
White, James F. *The Sacraments in Protestant Practice and Faith*. Nashville: Abingdon, 1999.
Whitmarsh, Tim. *Greek Literature and the Roman Empire: The Politics of Imitation*. Oxford: Oxford University Press, 2001.
Wilson, Brittany E. "Sight and Spectacle: 'Seeing' Paul in the Book of Acts." Pages 141–54 in *Characters and Characterization in Luke-Acts*. Edited by Frank E. Dicken and Julia A. Snyder. LNTS 548. London: Bloomsbury T&T Clark, 2016.
Wilson, Brittany E. *Unmanly Men: Refigurations of Masculinity in Luke-Acts*. New York: Oxford University Press 2015.
Williams, David J. *Acts*. San Francisco: Harper, 1985.
Wilson, Stephen G. *Luke and the Law*. SNTSMS 50. New York : Cambridge University Press, 1983.

Witherington III, Ben. *The Acts of the Apostles: A Socio-Rhetorical Commentary*. Grand Rapids: Eerdmans, 1998.
Witherup, Ronald D. "Functional Redundancy in the Acts of the Apostles: A Case Study." *JSNT* 48 (1992): 67–86.
Wright, N. T. *Paul and the Faithfulness of God*. 2 Vols. COQG 4. Minneapolis:Fortress, 2013.
Wright, William M. *Rhetoric and Theology: Figural Reading of John 9*. BZNW 165. Berlin: de Gruyter, 2009.
Yoder, Joshua. *Representatives of Roman Rule: Roman Provincial Governors in Luke-Acts*. BZNW 209. Berlin: de Gruyter, 2014.
Yoon, Joshua Seokhyun. "A Representative Outsider and the Inclusion of the Outsider in Acts 8:26–40." DMin diss., Duke University, 2016.

C. Newspapers and Online Sources

Adolf Hitler. *Mein Kampf*. The Noontide Press: Books On-Line. http://www.angelfire.com/folk/bigbaldbob88/MeinKampf.pdf.
Ahmed, Saeed. "Who were Syed Rizwan Farook and Tashfeen Malik?" *CNN*, December 4, 2015. http://www.cnn.com/ 2015/12/03/us/syed-farook-tashfeen-malik-mass-shooting-profile.
Choe, Sang Hun. "In Seoul, marking a somber anniversary of executions." *New York Times*, April 11, 2005. http://www.nytimes.com/2005/04/11/world/asia/in-seoul-marking-a-somber-anniversary-of-executions.html.
Cohen, Zachary and Kevin Liptak, "Trump praises Kim Jong Un as honorable, refuses to explain why." *CNN*, April 25, 2018. https://www.cnn.com/2018/04/24/politics/trump-kim-jong-un-honorable/index.html.
Fessler, Palm and Joel Rose. "Trump Administration Rule Would Penalize Immigrants For Needing Benefits." *NPR*, August 12, 2019. https://www.npr.org/2019/08/12/748328652/trump-administration-rule-would-penalize-immigrants-for-using-benefits.
Gun Violence Archive. "Last 72 Hours." https://www.gunviolencearchive.org/last-72-hours.
HHS Press Office. "New Rule Makes Clear that Noncitizens Who Receive Health or Other Benefits to Which They Are Entitled Will Not Suffer Harmful Immigration Consequences." *U.S. Department of Health and Human Services*, September 8, 2022. https://www.hhs.gov/about/news/2022/09/08/new-rule-makes-clear-noncitizens-who-receive-health-or-other-benefits-which-they-are-entitled-will-not-suffer-harmful-immigration-consequences.html.
Janowitz, Naomi. "Rethinking Jewish Identity in Late Antiquity." *UC Davis Previously Published Works*. Davis: University of California, 2001. https://escholarship.org/content/qt9vx1q0xd/qt9vx1q0xd.pdf.
Karimi, Faith, Jason Hanna, and Yousuf Basil. "San Bernardino Shooters 'Supporters' of ISIS, Terror Group Says." *CNN*, December 5, 2015. http://www.cnn.com/2015/12/05/us/san-bernardino-shooting.
Kim, Junghoon. "The Stealthy Rise of North Korean Sympathizer Rhetoric in Opposition to the Anti-THAAD Sentiment." *Nocut News*, July 11, 2016. http://www.nocutnews.co.kr/news/4620885.
Mansoor, Menahem. "Pharisees." *Encyclopaedia Judaica. Gale Virtual Reference Library*. New York: Macmillan Reference USA, 2007. http://link.galegroup.com/apps/doc/CX2587515688/GVRL?u=gradtul&sid=GVRL&xid=c142beb6.

Mansoor, Menahem. "Sadducees." *Gale Virtual Reference Library*. New York: Macmillan Reference USA, 2007. http://link.galegroup.com/apps/doc/CX2587517261/GVRLu= gradtul&sid=GVRL&xid=4ae7e20c.
Santucci, John. "Trump Says San Bernardino Shooting Appears Tied to Terrorism: 'Look at the Names.'" *ABC News*, December 3, 2015. http:/abcnews.go.com/Politics/donald-trump-san-bernardino-shooting- appears-tied-terrorism/story?id=35561319.
Steinfels, Peter. "Scholar Sees 4 Views of Jesus in Accounts of Death." *New York Times*, March 27, 1994. https://www.nytimes.com/1994/03/27/us/scholar-sees-4-views-of-jesus-in-accounts-of-death.html.
The History Place, "Adolf Hitler, 'Speech to the Reichstag,' January 30, 1941." http://www.historyplace.com/worldwar2/holocaust/h-threat.htm/.
Time Staff. "Here's Donald Trump's Presidential Announcement Speech." *Time*, June 16, 2015. http://time.com/3923128/donald-trump-announcement-speech.

Index of References

The letter *t* following an entry indicates a page with a table.

ANCIENT SOURCES

Appian
Civil Wars
5.7	74

Aristotle
Rhetoric
3.13.1	81
3.13.4	81
3.14	82

Politics
1273B-1274A	131

Babylonian Talmud Sanhedrin
3:6-8	111
90b	112

Babylonian Talmud Rosh Hashanah
16b–17a	112

Cicero
De inventione rhetorica
1.14.19	81

In Defense of Rabirius
4.12	72
12	101

On the Making of an Orator
1.19.27	81
1.23.34	81
1.41.77	82
1.52.98	82

Pro Archia Pro Archia Poeta
X.24	7

Rhetorica ad Herennium
1.3.4	81

Verr. Against Verres
2.4.66	72
2.5.66	106

Dio Cassius
Roman History
60.17.4–9	107

Dio Chrysostom
Orations
7	144
7.25	100

Epictetus
Discourses
4.1.12	73

Herodotus
Histories
4.134	131
7.237	132

Justinianus
Digesta Justiniani
49.6.1	140

Livy
History of Rome
10.9.3–6	72
10.9.5–7	106

Ovid
Metamorphoses
8.613–738	144

Plato
Apology of Socrates
28A	81

Phaedrus
267A	81

Republic
5.474A	100

Pliny the Younger
Epistles
10.96	101

Plutarch
Julius Caesar
29.2	102

Quintilian
The Orator's Education (Institutio Oratoria)
3.9.1	81
4.1	81
4.1,5	82
4.2	81
4.4–5	81
5.13	82
10.1.5	21

Strabo
Geography
8.6.15	74
14.5.9–15	74

Tacitus
Annals
12.54	140

Histories
5.9	140

Thucydides
History of the Peloponnesian War
3.10.52–60	82

JOSEPHUS

Antiquities of the Jews
4.70–2	59
4.207	133
12.271	86
13.171–3	113
13.297–8	112
13.397	24
14.186–285	119
16.5.2	141
16.10	130
16.205	130
16.262	130
18:1:1–2	2
18.11–25	120
18.13	113
18.16–17	112
20.7.1–2	140
20.9.1	111
20.103	111
20.169–72	70
20.202	108
20.205–7	111

Against Apion, or Contra Apion
2.147	81
2.237	133

The Jewish War, or De Bello Judaico
1.21.9	141
2.12.8	140
2.119–66	120
2.162–5	113
2.163–5	112
2.261–3	70
2:308	102
2.345–401	82
3.361–91	82
3.472–84	82
4.161	86
7.268–70	86
7.320–36	82
7.341–88	82

PHILO

Against Flaccus, or In Flaccum, or Contra Flaccum
144	100

De specialibus legibus
1.248	59

PSEUDEPIGRAPHA

1 (Ethiopic) Enoch
38:2	89

4 Maccabees
5	77

Letter of Aristeas
142:4	77

Index of References

Jubilees			24:2	52
22:16	77		Numbers	
			6:1-21	59
OLD TESTAMENT			19:12	59
			31:19	59
Genesis				
12:3	43		Deuteronomy	
15:1-6	84		1:6-17	111
15:6	76		2:30	132
18:11	119		10:16	132
21:1-7	119		13:15	127
28:3	48		19:16-19	111
35:11	48		20:17	127
38:6-11	120		23:1	51
41:12	138		25:5	120
48:4	48		28:22	111
Exodus			Joshua	
3:1-12	88		6:21	127
3:2-3	88			
3:4	88		Judges	
3:4-15	84		1:17	127
3:6	88		6:11-18	84
3:10	88		13:8-20	84
3:12	88		21:11	127
3:15	88, 89			
4:21	132		Ruth	
5:4	70		3:9–4:10	120
7:3	132			
8:19	132		1 Samuel	
13:15	132		15:3	127
16:1-36	135			
17:1-7	135		I Kings	
22:27	111		18:17	70
25:29	52		22:24	111
Leviticus			Job	
8:2	52		1:6	136
14:2-3	119		1:7	136
17–18	49		1:8	136
17:7-9	49		1:9	136
17:8	49		1:12	136
17:8-9	50		2:1	136
17:10	49, 50		2:2	136
17:10-11	49		2:3	136
17:13	49		2:4	136
17:15	49, 50		2:6	136
18:6-18	49		2:7	136
19:15	111			

Psalms		61:1-2	92
94:8	132	61:10	91
99:6	90	62:1	91
105:32	130	62:11	91
118	71	63:17	132
		66:1-2	67
Isaiah			
6:1	91	Jeremiah	
6:1-13	84	7:26	132
6:8-9	91	17:23	132
6:9	84	19:15	132
6:9-10	91		
6:12	91	Ezekiel	
9:2	88	1:28–2.8	84
12:2	91	1:28	84
12:3	91	2:1-2	84
17:10	91	2:307	84
18:3	89	13:10-16	111
25:9	91	40–48	78
33:2	91		
33:6	91	Daniel	
40:3	81	1:8-16	77
42:6	92, 93	12:2-3	84
43:6	92		
43:10	90	Joel	
43:12	90	2:28	55
44:8	90		
44:9	90	Zechariah	
45:8	91	3:1	136
45:17	91	3:2	136
46:13	91		
49:6	91, 92, 93	APOOCRYPHA or DEUTERO-	
49:7	92	CANONICAL BOOKS	
49:8	91, 92		
49:22	92	Book of Tobit	
49:23	92	1:10-13	77
51:5	91		
51:6	91	The Wisdom of Solomon	
51:8	91	6:10	81
52:7	91	18:1	88
52:10	91		
53:11	89	1 Maccabees	
56:1	91	2:20	86
56:1-8	43	2:24	86
57:19	84	2:26	86
59:11	91		
59:17	91	2 Maccabees	
60:18	91	7:14	84
61:1	71	7:20	84

Index of References

NEW TESTAMENT

Matthew
Ref	Pages
8:5-13	105
9:1-8	115
9:3	115
9:8	115
13:54-58	48, 88
23:1-36	115
23:27	111
26–27	20
26:1-5	20
26:61	68
27:25	149

Mark
Ref	Pages
2:1-12	115
2:5-7	115
2:12	115
3:6	115
6:1-5	88
6:1-6	48
8:32-33	142
11:12-21	68
13:1-2	68
14–15	20
14:1-2	20
14:57	68
14:58	68
14:62	22
15:29	68

Luke
Ref	Pages
1:1	8
1:1-4	17, 102
1:5-23	68
1:6	119
1:16	47, 94
1:17	115
1:26	88
1:51-53	114
1:52	22
1:59	76
1:68	47, 94
1:71	106
1:79	135
2:4	88
2:11	71
2:21	76
2:26	71, 91
2:32	95
2:34-35	113
2:39	88
2:51	88
3:3	94
3.7-14	94
3:8	95, 105
3:12	127
3:14	105
3:16	95
3:21–4:15	136
4:1-4	135
4:1-14	136
4:2	135
4:3	135
4:5-8	135
4:6-7	135
4:9-11	135
4:9-12	135
4:12	135
4:13	135
4:16	86
4:16-21	74
4:16-30	4, 28, 88, 89, 100, 137, 146
4:18	71, 84, 95
4:18-19	92, 106
4:19	91
4:20	110
4.22-30	113
4:23-27	92
4:24	91, 143
4:41	71
4:43	71
5:12	135
5:14	119
5:17	2, 71, 112
5:17-26	115, 130
5:21	2, 112, 114, 127, 129
5:26	115
5:27	127
5:29	127
5:30	2, 112, 114, 127
5:32	127
5:33	2
6:1-11	112
6:2	2, 114

6:7	2, 112, 114, 127	10:31	119
6:11	115	10:39	86
6:12	127	11:18	135
6:15	2	11:22	115
6:17	71	11:34	135
6:20	22	11:35	135
6:24	22	11:36	135
6:27-36	106	11:37–21:1	115
6:34-35	74	11:37	2, 112
6:35-36	74	11:37-54	114
6:39	84	11:38	2
7:1-10	105	11:39	2, 114
7:4	105	11:40	114
7:16	94	11:42-43	2
7:17	71	11:44	114
7:21	84	11:45	112
7:22	84	11:53	2, 114, 127
7:29	127	12:1	2, 114
7:29-30	115	12:10	129
7:30	2, 112	12:11	11, 81, 83, 104
7:34	127	12:11-12	95
7:36-37	2	12:16-21	114
7:36-50	16, 114	12:50	21
7:37	127	13:16	135
7:38	86	13:29	94
7:39	2, 114, 127	13:31	2
8:3	121	13:33	21
8:4	127	14:1	2, 114
8:12	135	14:1-24	114
8:35	86, 127	14:3	2, 112, 114
8:37	127	14:13	84
8:40	58	14:21	84
8:40-56	52	15:1-7	127
8:41	86	15:2	2, 114, 127
9:11	58	15:8-10	127
9:18-22	141, 142	16:14	2, 114
9:20	71, 91	16:15	114
9:21-22	9	16:19-31	22
9:22	104, 127	17:11	114
9:23	141	17:11-19	81
9:30	70	17:14	119
9:30-33	91	17:16	86
9:31	21	17:20	2
9:44	9, 141	17:25	104
9:51–19:28	21	18:3-33	9
9:51–19:44	9	18:9	114
9:51	9, 21, 57	18:9-11	2
9:51-53	9	18:9-14	114, 127
10:18	135	18:18-30	106

Reference	Page(s)
18:31-33	21, 141
18:32	141
18:35	84
18:35-43	81
19:1-10	106, 127
19:28-40	21, 142
19:36-40	142
19:37	21
19:38	72
19:38a	71
19:39	2, 114
19:40	71
19:41-44	9, 142
19:42	84
19:44	4
19:45-46	10
19:45-48	21, 142
19:47	127, 142
19:47-48	10
20:1	119, 127
20:1-8	10
20:9-19	71
20:19	127
20:20	119, 140
20:20-26	122
20:25	71
20:27	2, 112, 119
20:27-40	10, 112, 119
20:28	120
20:33	112
20:39	115, 127
20:43	86
20:46	127
20:47	127
21:12	140
21:12-13	17
21:12-19	83, 144
21:13	9
21:14	81
21:37–22:1	142
21:37-38	142
21:66-71	108
22–23	20
22:1	142
22:1-5	20, 21
22:1-6	135, 136
22:2	127, 142
22:3	135
22:4	127
22:7	142
22:7-20	142
22:15	104
22:31	135
22:39-46	142
22:42	22
22:45	142
22:47-53	21
22:52	127
22:52-54	142
22:53	10, 135, 142
22:54	65
22:56	110
22:63-65	10, 21, 142
22:64	84
22:65	129
22:66	127
22:66-71	10, 21, 142
22:67	4, 71
22:67-69	142
22:67-70	22
22:67-71	4
23:1-5	10, 18, 21, 69, 70
23:1-25	142
23:2	70, 131, 142
23:2-3	73
23:3	4, 70, 71, 106, 142
23:3-4	18
23:4	71, 105, 127, 142
23:5	71, 142
23:6-12	10, 21
23:10	127
23:12	105
23:13	10, 127
23:13-25	10, 21, 71
23:14	10, 105, 142
23:14-16	142
23:15	105
23:18	65
23:22	105, 142
23:25	73, 105
23:27	10
23:35	10, 91, 127
23:35-39	10
23:37	106
23:38	72, 106
23:39	129
23:43	71
23:44	135

23:44-46	135	2:25	88
23:46	10, 142	2:29	48, 104
23:47	67, 105	2:34	88
24:13-35	81	2:35	86
24:16	84	2:36	88, 143
24:19	88, 94	2:37	48, 127
24:20	127	2:37-42	25
24:26	71, 104	2:37-47	126
24:31	84	2:38	55, 94, 95
24:46	71, 104	2:39	88
24:47	94	2:40	82
24:50-53	68	2:41	94, 127
37	4	2:43-47	106
38	4	2:46	91
39	4	2:47	88
		3:1–4:22	104, 130
John		3:1	91
2:19-22	68	3:2	130
8:44	149	3:4	110
18–19	20	3:6	88
		3:9-10	130
Acts		3:12	110
1:1–5:16	51	3:13	89
1:1	102	3:14	67, 89
1:3	104, 106	3:17	11
1:5	95	3:18	104
1:6	88	3:20	88
1:8	50, 58, 81, 89, 91, 94, 96, 105	3:22	70, 88, 91
		3:23	48
1:10	110	4:1	2, 108, 111
1:12-14	68	4:1-3	82
1:12-42	68	4:1-4	112, 119
1:13	2	4:1-23a	127
1:16	48	4:2	113, 127
1:21	88	4:3	127
1:24	88	4:4	127
2	12	4:5-7	120
2:4	136	4:6	120
2:5	127	4:8	136
2:5-12	24	4:10	47, 88, 94, 113
2:5-42	28	4:12	47, 74, 94
2:7-11	127	4:13	136
2:11	29	4:15	108, 119
2:17-18	55	4:16	128
2:20	88	4:18	127, 138
2:21	88	4:20	136
2:22	80, 88	4:21	127, 128, 138
2:22-23	143	4:23	120, 127, 128
2:23	137	4:23-37	74

Index of References

4:24	88	6:9	64, 103
4:26	88	6:9-14	67
4:27	47	6:10	94, 136
4:29	88, 104	6:11	64, 67, 128, 132
4:31	104, 136	6:11-14	60, 130
4:33	88	6:12	64, 108, 119, 127, 128
4:35	86		
4:37	86	6:13	60, 64, 67, 68, 128, 132
5:1-11	106, 135, 136		
5:2	86	6:13-14	67
5:3	135	6:14	67, 68, 88, 128
5:9	88, 135	6:15	108, 110, 119
5:10	86	6:44	67
5:12-16	128	6:47	67
5:14	88	6:48	67
5:17–8:3	51	7:1	120
5:17	2, 100, 111, 120, 138	7:2	44, 80
		7:6	130
5:17-18	72, 128	7:7	67
5:17-21	156	7:8	76, 95
5:17-40	127, 128	7:17	94
5:17-41	119	7:19	130
5:17-42	104	7:31	88
5:18	138	7:32	89
5:19	88	7:33	67, 88
5:21	86. 108, 119, 120, 127	7:35-38	67
		7:37-38	67
5:24	120, 127	7:39-43	69
5:26	128	7:44	67
5:27	108, 119, 120	7:44-50	67, 69, 129
5:28	128	7:47	67
5:30	89, 113	7:48-50	132
5:33	128, 129, 137	7:49	88
5:33-40	114, 115	7:49-50	67
5:34	86, 119	7:51-52	4
5:34-39	2, 115, 119, 128	7:51-53	129, 145
5:39	86	7:51-60	44
5:40	128, 138	7:52	3, 67, 89, 143
5:41	119	7:53	67, 111
6:1–7:55	136	7:54	82, 129
6:1	48, 129	7:54-60	128
6:2	48	7:55	110, 136
6:3	48, 136	7:57	100
6:5	94, 95, 136	7:57-58	126, 129
6:7	48, 53, 119, 120	7:58–8:3	138
6:8–7:60	146	7:58	86, 103
6:8–8.3	28	7:58a	67
6:8	94, 128	7:59	73, 88, 89
6:8-15	128	7:60	88

8:1	79, 87, 137	9:24	136, 137
8:2	72	9:25	48, 137
8:3	87	9:26	48, 137
8:4-25	51, 136	9:26-30	9
8:4-40	58	9:28	79
8:12	94, 106	9:28-29	97
8;13	94	9:29	91, 129, 137
8:14-17	95	9:30	10, 48, 70, 91, 137
8:16	94	9:31	95, 96
8:26-40	10, 48, 50	9:32	48
8:29	136	9:36	55
8:36	52, 94	9:38	48
8:36-39	95	9:41	48
8:38	94	10	87
8:39	136	10:1–11:18	48, 52, 68
8:39-40	95	10:1	10, 105
8:40	10	10:1-48	10
9	96	10:2	51, 52
9:1	48, 53, 120	10:4	110
9:1-2	138	10:11	90
9:1-30	82, 83, 84, 88	10:14	52, 77, 95
9:2	2, 7, 81	10:15	52
9:3	88, 92	10:19	95, 136
9:4	84	10:22	51, 105
9:5	88	10:23	48, 53
9:7	88	10:24	10
9:8	84	10:25	86
9:9	134	10:28	52, 77, 95
9:10	48, 53, 89	10:35	51
9:10-18	68	10:36	47, 73
9:10-19	89	10:37	94
9:11	70, 91	10:38	88, 94, 95
9:13	48	10:39	137
9:13-14	89	10:44	82
9:14	120, 127	10:44-48	95
9:15	17, 47, 74, 89, 90	10:45	53, 94
9:16	104	10:47	52, 53, 94
9:18	84, 94	10:48–11:18	55
9:18-19	90	10:48	94
9:19	48	11:1	48, 94
9:20	84, 94	11:2-3	64, 95
9:20-22	97	11:3	77
9:20-25	136	11:5	90
9:21	120, 127	11:6	110
9:22	84, 94	11:8	95
9:23	11, 104, 136, 137	11:11	10
9:23-24	129	11:12	48, 136
9:23-25	84, 91	11:14	53
9:23-30	137	11:16	95

Index of References 189

11:17	52, 53	13:51	100
11:18	59, 92, 94, 96	13:52	48, 129
11:20	129	14:1	130, 137
11:24	70, 136	14:1-7	129, 137
11:25-30	96	14:2	48, 129, 130, 136, 137
11:26	48		
11:27-30	91	14:2-5	125
11:28	136	14:4	136
11:29	48	14:4-5	138
12:1	130	14:5	130, 136, 137
12:1-4	129	14:5-7	11
12:1-19	72, 156	14:6-7	137
12:12-17	68	14:7	130
12:17	48	14:8	130
12:23	139	14:8-18	144
12:25	9	14:8-20	130
13–19	57	14:9	110
13–28	9	14:11-12	130
13:2	136	14:13	130
13:3	91	14:14	100
13:4–14:28	12	14:15-17	132
13:4	136	14:18	130
13:4-12	136	14:19	11, 72, 125, 136, 138
13:7	89		
13:7-12	121	14:19a	130
13:9	95, 110	14:19b	130
13:9-10	136	14:20	48, 130
13:13-52	129	14:22	48, 106
13:16	51, 75	14:23	91
13:17	47, 94	14:27	94
13:24	47, 94	14:28	48
13:26	47, 51, 74	15:1	48, 50, 64, 95, 115
13:28	137	15:1-2	25
13:30	110, 113	15:1-5	96
13:37	110, 113	15:1-29	28, 91
13:39	62	15:1-35	48–50, 57
13:42	82	15:2	9
13:42-54	129	15:2-5	79
13:43	12	15:3	48, 94
13:44–14:7	3	15:4	9, 47
13:45	12, 100, 125, 129, 131, 136	15:5	95, 112, 114, 115
		15:7	48, 53, 94
13:46	94, 145	15:9	50
13:47	47, 74, 89, 94	15:10	48
13:47-48	92	15:10-11	50
13:48	12, 94	15:11	50, 92
13:50	72, 129, 130, 136, 138	15:12	94
		15:13	48, 80
13:50-51	11	15:14	93, 94

15:17	94	16:39	130
15:19	94	16:40	48, 72, 121, 130
15:19-21	95	17:1-9	69, 72, 73, 131
15:20	29, 49, 63, 95	17:3	104, 113
15:22	48	17:3a	73
15:23	48, 94	17:3b	73
15:28	63	17:4	131
15:28-29	49, 95	17:4-5	73
15:29	29, 63, 95	17:5	3, 12, 131, 136
15:32	48	17:5a	100
15:33	48	17:5-8	138
15:36–18:23	12	17:5-9	18, 121, 125
15:36	48	17:6	3, 48, 70, 73
15:40	48	17:6b	74
16:1	48	17:6-7	73
16:1-4	96	17:6-8	131
16:1-5	48, 53–4	17:7	73, 131
16:2	48, 53	17:7b	74
16:3	54	17:7c	74
16:6-7	136	17:9	131
16:6-10	54	17:10	48
16:11-15	48, 54–5	17:12	121
16:11-40	130	17:13	136, 138
16:13	91	17:13-15	11
16:14	55	17:14	48
16:14-15	72, 121	17:16	70
16:15	68, 94	17:16-34	131, 144
16:16	72, 91	17:17	131
16:16-24	69	17:18	110, 113, 131
16:16-40	104, 156	17:19	131
16:16-41	72	17:24-25	67, 132
16:17	47, 73, 74	17:30	48, 93, 94, 96
16:18	130	17:32	82, 110, 113, 131
16:18-19	72	17:34	121, 131
16:19	72	18:1-17	131
16:19-22	138	18:4-5	131
16:19-24	72	18:5	113, 132
16:20	72	18:5-7	11
16:20-21	130	18:6	100, 131, 145
16:21	72, 74	18:7	55, 61, 121
16:22	130	18:7-11	68
16:22-24	130, 131	18:8	94, 131
16:25	91	18:10	130
16:25-34	72	18:12	132, 136
16:27	72	18:12-16	125
16:31	94	18:12-17	15, 138
16:33	94	18:13	132
16:37	103, 106, 118	18:14-15	131
16:37-39	104, 130	18:15	132

18:17	132	20:17-38	57, 104
18:18	48, 59	20:19	133, 136
18:22	9, 10	20:20-21	68
18:25	81, 95	20:21	96
18:26	81	20:22	11, 21, 57, 136
18:27	48, 58	20:22-23	141
18:28	113	20:22-24	9, 21, 57
19:1–21:14	12	20:23	58, 136
19:1	48	20:28	136
19:1-7	95, 132	20:30	48
19:5-8	132	20:33-35	142
19:8	106, 132	20:36	82, 91, 142
19:8-10	25	20:36-38	142
19:8-41	132	20:37-38	21
19:9	48, 61, 62, 81, 125, 132	21–26	12
		21–28	12, 14
19:9-10	64	21:1–28:31	12
19:10-12	132	21:4	11, 21, 48, 57, 136
19:13-20	132	21:5	91, 142
19:21–21:16	9	21:7	48
19:21–21:17	21	21:8	10, 57
19:21	9, 10, 11, 57, 58, 136	21:8-14	68, 104
		21:10-11	21, 65
19:21-22	9	21:10-14	96
19:23	2, 7, 81	21:11	11, 58, 136, 141
19:23-29	132	21:11-14	57
19:23-41	24	21:12	11, 142
19:26	132	21:12-13	21
19:26-27	69	21:12-14	142
19:27	69	21:13	9, 11, 21
19:28	69, 132	21:14	21, 58
19:28-41	138	21:15–23:35	10, 12
19:29	69, 132	21:15-16	142
19:30	48	21:16	10, 48, 60
19:32	69, 133	21:17	10, 11, 48, 58, 139
19:33	69, 81	21:17-20a	21
19:34	132, 133	21:17-26	11, 13, 14*t*, 57
19:34-5	69	21:17–23:35	6, 133, 146
19:35	69	21:17-36	13, 63–6
19:35-41	133	21:17-40	57–78, 126
19:36	133	21:18	11, 61
19:37	133	21:19	58, 94
19:38	133	21:20	2, 59
19:38-39	133	21:20-25	64, 146
19:40	133	21:21	12, 58, 59, 62, 63, 67, 76, 77, 95
20:1	48		
20:3	21, 125, 133, 136	21:21b	63
20:4	11, 64	21:21-26	21, 142
20:16	11, 59, 142	21:23	59

21:23-4	59	21:38	70, 74, 106, 107
21:23-26	77	21:38-39	18
21:24	12, 64	21:39	74, 75, 100, 117, 147
21:25	29, 63, 94		
21:26	11, 21, 59, 91, 146	21:40	69, 75, 85
21:27–23:11	133	22–23	4
21:27–28:31	20	22–26	15
21:27	12, 69, 142	22:1	79, 80, 81, 82, 85, 110
21:27a	64		
21:27-28	11	22:1-5	80, 87
21:27-29	133	22:1-21	13, 14t, 16, 18, 19, 28, 62, 79, 82, 93, 100, 126, 142, 155
21:27-30	69		
21:27-31	146		
21:27-36	20, 21, 57	22:1-23	133
21:27-40	14t	22:2	75, 80, 85
21:28	11, 12, 18, 28, 58, 59, 62, 63, 67, 69, 77, 82, 118, 127, 142, 146	22:2-3	146
		22:2-21	15
		22:3	2, 12, 15, 19, 28, 63, 80, 85, 86, 87, 90, 110, 118, 146, 147
21:28a	64		
21:28b	63, 64, 82	22:3-5	61, 83
21:28-30	67	22:3-21	16, 80, 82
21:28-36	125	22:4	2, 7, 81, 87, 110
21:29	69	22:4-5	80, 146
21:29a	64	22:4-5a	80
21:29b	64	22:5	80, 87, 110, 120, 127
21:30	10, 60, 63, 64, 65, 68, 69, 87, 100, 127, 133		
		22:5b	80
		22:6	88, 92
21:30b	127	22:6-8	84
21:30-31	11, 133, 146	22:6-10	80
21:30-31a	82	22:6-11	80, 83
21:30-32	88	22:6-16	83, 88
21:30-36	100	22:6-17a	83t
21:31	87	22:6-21	87, 146
21:31-36	11, 134	22:7	84, 88
21:32	65, 68, 106, 133, 142	22:7-10	84, 146
		22:8	88, 89, 91, 94
21:33	142	22:9	88
21:33-36	133	22:10	88, 89
21:34-35	69	22:10-11	84
21:35-36	11, 88	22:11	84, 88
21:36	65, 69, 87, 127, 146	22:12	11, 89
21:37-38	69	22:12-13	80
21:37-39	18	22:12-15	80
21:37-40	11, 13, 57, 69, 79, 133	22:12-16	83
		22:13	89
21:37b	69	22:14	84, 89, 95
21:37c-38	69	22:14-15	80, 81, 89

Index of References

22:14-16	82	23:1-11	21
22:14-21	19	23:2	63, 111, 118, 120
22:15	89, 90, 132	23:2-3	118
22:16	80, 90, 94, 110	23:2-5	110
22:17	84, 90, 91	23:3	111, 142
22:17-18a	80	23:4	111, 120
22:17-21	80, 84, 90, 96	23:5	63, 120, 142
22:18	84, 89, 91	23:5a	111
22:18b	80	23:5b	111
22:19	89	23:5-6	142
22:19-20	80, 91	23:6	15, 17, 19, 84, 108, 109, 110, 112, 113, 114, 119, 121, 142, 146, 147
22:20	137		
22:21	28, 80, 81, 84, 89, 91, 92, 94, 96		
22:22–23:11	14t, 99, 126, 155	23:6-8	2
22:22	82, 92, 99, 100, 125, 127, 146	23:6-9	108, 110, 115, 133
		23:6-10	25, 110, 111
22:22-23	11, 82, 100, 116, 146	23:7	112, 113, 119
		23:7-9	114
22:22-24	82	23:8	112, 113, 119, 120
22:22-24a	134	23:9	16, 112, 113, 127
22:22-29	13, 99, 121	23:10	11, 119, 141
22:23	100, 127	23:11	12, 17, 83, 99, 108, 113, 125, 134
22:24	101		
22:24-29	11, 116, 133	23:12	125, 127, 134, 138
22:24b-29	134	23:12-15	82, 129, 134, 136, 141, 146
22:25	101, 103, 106, 117, 118, 142		
		23:12-22	11, 21
22:25-29	106, 147	23:12-35	11, 13, 14t, 104, 116, 125, 139, 155
22:26	101, 105, 106		
22:27	103	23:13	134
22:27-28	106, 142	23:14	120, 127, 134, 138
21:27-36	141	23:14-15	142
22:22-23	141	23:15	125
22:28	106, 117	23:15b	134
22:29	104, 106	23:15c	134
22:30	11, 106, 119, 120, 127	23:16	10, 134, 138
		23:16-36	138
22:30–21:10	82	23:17	106, 118, 134, 138
22:30–23:5	133	23:17-18	105
22:30–23:11	11, 13, 99, 116, 122	23:18	138
22:31	11	23:18-22	139
22:32	11	23:19	134, 139
23–26	133	23:21	134, 139
23:1	15, 19, 110, 111, 118, 142, 146, 147	23:22	138, 139
		23:23	10, 106, 139
		23:23-25	140
23:1-5	111, 141, 146	23:24	139
23:1-6	12	23:25	140
23:1-10	22, 134, 142		

194 Index of References

23:26	139	25:11	63, 108, 118
23:26-30	140	25:11-12	10, 83
23:27	103, 140	25:13–26:32	21
23:27-30	140	25:13-22	156
23:29	140, 142	25:15	120, 127
23:30	134, 136, 140, 141, 143, 146	25:16	81, 136, 143
		25:18	136, 142, 143
23:31	141	25:21	11, 83, 118
23:32	141	25:23-27	156
23:33–26:32	142	25:25	142
23:33	10, 139, 141	25:26	73
23:33-35	11	26:1	75
23:34	141	26:1-2	81
23:35	136, 141, 143	26:1-23	19
24–26	10, 125, 141	26:1-32	11, 82
24:1–25:12	21	26:2-18	82
24:1–28:31	12	26:2-23	82, 83
24:1	10, 11, 120, 127, 139	26:2-29	25, 96
		26:2-31	121
24:1-23	82	26:2-32	88
24:2	75	26:4-7	12
24:2-5	75	26:4-8	63, 115
24:5	48, 75	26:5	86, 110, 112, 114
24:5-8	106, 156	26:6	146
24:5-9	142	26:7	146
24:6	63	26:8	110, 113
24:8	136	26:9	88
24:10	81, 139	26:10	48, 120, 127
24:10-21	12, 19, 25, 82	26:12	120, 127
24:10-26	11	26:13	92
24:12-13	63	26:16	90
24:14	2, 7, 48, 84	26:16-18	74
24:15	109, 110, 113, 121, 146	26:17-18	96
		26:18	84, 92, 94, 96, 135
24:16-20	63	25:19-23	96
24:21	84, 109, 110, 113, 114	26:20	94, 95, 96, 97
		26:20a	97
24:22	2, 7, 82	26:20b	97
24:23	105, 106, 139	26:22-23	12
24:26	11, 106, 121	26:23	92, 94, 97, 104, 110, 113
25:1	10		
25:1-3	135, 136	26:24	82, 156
25:1-5	143	26:26-29	114, 121
25:2	120, 127	26:27	121
25:6	10	26:27-29	84
25:6-12	82	26:28	48, 156
25:8	12, 63, 81	26:29	91
25:8-12	11	26:30-2	156
25:9-12	11	26:31-32	142, 142

26:32	83, 118	3:9-20	76
27	125	3:20	77
27:1–28:10	156	3:28	77
27:1	106, 139	3:30	76
27:3	105	4:3	76
27:11	106	4:9	76
27:24	11, 81, 83, 108	4:9-12	76
27:29	91	4:11	54
27:31	106	4:12	76
27:43	105, 106, 139	7:1-6	60
27:44	139	8:33	76
28	125	9:11	76
28:1	139	11:1	86, 109
28:1-6	144	11:1-36	76
28:4	139	11:7	76
28:7-10	121	11:28	76
28:8	91	15:8	76
28:14	48, 83		
28:15	48	1 Corinthians	
28:16	83	3:12	77
28:16-28	105	3:16	77
28:16-31	25	3:16-17	76
28:17	63	3:17	77
28:17-28	25	6:19	77
28:17-31	11	7:17-20	76
28:19	11, 83, 108, 118	9:1	88
28:20	15, 19, 114, 121, 146	11:17-34	77
		12:13	77
28:22	48, 69, 74	14:12	3
28:23	106	15:8	88
28:23-25a	83	15:45-49	110
28:23-27	143		
28:23-28	113	2 Corinthians	
28:23-31	68	6:16	76, 77
28:24-28	3	11:22	86, 109
28:24-31	145	11:25	101, 102
28:25-28	145		
28:27	84	Galatians	
28:28	47, 74, 91, 94, 145	1:6-10	156
28:30	58	1:11–14	86
28:30-31	68, 105, 121, 142, 143	1:14	3, 86, 109
		1:16	97
28:31	4, 53, 104, 106	1:22-24	91
		2:1-10	91
Romans		2:1-14	156
2:25–3:1	54	2:3-5	54
2:25-3:2	76	2:11-14	77
2:29	76	2:11-21	76
3:1	76	2:12	77

2:13-21	77	6:14	77
2:14	77	6:15	61, 76
2:15	95	6:17	102
2:15-21	60	28–5:21	156
2:16	76, 77		
3:1	76	Philippians	
3:2	77	1:27	110
3:3	76	3:5	109
3:5	77	3:7-11	110
3:6	76	3:17	90
3:8	76	4:22	121
3:10	76, 77, 149		
3:10-14	156	Colossians	
3:11	76	2:5	61
3:12	77		
3:23-25	77	Titus	
3:24	76	2:14	3
3:28	77		
4:8-20	156	Philemon	
4:10	77	3:2-11	76
5:2-6	54	3:3	76
5:2-12	76	3:5-6	86
5:4	76	3:5	76
5:6	61	24	102
5:11	77		
6:12	77	1 Peter	
6:12-16	76	3:13	3

Index of Authors

Abrams, Dominic 29, 30, 31, 33, 34, 36, 38, 39
Adams, Sean A. 101, 102, 103, 106
Ahmed, Saeed 32
Alexander, Loveday C. A. 107
Allison, Dale C., Jr. 84, 88
Allport, Floyd 30
Amir, Y. 41
Andreoli, Virginia A. 41
Anh, Yong-Sung 10
Argote, Linda 43
Ashcroft, Bill 45, 150
Aune, David E. 8

Baker, Coleman A. 39
Balch, David L. 8, 118
Baltzer, Klaus 68
Bar-Tal, Daniel 38
Barensten, Jack 38
Barreto, Eric D. 54
Barreto, Manuela 38
Barrett, Charles K. 14, 18, 51, 60, 143
Barth, Fredrik 46, 50
Basil, Yousuf 32
Bass, Kenneth 99
Bauernfeind, Otto 103
Baur, Ferdinand C. 23
Beale, Gregory K. 68
Beavis, Mary A. 68
Béchard, Dean P. 83, 107
Beck, Norman A. 16, 67, 71
Bell, David 99
Bennett, Mark 34
Berger, Peter L. 57, 122
Bhabha, Homi K. 45
Billig, M. G. 31
Blair, Edward P. 91
Bock, Darrell L. 8, 12
Boesenberg, Dulcinea 48
Bonz, Marianne P. 8, 21
Boring, M. Eugene 68

Bosman, Jan Petrus 38
Bovon, François 71, 119, 120, 135, 137
Boyarin, Daniel 25, 147
Brawley, Robert L. 19, 111, 115, 119, 120, 126
Brenner, Michael 16
Brodie, Thomas L. 8, 67
Brown, Raymond E. 23, 144
Brown, Rupert 37, 39, 40, 42
Brown, Schuyler 135
Bruce, F. F. 8, 14, 23, 61, 102, 105, 112
Brunner, Jerome S. 117
Bryan, Christopher 122
Bundy, R. P. 31
Burke, Sean D. 51
Burridge, Richard 8
Burrus, Virginia 25
Bush, Stephen S. 75
Butticaz, Simon 84
Byrskog, Samuel 39

Cadbury, Henry J. 7, 11, 50, 105
Carroll, John T. 115
Cassidy, Richard 11, 103, 107, 140
Chance, J. Bradley 68
Chen, Jian 37
Chepey, Stuart 59
Choe, Sang Hun 1, 157
Cohen, Shaye J. D. 24, 29, 48, 50, 51, 53, 55
Cohen, Zachary 79
Cohn-Sherbok, Dan 110
Commins, Barry 42
Conzelmann, Hans 15, 18 , 23, 60, 105, 112, 135, 146
Cooley, Charles H. 149
Corley, Bruce 83, 84
Crabbe, Kylie 58
Croatto, J. Severino 70
Crossan, John D, 144

Daube, David 113, 120
de Vos, Craig S. 72

Devine, Christopher J. 120
Devine, Patricia G. 150
Diab, L. N. 41
Dibelius, Martin 48, 67
Dickow, Helga 42
Dietze, Carsten 39
Dinkler, Michal Beth 14
Donahue, John R. 68
Doosje, Bertjan 38
Douglas, Mary 65
Dovidio, John F. 41, 42
du Toit, Andrie 86
du Veil, C. M. 111
Dunn, James D. G. 77, 93, 95

Easton, Burton S. 18
Edwards, James R. 141, 142
Eisenbaum, Pamela 84, 149
Ellemers, Naomi 38
Elliott, John H. 68
Esler, Philip F. 30, 31, 33, 34, 40, 45, 55, 68, 122
Esmail, Aziz 125
Euripides 74
Evans, Christopher F. 71, 94

Fairchild, Mark R. 86, 102
Fee, Gordon D. 77
Fessler, Palm 158
Fitzmyer, Joseph A. 16, 49, 50, 54, 60, 67, 71, 74, 80, 112, 134, 139, 140, 141
Flament, Claude 31
Flessen, Bonnie J. 53
Foakes-Jackson, Frederick J. 51
Folger, Roger 41
Foxhall, Lin 7
Franzoi, Stephen L. 150
Fredriksen, Paula 151

Gaertner, Samuel L. 37, 41, 42, 43, 46, 95, 96
Gans, Eric 89
Gaventa, Beverly R. 14, 17, 57, 62, 138
Gibson, James L. 42
Gilbert, Gary 106
Goffman, Erving 40, 46, 47, 85, 87
Golding, Thomas A. 67, 69
González, Justo L. 22
Goodman, Martin 50

Green, Joel B. 70, 71
Griffiths, Gareth 45, 150
Grindheim, Sigurd 94
Gruca-Macauley, Alexandra 55
Gruen, Erich S. 24
Grünert, Melanie 39
Gutzke, Manford G. 61

Haeger, Gabi 39
Haenchen, Ernst 8, 18, 48, 60, 104, 142, 145, 146
Hakola, Raimo 38, 39, 146
Hamm, Dennis 82
Hanna, Jason 32
Hanneken, Todd R. 49
Hanson, John S. 70
Harnack, Adolf 23
Harrington, Daniel J. 68
Harrisville, Roy A. 88, 89
Hartsock, Chad 84
Harvey, O. J. 31
Haslam, S. Alexander 33, 34, 38, 66, 117
Haya-Prats, Gonzalo 136
Hayes, Christine 52, 97
Hemer, Colin J. 140
Hengel, Martin 7, 102
Herriot, Peter 31
Hewstone, Miles 42, 43
Hinkle, S. 39
Hitler, Adolf 2
Hock, Ronald F. 21, 101
Hodge, Caroline J. 97
Hogg, Michael A. 29, 30, 31, 33, 34, 36, 38, 39
Holladay, Carl R. 12, 14, 23, 51, 60, 63, 70, 73, 75, 80, 81, 82, 83, 84, 86, 89, 90, 91, 96, 100, 101, 103, 107, 108, 110, 111, 113, 120, 132, 133, 134, 138, 139, 141
Holland, Tom 86
Homer 7, 22
Hood, William R. 31
Horn, Friedrich W. 59
Horrell, David G. 40
Horsley, Greg H. R. 82
Horsley, Richard A. 70
Howard Marshall, I. 16

Im, Pong D. 38
Immanuel, Babu 107

Irudayaraj, Dominic S. 30, 33, 38, 40, 46, 122, 148
Izenberg, Gerald 97

Janowitz, Naomi 24
Jeffers, James S. 103
Jenkins, Richard 27, 36, 46, 47, 87, 90, 93, 95
Jeremias, Joachim 109
Jerome 102
Jervell, Jacob 19, 47, 51, 58
Johnson, Luke T. 8, 14, 16, 19, 22 49, 52, 53, 60, 62, 63, 70, 71, 75, 81, 82, 86, 89, 91, 100, 101, 108, 111, 112, 115, 121, 125, 127, 129, 131, 132, 134, 138, 139, 141, 143, 144, 145, 148, 149, 150, 151
Johnson, Sherman E. 74
Jokiranta, Jutta 38, 39
Joseph, Suppogu 114

Kafati, Gladys 41
Kaminsky, Joel 92
Kane, Aimée A. 43
Kang, Wi Jo 1
Karakolis, Christos 136
Karimi, Faith 32
Keener, Craig S. 10, 15, 60, 82, 103, 104
Kelhoffer, James A. 87, 100
Kennedy, George A. 82
Kessler, Sabine 39
Kiernan, Victor 32
Kim, Junghoon 157
Kim, Seyoon 122
Kipling, Rudyard 32
Kister, Menahem 110
Klawans, Jonathan 113
Klijn, Albertus F. J. 115
Kollman, Bernd 51
Krodel, Gerhard A. 14, 16, 61, 67
Kuecker, Aaron 38, 39, 42
Kurz, William S. 14, 20, 59

Lampe, Peter 101
Landolt, Jean-François 90
Lappenga, Benjamin J. 87
Lau, Peter H. W. 38, 40
Le Bon, Gustav 29
Lee, Doohee 8, 145
Lehtipuu, Outi 150

Lenski, Richard C. H. 60
Lentz, John C. 15, 102, 108, 109
Lettgen, Stephan 39
Levine, Amy-Jill 114, 149
Levy, Leonard W. 128
Linafelt, Tod 151
Liptak, Kevin 79
Lockwood, John 42
Long, William R. 82
Longenecker, Bruce W. 121
Lucian 52, 144
Luckmann, Thomas 57, 122
Lüdemann, Gerd 7, 102, 108

Maccoby, Hyam 109
MacCulloch, Diarmaid 2
MacDonald, Dennis R. 21, 22
McDougall, William 29
McGarty, Craig 40
McGarvey, John W. 14, 67
Maddox, Robert 18, 142, 146
Malina, Bruce J. 3, 17, 49, 66
Mallen, Peter 84, 113
Mandell, Sara 23
Mann, Jeffrey 42
Mansoor, Menahem 111, 112
Marguerat, Daniel 10, 18, 60, 61, 85, 121
Marohl, Matthew J. 38
Marques, José M, 38
Marshall, I. Howard 16, 115
Marshall, Mary 116, 122
Martin, Clarice Jannette 51
Martin, Troy W. 81
Mason, Steve 86
Mather, P. Boyd 90
Matthews, Shelly 67, 68, 129, 145
Maxwell, Kathy R. 82
Meeks, Wayne A. 121
Metzger, James A. 114
Michaels, J. Ramsey 68
Miller, Norman 42
Møller, Valerie 42
Monteith, Margo J. 150
Mor, Menahem 23
Morris, H. S. 117
Mullin, B. 39
Mummendey, Amélie 39, 43
Muñoz-Larrondo, Rubén 11, 19, 73, 106

Murphy-O'Connor, Jerome 102
Murrell, Audrey 42

Nadella, Raj 150
Neagoe, Alexandru 14, 15, 17
Neusner, Jacob 109
Neyrey, Jerome H. 3, 65, 66, 74
Nicklas, Tobias 147
Nicols, John 74
Nirenberg, David 25, 136
Nolland, John 71, 114

Oakes, Penelope J, 33, 34, 38, 66, 117
Oswalt, John N. 91
O'Toole, Robert F. 115

Páez, Dario 38
Pao, David W. 71
Park, Hyun Ho 10, 157
Parker, Floyd 113
Parry, Donald W. 91
Parry, Jay A, 91
Parsons, Mikeal C. 10, 14, 17, 60, 113, 143
Paterson, Jeremy 106
Penner, Todd C. 8
Pervo, Richard I. 8, 15, 23, 49, 62, 70, 74, 134, 138, 140
Peterson, Tina M. 91
Phillips, Thomas E. 8
Pickett, Raymond 11, 74, 105, 106
Pilch, John J. 17, 49, 67, 83
Plummer, Alfred 71
Polhill, John B. 14, 61
Porter, Stanley E. 19, 61, 103
Powell, Mark A. 71

Racine, Jean-François 51
Rackham, Richard B. 16
Rapske, Brian 109
Reade, Winwood 32
Regev, Eyal 112
Reinhartz, Adele 151
Riesner, Rainer 102
Roberts, Jimmy J. M. 91
Røsæg, Nils Aksel 84, 88
Rose, Joel 158
Rosenblatt, Marie-Eloise 15
Roskam, Hendrika N. 23
Ross, Gordon F. 40

Rothschild, Clare K. 8
Rowe, Kavin C. 3, 73, 74

Saguy, Tamar 42
Saldarini, Anthony J. 110
Samkutty, V. J. 51
Sanders, Ed P. 77
Sanders, Jack T. 47, 60, 114, 115, 126-7
Sani, Fabio 34
Santucci, John 32
Scaer, Peter J. 22
Schäfer, Peter 45
Schäferhoff, Stefanie 39
Schmithals, Walter 102
Schoenfeld, Andrew J. 52
Schreiner, Thomas R, 76, 77
Schwartz, Daniel R. 72
Seccombe, David 48
Seesengood, Robert P. 7
Segal, Alan F. 84
Semin, Gun 38
Sevenster, Jan N. 70
Shalom, M. Paul 92
Shauf, Scott 8, 9-10, 51
Shepherd, William H. 136
Sherif, Carolyn W. 31
Sherif, Muzafer 31, 41
Sherwin-White, Adrian N. 73, 101, 102, 103, 107, 140
Shillington, V. George 39
Sim, David C. 52
Simon, Bernd 39
Skinner, Matthew L. 14, 15, 104
Slingerland, Dixon 145
Smith, Jonathan Z. 27, 44
Smith, Mitzi J. 148
Smith, Steve 69
Soards, Marion L. 80
Songer, Harold S. 14
Southwood, Katherine 44, 47
Spears, Russell 38
Spencer, F. Scott 14, 17, **60**
Spivak, Gayatri 150
Squires, John T, 15
Stallybrass, O. 33
Stegemann, Wolfgang 101, 102
Steinfels, Peter 144
Stendahl, Krister 84
Sterling, Gregory E. 8, 22, 23

Stewart, Anne 92
Still, Todd D. 101
Strauss, Barry 7
Strauss, Stephen J, 17
Strelan, Rick 120
Stroup, Christopher 48

Tajfel, Henri 30, 31, 32, 33, 37, 41, 45, 46, 117
Tajra, Harry W. 109, 119
Talbert, Charles H. 8, 21, 54, 80, 141
Tannehill, Robert C. 16, 19, 51, 79, 113, 114, 115, 121, 130, 132, 137, 140, 145
Taylor, Charles 27, 118
Taylor, Nicholas H. 68
Tertullian 18
Thiessen, Matthew 50, 76, 97
Thompson, George H. P. 71
Thompson, Richard P. 59, 60, 61, 62, 133
Thornton, Timothy C. G. 50
Tiede, David L. 119, 145
Tiffin, Helen 45, 150
Trebilco, Paul 39, 81
Tripp, Jeffrey M. 67
Tucker, Brian 39
Turner, John C. 30, 33 35, 36, 37, 40, 66, 117
Turner, Nigel 86
Tutu, Desmond 42
Tyson, Joseph B. 45, 77

van Minnen, Peter 102, 103
van Unnik, Willem C. 86

Verheyden, Joseph 8
Vielhauer, Philipp 7
Vinson, Richard B. 70

Waddell, James A. 89
Walaskay, Paul W. 11, 18
Waldzus, Sven 43
Walker, William O., Jr. 61
Wall, Robert W. 19, 54
Walton, Steve 11, 105, 107
Watson, Alan 68
Weatherly, Jon A. 145
Wenzel, Michael 43
White, B. Jack 31
White, Devin L. 57
White, James F. 94
Whitmarsh, Tim 20
Wigbodus, Daniel 38
Wilder, David A. 42
Wilkes, A. L. 31
Williams, David J. 139
Wilson, Brittany E. 50, 51, 85
Wilson, Stephen G. 49, 62
Witherington, Ben 60, 67, 82, 85, 88, 89, 101, 103, 108, 109, 110, 112, 113, 125, 127, 132, 134, 139, 140, 141, 149
Witherup, Ronald D. 83
Worchel, Stephen 41
Wright, N. T. 86
Wright, William M. 150

Yoder, Joshua 105, 107
Yoon, Joshua Seokhyun 51

www.ingramcontent.com/pod-product-compliance
Lightning Source LLC
Chambersburg PA
CBHW051523230426
43668CB00012B/1713